Virgi

MW01156860

THE CUTTING EDGE
Lesbian Life and Literature

THE CUTTING EDGE
Lesbian Life and Literature

Series Editor: Karla Jay

Professor of English and Women's Studies
PACE UNIVERSITY

EDITORIAL BOARD

THE CUTTING EDGE
Lesbian Life and Literature

Series Editor: Karla Jay

Virginia Woolf

Lesbian Readings

EDITED BY

Eileen Barrett and
Patricia Cramer

NEW YORK UNIVERSITY PRESS
New York and London

NEW YORK UNIVERSITY PRESS
New York and London

Copyright © 1997 by New York University

Library of Congress Cataloging-in-Publication Data
Virginia Woolf: lesbian readings / edited by Eileen Barrett and
    Patricia Cramer.
        p.   cm. — (The cutting edge)
    Includes bibliographical references and index.
    ISBN 0-8147-1263-0 (clothbound : alk. paper). — ISBN
0-8147-1264-9 (paperbound : alk paper)
        1. Woolf, Virginia, 1882–1941—Criticism and interpretation.
    2. Homosexuality and literature—England—History—20th century.
    3. Feminism and literature—England—History—20th century.
    4. Women and literature—England—History—20th century.
    5. Lesbianism in literature.   6. Lesbians in literature.   7. Sex in
    literature.   I. Barrett, Eileen.   II. Cramer, Patricia, 1948 Mar.
    17-   III. Series: Cutting edge (New York, N.Y.)
    PR6045.O72Z8936   1997
    823.912—dc20   97-4667
                          CIP

New York University Press books are printed on acid-free paper,
and their binding materials are chosen for strength and durability.

Manufactured in the United States of America

10 9 8 7 6 5 4 3 2 1

Contents

Acknowledgments

The idea for *Virginia Woolf: Lesbian Readings* was conceived and developed at the annual conferences on Virginia Woolf, where many of the essays published here were first presented. Originally organized by Mark Hussey in 1991, these ongoing conferences continue to provide a stimulating, supportive environment for lesbian readings of Woolf. We thank Vara Neverow, Jane Lilienfeld, Paul Connolly, and Beth Rigel Daugherty for organizing succeeding conferences. Special thanks to conference participants Krystyna Colburn, Elizabeth Lambert, Heather Levy, Vara Neverow, Pam Olano, Donna Risolo, and Diana Swanson, whose ground-breaking work has helped to create the community of lesbian readings of Woolf that inspired this project and helped shape its ideas. Other essays in this volume were presented at the 1993 Modern Language Association convention in Toronto; we thank the Virginia Woolf Society for sponsoring this panel. Thanks to Pace University Press for its annual publication of the *Selected Papers* from the Woolf conferences, as well as the *Woolf Studies Annual*; both have been valuable resources.

Thanks to our reader at New York University Press who provided astute, helpful suggestions. Karla Jay, Niko Pfund, Jennifer Hammer, Despina Papazoglou Gimbel, and the production staff at New York University Press guided us from idea to manuscript with grace, wit, and professionalism. Laura Moss Gottlieb, our indexer, brought to the task her expertise on Virginia Woolf.

Eileen Barrett thanks the faculty, staff, and students at the English Department of California State University, Hayward. Special thanks to Deitra Taylor, department secretary extraordinaire, and to Jennifer Bohner who assisted me during the final stages of this project. The School of Arts, Letters, and Social Sciences generously granted me release time from teaching in the fall of 1995 and the winter of 1996 to complete work on this project. Family and friends encouraged me during all stages of this project; as always, Linda Scaparotti offered welcome support. Elissa Dennis is my first and last reader, my partner in life and in love. I dedicate my work on this volume to her.

Pat Cramer would like to thank the University of Connecticut for grant support during the editing process. Thanks also to Angela Yorweth, from the Stamford branch library, for her patient and expert research assistance. I am grateful for the friendships that have sustained and inspired me throughout this project. Thanks especially to Nechama Tec and Mary Cygan for their keen insights and professional advice, and to Mary Farrington, whose kindness, integrity, and proofreading skills have provided such reliable support. I thank Mark Hussey for his characteristic generosity in sharing with me his considerable knowledge of Woolf scholarship and for his sound editorial advice when I most needed it. I dedicate my work on this volume to the complexities and joys of lesbian friendship: to Krystyna Colburn, Susan DeMark, and Vara Neverow. I believe they know how much their radical feminist honesty, intelligence, loyalty, and humor mean to me.

A Note on the Text

Virginia Woolf's personal writings include idiosyncrasies of spelling and punctuation that we have left unaltered, using [*sic*] only when the error might be mistakenly attributed to the essay's author. When quoting from the holograph versions of *Orlando, The Waves,* and *The Years,* [*word*] indicates words Woolf deleted in the draft; <word>, an insertion made by Virginia Woolf, and [word], a word editorially added.

Abbreviations

Contributors

TUZYLINE JITA ALLAN is Associate Professor of English at Baruch College of the City University of New York (CUNY). She is the author of *Womanist and Feminist Aesthetics: A Comparative Review* and coeditor of *Literature Around the Globe*. Presently, she is codirector of *Women Writing Africa*, a multivolume publishing project sponsored by the Ford Foundation and the Feminist Press.

EILEEN BARRETT is Associate Professor and Coordinator of Graduate Studies in the English department at California State University, Hayward. She is coeditor of *American Women Writers: Diverse Voices in Prose Since 1845* (St. Martin's Press, 1992) and of two volumes of *Selected Papers* from the annual Virginia Woolf conferences. Her work on Woolf includes articles on *Between the Acts,* on teaching *To the Lighthouse,* and on Woolf and Toni Morrison.

SUZANNE BELLAMY is an Australian artist and writer with a teaching background in history and women's studies. She lives in rural New South Wales, operating a sculpture and printmaking studio, and exhibits internationally. Her artwork and writing attempt to illuminate the story of contemporary feminism and the creation of new cultural forms, both verbal and visual. Virginia Woolf has been her most sustaining muse since the 1970s, and Bellamy has written and broadcast ideas and thought on Woolf in many essays.

CORINNE E. BLACKMER is an assistant professor of lesbian and gay and American literature at Southern Connecticut State University. She has coedited *En Travesti: Women, Gender, Subversion, Opera* (1995) and written articles on Elizabeth Bishop, Gertrude Stein, and Nella Larsen. She is currently completing *The Presence of the Thing Not Named,* a study of race, lesbianism, and censorship in literature and film.

PATRICIA CRAMER is Assistant Professor of English and Director of Women's Studies at the University of Connecticut, Stamford. She is coeditor of the *Selected Papers* from the Fourth Annual Virginia Woolf Conference and is currently working on a book on Virginia Woolf and lesbian autobiography. Her work includes articles on William Blake, Chaucer, and feminist teaching, and on Jane Harrison and Virginia Woolf.

NOEL FURIE is a founding member of Bloodroot, a vegetarian restaurant and feminist bookstore in Bridgeport, Connecticut. For twenty years she has been cooking vegetarian food and selling feminist books with copartners Selma Miriam and Betsey Beaven. Photography is a means to express her feminist and lesbian point of view. Sometimes she thinks of the camera as her "third eye"—the one through which she is most insightful. In the past couple of years she has also done some local political work, helping neighbors organize in the West Side of Bridgeport.

LESLIE KATHLEEN HANKINS is Assistant Professor of English at Cornell College in Mount Vernon, Iowa. She is writing a book on Virginia Woolf and the challenge of cinema, and regularly presents multimedia work in progress at the annual Virginia Woolf Conferences and the Modern Language Association conventions. With Diane F. Gillespie, she is editing the *Selected Papers* from the Sixth Annual Virginia Woolf Conference, to be published in 1997 by Pace University Press as *Virginia Woolf and the Arts*.

JANE LILIENFELD teaches at Lincoln University, a historically black college, and has published essays on Woolf, Atwood, Cather, Colette, Joyce, and feminist theory. She is at work on *Reading Alcoholism: Theorizing Character and Narrative in Selected Novels by Hardy, Joyce, and Woolf*.

TONI A. H. McNARON is Professor of English and women's studies at the University of Minnesota, where she has taught for the past thirty-two years. Her publications include *Voices in the Night: Women Speaking about Incest, The Sister Bond: A Feminist View of a Timeless Connection, I Dwell in Possibility: A Memoir, The New Lesbian Studies: Into the Twenty-first Century,* and *Poisoned Ivy: Senior Professors Confront Academic Homophobia*. When she is not teaching and writing, Toni enjoys gardening, time with her partner and animals, and travel.

ANNETTE OXINDINE is Assistant Professor of English at Wright State University, where she teaches twentieth-century British literature and women's literature. She is currently working on a book entitled *Decoding Desire in Virginia Woolf's Fiction.*

PATRICIA JULIANA SMITH is Visiting Professor of English at the University of Connecticut. She is coeditor of *En Travesti: Women, Gender Subversion, Opera* (1995) and author of *Lesbian Panic: The Homoerotics of Narrative in Modern British Women's Fictions.* She is at work on a study of the shifts in cultural perceptions of gender and sexuality in 1960s literature, film, and popular culture, and has published articles on Angela Carter, Fay Weldon, Brigid Brophy, and Dusty Springfield.

RUTH VANITA is Associate Professor of English at Delhi University. She is the author of *Sappho and the Virgin Mary: Same-Sex Love and the English Literary Imagination* (1996) and *A Play of Light: Selected Poems* (1994). She was founding coeditor of *Manushi: A Journal about Women and Society* from 1979 to 1990. She is currently coediting an anthology of Indian writings on same-sex love.

LISE WEIL lives in Montreal and teaches at Goddard College in Vermont. She has published numerous translations from French and German, including Christina Taurmer-Rohr's *Vagabonding: Feminist Thinking Cut Loose,* and is now working on a collection of stories. She was editor of *Trivia: A Journal of Ideas* from 1982 to 1991.

JANET WINSTON is completing her dissertation at the University of Iowa on Queen Victoria's image as an icon of imperialism in twentieth-century narrative. Her publications on Woolf include "'Something Out of Harmony': *To the Lighthouse* and the Subject(s) of Empire" in *Woolf Studies Annual 2.* She is the recipient of a 1996 Woodrow Wilson Dissertation Grant in Women's Studies and is a 1996–97 American Fellow of the American Association of University Women Educational Foundation.

• PART I •

Lesbian Intersections

ONE

Introduction

EILEEN BARRETT

In the 1970s, feminist scholars inaugurated a resurgence of critical and popular attention to Virginia Woolf's life and work. Woolf's writings are now essential to classroom and critical studies of modernism, women writers, feminist theory, and lesbian and gay studies. Interest in her life and writing extends beyond the universities to those whom she called common readers, and her image is prominently displayed in a range of venues, from Hanif Kureishi's avant-garde film *Sammy and Rosie Get Laid* to an episode of the popular television program *Murphy Brown,* to evoke the radical feminist politics with which she is associated. Sally Potter's film version of *Orlando* and Eileen Atkins' *Vita and Virginia,* a stage adaptation of the love letters between Sackville-West and Woolf, have increased public awareness of Woolf's lesbianism. Visitors to the Lesbian and Gay Reading Room of the new San Francisco Public Library will see Virginia Woolf among the names of other famous lovers of their sex inscribed in the ceiling mural. Clearly, Virginia Woolf is one of the twentieth century's best-known lesbians.[1]

Virginia Woolf: Lesbian Readings represents the first book devoted to Woolf's lesbianism. Emerging out of the groundbreaking scholarship that precedes us, our collection develops a range of reading practices that shows how Woolf's private and public experience and knowledge of same-sex love influence her writings. The thirteen personal narratives and scholarly essays reflect the latest approaches in lesbian-feminist criticism. Intertextual readings cover Woolf and lesbian love in the life and work of such figures as Katherine Mansfield, Gertrude Stein, and Nella Larsen. Our writers provide interpretations of the novels and shorter fiction aimed at deciphering Woolf's complex lesbian codes, analysis of

Woolf's reactions to contemporary sexologists' definitions of lesbians and gay men, and discussions of Woolf's relationships to authors who also coded lesbian and gay themes in their writing.

We have divided *Virginia Woolf: Lesbian Readings* into two parts that we hope enhance the appreciation of Woolf's significance to conceptions of lesbianism both in her own and in our times. "Lesbian Intersections" includes work that explores how Woolf reads love between women in the work of her nineteenth-century precursors. It also contains personal narratives that trace the experience of reading Woolf through the 1960s, 1970s, 1980s, and 1990s. Three of its essays consider Woolf in the context of her lesbian contemporaries; juxtaposing Woolf with Mansfield, Stein, and Larsen, these essays suggest how techniques for inscribing lesbianism compare to developing concepts of modernism. "Lesbian Readings of Woolf's Novels" includes seven essays that provide lesbian interpretations of the individual novels: *The Voyage Out, Mrs. Dalloway, To the Lighthouse, Orlando, The Waves, The Years,* and *Between the Acts.* These essays break new ground in our understanding of the role Woolf's love for women plays in her major works. More important, they shift the emphasis of lesbian interpretations from Woolf's life to her work.

Women were always central to Virginia Woolf's life and work. She lived in a milieu that included many lesbians and gay men, and she had passionate relationships with a number of women. As this collection demonstrates, her lesbian experiences, explicitly expressed throughout her letters and diaries, influenced her short fiction, essays, and novels. Throughout her writing, Woolf resisted what she referred to as the "perpetually narrowing and naming" of lesbian and homosexual love; instead, as our essays show, she developed an intricate, multifaceted style to convey "these immensely composite and wide flung passions" (*L* 4: 200). Familiar with the literary tradition of same-sex love and with the social tradition of romantic friendships, Woolf created an expansive language with which to depict women loving women. By the late 1920s, she was referring proudly to herself as "the mouthpiece of Sapphism" (*L* 3: 530).

Woolf's lesbian attractions were common knowledge to her intimate friends and family. Her flirtatious correspondence with Violet Dickinson includes such disclosures as "I am so susceptible to female charms, in fact I offered my blistered heart to one in Paris, if not two" (*L* 1: 69–70). Well informed of her sister's attractions for women, Vanessa Bell teased Virginia in a 1906 letter: "Naughty Billy, to get up a flirtation in the train. You really aren't safe to be trusted alone. I know some lady will get a written promise of marriage out of you soon and then where will you be?" (37). Although there is no evidence that Woolf ever promised marriage to a lady, her first engagement was decidedly unconventional. In 1909, she accepted Lytton Strachey's marriage proposal knowing that his attractions were for men. "I should like Lytton as a brother in law better than anyone I know," Bell jested with her sister six months before the proposal, "but the only way I can perceive of bringing that to pass would be if he were to fall in love with [their brother] Adrian" (67). Most likely, Woolf sought the companionship in marriage with Strachey that she eventually achieved with Leonard Woolf. Bell implied as much in a letter of 1910, when she compared her sister's powers of homoerotic seduction to Strachey's. "Really, what with your cultivation of Sapphism . . . and Lytton's of Sodomism . . . you will be a fine couple worthy of each other when you both come out" (94). Although they agreed to call off the marriage, Lytton remained, in Woolf's estimation, "perfect as a friend, only he's a female friend" (*L* 1: 492).

In *Moments of Being* Woolf describes her relief upon discovering that like Strachey "the majority of the young men who came" to visit in Bloomsbury "were not attracted by young women" (194). This homoerotic environment enabled her to continue to explore her own same-sex attractions. For example, Vanessa Bell considered Ottoline Morrell a serious contender for her sister's affections, writing to Virginia in a 1909 letter, "You will have a desperate liaison with [Ottoline] I believe, for I rather think she shares your Sapphist tendencies and only wants a little encouragement" (84). Twelve years later, Woolf vividly recalled the erotic relationship with Morrell as "full of 'lustre and illusion'" (*MOB* 195). In 1912, when she accepted Leonard's marriage proposal, she bluntly admitted: ". . . I feel no physical attraction in you. There are moments—when you kissed me the other day was one—when I feel no more than a rock" (*L* 1: 496). Although, as Mark Hussey suggests, in marrying Leonard, Woolf "checked her homoeroticism by entering a heterosexual relationship" ("Refractions" 144), her interest in heterosexuality did not increase with sexual consummation. "Why do some of our friends change upon losing chastity?" she asked Katherine Cox in a letter written shortly after her marriage. "Possibly my great age makes it less of a catastrophe; but certainly I find the climax immensely exaggerated" (*L* 2: 6).

Woolf knew many women who lived with other women in a variety of arrangements. She once described a vacation she and Leonard shared with Margaret Llewelyn Davies and Lilian Harris. "When Margaret gets excited she calls her 'John,' and Miss Harris calls Margaret 'Jim'" (L 2: 119). In the 1930s, she recounted a memorable meeting with Charlotte Wolff, the author of the famous study of English lesbians, *Love between Women* (D 4: 357); and toward the end of her life she fell in love with Octavia Wilberforce, the life partner of Elizabeth Robins (L 6: 462, 465). Such attractions for women and interest in lesbian relationships led her to avow, "Much preferring my own sex, as I do, . . . [I] intend to cultivate women's society entirely in future. Men are all in the light always: with women you swim at once into the silent dusk" (L 3: 164).

The woman whose society Woolf most cultivated was Vita Sackville-West. "She is a pronounced Sapphist," Woolf wrote with excitement shortly after meeting her, "& may, thinks Ethel Sands, have an eye on me, old though I am" (D 2: 235). But far from waiting passively for this seduction, Woolf also declared, "To tell you a secret, I want to incite my lady to elope with me next" (L 3: 156). Although not without its complexity and pain, this love affair remained the most profound of Woolf's life. In the 1930s, when the passion between Woolf and Sackville-West was in its decline, Woolf met Ethel Smyth, another woman who stirred her lesbian imagination. Of Smyth's energetic correspondence Woolf exclaimed, "I get, generally, two letters daily. I daresay the old fires of Sapphism are blazing for the last time" (D 3: 306). She admired Ethel's creativity and respected her worldliness; as Woolf put it, she has "taken her own way in shirt & tie vigorously unimpeded" (D 3: 313). Encouraged by Smyth's feminist activism and friendship, Woolf urged other women to write openly about sexuality: "All that we have ought to be expressed—mind and body—a process of incredible difficulty and danger" (P 164). Finally, Woolf not only loved, but loved being loved by Ethel: "'D'you know Virginia, I dont like other women being fond of you.' 'Then you must be in love with me Ethel.' 'I have never loved anyone so much'" (D 3: 314).

Despite such overtly lesbian material in the letters and diaries, biographers continue to view Virginia Woolf as Quentin Bell's "sexless sappho." In his recent biography *Virginia Woolf* (1995), James King exemplifies the pervasive obtuseness about Woolf's lifelong attractions for women, which he suggests are "triggered by a psychic search for the dead mother" (79). Ignoring the exuberant eroticism of the letters, he reduces the affair between Sackville-West and Woolf to a Freudian simplification: "Vita wanted to become a male lover who could compete for and win her mother's embraces, whereas Virginia's desire was to be hugged and cared for by a maternal woman" (336). In King's final analysis, Woolf is a "eunuch" (386). Twenty years separate the Bell from the King biography; still, the portrait remains of what Ellen Hawkes called "The Virgin in the Bell Biography."

Meanwhile, critics continue to contest Woolf's lesbian identity. In an essay that explores explicit homoerotic imagery in the drafts of *A Room of One's Own,* Ellen Rosenman nonetheless insists that "contemporary definitions of lesbianism are not applicable to Woolf's work" ("Sexual Identities" 648). Yet as Bonnie Zimmerman points out, that rationale would never be used to argue, for example, that current definitions of marriage should not be applied to the work of modernist heterosexual writers. "Why can we not use the word lesbian," Zimmerman asks, "as we use marriage or wife or mother: to refer to a recognizable structure with content and meaning that may vary according to era or culture?" ("Chloe" 174). After all, when Rosenman considers the meaning of lesbian identity in England of the 1920s, she divorces it from any historical tradition and sees only the category of mannish lesbian. In contrast, Patricia Cramer argues that Woolf's lesbian identity belongs within a "particular lesbian tradition" of writers who "adopt the homoerotic self as a center from which to oppose patriarchal values and to reimagine self and community" ("Underground" 177). *Virginia Woolf: Lesbian Readings* challenges such narrow definitions of lesbianism as Rosenman's to reveal further the myriad ways in which Woolf expressed her lesbian-feminist identity.

Indeed, as Karla Jay and Joanne Glasgow suggest and as the title of their collection *Lesbian Texts and Contexts* illustrates, once we shift the context in which we read Woolf's and other writers' work, their lesbian content becomes apparent. One of the earliest discussions of Woolf's lesbian plots appears in Jeannette Foster's formidable study of lesbians in Western literature, *Sex Variant Women in Literature*, which was published in 1956 at the author's expense. With remarkable insight into the range of lesbian experience in Woolf's work, Foster discusses Clarissa's attraction to Sally Seton, notes Lily's lasting desire for Mrs. Ramsay, and praises Woolf's defense of the "lesbian woman of personal integrity" in *Orlando* (287). Blanche Cook's influential "'Women Alone Stir My Imagination': Lesbianism and the Cultural Tradition" highlights Woolf's role in the literary history of modern lesbianism and connects Woolf's feminism to her woman-identified sensibility. Considering *Orlando* with Djuna Barnes's *Ladies Almanack* and Radclyffe Hall's *The Well of Loneliness,* Cook's essay underscores the varied representations of women-loving women that traditional literary history elides. In "Is 'Chloe Liked Olivia' a Lesbian Plot?"

Bonnie Zimmerman uncovers the lesbianism in Woolf's sapphic vision of female collaboration and friendship. Jane Marcus reads *A Room of One's Own* alongside Hall's *The Well of Loneliness,* names Woolf's subversive writing style "Sapphistry," and explores how through an array of rhetorical strategies, Woolf seduces her female readers. Such attention to Woolf's relationship to other lesbian writers and traditions of lesbian literature, as well as to her lesbian audience, has enabled the current generation of critics to decode even further the erotic in Woolf's lesbian plots.

Audre Lorde defines the erotic as "an assertion of the lifeforce of women" (55). And although she recognizes that we live in a culture that "robs our work of its erotic value, its erotic power and life appeal" (55), Lorde conceives the erotic as "a well of replenishing and provocative force to the woman who does not fear its revelation, nor succumb to the belief that sensation is enough" (54). Woolf, like Lorde, struggled to express the erotic, to describe "womens bodies for instance—their passions" (*P* xxxix). Still, as this collection reveals, she persisted in her search for an erotic language that would embody the sensation as well as the replenishing force of women loving women. As Woolf puts the question: "If one could be friendly with women, what a pleasure—the relationship so secret & private compared with relations with men. Why not write about it? truthfully?" (*D* 2: 320).

"Lesbian Intersections" opens with Toni McNaron's reflective essay "A Lesbian Reading Virginia Woolf." In describing her experience of reading Woolf over the past thirty years, McNaron sheds light on critical issues involved when one reads Woolf as a lesbian. McNaron notes how many of us read in an environment that forces us to hide our own lesbianism; we are trained to read, as she puts it, through "heterosexist blinders." Trying to understand why and how she had missed the lesbian significance of Woolf's erotic scenes, McNaron developed her own "lesbian-feminist theorizing about reader response." Suzanne Bellamy describes her essay, "The Pattern behind the Words," as a love story tracing Woolf's influence on her own life as a writer and sculptor. Claiming the freedom of the common reader, Bellamy envisions Woolf as her lesbian muse, as her "most potent mythic companion." Bellamy conveys how Woolf's writing inspires, resonates, and intersects with her own creative work. Noel Furie's perceptive photographs of Bellamy's sculpture illustrate another intersection of the lesbian aesthetic.

Jane Lilienfeld's "'The Gift of a China Inkpot': Violet Dickinson, Virginia Woolf, Elizabeth Gaskell, Charlotte Brontë, and the Love of Women in Writing" explores lesbian intersections between Woolf and her nine-teenth-century precursors. Woolf's erotically charged friendship with Violet Dickinson encouraged her to write; it also, as Lilienfeld demon-strates, enabled her to see the lesbian loves in other women writers' lives.

Katherine Mansfield shared not only Woolf's love for women but also her interest in modernist technique. In "Reading Influences: Homoeroti-cism and Mentoring in Katherine Mansfield's 'Carnation' and Virginia Woolf's 'Moments of Being: "Slater's Pins Have No Points,"'" Janet Winston captures how Mansfield, alone among Woolf's literary friends, understood the artistic and personal effort required to write about erotic love for women. Winston interprets the complexity of Mansfield's and Woolf's homoerotic "reading influences," naming their relationship a mutual mentorship that validates each woman's life and work.

Looking at the critical reception of Woolf and Gertrude Stein, Corinne E. Blackmer wonders why they have never been considered in tandem as the most significant lesbian modernists. Blackmer's juxtapositions of both writers' lesbian short fiction in "Lesbian Modernism in the Shorter Fiction of Virginia Woolf and Gertrude Stein" supports her contention that these writers' intersecting vision of creative, independent lesbians is a defining moment in modernist writing. Tuzyline Jita Allan demonstrates intersec-tions between the personal and intellectual histories of Woolf and Nella Larsen. Pairing *Mrs. Dalloway* with *Passing,* Allan reveals the striking sim-ilarities between both novels' expressions of same-sex love; at the same time, "The Death of Sex and the Soul in *Mrs. Dalloway* and Nella Larsen's *Passing*" explores how race and class affect lesbian passing.

Blanche Cook notes that throughout the first half of the twentieth century, a "variety of lesbian literature coexisted with the vigorous denial of lesbianism in general and the unending difference in manner and style among lesbian women in particular" (719). By interpreting Woolf in the context of some of this literature, the essays in "Lesbian Intersections" reclaim the varied styles and manners not only of lesbian writing but also of lesbian life.

NOTES

1. See Silver, "What's Woolf Got to Do with It?" for a probing analysis of Woolf as an icon of popular culture.

TWO

A Lesbian Reading Virginia Woolf

TONI A. H. MCNARON

In 1964, I received a Ph.D. in English literature and history without ever having been required or even encouraged to read Virginia Woolf. Granted, my training was in the Renaissance, and at that time most academics would not have known of Woolf's many critical essays about that period and its great writers. The only novel of hers that I knew about was *To the Lighthouse,* pressed into my hands by a lover, not a professor. But she definitely was an ardent fan of the tall, horsey British woman and was eager to have me be knowledgeable enough to hold up my end of a discussion of her fiction.

In this reflective essay, I want to trace the progress of my continuous exploration of Virginia Woolf's works and the parallels that intellectual path has with my personal development, especially as a lesbian-feminist scholar working at a major research university in North America.

I began reading *To the Lighthouse* eagerly, wanting to please my lover more than to learn of yet another early-twentieth-century novelist. After all, I had successfully completed a whole semester on the Edwardian novel, immersing myself in the likes of Forster, Ford, Huxley, and Lawrence. I am afraid I responded only to formalistic elements during that first read; that was how I had been told to treat the period, and so I simply transferred skills used to interpret *Chrome Yellow* and *Howards End* to Woolf's clearly modernist and psychoanalytic novel about a phallic lighthouse and the characters held in its beams.

My lover was very literary, though she was a civilian in the world of academe, and very persistent. Under her auspices, I learned about Virginia Woolf as a person once I'd dutifully begun to read her work. What I heard drew me to her like a filing to its magnetic home. Soon I was asking for photographs of the young Virginia Stephen, staring intensely into that long, sensitive face, making up stories about the kind of person she must have been with that distinctive physiognomy.

My lover also told me about Vita Sackville-West and their idyll in Burgundy, which, though brief, raised questions and anxieties in their respective husbands' minds. I knew I was in the presence of a lesbian even if she did live with Leonard all those years. I identified with her melancholy search for a genuine connection to other human beings even as she knew deep down the impossibility of any such utopian state.

Her melancholy matched my own, though I was sure my causes were far less exotic than hers. Heavily into alcohol and denial of the everydayness of my lesbianism in the late 1960s and early 1970s, I identified with Virginia Woolf in what now seem distinctly dangerous ways. Romanticizing her suicide while simultaneously trivializing her mental instability, I turned her into the classic tragic heroine who achieved what she did under the most severe hardships and who had to suffer even more fools than I believed I did.

But through it all, I just kept on reading. Novel after novel until I'd been through them all at least once; then on to the only two volumes of essays then available to the general public (*CR 1* and *CR 2*). This process went on long after my separation from the woman who first placed Woolf's work in my hands; in fact, it continues to this day, some thirty years later. Certain landmarks persist even amid the rich blur that surrounds my engrossment. Reading *Mrs. Dalloway* for the first time thrilled me beyond measure, though I must confess I completely glossed over the key lesbian scene that now seems central to the entire book. I cannot remember what I told myself from my closet about the significance of Sally Seton's kissing Clarissa, but it was not until I first taught that novel in 1973 that the scene stood out from the overall narrative canvas. Perhaps I read that moment the same way I did scenes between Romeo and Mercutio or Rosalind and Celia—through tightly fitted heterosexist blinders, which prevented me from attaching sexual or intimate excitement to anything other than a male-female liaison. Nevertheless, the opening scene of *Mrs. Dalloway,* with its memory of sensuality and unbounded joy, bowled me over from the start. I also reveled in the sheer artistic achievement of that opening, where every detail suggested an ambiance around the central character even as it teased my imagination and wove its part of the web that would soon catch me up. The first time I taught that novel, I spent an entire class period on the first

two pages, drawing responses from students until they felt entirely inside the world they were to discuss.

Though I missed the erotic center of Sally and Clarissa's relationship,
I did not relinquish my firm belief that Clarissa and Septimus (who
always seemed her shadow self to me, long before I learned that Woolf
only added him to a later draft, deciding it was too unrealistic to have
Clarissa throw herself out of a window) were clearly ill-suited to marriage. After all, I had spent years trying to fit myself into that pattern,
only to come to my late twenties resolved to live my life as a lesbian
even though that would mean disapprobation from the culture at large
and the loss of certain domestic and financial securities I had long
assumed would be mine.

What I perceived about Clarissa and Septimus was that they could
not surrender themselves to their heterosexual marriage partners; and, it
never seemed puzzling to me that Clarissa chose to marry Richard rather
than Peter. Peter wanted full engagement from her, passionate sharing
on many levels; she had enjoyed this kind of intimacy only with Sally.
That much I had registered, since it corresponded to my own non-sex-
ual attachments to women throughout my life.

When the crucial scene finally pierced my consciousness, I spent a
long time figuring out why and how I'd missed it during my several previous readings. The resulting conclusions became helpful to my lesbian-
feminist theorizing about reader response. I understood that I had been
so thoroughly and successfully trained (brainwashed?) to read for heterosexual romance that nothing else registered as excitement or eroticism.
The fact of my own passionate relationships with women did not offset
that indoctrination into compulsory heterosexuality as a literary scholar.
Anger and sadness vied with one another until I forgave myself for being
a good learner and began using my new insight to scour off years of heterosexist rust from my reading antenna.

Having picked up the thread of women's lot in incompatible marriages, I quickly moved to examine Woolf's single women characters,
beginning with Lily Briscoe simply because she was the only one I knew
about at the time. (In 1976 or so, I still had not read *Night and Day* or
The Years.) Critics told me Lily and Mrs. Ramsay were polar opposites,
with Mrs. Ramsay representing the essential earth mother/match-
maker/caretaker, while Lily depicted a too-rigid creature in both her personal and artistic behavior. But I read *To the Lighthouse* rather differently
when I put the critics aside. It seemed to me then, and I am even more

convinced of it now, that Lily and Mrs. Ramsay are much more closely aligned than they have often been considered to be. What unites them is a desire to know their center—Mrs. Ramsay alone at night watching her favorite languorous beam of the lighthouse and Lily in her quest for the correct location for the tree in her painting.

I also felt there was erotic energy between them, not only coming from Lily's fervent wish early in the novel to become one with Mrs. Ramsay but significantly in a scene in which Mrs. Ramsay goes up to Lily's tiny attic room late one night after an evening of philanthropic activity. In this scene, Mrs. Ramsay initiates contact, both verbal and physical, and no matter how she insists on their difference because she is married and Lily is not, Lily counters by pointing out similarities. Furthermore, the stillness at the center of this encounter mirrors an earlier scene in *Night and Day* where Katherine and Mary sit in intimate silence, Mary fingering the soft hem of Katherine's skirt.

Scenes like these turn up not only in Woolf's novels, but in her short stories as well. I can still recall the intake of my breath when I first encountered the story "Kew Gardens," in which a young girl feels the presence of an older woman she admires behind her, kissing her hair ever so gently and quickly, giving her "the mother of all [her] kisses" (91). Unlike her coded eroticism in such stories as "Slater's Pins Have No Point," these scenes stand out in many readers' minds as carrying a charge quite beyond their length or surface content. For me, they constituted a direct lifeline to my own emerging lesbian existence, confirming my latent hope that such an existence could be shaped into moving art, countering negative stereotypes about lesbians that had become part of my view of myself.

As long as I harbored such internal homophobic ideas about lesbians as women not to be trusted with other people's daughters, I desperately needed writers like Virginia Woolf to render lesbian characters in a positive light. During this phase of my relationship with my literary hero, my dearest friend agreed when I proposed taking her young daughter off alone to shop for a birthday present and have ice cream together. I still remember how terrified I was to ask, sure that she would hesitate and in that moment confirm my worst scripts about myself. When she easily and cheerfully assented to the idea, I burst into tears. Later I began to consider that perhaps I was not someone to be feared. Once this epiphany occurred, I was able to acknowledge that not all lesbians in life or literature were sterling individuals and that I did not have to like or admire or, most important, identify with negative representations of lesbians any more than I had ever felt compelled to respond positively to characters like Iago, Fagan, or Claggart.

About ten years ago, I began examining less flattering images of lesbians in Woolf's fiction, beginning with Miss Kilman. My puzzlement over Woolf's juxtapositioning her with Clarissa and Sally gradually gave way to a regretful admission that Virginia must never have resolved her own ambivalence about sapphism. I tried to give extra weight to Clarissa's comment that only Miss Kilman was a thoroughly fit adversary, but the force of the unpleasantness surrounding her did not abate. Not only does Woolf present her as a pathetic and unattractive individual, but perhaps the most damning aspect of the characterization lies in her seemingly predatory possessiveness about the willowy young Elizabeth Dalloway.

Emboldened by this investigation into an obviously uncomplimentary portrayal, I turned to a much more problematic character, Mary Datchet, in *Night and Day*. On my first reading of this novel, I felt both pity and identification with Mary, finding her desire to have meaningful work admirable and yet ludicrous, since she never commits to the cause she serves. In response to her loss of Ralph to a more attractive woman, I was propelled back to Vanderbilt University in 1958. While pursuing a master's degree, primarily because there wasn't anything else I wanted to do at age twenty-one, I fell in love with a tall, handsome, sensitive poet who turned out to be engaged to a musician back home. Not only did I refrain from making any of the possible moves that were available to me, since I was, after all, in closer proximity than my competition, I drove the man I would have gladly married from Wisconsin to Florida so that he could attend his fiancée's piano recital. Yes, I knew Mary very well.

On subsequent readings, I was able to move out of my failed heterosexual mode and into my lesbian-feminist self. Looked at from that perspective, Mary becomes considerably more sympathetic, even heroic. Her determination to tell Katherine the truth about Ralph's affections seemed radical because it completely rejected the conventional mandate that the rejected woman can feel only bitterness and envy toward her more successful rival. I also decided that Mary's not being totally caught up in her work could be read as a more balanced characterization than Woolf's depiction of Mrs. Seal. Mary does not delude herself into seeing work as a substitute for life.

Reading *Night and Day* a couple of years ago, I was newly moved by the final scene, in which Ralph and Katherine seek out Mary's flat after their tenuous intimacy down by the river, only to be unable to climb the necessary stairs to reach the inviting light in her window. They sense in that upstairs room a level of satisfaction and integrity that may elude them, even though they are now an entirely socially acceptable couple and Mary is defined as alone. Even at this early stage, Woolf may be looking ahead to later works such as *Mrs. Dalloway* and *To the Lighthouse,* where she represents marriage at its best in a deeply ambiguous light.

The whole question of identification became central to my evolving connection with Virginia about seventeen years ago. I had recently fallen in love with the woman who has become my life partner. I had also been awarded a spring quarter leave from my academic institution and was planning a six-week pilgrimage to Woolf territory. Beginning with three weeks in London poking around Bloomsbury and Hyde Park Gate, my journey would eventually take me to St. Ives, where, for three luxurious weeks, I intended to sit on the same beaches where she sat as a little girl, walk in the same cold Atlantic waters, and stand before her family's summer place in order to absorb whatever magical atmosphere I could conjure up. I think what I wanted was to get as close to Virginia as humanly possible. In my own life, sustained intimacy seemed beyond my capabilities, yet I was lonely for someone to know me deeply. My wish, then, mirrored Lily Briscoe's initial desire to fuse with Mrs. Ramsay—a desire I consistently defended when teaching *To the Lighthouse* to skeptical students who quoted Freudian theories of mother-daughter enmeshment to my quite deaf ears.

This kind of fantasy identification with literary figures is foolish, if not downright dangerous. I myself had made great fun of American television viewers who sent birthday or anniversary or get-well cards to the women and men who peopled the daily soap operas. Yet I was exhilarated to be about to engage in activities that now seem to me only more sophisticated or arty versions of the same confused conflation of art and life.

By the time my ticket came due, my lover had found a way to take off two weeks from her work to join me in London. My ecstasy over this real-life adventure began to compete with my dream trip to "find" Virginia in the ether. During the week when I was in London on my own, I began to feel overwhelmingly incapable of remaining in England for the

projected three weeks in Cornwall. After much deliberation and a daunt-
ing trip to the airline ticket office, where I discovered just how much I
would have to pay to change my return date, I decided to spend an afternoon in Virginia Stephen's favorite squares around the British Museum.
What I did in those secluded and cool inner-city retreats was attempt to
commune with my heroine, seeking her advice about my pending flam-
boyant decision. What came to me late in the afternoon, clear and whole,
was a reply in the form of a very short poem. Convinced that I had
"heard" Virginia, I quickly scribbled the words on the slightly greasy
paper bag in which my shepherd's pie had been placed by a server at one
of the numerous luncheon shops across from the park near Gordon
Square. Here is that message: "Your waves will lose my echoes for the
present / I'll not go west to see your childhood shore / I need to hear
and feel my own concentrics."

Eventually I recognized these words as my reply to whatever voice I
thought I had heard. They proclaim my choice to live in my own present
rather than in her past. As such they do two paradoxical things: they fulfill Woolf's frequent injunction to stay focused on what is in front of
one; and they accomplish something she could not by acknowledging
and celebrating the keen and forceful pull of lesbian attachment as a
source upon which to build a life.

When the journals and letters began to appear, I bought cloth copies
with avid anticipation. At last I would hear Virginia unfiltered through
husband or nephew or academic critics with theories to advance. Immersing myself in each new volume was like having an extended gossip
session interspersed with amazing insights about her own feelings and
motives, the world around her, various of her associates and detractors.
The voice in these somewhat more private works was different from the
one in her public writing but only in degree: I could finally see how her
journals functioned as exercise books for her fiction and how many of
her letters were springboards for political and cultural analyses less
overtly rendered in the novels and stories. Given my connection with
her, I took her journals as strong proof of the need for me to keep my
own, no matter how trivial the entries might seem.

I also found a woman-identified woman, beyond any doubt. In entry
after entry, she spoke lovingly of her women friends, of other women
writers whom she knew or read, of her female literary ancestors, especially George Eliot. Never having given Eliot much serious consideration,
I eventually would be amazed to find such marked agreement between

the two women on the nature of marriage for white, middle-class, intelligent women who, like Jane Eyre before them, thirsted after knowledge and meaning in their lives.

One journal entry stands out among the rest. I remember thinking the first time I stumbled upon it, "This sentiment could only come from someone who loved women in general as well as in particular." She writes of traveling on the top of a London omnibus, from which perch she can see the streets below. She catches a headline in a daily paper asserting that a well-known writer has died unexpectedly. Her first thought is of which male it might be, only to be shocked to find out later that it is one Stella Benson, an up-and-coming novelist a generation younger than she. Her shock and grief seem genuine: she wonders why it should be this young woman and not she, a published author with major works to her credit. She also allows herself to recall their one brief tea together, admitting to having thought they might develop a friendship. Finally, Woolf mourns the permanent loss of subsequent books by Stella Benson, whose talent she recognizes and whose literary future she had anticipated. The sheer generosity of spirit in this entry spoke volumes to me about Virginia's desire for community. Because of the deep impression made on me by this entry, it came as absolutely no surprise when I later found the famous pronouncement: "Women alone stir my imagination" (L 4: 203).

I essentially liked the person I met in the letters and diaries, even though her prejudices and lacunae were often glaringly present. She began to descend from the pedestal upon which I'd placed her many years before and upon which it was easy to keep her as long as I depended only on her fiction for evidence.

My response to the self-referenced writings was not unlike her own to the many biographies she would read or indeed to Lytton Strachey's radical new definition of the entire genre of biography. I became fonder of the person with warts than I had ever been of the distant, esoteric artist. No longer was I in vague awe of the sheer talent of this literary giant. Rather, I argued with her views of Jews, people of color, other writers, or the state of fiction in the 1930s. The result was a healthier positioning of myself in relation to Virginia Woolf. I grew up in relation to her by reading the letters and journals, by giving up wanting to be like her, and by recognizing that I could stand free of her shadow without losing respect for and excitement over her and her accomplishments.

The last chapter in the saga of Virginia and me turns on her essays—

all several hundred of them—and on *Orlando*. After devouring the essays, I have returned repeatedly to certain favorites: the story of the moth's beating itself to death on her windowpane; her reflections on lumber rooms both architectural and mental; the stunning description of the eclipse of the sun that she witnessed; her wry analysis of changing tastes in fiction writing, complete with the implications of such changes on her own reception by readers and critics alike. I grasped the abiding love and admiration she felt for Shakespeare across sex and time, coming to understand why she strove to write from inside her characters with the same adroitness and sympathy as he had.

In addition to glorying in Shakespeare's use of language, Woolf found in him the androgyny she believed essential for any truly great artist. As someone caught up in what androgyny might mean in relation to my own lesbian identity, as well as someone who enjoyed cross-dressing, I was sufficiently encouraged by Woolf's references to Shakespeare's success at empathizing with male and female characters to begin presenting him to undergraduates as bisexual.

At about this time, I offered my first seminar on Woolf as the prototypic feminist critic. I invited graduate students to meet her challenge in those essays: to climb up on the shoulders of each writer one reads and make the heroic attempt to see what she or he sees. To look out of the author's eyes rather than our own is one of the hardest feats imaginable because it involves giving up so much of our own egos. It may well be in her essays, then, that Woolf comes closest to being like her model, Shakespeare. The fiction never entirely effaces her own political and sexual beliefs, but many of the essays are incandescently about their subject matter, not about their author. As my politics and my literary standards mature, I become increasingly sensitive to the potentially claustrophobic "I" about which Woolf speaks so acerbically in *A Room of One's Own*. I find myself in arguments about what constitutes a "lesbian novel." Whereas I believe that any fictional work by lesbians qualifies, many of my friends and colleagues insist that a novel has to be about a lesbian relationship to warrant the classification. Having Woolf's essays to support me makes it easier for me to stand my ground against what seems an unduly hermeneutic definition.

And so I come at last to *Orlando,* where some might have thought I would have begun this journey about reading Virginia Woolf as a lesbian. But this celebration of her love for Vita Sackville-West seems terribly private to me. In the late summer of 1993, my partner and I spent our fifth vacation in England. This time we determined to visit Knole and Sissing-hurst to feel something of what their environs might have been like. Unlike my earlier projected pilgrimage to St. Ives, this trip was motivated by a love of gardens and history not very different from their own. The moment I set foot on the grounds at Knole, I felt an aura of sadness and emptiness. I was sure that Vita and Virginia would resent the intrusion of casual picnickers and of voyeuristic tourists tramping the deer-cropped grass on the lawn where once I fancied their chasing one another in sheer delight to be together in so spacious and regal a locale. We went inside but stayed only a short time; I felt uncomfortable being there. The old house should be left to itself and its current inhabitants, distant relatives of the tall, angular woman for whom Woolf would write perhaps her most elusive and profound study of time and place and gender.

Sissinghurst was a sunnier place literally and metaphorically, with its obvious focus on living things in the many different gardens Vita planted over the years. As I climbed the steeply curved tower steps, my heart beat faster from more than cardiac exertion. I knew we had come to her study, with the tiny desk on which the lovely photograph of Virginia always stayed and to which her husband, Harold, was denied entrance. When I peered into that room, I felt the way I do on the third floor of my own home. That floor is where my lover and I have our desks and our computer, where we spend hours interspersing work with affection-ate contact and casual conversation. Like us, Vita made a physical space in which she could combine love and work. I tried to ignore the fact that some public relations person had put a picture of Harold in plain view and pushed the one of Virginia into a corner discernible only to some-one like me who craned my neck to find it.

My response to Knole and Sissinghurst seems in retrospect to have very much to do with my being a white Southern lesbian, steeped in class distinctions, surrounded by equally compromised mansions that both enchant and appall my sensibilities. Additionally, my mother loved an-tiques, surrounding herself with a vast array of inherited or acquired fur-niture, china, crystal, and silver until our house seemed different from any I ever visited. Furthermore, she singlehandedly designed and planted a magnificent flower garden in the next-door vacant lot, introducing me to the joys of gardening *in utero*. All this gothic and botanical history had prepared me to be moved by Vita's stunning gardens and by her and Virginia's privileged romps among the 365 rooms and untold acres of the Knole estate.

Spending thirty-odd years reading Virginia Woolf within academic settings means that I have been both the victim and the beneficiary of university life. Being in such an intellectually privileged setting has meant easy access to more of her work than is available to the common reader she so admired. Yet at crucial moments in my own academic history, her work was kept from me by sexist and homophobic professors. But it is futile to ask what I might have done in terms of my own research had I been fully introduced to this major figure by the wise men who taught me about other wise men. Maybe I am fortunate never to have been required to read her for a course. She came to me as part of a passionate relationship, and I have maintained an unbroken if necessarily changing relationship with her all these years. She still seems unofficial, peculiarly mine, because I never listened to experienced scholars opine about her stylistics or meaning.

My current theoretical work concerns my conviction that lesbian-feminism has the potential to articulate a new aesthetic based on likeness rather than the militantly oppositional foundation for traditional aesthetic standards. When I think of which writers stand behind my efforts, urging me to continue my formulations, Virginia Stephen Woolf is near the front of the line. Laced throughout all her work is a luminous commitment to other women, partly because they appeal to her physically and emotionally but also, and largely, because there is a charge she feels in the presence of others like herself, who send her back mirror images that resemble her more than do the men with whom she spent her life. Writing in her journal shortly after a visit from Katherine Mansfield and her husband, she remarks on the relief she felt when John Middleton Murry stepped out of the room for some reason. She found it easier and quicker to communicate when it was just the two of them, naming their likeness "shorthand." Even if I now shy away from the potential essentializing in such a statement, I resonate to its absolute truthfulness for her and for me. I profoundly agree that women alone stir the imagination. So I, as the lesbian I am, will go on reading Virginia Woolf, as the lesbian she was, for as long as I go on reading at all.

THREE

The Pattern behind the Words

SUZANNE BELLAMY

Among the clutter of my studio is a very large photograph of Virginia Woolf taken in her late thirties, a beautiful one with her long fingers stretched up to her cheekbones and deep-set, melancholy eyes. It has lived in my changing work spaces, among books, clay, etching inks, and tools for twenty years, and holds the place of honor and the muse. Along with this photo are a number of large, hand-printed quotations from Woolf about work, the brain, shapes, and the creative process. As they yellow, tear, stain, and deteriorate, I make them again, and again, and again.

This is the one I look at after an exhibition, after the weariness and emptiness settle, or with a looming deadline:

> [N]ow I must press together; get into the mood & start again. I want to raise up the magic world all round me, & live strongly and quietly. . . . The difficulty is the usual one—how to adjust the two worlds. It is no good getting violently excited: one must combine. (*D* 4: 202)

Every woman who knows me intimately, or has ever lived with me, knows about the centrality of Virginia Woolf in my life. There is a dynamic in the relationship that has always been erotic, though like many affairs it deepened slowly, and the passion comes and goes.

I was blessed to be a young artist and scholar just as the publishing world blossomed with Woolf's biographical, diary, and letter material in the early 1970s. Something started in me then, something I needed as a lesbian artist, as a writer, as a political activist, as an explorer of the hidden and mystical. We linked arms, Virginia and I, our garden grew and grew, and our metaphors mixed and flourished.

This then is a love story, one of those really good long ones, in the manner of the eighteenth century, where the space between vibrates with a thrilling inquiry, with probing intimacy and incalculable respect, projection, correction. The hot and the cool. It is time for me to look more closely at this passion, to find out why this great artist has been my most potent mythic companion. How did it begin? What are its shapes? How has it illuminated my own creative life?

I have written about Woolf often, bounced off a sentence, an image, played Bloomsbury games with my friends. I have written a series of partly autobiographical essays over a number of years, each of which has a Woolf title and philosophical underpinning.[1] I have lived with the dilemmas of dual creativity, sister love and envy, child abuse memories, madness, sibling suicide, the failings of love and lust and loyalty, the drive and passion of work. In all of this and in degrees, Virginia Woolf has had something to say. She has given me contexts, windows, parts in the play.

> [I]t is a constant idea of mine; that behind the cotton wool is hidden a pattern; that we—I mean all human beings—are connected with this; . . . we are the words; we are the music; we are the thing itself. (*MOB* 72)

The clarity and seriousness of this passage thrills me to the core; all the more so for knowing how tenuous is the effort to make it happen in a life or a piece of work, to bring the world into focus as if for the first time. "I am the thing in which all this exists." This "thing" Woolf writes about so often rings in my brain, "the thing itself," over and over again, the core, the form, the life force, the mystery, the point of everything. How daring the use of this word is, how precise its evocation. This thing, a life, something, her life, my life, patterns and connections, finding patterns behind the words. "I think I am about to embody, at last, the exact shapes my brain holds. What a long toil to reach this beginning" (*D* 4: 53).

For twenty years I have imagined and explored those shapes in her brain, and in the process have grown my own story. The formal academy could not offer me this fare. I needed to find it myself. Teacher, muse, companion, beloved—a potent mix.

This story really begins with another wonderful friendship in the great lesbian tradition, an Australian story. In my women's liberation group in Sydney in 1970 I met Bessie Guthrie. I was twenty-one, a Ph.D. student in history at the University of Sydney. She was then in her late sixties, an intellectual, a political campaigner, and a children's rights activist. We became devoted friends until her death in 1977, and in those few years she opened up a new world to me. She had been Australia's first woman publisher, in the 1930s, and had a great library.[2] Bessie loved Virginia Woolf, and she ignited that love in me. A Woolf bibliophile, she had all the old hardcover colonial editions of the novels, a first edition of *Three Guineas, Granite and Rainbow, The Captain's Deathbed,* and *The Common Reader,* as well as Vita Sackville-West's *The Garden, Collected Poems, Volume 1,* the Winifred Holtby biography of Woolf, and a vast collection of Bloomsbury material in fragile old blue early Penguins: Clive Bell, Lytton Strachey, Leonard Woolf. When she died we had just received the first of the new material, two volumes of letters and the first diary. How she would have loved what was to come. I inherited her books and continue to add to them, in hardcover whenever I can. It has become a joyful responsibility and in time will pass on to another. This is the tradition of the common reader.

> It seems to me indisputable that the conditions which make it possible for Shakespeare to exist are that he shall have had predecessors in his art, shall make one of a group where art is freely discussed and practiced, and shall himself have the utmost freedom of action and experience. Perhaps in Lesbos, but never since, have these conditions been the lot of women. (*D* 2: 341)

I wonder if that is true. It is hard to recreate now what it was like to be in those women's liberation groups of the early 1970s, in the gritty inner-city suburbs of Sydney. Not since Lesbos? Perhaps. The preconditions Woolf listed were there: a passionate community of women in fierce debate, confident, optimistic, able and beginning to acquire resources to work creatively, to write, make art, make choices about institutions, the academy, loyalty, the critical tradition; to be serious and to take each other seriously. "I dont mean that one ought to strain . . . only that one ought to stand outside with one's hands folded, until the thing has made itself visible" (*L* 3: 321).

I like this idea. It suits me and the way I work as an artist. I have read and thought and wondered about Virginia Woolf's influence, our creative partnership. I have waited until the thing has made itself visible. What comes is a mirror, the present, a love affair, and the need to shed the quest for analysis: inspired by my favorite, Miss La Trobe, "You've stirred in me my unacted part"; "You've twitched the invisible strings" (*BTA* 153).

My method in writing this essay is discursive, as is the freedom and privilege of the common reader, shedding the quest for answers, allowing germination. For so long the spotlight has been on Woolf, endless inquiry, endless questions—is she mad, is she a genius, is she a lesbian, does she hate men, is she a separatist? Her work and story spiral ahead of all these attempts. Enough! The spotlight can now shift and be on the seeker. Everyone finds what they are looking for; the rich, deep veins lend themselves to it all. For myself here I am content and thrilled that, as a lesbian artist, I can find resonances.

That Woolf's work at all levels continues way beyond its time to ignite inquiry and lead to links with me, my work, my life, for twenty years already, and with a community of women internationally is greatly significant. She found a form of writing and speculation that straddles at least the twentieth century and, like Orlando, perhaps will go further. Perhaps she did crack the pattern behind the words, fusing work and life form, moving in the stream past time.

Jane Marcus brilliantly speaks to Woolf's writing as seduction. Noting that for Woolf writing is a sexual act, Marcus writes,

> What, then, will we call it when the woman writer seduces the woman reader? . . . The seduction of the woman reader . . . has two purposes, to inculcate sexual solidarity by establishing difference and claiming that difference as superior, and the recruitment and enlistment of a new generation of women in the cause of feminist scholarship. The artist, the historian, or the critic have all been assigned their tasks in the conspiratorial "cell" of our "room." ("Sapphistry" 169, 176)[3]

This fits me so well. Certainly I began making creative choices in Woolf's wake, in her line. In July 1979 I made two fifty-minute radio programs for the Australian Broadcasting Commission on Virginia Woolf's life and work. It was a big project in a big year at the end of which I walked out of the university for the last time, away from an academic career, teaching, working in a hierarchy, a comfortable salary, an identity. It was fantastic, one of those pivotal moments of being for me. I chose to find a way to become an independent scholar and artist in the Woolf tradition.

She was not my only inspiration, but she was the one who has lasted the distance. Those of you who have taken this path know it is only for thrill seekers, crossed with nightmares and phantom terrors, economic strictures, and self-doubt. You learn to work from within your own imperative, invent a creative process, be self-motivated, and survive tough times. Not once have I regretted my choice, but I have foundered regularly, and it's the story of Virginia Woolf that picks me up. I chose independence in as many ways as possible, moving to the country where it was cheaper to have studio space and a garden. I chose to exhibit and sell my sculptures and installations in spaces where I had creative control, rejecting the gallery system without compromising the best available professional standards. I sought and built my audience from a community of women, artists and writers, activists, and readers, and all kinds of feminists and lesbians. I saw my role as that of a cultural worker but independent, following my own demons, my own patterns. I work with the expectation that the thing will make itself visible.

In 1980, at the start of this new life, I went on a pilgrimage—my country: the whole world. After the certainties of the 1970s, it was time for some shocks. How seamless it can all look with distance from the view, but journeys are turbulent. Thanks to Woolf, I had become a serious diarist, which is helpful then and now in finding the pattern.

On my first trip ever to New York in 1980, I sat at the Berg Collection and held the manuscript fragments of *Three Guineas*. Even now I am hard pressed to communicate the importance of this. Reading is one thing; touching and seeing is something else again. Perhaps because I make things, it meant more to me. Certainly it still matters when I think about it. It was such a wonderfully lesbian experience at the Berg, feeling the mistrustful eyes of guards who sensed I didn't belong there despite my ticket, the last privilege of academe I ever got. Now as an independent scholar, I daresay I wouldn't get a ticket. No Entry, and an antipodean colonial to boot.

It was so intimate, this reading of fragments. And the handwriting was atrocious. It was all quite agitating. There I read and copied Vita Sackville-West's diary of a journey to France with Virginia Woolf in September 1928: "We had breakfast in my room, and entered on a heated argument about men and women. V. is curiously feminist. She dislikes the possessiveness and love of domination in men. In fact she dislikes the quality of masculinity. Says that women stimulate her imagination, by their grace and their art of life."[4]

What a dilemma, I thought. A lover who doesn't share your politics. How can that love work? As usual I was taking Virginia's part, and reflecting my own experience of love and politics. Jane Marcus grasps this tension between two women as it develops around the whole *Orlando* business, *A Room of One's Own,* and the trip they made together to Girton for Virginia's talk. The creative dynamic between them seems more important than the sex. Marcus quotes Kathleen Raine, then a young Girton student, who described Virginia and Vita being together there on that day, "descend[ing] like goddesses from Olympus" (Raine 16). Such a picture of the two of them! Marcus says, "Much of *A Room* was meant simply to convert her beloved Vita to feminism, its seductive tone an extension of her love letters" ("Sapphistry" 166).

This business of sex and politics, passion in the body and in the work, is not simple, but it all belongs, it all matters. Can the muse come so close? Is it impossible to be stirred and stimulated by a lover one cannot convert, seduce, hold, and transform? Conversely, is the muse always best just beyond the grasp? Creative tension has its price for lovers who are artists, I decided. And wanting Virginia to have been a little happier in life, I realize, flows from my own love of her but is not especially helpful to my understanding of the creative process. Its great use for me is to expose youthful folly in me, which has nothing to do with Woolf at all.

Rethinking earlier ideas about Woolf became part of my work throughout the 1980s. As a common reader, I shifted some ground, as I discovered when I listened again to my old radio programs. Some certainties dissolved; some views extended. Lily Briscoe's yearning for Mrs. Ramsay was then hot, painful, and pivotal: "[T]o want and want and not to have" (*TTL* 202). My reading of Mr. Ramsay was severe, and I loved the scene where Lily resisted his demands for sympathy, pulling back her skirts, "grasping her paint brush" (*TTL* 153). Lily Briscoe, the independent lesbian artist, still shines for me, but I feel her depths more now, explore her palette and her perspective with more attention, and I can stay connected emotionally with the gigantic spirit of Mrs. Ramsay in her grace and impossible choices.

With *Three Guineas,* I experienced an extension on my return visits. I hold it to be the most brilliant piece of political writing I've ever encountered in the English language, other than some of the works of Mary Daly in my own time.[5] In 1979 I analyzed it as an invocation to establish our own traditions and centers of learning, to flourish as an outsider. I read the analysis of fascism within patriarchy in a historical sense primarily. What has changed for me now is how contemporary a document it remains. The *Three Guineas* world remains, with the rise of more blatant anti-feminist forces among intellectuals, as well as in the resurgence of male militias, neo-Nazis, and racist sects. As in the 1930s, we can witness radical-sounding aesthetics, invented by critics, that mock and erode feminism with fashionable rhetoric—the subtext of "post-modernism" feeling very similar to that of high and mighty male "modernism."

In the current debates about post-feminism and post-modernism, there are useful reminders for feminists about Woolf's modernist tag.[6] Contrary to the myths of Bloomsbury unity, there were always uneasy relations. As Marcus suggests, E. M. Forster, Lytton Strachey, and Goldsworthy Dickinson tended toward misogyny in their lives and writings, and certainly didn't like sapphism or lesbianism ("Sapphistry" 175n). E. M. Forster, in his speech about Woolf after her death, mocked "the cantankerous *Three Guineas,*" claimed "feminism responsible for the worst of her books," that she had little to complain of, "grumbling from habit," and that in any case she failed to address the two great (male) concerns of that time—sexuality and class ("Rede Lecture"). Are we reading the same author, I wondered, when I first encountered this. Gracious enough though he is to add that he was not the person best positioned to judge these matters, Forster nonetheless maintained what became a continuous point of tension within Virginia Woolf's social circles. Although the Apostles formed largely a male homosexual culture, they were not politically motivated toward any radical defense of the rights of women. Once the high modernist reactionaries around T. S. Eliot began to attack Woolf, her critical position began to look quite embattled. She was able to be resilient in the face of growing criticism—for example, that mounted by Q. D. Leavis—but it seems to me that terms like "modernism" require expansive qualification if used about Woolf.[7]

I am left with the sense that the broad cultural terms "modernism" and "post-modernism" are calculations fitted to the male tradition principally, with only partial application to writers like Woolf. We women artists have a tradition of our own like another language. Working within patriarchal culture becomes something like speaking in a second language, whether verbal or image-based. The rise of post-modernist attacks on feminism remind me of my years as a student in Leavisite-dominated English university departments of the late 1960s. It feels the same to me; the agenda has a snobbish, mocking anti-feminism about it.

The crucially important work of articulating the forms of cultural shift that are happening to women's creative work simply has to shed this recurring bitter and unhelpful debate, or at the very least decenter it. The cat in the bag is still a tom. As to *Three Guineas,* it has lasted the distance beyond the Leavisites and is due for a major rereading.

What has in fact changed for the lesbian outsider in the *Three Guineas* tradition is not at all structural but cosmetic, though there's something to be said for a little of that. Lesbian chic, sadomasochism at women's festivals and on the covers of magazines—this is more about the infection of the patriarchs than about the end of power politics. Rising anti-lesbian violence is a fact; death lists, threats, and recent murders in Oregon and other cities all coexist with the phenomenon in Australia of the Sydney Mardi Gras, which is interpreted by many as an indicator of community tolerance and acceptance. The *Three Guineas* world reappears for me when it is seen yet again as cantankerous to spoil the Mardi Gras–style party mood by challenging this assumption, by showing, as Woolf did in *Three Guineas,* the real growth of violence under the surface of the myth of greater freedom. Lovers without politics, a dynamic of dangerous times.

There are, of course, women everywhere inventing new pathways, living not as fragments, not in exile, not without our own language, creating the practice of post-patriarchal creative form. I try to live and work in this way. It's no harder than any other way. One thing I know intuitively from twenty years of reading Woolf, where texts merge, novels run into letters, diaries into reviews, is that it's living that is hard. It's being alive to life that is almost impossible. Beyond and because of all the wounding, there's the living. Not a half-lived, compromised life, but engagement—"real things behind appearances" (*MOB* 72). My hope in this is that we can be happier than Lily Briscoe, not so bad tempered as Miss LaTrobe, live in some community—but I doubt that the creative process will lighten at some level. Beyond our temperaments, there is still work to do. Central to that work is putting the time into each other's creative best. Like Orlando, Virginia Woolf can stay alive while I and others still find points of dynamic exchange with her. I don't stay in my relationship with Woolf from duty or career or nostalgia, but because it still ignites me, because in her and through her I drop down into my tradition, I play my part. I give my work context. I satisfy some of the lust of my own brain.

It has taken me a long time to think through the intersections of Woolf, lust, love, climax, and after. I have had to be brutally honest about myself and my relationships, and to allow for some insights to come through aging. In the sculptural non-verbal work I produced through the 1980s, mainly in clay, I moved through erotic forms, the female landscape, mythic journeys, memory, and the lesbian brain.[8] In a long

The Lesbian Common Reader (from "Lesbian Salon Series," 1992). Porcelain miniature. Artist Suzanne Bellamy. Photograph by Noel Furie.

sequence of porcelain studies, my Lesbian Salon Series, I tried to create the tense intimacy of a community of ex-lovers, pompous, fragile, epic, and ridiculous in one breath. This series spun off from a major work called *And We Hid Our Secret Knowledge, Even from Ourselves,* a great wooden barge and sail, full of porcelain figures and objects, women carrying books, instruments, artifacts, boxes, scrolls, fleece, statuary—a culture in flight, waiting and wanting to be remembered. Like an ancient dynamic artifact, this journey boat seemed to come alive in my own life. I began to travel again, to meet the women on it, scholars, artists, minstrels, holy women, storytellers, archivists, musicians, navigators, chatelaines. These women, my spiritual peers, ancestors, and contemporaries, had gathered up into the secret recesses of my ancient memory the key ideas and forms of a separate heritage, mythic if not real. They floated on the sea of my amnesia, waiting to be made and spoken back to form.

As in Miss LaTrobe's play, the distinctions of character and time blurred. These boatwomen shared with us the same ordinariness, limita-

Lesbian Bus Stop (from "Lesbian Salon Series," 1993). Porcelain miniature. Artist Suzanne Bellamy. Photograph by Noel Furie.

tions of trust, arrogance, irritability, small-mindedness. Invoking a per-fect humming past is nonsense, simply unbelievable, as Woolf knew. Some acknowledgment of the fierceness in us, the lust for nourishment and nurturance, is a good idea. What I have always found in Woolf is this marvelous battle among women, whether it is in her novels or in her lived story. It is not the battle between men and women, but battle it is, biophilic battle at its best. Once you throw out the angel in the house, keep her out. Save us from the new tyranny of the perfect femi-nist and perfect lesbian, reincarnated killers of the independent spirit. "With me and I think many women the root of love is in the imaginative part of one—its violence, its tenderness, its hunger" (qtd. in Marcus, "Thinking" 14).

For myself, cerebral/imaginative passion is what gets me near the peak. The key to erotic charge is a kind of sex in the mind, a complex experience of words and shapes and potencies that can be shared, but not essentially—that can be physical but will not stay there. My heights come when a personal connection or experience or place ignites the cerebral revolution.

For Woolf, there's no question that Vita Sackville-West provided something of that charge. Many writers have appreciated this intensely fruitful collaboration.[9] The byplay is delicious to consider, and Vita acknowledged at least something of Virginia's ability to educate her. "It is quite true that you have had infinitely more influence on me intellectually than anyone, and for this alone I love you. I feel my muscles hardening" (Sackville-West, *Letters* 165).

As to *Orlando,* Vita claimed to have found herself "in love with Orlando . . . a complication [she] had not foreseen" (Sackville-West, *Letters* 289). It would seem that as Vita took on another lover, Virginia created an immortal one—a stylish seduction indeed.

Another relationship that has come to fascinate me in recent years is the one of the two sisters, Virginia and Vanessa. I have seen a few of Vanessa's paintings at the Tate, and there is much new material now so that she can be really approached at last. The intimacy of sisters has been a difficult subject for me to approach. I have an older sister who is a painter and has two children and four grandchildren. Our brother committed suicide in 1981. Our relationship has been given friction by my lesbianism and by child abuse memories throughout the 1980s. The long break in our bond as sisters has only recently begun to mend, with lots of attention on both sides. In my family, my sister was "the artist" and I was "the intellectual." Both of us have needed to expand on these identities, give each other space and separation, and now piece together a new relationship. I also needed to settle with the dilemma and pleasure of dual creativity, needing both to write and to make artifacts and images. These territorial matters between Virginia and Vanessa draw me in and take on new importance in my reading and understanding of Woolf. Their letters are a monument.

> People will certainly think that we had a most amorous intercourse. They read more like love-letters than anything else. (V. Bell 71)
> [Vanessa to Virginia]
>
> Now if you sometimes kissed me *voluntarily* perhaps I wd. not be afraid. (L 4: 68; emphasis in original)
> [Virginia to Vanessa]
>
> [A]re you too much engrossed in me as a subject for your art to be able to think of me in the flesh? (V. Bell 59)
> [Vanessa to Virginia]

my own proper science; the theory of Vanessa. (*L* 1: 289)
[Virginia to Clive Bell]

They seemed very happy, but are evidently both a little exercised in their minds on the subject of the Goat's coldness. I think I perhaps annoyed her but may have consoled him by saying that I thought she never had understood or sympathised with sexual passion in men. Apparently she still gets no pleasure at all from the act, which I think is curious. (V. Bell 132)
[Vanessa to Clive Bell]

Their intimacy here founders, as it can between sisters on the differences in sexual orientation and with differing experiences of child abuse. I flinch at this letter to Clive on the subject of sex with Leonard, smelling as it does of compulsory heterosexuality and insensitivity to the effects of rape. Their love survived deaths, betrayals, the burdens of care, too much grieving and too many losses, partly, I feel, because each expected the other to work and respected that work profoundly. This makes for the most sustainable model of a partnership, which is crucial for women. Only Virginia's death breaks the pattern.

I often think how Virginia would have adored your having 4 daughters and have enjoyed the feminine atmosphere. (V. Bell 525)

I wish dolphin were by my side, in a bath bright blue, with her tail curled. But then I've been always in love with her since I was a green eyed brat under the nursery table, and so shall remain in my extreme senility. (*L* 6: 153)

What emerges beyond the family intimacy is the profound professional influence each had on the other. Vanessa's experiments in painting, the Omega Workshops, the country living, the gardens, the domestic aesthetics were all large influences on Virginia Woolf. An ambience grew around both women of rich sensuality. In their way, they each lived out "the personal is political" notion as well.

When I first began to read Virginia Woolf's novels, I felt she wrote like a sculptor. She was able with words to build forms, strip away surfaces, shed representation in a way different from abstraction. "I shall reform the novel and capture multitudes of things at present fugitive, enclose the whole, and shape infinite strange shapes" (*L* 1: 356–57).

Watching Vanessa's paintings evolve, participating in her art theory discussions of postimpressionism, and then immersing herself in the physical act of printing and making books was an expansive experience for Woolf. The decision to self-publish, to buy a press, to set the type with her own inky fingers, to commission art work—all this put Virginia and Leonard in the flow of an art movement. What I feel is that she pushed past the limitations of painting as a way ahead, drawing from another, more robust form of construction, literary but breaking into the same new territory as a maker of physical shapes that free themselves from direct representation but take on independent form. Things themselves, coming from a place in the brain not often visited. Something different from abstraction and not random.

> If I could catch the feeling, I would: the feeling of the singing of the real world . . . (D 3: 260)

> [I]nwardly I am more full of shape & colour than ever. (D 3: 219)

> I believe these illnesses are in my case . . . partly mystical. Something happens in my mind. It refuses to go on registering impressions. It shuts itself up. It becomes a chrysalis." (D 3: 287)

This embodies the paradox at the heart of Woolf's creative process. The madness business is beyond my present scope. As an incest survivor myself, I have many thoughts about the potent infusion of that experience into Woolf's work and life. It is a rich area of exploration for me and deeply familiar territory.

Her articulation of the mental landscape when the brain turns within is the peak of her genius and her courage. Sometimes chrysalis, sometimes only to "wish for death" (D 4: 319), she articulates the extremes. No writer gave more of her life force to the exploration of the world beyond the surfaces.

Woolf's creative courage and influence led to an explosion of experiments among women artists and writers. In my work this influence manifested itself unexpectedly some years ago within a personal meditation practice. For over twenty years I have developed a creative meditation I call the "workshop of my own mind": a dynamic studio tool for accessing work images, stories, and solutions to problems. I first wrote about this meditation practice in 1982, using personal journal stories ("Form"). The idea of the workshop developed over time to encompass an expansive world of women, a great city, studios, teachers, complex art practices, journeys, a forum for ideas. It became a multitudinous form and is still expanding.

In this world of my mind, there is a studio complex where I work, discuss projects, and in particular meet with a teacher, Hephaista, who is both a mathematician and a "mosaic scientist." In one of these meditations, Hephaista showed me a studio where this mosaic process was being researched. We went through a maze-like garden of exuberant color to a beautifully light-flooded room where a woman was working. It was Virginia Woolf. It is no surprise to me that I should invent her in my work world, but the detail of our ensuing contacts has been marvelous and continuous. I have never written of this before outside of my journals, but it seems insistent now to be included in this essay.

When I first saw the Woolf persona, she stood absorbed at a huge easel-like circuit board, tipped at an angle like an architect's bench. On both sides of her were hundreds of tiny objects in containers and trays, exotic materials unknown to me, like jewels and unknown metals, tiny shapes. She had an array of tweezers and tools that she used to pick up these objects, and obviously amazing eyesight, I thought, helped by the abundant prismatic light in her studio.

The board she worked on seemed to be moving as she built shapes in intricate detail. I asked her whether she could tell me what her current work involved. "The pattern behind the words," she said. Speaking very much in character, with comfortable references to her earlier corpus, she said she was now absorbed at a deeper level, creating forms in the shape of brain patterns themselves, synaptic constructions with patient experimentation. Now when I recall my first sighting of Woolf's work in progress, it was like a computer-generated circuit board. It had dynamic energy and seemed to make me dizzy, or at least cerebrally agitated, and at sea. It's hard to explain exactly. She was quite seriously courteous but not wanting to encourage silly questions or any gee-whiz responses, so I withdrew on the invitation to return by the courteous "Woolf character." This I have done often, and I am studying mosaic science directly with Hephaista. As to "Virginia," she is not a teacher there, not overly familiar at all, but we have had some conversations and sat together on deck chairs in the garden, smoking rollies. I like it a lot.

Of course, after I saw her and was trying to write it up in my journal, I realized the parallels with setting type. The tweezers, the tiny objects— it could all have been at the Hogarth Press but for the light, color, and absence of words and letters. "Thoughts without words. Can that be?" (BTA 55). Recently I read the essay by Ellen Hawkes, "Woolf's 'Magical Garden of Women,'" in which she mentions an enclosed garden where women can tell their tales, where the outsiders come in. I can happily report that in my mind at least this garden flourishes.

The book I turn to now, as if pursuing some urgent puzzle in my own work, is *Between the Acts*. Miss LaTrobe and Mrs. Swithin speak to me from scraps of paper on my studio walls. "But we have other lives, I think, I hope.... We live in others.... We live in things," says Mrs. Swithin (*BTA* 70). "'We haven't the words—we haven't the words,' Mrs. Swithin protested. 'Behind the eyes; not on the lips; that's all.' 'Thoughts without words,' her brother mused. 'Can that be?'" (*BTA* 55).

This last great work of Virginia Woolf puts the lesbian artist at a historic turning point. Does she go back to merge with Anon or will she come into her greatness at last? It's a matter of attitude, of self-invention.[10] Miss LaTrobe, like Woolf, the embodiment of the Elizabethan fool/scapegoat, is my personal nemesis. She is drawn to great projects, doomed to work with available materials and people, between worlds, cranky, depressive, driven. Her village play is not a failure. It is both an ancient passion play and a radically experimental revitalization of ritual. She is a shaman. She can live in things. She suffers the despair of emptying out before the next thing comes. She sits at the pub alone:

> She raised her glass to her lips. And drank. And listened. Words of one syllable sank down into the mud. She drowsed; she nodded. The mud became fertile. Words rose.... Words without meaning—wonderful words.... She set down her glass. She heard the first words. (*BTA* 212)

And so the creative cycle begins again. Transcending the great patriarchal forces that demand our attention and refuse to give us our liberty, there are other places. In the world of Chloe and Olivia, in the place through the looking-glass, there is magic to be had from the gift of Virginia Woolf to lesbian artists with the wit to go looking.

She is one of us; she is us; and the work continues.

NOTES

1. See Bellamy, "Form—'We Are the Thing Itself,'" "Freedom from Unreal Loyalties," "The Creative Landscape," and "The Narrow Bridge of Art and Politics."

2. See my essay "Bessie Guthrie" and the entry by me in the *Australian Dictionary of Biography, 1940–80,* on Bessie Guthrie.

3. After reading Marcus, I can never use three dots the same way again . . .

4. Victoria Mary Sackville-West, "Diary of a Journey to France with Virginia Woolf in 1929." Holograph, unsigned, dated September 24–30, 1928, 5 p. with Nigel Nicolson's MS identifying note. Berg Collection, New York Public Library.

5. In particular, Mary Daly, *Gyn/Ecology: The Metaethics of Radical Feminism*. Mary Daly makes strong links with *Three Guineas* and Woolf's outsider vision.

6. See Bell and Klein for a variety of critiques of post-modernism.

7. See Willis (46–47). See also L. Woolf, *Downhill,* for a good discussion of Virginia Woolf's handling of criticism and "thorns" (148–49).

8. A book of photographs and text from this fifteen-year period of my work, *Mapping the Coming Women,* is to be published by Sanguinary/Spinifex.

9. See Raitt for a mapping of the work relationship.

10. See Eisenberg.

FOUR

"The Gift of a China Inkpot"
Violet Dickinson, Virginia Woolf, Elizabeth Gaskell, Charlotte Brontë, and the Love of Women in Writing

JANE LILIENFELD

Virginia Woolf loved women. Virginia Woolf's deepest emotional resources developed from her dependence on women and her occasional resentment of that dependence. Virginia Woolf envied women; she got angry at women; she needed women; she hungered to be joined with other women, in imagination, through learning, through creating fictional women, through friendship. Discussing feminist ethics as a form of epistemology, Sandra Harding questions the concept of scientific truth, making a strong case for the fact that seeking knowledge requires empathy as well as inductive reasoning. To substantiate this argument, Harding hypothesizes that a lesbian perspective offers a series of political positions that situate lesbians outside heterosexist social constructions, a perspective substantiated by Sarah Hoagland's philosophical inquiries in *Lesbian Ethics* (Harding 249–67). Virginia Woolf demonstrated the truth of this epistemological argument, creating fiction in which many of her women characters loved and mingled themselves empathically with the hidden selves of other women and so gained knowledge of the inner life of another woman character while retaining their own selfhood.

Not only were Woolf's deepest emotional bonds to women, she recognized other women for whom connection to women was a psychic necessity. Throughout her life, Virginia Woolf eagerly studied women's lives and writings, seeking alternatives to prevailing cultural norms. Doing so, Woolf imagined and thus reconstituted what Nina Auerbach (in her discussion of Gaskell and Brontë) has called "a community of women" in past time to whom Woolf could look for example and support through their practice of loving and supportive friendship (Auerbach; Hawkes, "Magical").

Though not always sexually involved with women, Virginia Woolf was a woman-identified woman who can certainly be seen as lesbian (Cook; DeSalvo "Cave"). To explore the argument of this essay, I define lesbian according to one aspect of Julia Penelope's definition of the term in *Call Me Lesbian*:

> what it means to *be* a Lesbian in heteropatriarchy . . . [includes] one who *resists efforts to make her into a "woman"*; one who *defies the male descriptions and prescriptions that would limit her possibilities;* one who *refuses the very foundations of heteropatriarchal reality.* (78; emphasis in original)

In this essay, I will argue that both Virginia Woolf and her evolving conceptions of Charlotte Brontë meet this definition of lesbian. Additionally, I will argue that Woolf's evolving reconstruction of the idea of Brontë was inextricably connected to Woolf's relationships with Violet Dickinson, Vita Sackville-West, and Ethel Smyth. Loving and being loved by these three women increasingly enabled Virginia Woolf to view Charlotte Brontë through a lens as defined by Harding, a re/vision that challenged and clarified many of the political and literary beliefs Woolf had retained from her Victorian upbringing and education. Space constraints, however, permit me to focus at length only on Violet Dickinson's centrality to Woolf's reassessment of herself and to her idea of Charlotte Brontë.

Through loving a woman and being loved by her, Virginia Woolf was able to begin publishing her writing. In her 1979 introduction to her edition of "Friendships Gallery," Ellen Hawkes pointed out that Violet Dickinson "came to play a major part in Woolf's life, serving as a surrogate mother, an older sister, a confidante, a tutor in her reading and a mentor for her writing" (271). In "Virginia Woolf and Her Violin," Jane Marcus includes Violet Dickinson as one of a group of strong, inviolable single women whose courage, humor, endurance, and ability to live full lives without men enabled them to "mother" Woolf's mind (104–5). Developing Hawkes's and Marcus's ideas further, Louise DeSalvo connects Violet Dickinson to Woolf's survival of her half-brothers' incestuous attacks: "Violet Dickinson who, [cared for Virginia Woolf after her father's death] quite literally, saved her life by offering her maternal care and protection, and a respite from the abuse that she had lived with up to this time" (*Impact* 303).

Interpreting the pastoral idyll, the second section of "Friendships Gallery," DeSalvo reads "The Magic Garden" as a remembrance of Virginia Woolf's recuperation from her second nervous breakdown under Violet Dickinson's care for her in Welwyn in the summer of 1904 (*Impact* 303). Pointing out that Violet Dickinson had supervised the building of her own house in Welwyn, Hertfordshire, DeSalvo suggests that this fact symbolized to Woolf "that it was indeed possible to think about the kind of psychic space you yourself wanted to inhabit, which meant that it was necessary to reject those patterns of behavior erected by others" (*Impact* 304–5). Violet had even supervised the building of the drains, a fact DeSalvo interprets as "finding out how the houses ["and foundations"] of the fathers were built" thus modeling the fact that, "like Violet, [Woolf] had to find out for herself" (*Impact* 304–5).

In agreement with Hawkes, DeSalvo notes that it was Violet who "insisted that Woolf take herself seriously as a writer, that she convert her private diaries, essays, and fragments into published works" (*Impact* 305). Virginia Woolf was, in fact, launched as a book reviewer and essayist because Violet Dickinson's introduction to "Margaret Lyttleton, editor of the Women's Supplement of *The Guardian,* was a crucial first step for Woolf—who shortly thereafter became a published and a *paid* writer" (Hawkes, Introduction 271; emphasis in original). As Sir Leslie Stephen's daughter, Virginia Stephen might have begun publishing through her father's connections. Significantly, she did not; she published through her connections to someone she called "My Beloved Woman."

One of the first of these publications began a lifelong writing relationship with the idea of Charlotte Brontë. Sustained by Violet's love for her, and enabled to publish because of a connection Violet helped her establish, Woolf published her essay on Haworth Parsonage in *The Guardian* on December 21, 1904. The essay centers on Charlotte Brontë, initiating Virginia Woolf's long struggle to conceptualize Brontë as a radical female model. Woolf's essays, letters, diary entries, and two feminist polemics record the fluctuations in her assessments of Charlotte Brontë from this 1904 essay to *Three Guineas,* where Woolf seems to return to the admiration evinced in 1904. This admiration is clear in a letter to Madam Sue Ling written on July 27, 1938, suggesting that the positive view of Brontë was sustained throughout the rest of Woolf's life.

As a friend of Stella Duckworth, Violet frequently visited the family at

Hyde Park Gate during Woolf's childhood (*L* 1: xviii). Violet was socially very well connected; her mother was a daughter of the third Earl of Auckland. Financially independent, Violet Dickinson did not have to work—or marry. Her sexuality, independence, and stature seem to threaten the editor of Woolf's letters, Nigel Nicolson, who introduces Violet as "6 feet 2 inches tall, gawky, even graceless" (*L* 1: xviii). However, even he is forced to admit that "everybody who knew her, in the literary and fashionable world which she frequented, adored her" (*L* 1: xviii).

Significantly, Virginia Stephen's first impression of Violet Dickinson, recorded in the summer of 1902, is astute and respectful, differing greatly in tone from that of Nicolson. She noted Dickinson's height and "certain comicality of face," but also that "she treats her body with dignity." Violet's clothes are "suitable and harmonious." Not ashamed of her spinsterhood or her age, Violet was truthful about emotions. "She had her times of depression, & her sudden reserves." Violet Dickinson is not "one of those cleverish adaptable ladies of middle age who are welcome everywhere and not indispensable anywhere." In fact, "[s]he has a very wide circle of acquaintances mostly of the landed & titled variety . . . with whom she seems to be invariably popular" (qtd. in Hawkes, Introduction 270–71).

In a letter to Violet Dickinson, Virginia Woolf named the relationship that developed between her and Violet Dickinson a "romantic friendship" (*L* 1: 75). As Lillian Faderman has analyzed such friendships in her *Surpassing the Love of Men,* they consist of passionate, intense friendships with deep trust and involvement in one another's lives, frequent if not daily contact, and a supportive, loving sharing of confidences, details of daily life, thoughts, and values. Such relations were the accepted norm of friendship between women in nineteenth-century Britain and America.

Although not universally acknowledged at the time, such relations were sometimes physical (Faderman, *Surpassing* 18–19, 328–31). Read in light of current lesbian theory, the language of Virginia Woolf's letters to Violet Dickinson hints strongly at a physical component to their relationship. Ellen Hawkes states unequivocally that "it is clear from her letters that Woolf fell in love with the older woman" ("Magical" 36). However, Hawkes's refusal to focus on the possibility of a physical component in Violet Dickinson's and Virginia Stephen's relationship is suggested by Hawkes's reaction to the known facts about the sexual love of Vita Sackville-West and Virginia Woolf. Although Hawkes notes that Carroll Smith-Rosenberg specifically cites the sensual ("Magical" 37) as part of "'the female world of love and ritual,'" Hawkes rejects such a focus when talking about Vita Sackville-West and Virginia Woolf: "I want to say from the outset that I am not interested in what Quentin Bell once called the 'coarse physiological facts' of their sexual affair. Their love, like most deep relationships, encompasses so much more than the simple fact that they went to bed together" ("Magical" 49).

Hawkes's essay was published in 1981, before strategies of lesbian interpretation had received academic acceptance. In her essay "'Throw Over Your Man . . . ,'" arguing that "homoerotic desire . . . is expressed in an intertextual code," Pam Olano theorized several reading strategies that I follow here (17). When read according to Olano's strategies of interpretation, images of cuddling, burrowing furry animals, of touching, tasting, digging, twining, hugging, delving, and metaphors of ecstasy in Woolf's letters to Dickinson may reveal one of Woolf's lesbian languages, a textuality of sexual desire that forms a part, but not the whole, of Woolf's correspondence with Violet Dickinson in Volume One of Woolf's published *Letters*. Just as "Friendships Gallery" is named a precursor to *Orlando* (Hawkes, Introduction 271), so Woolf's letters to Dickinson resemble her later love letters to Vita Sackville-West in their arch tone and playful sexual allusions.

DeSalvo and Cook suggest that not only was "Friendships Gallery" the prototype of *Orlando,* the mutual love of Violet and Virginia "lighted the caves" wherein Virginia loved Vita. A language of lesbian desire flows through both sets of letters. The encoded imagery of "wallabies" and "kangaroos" found in Woolf's letters to Violet Dickinson is transformed into the mongrel squirrel, the hooked dolphin, and the muddy Grizzel of Woolf's letters to Vita. Similarly, the truths confided to Violet about her feelings for Leslie Stephen become the truths shared with Vita about the emotional fluctuations of Woolf's reactions to her insights about her life. When Virginia fell in love with Vita, Virginia initiated the relationship by telling Vita two truths. One was of the Duckworths' molestations; the other was the history of her love for Violet Dickinson (*L* 3: 305–6; DeSalvo, "Cave" 199; Hawkes, "Magical" 50). Both Virginia Woolf and Vita Sackville-West acknowledged that their love was sexual. With Violet Dickinson so clearly woven into the early moments of the relationship to Vita, I can suggest, if not prove, that Woolf's relation with Violet was a consummated lesbian love.

The same code that Pam Olano and Blanche Cook have demonstrated in the works I have cited above authorizes my interrogations of Nigel

Nicolson's tone in his edition of Woolf's letters. I have noted, for example, that Nicolson's "awkward" becomes Woolf's "self-respect" in descriptions of Violet. But even Nigel Nicolson, writing for a British audience rather than an American feminist one and hence apparently intent to "protect" Woolf from the charge of lesbianism, notes that Woolf calls some of the letters "hot" and he gives the examples of "Nos. 91 and 296" (*L* 1: xviii). Numerous additional examples can easily be found. In September 1904 Woolf asks, "Why the D——— cant you come up to London? Then I should be petted again perhaps" (*L* 1: 54). In October she demands "a good hot letter" (*L* 1: 60) and announces in March 1903 that "she [Woolf] has tender memories of a long embrace, in a bedroom" (*L* 1: 71).

Teasing allusions to physical relations are intertwined with flirtatious innuendos. Woolf addresses Violet as "My woman" and "My beloved Woman" (*L* 1: 74–75), titles Hawkes dismisses as Victorian conventions without sexual significance ("Magical" 38). "Dont get too Holy" (*L* 1: 58) shades into "I hope your grinders are all right, and the rest of your works well oiled" (*L* 1: 61). Herself in Surrey, Woolf writes to her friend, "I have got a double bed—some strange foresight made them give it me—I wish you could come" (*L* 1: 73).

Sexually suggestive language that alludes to the maternal increases in the letters as Violet Dickinson's back injury worries Woolf and intensifies her feelings about their separation. Playing on her intimate nicknames for herself and Violet, Woolf's desire that "I wish you were a Kangaroo and had a pouch for small Kangaroos to creep to" (*L* 1: 79) soon becomes "When are you coming back to your Sp's bosom? . . . I shall have earned my kangaroo nest before I die" (*L* 1: 83). Given permission to visit, Woolf writes, "I will come with joy on Friday, but it grieves me to think that your works are rusty. I see they want a good licking by the devoted Sparroy" (*L* 1: 84). Thus it is no surprise to find that one of the letters Nicolson cannot avoid calling "hot" is indeed so: In Letter 91, Woolf writes, "it is astonishing what depths—hot volcano depths—your finger has stirred in Sparroy—hitherto entirely quiescent" (*L* 1: 85). Calling Violet her "illegitimate Aunt," Woolf recalls a coded scene: "it is marvellous what a blind ostrich Sparroy can be—do you remember the incident of her and her intimate in the early days? and now hasn't that blossomed?" (*L* 1: 90).

Noting the intermingling of Violet's nurturing, maternal role with what she had earlier called the "romantic" aspects of their relationship, Woolf queries, "would you like to feel the Wallaby snout on your bosom?

Say Come and I Come, Go and I Go" (*L* 1: 96). Apparently this Wallaby could signal Woolf's passion for truth as well as for tenderness. In December 1906, apologizing for having delayed telling Violet the truth about her brother Thoby's death, Woolf tells her friend that "you must imagine the most compassionable and soft of Baby Walls just climbing on to your bed." In this same letter she tells Violet, "I shall come to you very soon for—well, not for consolation, but for all the things that make life worth having" (*L* 1: 267). Having seen Woolf's merger of the maternal with the sexual image, the reader might ask whether maternal images, in addition to acknowledging the lost mother, may also have provided Woolf a safe and available language of female love. If so, it may be illuminating to place the maternally sensual images of the Violet Dickinson letters next to Woolf's well-known remark in her diary that Vita Sackville-West "so lavishes on me the maternal protection which, for some reason, is what I have always most wished from everyone" (*D* 3: 52).

Playing on the stereotype of the older lesbian seducing innocent girls into "the life," Woolf teases Violet, "you are one of those dangerous women who exercise not at all the right kind of influence over young girls—and Virginia should be careful whom she knows—I dont think Violet Dickinson is at all the friend I should like for my girls" (*L* 1: 191). But the passage that Nicolson refers to as "hot" does not seem to be teasing in its tone: "Shall we say Love? If you could put your hand in that nest of fur where my heart beats you would feel the thump of the steadiest organ in London—all beating for my Violet. Sometimes, when I am ordering dinner, or emptying—a flower vase—a great tide runs from my toe to my crown, which is the thought of you" (*L* 1: 245). Discussing this letter, Pam Olano insists on foregrounding its passionate love, advising readers that "the sensual references should be understood as exactly what they are—a twenty-four year old woman's sensual description of her female anatomy and her knowledge of its sexual capacity" ("'Throw'" 29).

Sexual innuendoes and flirtatiously worded invitations continue through 1908 and even occasionally into 1911, five to seven years after the first intensity of Virginia Woolf's love. A letter of 1906 ends with "I wish we could put our pens in the fire, and take to the material embrace" (*L* 1: 261). Speaking of their recent visit in July 1908, Woolf asks, "but how did you sleep . . . after the sudden revelations I made you . . . I think with joy of certain exquisite moments when Rupert [Violet's dog] and I lick your forhead [*sic*] with a red tongue and a purple tongue; and twine your hairs round our noses" (*L* 1: 338). Woolf's playful wit may have enabled her to suggest a lesbian love encoded in a domestic animal, Violet's dog, perhaps serving here as another sort of wallabie or kangaroo image. Could "forehead" be a euphemism for the vagina? If so, might "a red tongue and a purple tongue" allude not to Rupert's but to Woolf's and Dickinson's instruments of lesbian desire?

However, in August 1908, Woolf admits that her longings for Violet are less intense. Moving away emotionally, she asks Violet: "Supposing we drift entirely apart, in the next 3 years, so that we blush when we meet and remember our ancient correspondence. Will it be your fault or mine? Yours, I think; because you are always so unselfish" (L 1: 367). Woolf's letters to Violet become less frequent, but even as late as March 1909, she clothes Violet once more in the sensual imagery of their love: "Well—I wish I ever saw you: a fine spirit, like some pale taper in a gale— Do you ever see yourself—flowing all night long—the flame streaming like a river" (L 1: 389). Continuing in this tone, Woolf acknowledges in April 1909 that Violet was "very exquisite the other night, and I suppose I was very egoistical [sic]" (L 1: 389). If her letter discussed their relations and not others, then sadly, Woolf seems to have implied more than she could give to Violet. She advises the friend whom she had once passionately importuned, "Please dont dwell upon my exaggerated account of love; as a matter of fact I am a woman with very little sexual charm. Warming to the task, I often represent myself as irresistible" (L 1: 392).

Violet Dickinson's actions demonstrate that she joined Virginia Stephen in "A Gallery of Love and Friendship." Acknowledging their shared cuddly-animal language, Violet had signed a gift book to Woolf "A Tract for the Sp[arrows] fr[om] V[iolet] D[ickinson]" (PA 221 n. 1). Violet had bound and saved Woolf's letters for many years, as Woolf found when these were returned to her. Before giving "Friendships Gallery" to Violet in 1907, Virginia Woolf had "typed [it] with a violet typewriter ribbon and bound in violet leather with the title embossed in gilt on its cover." Although Woolf requested the book back, Violet Dickinson never returned it. That it was still among Violet's papers at her death in 1948 suggests its importance to her (Hawkes, Introduction 272).

As Diane Gillespie's The Sisters' Arts and numerous of Woolf's published letters reveal, for Woolf the physical act of writing was an emotional exercise, inseparable from the creation of meaning. She was quite particular about paper quality, pens, and their nibs. More than the playful punning that marked her letters to Violet is suggested by Woolf's typing her manuscript in violet ink, possibly physically recalling the loved one—Violet, the color of whose name Woolf may have punned on more than once. Did Woolf use the images associated with Violet's name as a means to gain writing fluidity while composing "Friendships Gallery"? What did it feel like, for example, for Woolf to strike each key onto the page and see a violet mark spread out on the paper like the spreading folds of the many-hued purples of the vulva? Did the flow of ink on paper recall Woolf's haunting image of Violet's "flowing all night long—the flame streaming like a river" (*L* 1: 389)?

It is significant that the maternal and sensual image of the furry pouch into which the younger woman imagined she could climb in with Violet Dickinson became a cornucopia of the materials needed for writing. On November 8, 1904, just prior to her first publication, Violet Dickinson made the younger woman a gift of a china inkpot (*L* 1: 153; *PA* dates this as a birthday present on January 25, 1905). It was so large that it had "a well for ink deep enough to write a dozen articles for the Guardian [*sic*]" (*L* 1: 153). Discussing the gift in her diary, Woolf noted that it "holds almost a jar full of ink, & is rather too large to be practical" (*PA* 227). Had Dickinson meant it to be practical or to inspire courage? Woolf notes that such reserves of ink will force her to "cultivate a bold hand" (*PA* 227).

Read according to the codes Woolf seems to have employed when writing letters to Dickinson, this ink pot suggests symbolic as well as literal meaning. Like Violet's love for Virginia, it is "deep." For me as a reader, its shape, "a pot," recalls the locution "honey pot" for the vagina. The "ink pot" iconographically recalls the wallabie's pouch that in Woolf's letters to Violet symbolized and provided comfort, protection, and sexual delight in one image. As I have suggested above, Woolf's letters to Violet are full of demonstrations of a "bold hand," a delightful pun on authorial and sexual explorations. In writing these letters, Woolf's hand has lingered on Violet Dickinson's chest, traced patterns of Violet's "works" and entered Violet's "pouch." Having gone deep into these depths of strength and love for its fluid, its ink, for the physical technology of the production of writing, such a hand might boldly write the truth, having dipped its pen into such a Well/wyn.

Virginia Woolf's article on Haworth, perhaps written with ink from Violet's china ink pot, with its focus on Charlotte Brontë as the most accessible of the Brontë daughters was a harbinger. Her romantic friendship with Violet Dickinson seems to have made her feel safe enough to undertake a feminist pilgrimage of knowledge, to move from judgment to empathy with aspects of Charlotte Brontë, a journey that began with this 1904 essay. Woolf's subsequent relations with two other lesbians important in her life, Vita Sackville-West and Ethel Smyth, were gateways to a deeper understanding of and identification with Woolf's changing conception of Charlotte Brontë.

Like Virginia Woolf, Charlotte Brontë might never have existed as a writer, or even survived her childhood, had she not had strong, woman-centered roots, first with her sisters, then with the closest friends of her youth, Ellen Nussey and Mary Taylor, and then with the great writers of her day, among them her sometime friend Harriet Martineau and her biographer, Elizabeth Gaskell (Lilienfeld, "Sisterhood"; E. Miller).

Virginia Woolf apologized to Violet for the article on Haworth, trivializing it: "I wrote it in less than 2 hours, so I dont suppose it is very good" (L 1: 158). Yet there is nothing in Woolf's article, reprinted in Volume One of the *Collected Essays*, to apologize for. Woolf seems to have prepared herself for her trip to Haworth Parsonage by reading the later edition of Elizabeth Gaskell's *Biography of Charlotte Brontë* (a copy of which was catalogued in Leslie Stephen's library, which Virginia Stephen inherited [Holleyman and Treacher]), as Woolf several times quotes the biography in her essay. Elizabeth Gaskell made no pretense of objectivity, inserting herself into her biographical narrative by interpreting events, working always to make Charlotte appear as socially acceptable as possible by reinterpreting those traits that had repelled and fascinated the Victorians, Gaskell among them.

The figure of Elizabeth Gaskell has long been a contested scholarly site and, like Virginia Woolf, the object of competing British and American feminist views. Heated charges against Gaskell as bourgeois appropriator of workers' lives are met with countercharges of Gaskell as revolutionary woman artist or morally indignant minister's wife and mother.[1] Elizabeth Gaskell's representations of Charlotte Brontë cannot be extricated from this scholarly debate, which here intersects with new directions in lesbian literary theory (E. Miller). Gaskell, who, like Woolf, sought knowledge through empathy and identification, responded complexly to Charlotte Brontë, in whose life she may have seen reflected, as through a prism, her own struggles with her Victorian roles as wife of a minister, mother, community worker, and creative artist (Lilienfeld, "Sisterhood"; Gerin, *Gaskell*).

Brontë's family and friends had been determined to counteract the popular portrayal of Charlotte Brontë as sexually impure, a view that had been created in part by the reactions to Brontë's books such as Lady Eastlake's review (Poovey 130, 132–36), the content and tone of the novels, and the rumors of Brontë's having been Thackeray's governess and mistress. Ellen Nussey had suggested to Reverend Brontë that he choose Gaskell as his daughter's "official biographer," a task Gaskell told George Smith she accepted as "a grave duty" (Gaskell, *Letters* 349). She repeatedly informed Smith and other correspondents that "the more [Brontë's] character and talents are known the more thoroughly will both be admired and reverenced" (Gaskell, *Letters* 395). To that end, Gaskell informed Nussey, her book would emphasize "Charlotte Brontë—the friend, the daughter, the sister, the wife" (Gaskell, *Letters* 376), the subservient female role. Gaskell actively counteracted "the common ideas of her being a 'strong-minded emancipated' woman" (Gaskell, *Letters* 430).

In many areas of her life Elizabeth Gaskell was quite radical. She challenged Victorian novel conventions in depicting the roles of workers and women.[2] Reverend and Elizabeth Gaskell insisted that their daughters be highly educated and allowed them more intellectual freedom than was normative for Victorians of their social class. However, demonstrating some of the more conservative aspects of Gaskell's nature, her relations with Brontë were inflected by her own conflicts between creativity and the female duties of wife and mother, which she often alluded to in her correspondence (Gaskell, *Letters* 106–7, 109, 694–96). Elizabeth Gaskell knew that Charlotte Brontë, like herself, lived divided. Gaskell knew Brontë the gentlewoman and exemplary Christian daughter, as well as Brontë the impassioned follower of her own conscience. Representing a more socially acceptable Charlotte, Gaskell interrogated her own conflicts and choices.

Complicated and honest as it was, the relationship between Gaskell and Brontë was not a romantic friendship like that of Dickinson and Woolf. Gaskell frequently invited Charlotte to visit her in Manchester and "encouraged her to greater independence [from her father]," if not from the socially accepted roles for women (Gerin, *Brontë* 529). Uncertain, Charlotte involved all her friends in her decision on whether or not to marry Reverend Nicholls (Gerin, *Brontë* 532). Visiting Gaskell in Manchester about a month before her marriage, Brontë confided her fears to Gaskell. Gaskell praised her own and her friends' husbands and marriages, a generous response, for Gaskell feared that after the marriage, Reverend Nicholls would prevent Charlotte's further relations with her, a Dissenter (Gaskell, *Letters* 280). Charlotte Brontë married not for romantic love but for financial reasons, to ensure an income and a secure home for her father in his old age (Gaskell, *Letters* 289). Hence it is unlikely that the strong-willed Charlotte Brontë would have been persuaded by Gaskell's appeals to romantic love, no matter how much she valued her friendship with Elizabeth Gaskell.

Gaskell may have seen herself in those aspects of Brontë that Gaskell felt it her biographer's "duty" to eradicate from the public's mind. Comparing herself to Brontë, Gaskell humorously speculated that

> the difference between Miss Brontë and me is that she puts all her naughtiness into her books, and I put in all my goodness. I am sure she works off a good deal that is morbid *into* her writing, and *out* of her life; and my books are so far better than I am that I often feel ashamed of having written them and as if I were a hypocrite. (Gaskell, *Letters* 228; emphasis in original)

Gaskell's books were not so "good" that she escaped without censure from Victorian readers. *Mary Barton* was condemned by some contemporary readers for deliberately stirring up class hatreds (Gaskell, *Letters* 66–67), the very charge, in fact, that Lady Eastlake had leveled against *Jane Eyre*. Shaken by readers' reactions to *Ruth,* Gaskell said to her close friend Tottie Fox, "I think I must be an improper woman without knowing it, I do so manage to shock people. Now *should* you have burned the 1st vol. of *Ruth* as so *very* bad?" (Gaskell, *Letters* 222–23; emphasis in original). Interestingly, Charlotte Brontë had questioned her friend Gaskell's decision to kill the redeemed though once fallen Ruth (Gerin, *Gaskell* 132).

Perhaps seeking knowledge of herself as an artist, as well as the means to protect Charlotte Brontë's memory and artistic achievement, Gaskell began writing *The Life of Charlotte Brontë*. She had joked with her publisher, George Smith, also the publisher of Brontë, that "I have three people I want to libel—Lady Scott (that bad woman who corrupted Branwell Brontë) Mr. Newby, [the unscrupulous first publisher of the Brontës' novels] & Lady Eastlake" (Gaskell, *Letters* 418). In fact, in order to escape threatened law suits from Lady Scott and the family of the director of Cowan's Bridge School, which Brontë fictionalized as Lowood Institution in Jane Eyre, Gaskell had to retract the first edition of the biography, making numerous corrections to the text for the revised edition (Gerin, *Gaskell* 186–97). It is now well known that Gaskell was dismayed by what many later biographers have described as Charlotte's sexual obsession with a married man, M. Heger, with whom Brontë studied French in Brussels. Winifred Gerin asserts that in order to suppress what might be construed as further impropriety, Gaskell deliberately falsified the dating of what Gaskell hinted was Branwell's dissolution through addiction and sexual depravity in order to account for Charlotte's severe depression after her return from Brussels (Gerin, *Brontë* 572–74; Gaskell, *Letters* 401, 409–10). Inadvertently, thus, Gaskell also suppressed what some twentieth-century readers might term the lesbian Charlotte Brontë (E. Miller 35, 37, 48, 51–52).

Elaine Miller's passionate scholarship has focused renewed attention on the romantic friendship between Ellen Nussey and Charlotte Brontë. Miller, like Gaskell, eschews an objective stance. From a lesbian perspective, Miller reassesses the known facts, circumstances, and supporting documents, hence, of necessity, interrogating Gaskell's (as well as other constructions) of Brontë. Miller describes Ellen's and Charlotte's running away together, their "capture" as Ellen herself called it, their magical week together at Bridlington (37–39). Arguing in favor of an emphasis on Ellen's importance to Charlotte as opposed to that of M. Heger, Miller points out that on "the evidence of language alone it is clear that any word or phrase that can be construed as expressing affection to Heger can be easily matched by similar words and phrases expressed to Ellen" (42). Miller counteracts Brontë's biographers' belittling of and prejudice against Nussey and their relationship (51–54). Thus Miller builds a strong argument to substantiate her claim that

> on the evidence of the letters between 1832 and 1839, it seems inconceivable that these two women in their twenties would not have chosen to live together as friends and lovers had they been offered different economic, social and sexual choices. . . . [However, they] were allowed to be "romantic friends" so long as this did not challenge accepted conventions by becoming an openly committed relationship in which their energies were withdrawn from men and given to each other. (39)

In contrast to Gaskell's image of Brontë, the reconstructed figure of the lesbian Brontë reshaped Woolf's earlier conception of Brontë. As Woolf sought literary foremothers, apparently Vita Sackville-West sought lesbian herstory, keeping, for example, "a photograph of Charlotte Brontë on her desk, [and writing] in her journal that the letters of Charlotte to Ellen were 'love letters pure and simple' and 'left little doubt in one's mind as to what Charlotte's tendencies really were'" (Glendinning qtd. in E. Miller 29). Significantly, this writing desk was at Long Barn, where in December 1925 Woolf spent the first three of her nights with Sackville-West (*D* 3: 51 n. 10). Noting her longing for Vita, Woolf described "[h]ow Vita's inkpot flowered on her table," an image that clearly haunted Woolf (*D* 3: 118). The "gift of a china ink pot" has become this flowering ink pot; from involvement with each beloved woman Woolf had drawn materials for writing. It is tempting to speculate further about the l/ink connecting Violet to Vita to Woolf, whose changing view of the life of Charlotte Brontë was illuminated perhaps by the flame streaming in the wind (*L* 1: 388), by whose light Woolf might see another truth than the one taught her in her parents' household.

Victorians such as Lady Eastlake and Matthew Arnold interpreted what they called Charlotte Brontë's "coarseness," her mingling of sex and anger, as a political attack on hegemonic patriarchy in the family, the church, the culture. It was increasingly this political aspect of Brontë that Woolf grew to admire. As the lesbian ethicist Sarah Hoagland has argued, the lesbian exclusion from patriarchy enables an active, creative stance against the dominant male culture (296–302), a point Sandra Harding also uses in basing certain aspects of her study of epistemology on the viewpoints of several excluded communities, among them lesbians and women of color (191–217, 249–67). But in order to recognize, to admire, and later to emulate Brontë's clear-eyed rage at women's cultural position, Woolf had first to move beyond Elizabeth Gaskell's interpretation of Charlotte Brontë.

Gaskell, Brontë, and Woolf understood that women's love for women provided an antidote to the socially sanctioned negative images of women. When writing as adults, Charlotte, Emily, and Anne Brontë circled their cramped parlor, sharing their stories and critiquing them in the striking image in Gaskell's biography (Gaskell, *Life* 307–8). This image may have helped shape Woolf's sense of women writing and working together to create a space for the reborn Shakespeare's sister (*AROO* 118). Notably, Woolf and Gaskell had emulated this involving of others in one's creations as one wrote them. Gaskell had talked so much about her stories to her family that they were able to finish Gaskell's novel *Wives and Daughters,* left incomplete at her death. As a young writer, Woolf had shared her drafts with Violet Dickinson, looking to her for support more than for guidance.

Virginia Woolf had been raised by parents whose lives were sustained by the Victorian views of women (Lilienfeld, *Necessary* 22–121) that had hampered Gaskell and Brontë, for after all, Gaskell and Brontë were contemporaries of Woolf's father, Sir Leslie Stephen. Hence it is not surprising to find that in her first essay on Brontë, Woolf's writing seems to imply areas of identification with the Victorian novelist, for the imagination that saw the parsonage saw it with a view of Woolf's own life. Asking whether "pilgrimages to the shrines of famous men [*sic*]" ought perhaps to be "condemned as sentimental journeys," the writer decides that her curiosity is "legitimate" (*E* 1: 5). She claims her trip as "a pilgrimage to the home and country of Charlotte Brontë and her sisters," although Emily and Anne are mentioned only in a sentence or two (*E* 1: 5).

Along with Gaskell, Woolf notes that the graves in the graveyard behind Haworth Parsonage come almost into the back wall of the dwelling, an emblem of the dead overtaking the living, a theme of Woolf's short essay (*E* 1: 7; Gaskell, *Life* 56). Brontë had been left motherless, as had Woolf and Gaskell. Other deaths pointed to startling family similarities. Charlotte's two oldest sisters had died, as had Woolf's older half-sister, Stella Duckworth. Charlotte Brontë had had Branwell, her literary mentor and rival, the brother whose drinking and drug taking shamed the family, broke her father's heart, and caused Charlotte to turn from him to save herself (Lansbury 136–37; Gerin, *Brontë* 321, 331–32). Woolf, too, had had rivalrous relations with her beloved older brother, Thoby, and had been the repeated object of incestuous assaults by her half-brothers Gerald and George Duckworth (DeSalvo, *Impact* 100–101, 113–14, 119, 124).

Other family relationships perhaps came to mind as Woolf walked inside the house and around the grounds of Haworth Parsonage. The children, according to Gaskell's biography, had lived under the stern rule of Reverend Brontë, their embittered and authoritarian father, a view of him Gerin actively disputes (*Brontë* 528). There are indeed similarities between this father—who, according to Gaskell's letters, had once burned a rug from rage and who sat down to breakfast at the table every day of her visit with "the deadly little pistol"—and the reductive portrait of the emotionally violent Mr. Ramsay of *To the Lighthouse* (Gaskell, *Letters* 125, 245; Lilienfeld, "Critic"). Reverend Brontë's passionate preference for his son, Branwell, over his many daughters may have reminded Woolf of her own father, who had educated his sons, Thoby and Adrian, at preparatory schools while not allowing Woolf and her sister, Vanessa, to attend school or the new women's colleges, even though their own cousin was the principal of one of these. Both fathers were extremely possessive, a fact Woolf knew in 1904, although she wrote about it only in 1938, suggesting in *Three Guineas* that Reverend Brontë's delay of Charlotte's marriage had incestuous overtones (*TG* 130–31). DeSalvo has suggested a similar motive in Leslie Stephen's refusal to give his consent for Stella Duckworth's marriage to Jack Hills (*Impact* 56–59).

In seeing Haworth, Woolf might have seen mirrored there another mother dead too soon, leaving an "abandoned" father full of passion and pain. Branwell's dissipations, a secret the family tried to hide, had an analogue in Woolf's family's refusal to acknowledge the realities of Laura Stephen's retardation (Bicknell) and the necessity to suppress the disclosure of brother-sister incest (Q. Bell 1: 45). According to Gaskell's biography, the freedom allowed the father in the Victorian family had in the Brontës' case exacerbated the eccentricities of the father, which in turn had contributed to the children's isolation from other experiences than were contained in the Brontë family itself. Fortunately for them, the Stephen children were able to break away from the Duckworth brothers after their father's death in 1904, a separation from family that was unthinkable to Charlotte, whose conception of duty meant that she could never have settled in London once she became famous (Gaskell, *Life* 309–10). When she married, her husband came to live with her and her father, and after her death, Reverend Nicholls remained in Haworth Parsonage, caring for Reverend Brontë until the older man's death.

Gerin's insistence that Gaskell's mature fictional voice resembled that which was best in her letters seems to point to Woolf's insight, in *A Room of One's Own,* that women's fiction evolved from letters, diaries, talk, and their keen observation of others as women sat immured in their drawing rooms rather than roamed the external worlds of business and commerce (*AROO* 70–71; Gerin, *Gaskell* 119). In fact, Gaskell's biography of Brontë might be said to have begun in her letters to her women friends about the writers' first meeting, letters that champion Brontë's noble nature and emphasize the difficulties over which Brontë had consistently risen by self-control and genius (Gaskell, *Letters* 123–31).

Like Woolf's, part of Gaskell's fascination with Charlotte Brontë arose from the power and rage of Brontë's narrative voice. Just as she had once chastised Thackeray to his face about failing to fulfill what Brontë thought were his duties as a great author whose gift came from a divine source (Gerin, *Brontë* 431–32), Brontë refused to shape her novels to accord with Victorian narrative conventions. Elizabeth Gaskell's access to her own aggression changed after she had written both the original and expurgated editions of her biography of Brontë. The controversies and threatened law suits brought on by the first edition led her to tell Ellen Nussey that "I think I *am* so *angry* that I am almost merry in my bitterness" (Gaskell, *Letters* 454; emphasis in original). Having known her since they were fifteen-year-old girls, Ellen had witnessed Charlotte Brontë's rage. In fact, as Miller points out, imagining their life together, Brontë wrote to Ellen that "'it is not in my nature to forget your nature—though I daresay I should spit fire and explode sometimes if we lived together continually'" (E. Miller 39). As I have suggested elsewhere, the liberating influence of Brontë's refusal to muffle her voice is evident in Gaskell's choice of incidents, authorial tone, and widened scope of action in *Sylvia's Lovers,* the novel written immediately after the Brontë biography (Lilienfeld, "Verbal Violence"). Similarly, increased courage and confidence inform the narrative choices and depiction of women in *Wives and Daughters,* Gaskell's last novel (Lansbury). Researching, writing, publishing, expurgating, republishing, and then surviving her *Life of Charlotte Brontë* were among the factors that encouraged Gaskell to revise her authorial voice so that it became more complex, direct, satirical, and—angrier.

Like Gaskell, Woolf was increasingly influenced by Charlotte Brontë's refusal to be silenced. Jane Marcus was the first to suggest that the stifled anger of *A Room of One's Own* was unleashed cleanly in *The Years* and in *Three Guineas,* in no small part because of the lesbian Ethel Smyth's liberating influence on Woolf ("Violin" 112). Before Smyth's passionate eloquence modeled successful use of rage in writing, however, Woolf became lovers with Vita Sackville-West, whose insights into Brontë's lesbianism I have cited above. Vita Sackville-West accompanied Woolf to present the lecture that later became the feminist polemic, for Woolf wrote *A Room of One's Own* after her love affair with Sackville-West. Virginia Woolf's fictional self-presentation in *A Room of One's Own,* what she described as a female figure created by "the lies which will flow from my lips," appears to fear the female passion of rage (Rosenman, *Invisible* 164–66; Marcus, *Patriarchy*; Restuccia). That protean narrator seems to disapprove of Brontë's rage, pointing to it as the disruptive force that shatters the unity of *Jane Eyre.* The fact that Woolf stops her own narrative in order to rupture it by the appearance of a rage she imputes to Brontë, however, should give the reader pause. Perhaps Woolf's denial of Brontë's anger is not denial at all; perhaps it is a subversive attempt to replicate Brontë's rhetorical strategies (Rosenman, *Invisible* 164–66). Just as Woolf claims that Brontë disrupts her own text by a volcanic eruption of anger that brings the narrative to a halt while the anger scalds the reader, Woolf halts her own narrative in order to have Brontë's anger serve as the mouthpiece by which to express her own outrage at women's circumscribed lives and the distorted mirroring women receive from men in the home and in the academy (*AROO* 71–78).

Important changes in Woolf's use of rage were among the gifts given to her by involvement with lesbian women. Penelope's, Hoagland's, and Harding's views that excluded women can see and describe more clearly the injustices against women help readers understand why the subversive anger, disguised in *A Room of One's Own* but present nevertheless, can become fully expressed in *Three Guineas*. Virginia Woolf noted that Ethel Smyth's power made her like an icebreaker in arctic seas, able to cut a passage for more vulnerable ships as they navigated the dangerous waters (Radin, *Evolution* 3). Although Ethel's demands occasionally exhausted her, Woolf makes the same point in her diary as in her draft of "Professions for Women": "Her speech rollicking & direct: mine too compressed & allusive" (*D* 4: 7). Because Woolf's diaries and letters remark on Ethel's lesbian sexuality, it is clear that Woolf connected Smyth's power and fearlessness to a life lived against British sexual convention.

In *Three Guineas,* Woolf did not need to hide behind Charlotte Brontë's reputation as a firebrand. No longer voicing many of Gaskell's and Leslie Stephen's views of Charlotte Brontë, as Woolf had in her essays of 1910, 1916, and even 1929, Woolf adopts not only the fearlessness of Charlotte Brontë, but one of her central images. Fires rage in *Jane Eyre* as they do in *Three Guineas*. The heath rages from Jane Eyre's anger in chapter 10; the narrative insistently foregrounds the presence or absence of firelight in the many rooms mentioned in the narrative; these images culminate in Bertha Mason Rochester's burning her husband's bed curtains and then his house in understandable retaliation for his racialized mistreatment of her. In *Three Guineas* the flames of the cities bombed by fascists become transformed into the burning house set ablaze by the "daughters of educated men," a class to which both Woolf and Brontë might be said to belong (13). Using evidence from Elizabeth Gaskell's biography of Charlotte Brontë, Virginia Woolf takes Charlotte's part against the "infantile fixation" of the possessive Victorian father (*TG* 130–31). Here her suggestion of emotional if not physical incest is a courageous refusal to be silenced by the need to maintain ladylike respectability. The Charlotte Brontë represented by Elizabeth Gaskell's biography, the subject of Woolf's first published essay, no longer requires dismissal for inappropriate self-assertion, but seems to have become instead an inspiration. Is it a coincidence that flames like Charlotte Brontë's images for passions surged first in Virginia Woolf's love letters to Violet Dickinson and to Vita Sackville-West? The streaming flame of Violet, shining in the night (*L* 1: 388), becomes Vita's fire, "for if ever a woman was a lighted candlestick, a glow, an illumination . . . it was Vita" (*L* 3: 226).

Circumstantial evidence, thus, suggests that three lesbians helped Virginia Woolf reassess Charlotte Brontë. As she renegotiated her relation to Charlotte Brontë within "the china ink pot" of lesbian artists' insights, Virginia Woolf renegotiated her relation to her own rage against social constriction, violence, and injustice. But the growth of Woolf's insight into Brontë depended in part on Woolf's developing what Penelope and Hoagland have both cited as a lesbian ethic of resistance to and outspokenness against heteropatriarchy. Woolf's increasing empathy for and identification with Brontë as the flame-throwing figure of the woman oppressed by "the fathers" depended on strong support from women. Only when joined with other women such as Violet Dickinson, Vita Sackville-West, and Ethel Smyth, among others, could Woolf have moved beyond Elizabeth Gaskell's official view of Charlotte Brontë, a movement that symbolized her leaving her father's library in order to help other women excavate and establish another literary tradition.

The mutual love between Gaskell and Brontë and between Dickinson and Woolf demonstrates that women's empathic love for women can create a safe space for the discovery and expression of feelings. This safe space, "the gift of a china ink pot," may increase creativity and illumination, as well as model the challenge to love within the acceptance of difference. When Charlotte Brontë's heroine Jane Eyre faces Mr. Rochester and courageously informs him that they speak as equals, Mr. Rochester stops her voice by his bigamous kiss. Having supposedly disclaimed Jane Eyre's verbal violence as propaganda rather than art, Virginia Woolf's narrator nevertheless closes *A Room of One's Own* with a peroration advising women writers to "have the habit of freedom and the courage to write exactly what we think" (113), an admonition repeated almost verbatim in *Three Guineas* (91). The courage not to be silenced by Mr. Rochester's kiss, but instead to use her own voice to challenge the received opinions of heteropatriarchy, arose in part from Woolf's love for women. Re/viewing other women's lives, loving and being loved by such lesbian women as Violet Dickinson, Vita Sackville-West, and Ethyl Smyth, Virginia Woolf not only freed her own voice from its constraints but helped inspire other writers to do the same.

NOTES

1. See Stoneman; Marxist-Feminist Literature Collective; Lansbury; Boden-heimer; Uglow; and Easson.

2. See Lilienfeld, "Sisterhood" and "Verbal Violence"; see also Lansbury 7–10, 212–14; Bodenheimer; and Marxist-Feminist Literature Collective.

FIVE

Reading Influences
Homoeroticism and Mentoring in Katherine Mansfield's "Carnation" and Virginia Woolf's "Moments of Being: 'Slater's Pins Have No Points'"

JANET   WINSTON

On January 9, 1923, Katherine Mansfield died of tuberculosis, from which she had suffered for much of her young life. Yet, Mansfield continued to live on acutely in the minds of those who had known her and her work. Her literary friend and rival, Virginia Woolf, records in her diary how Mansfield haunted her imagination for years (Tomalin 204). For example, just one week after Mansfield's death, Woolf saw a vision of "Katherine putting on a white wreath, & leaving us, called away; made dignified, chosen" (*D* 2: 226). Five and a half years later, Woolf recounts:

> All last night I dreamt of Katherine Mansfield & wonder what dreams are; often evoke so much more emotion, than thinking does—almost as if she came back in person & was outside one, actively making one feel; instead of a figment called up & recollected, as she is, now, if I think of her. Yet some emotion lingers on the day after a dream; even though I've now almost forgotten what happened in the dream, except that she was lying on a sofa in a room high up, & a great many sad faced women were round her. (*D* 3: 187)

Three years after this vision, Woolf was still dreaming about Mansfield, "how we met, beyond death, & shook hands; saying something by way of explanation, & friendship" (*D* 4: 29).[1]

Numerous critics and biographers have written extensively on this friendship, drawing from Woolf's and Mansfield's letters, diaries, and fiction. They discuss the women's mutual rivalry and jealousy, their criticisms of each other's work and lives, as well as their shared sense of an aesthetic, their mutual influence, respect, and admiration.[2] Several critics suggest that one woman had a passionate, perhaps erotic, attachment to the other, while others stress the keen sense of intellectual support they found in talking together.[3] As if anticipating Sydney Janet Kaplan's wise warning against "overemphasiz[ing] their competition and thus play[ing] into the stereotype of women as enemies, conspiring against each other for the favors of men" (*Katherine Mansfield* 146),[4] Louise DeSalvo offers an optimistic appraisal of their relationship: it was that which exists between a woman writer and "her ideal reader" ("Cave" 196). More cautiously, Ann McLaughlin characterizes it as "an uneasy sisterhood" ("Sisterhood" 152).

I propose that we think of their relationship—in all of its complexity and indeterminacy (Kaplan, *Katherine Mansfield* 149)—as one of mutual mentorship. Each looked to the other for approval, intellectual stimulation, and competition as a spur to creative progress, professional opportunities and connections, love and affection,[5] and validation of her life's work through a mutuality of thought and vision, or as Woolf describes, "the queerest sense of echo coming back to me from her mind the second after I've spoken" (*D* 2: 61).

Let us consider for a moment this "echo" resonating between them in its "queerest sense." How did Woolf's and Mansfield's passion for women influence their mentoring relationship? As I mention above, several critics suggest that the relationship was tinged with eroticism. Indeed, in a letter to Vita Sackville-West, Woolf implies that while she and Mansfield did not actually have a sexual union, the suggestion that they might have had one was not unwarranted: "As for Katherine, I think you've got it very nearly right. We did not ever coalesce; but I was fascinated, and she respectful, only I thought her cheap, and she thought me priggish; and yet we were both compelled to meet simply in order to talk about writing. . . . I dream of her often . . ." (*L* 4: 366). That Woolf and Mansfield's relationship was infused with eroticism seems likely given suggestive quotes such as this one and the intensity of their creative bond. More important to this essay, however, is the question of how they approached lesbian eroticism in their fiction and of what influence, if any, their differing approaches had on each other.

For instance, much has been made of Woolf's dismissal of Mansfield's "Bliss" (1918), her story about a married woman's awakening to her sexual desire for another woman, whom she later discovers to be her husband's lover. Woolf thought the story "so hard, and so shallow, and so sentimental," revealing Mansfield's own "callousness & hardness as a human being" (*L* 2: 514; *D* 1: 179). Critics, and Woolf herself, read such comments as evidence of Woolf's jealousy over Mansfield's literary talents and public recognition. Yet, I wonder if Woolf's horrified response to "Bliss" in her diary—"'She's done for!' Indeed I dont see how much faith in her as woman or writer can survive that sort of story"—betrays Woolf's disapproval of Mansfield's portrayal of lesbian desire (*D* 1: 179). Are we to conclude from this remark that Woolf's response is fueled by homophobia? Is she condemning "that sort of story" because of its overt lesbianism? I think not. For how then do we reconcile such conclusions with Woolf's own passionate desire for women expressed in letters as early as 1903 (Cook 728)? And what of Woolf's criticism of Mansfield in this same passage from her diary for not "going deeper" with "Bliss" (*D* 1: 179)?

Perhaps Woolf loses "faith in [Mansfield] as woman or writer" or as woman writer because of what she perceives to be the "superficial smartness" of her portrayal of love between women (*D* 1: 179). After all, in "Bliss," Mansfield represents a woman's passion for another woman as something foolish, impulsive, and untrustworthy. The protagonist, Bertha, who "always did fall in love with beautiful women who had something strange about them" ("Bliss" 340–41), is infatuated with Pearl Fulton and mistakenly imagines the sexual passion she feels to be reciprocal. In contrast, Woolf's early story "Memoirs of a Novelist," written in 1909, shows women's intimate bonding as genuine, enduring, and to a large extent reciprocal[6]—a relationship between two "dearest friend[s]" who, according to one, "bear the secrets of my soul and the weight of what the poet calls this 'unintelligible world'" until the "abyss" of heterosexual marriage divides them (72–73). Woolf's later fiction would provide many inspired portraits of women loving women, often emphasizing an idealized, sacred communion between them.[7] In contrast, Mansfield's stories most often represent erotic desire between women as fleshly, exotic, reckless, and menacing.[8]

With this contrast and their mentorship in mind, I want to return to the passages from Woolf's diary with which I began this essay—to the persistence of Mansfield's presence in Woolf's imagination, to the "sad faced women" of Woolf's dream. Who are these "sad faced women"? The dream suggests an act of collective female mourning. Might these women represent the writers and readers who, like Woolf herself, over the years would be visited by the specter of Mansfield through the power of her artistic vision?

Woolf's image of Katherine's recumbent body surrounded by mourning women uncannily resonates with a passage from *A Room of One's Own*: "For masterpieces are not single and solitary births; they are the outcome of many years of thinking in common, of thinking by the body of the people, so that the experience of the mass is behind the single voice" (65). The metaphoric "body of the people" described here collides with the image of Mansfield's body in Woolf's dream, while the "births" of women's artistic achievements correspond to the death of one woman's masterful "single voice." It is as if Woolf's dream about Mansfield, recorded just one month prior to her talks at Cambridge on "Women and Fiction" that would become *A Room of One's Own,* encodes through reverse images—the death of a singular body equals the birth of a communal voice—one of her central ideas about writing, what Jane Marcus describes as Woolf's belief in "a democratic feminist 'collective sublime'" ("Thinking" 10). In discussing Woolf's famous phrase in *A Room of One's Own,* "For we think back through our mothers if we are women" (76), Marcus explains that Woolf "saw herself as a link in a long line of women writers; she knew just where her own work fitted and what heritage she was leaving for the women writers who would come after her" ("Thinking" 9).

During the process of writing an early draft of this essay, I had a dream that seems in some way oddly connected to Woolf's dream about Mansfield and that takes up Woolf's notion of a cross-generational trajectory of collective female influence. In my dream, my maternal grandmother, who has been dead for over twenty years, was living in Virginia Woolf's house and had the responsibility of maintaining it for the public. I learned from my mother that upon my grandmother's death, the house would be inherited by a married academic couple, neither of whom had any interest in Woolf. As a descendant of my grandmother and of Woolf's writing, I remember feeling angry and pained that I would be cut off from this joint heritage. Clearly, the dream projects my desire to claim Woolf as my intellectual grandmother, as well as my fear that such entitlement might be usurped by an uninterested heterosexual academy.

Working against Woolf's assimilation into a heterosexual analytical framework, the reading that follows situates two stories, one by Mansfield and the other by Woolf, within a larger tradition of lesbian story-telling and situates itself among other essays of lesbian feminist criticism: reclamations of Woolf and Mansfield that recognize them as writers who shared not only an "aesthetic sisterhood based on shared traditions" (Banks, "Mansfield" 79) but also a passionate love of women. By recognizing women's and specifically lesbian writing as a collective tradition and by acknowledging Woolf's and Mansfield's mutual influence in its "queerest sense," we might think of Woolf's story as emerging from and in some ways revising Mansfield's.[9]

Mansfield's "Carnation," written in 1918 (just a few months after "Bliss") (L. Moore 107, 115), and Woolf's celebrated "Sapphist story" (L 3: 431) "Moments of Being: 'Slater's Pins Have No Points,'" written in 1927, examine homoerotically imbued mentoring relationships, a subject Woolf and Mansfield knew well. Though representing lesbian passion in differing ways, these stories illustrate several of the conventions of lesbian fiction that Catharine Stimpson and Elaine Marks describe: the schoolroom setting, the erotic intrigue between teacher and student, the use of nature imagery to symbolize lesbian desire, and the reliance on Christian and ancient Greek models to reinforce or reject such desire. Both stories represent mentors who model same-sex passion in the classroom and who thereby facilitate the development of a gay consciousness in their students. Within the mentoring relationship, the act of reading becomes *the* site of narrative tension where the politics of homoeroticism are played out. Just as Woolf's reading of Mansfield's lesbian stories may have influenced Woolf as she wrote her own, so reading in these stories inspires the protagonists to recognize, if not overtly express, lesbian desires of their own.

In "Lesbian Intertextuality," Marks explains that the schoolroom setting is part of a larger "Sappho model" of lesbian storytelling, which dominates the genre (Marks 356; Stimpson, "Zero Degree" 307–8, 310). According to this model, a seductive female teacher at a women's school awakens one of her "innocent" students to the pleasures of lesbian love (Marks 357). Woolf's and Mansfield's stories follow this model. Set in the schoolroom, each story describes a young female student's psychic and sexual awakening to the possibility of lesbian desire, facilitated by her relationship with her teacher (and, in the case of Mansfield's story, with another student).

"Carnation" is an evocative sketch of a French lesson at a women's college. A teacher reads poetry to his students while one of them plays with a carnation. The young women are bored and fidgety; the room is hot and stuffy. The scent of the carnation wafts from one woman to another.

Read with attention to its symbolism, the sketch chronicles a seduction. "Carnation" loosely belongs to the genre of lesbian fiction known as "the dying fall, a narrative of damnation, of the lesbian's suffering as a lonely outcast attracted to a psychological lower caste," of which Radclyffe Hall's *The Well of Loneliness* is the touchstone (Stimpson, "Zero Degree" 301–7). Like Hall, Mansfield borrows from Christian mythology to set the tone. "Carnation" revises Genesis, offering a fable of lesbian temptation and knowledge as a fall from sexual innocence.[10] In Mansfield's Eden, a seductive female classmate, appropriately named Eve, and a lecherous male professor, M. Hugo, dwell—both predatory beasts out to capture and devour the protagonist, Katie. As if personifying the "sea serpents" and "winged creatures" in Genesis (1.21), M. Hugo wears a "white waistcoat [which] gleamed like the belly of a shark," while Eve has a "cruel . . . little thin laugh" with "a long sharp beak and claws and two bead eyes" ("Carnation" 322).[11]

In place of the apple, Mansfield employs the carnation as the instrument of temptation. Eve "always carried a flower. She snuffed it and snuffed it, twirled it in her fingers, laid it against her cheek, held it to her lips, tickled Katie's neck with it, and ended, finally, by pulling it to pieces and eating it, petal by petal" ("Carnation" 321). On the day the story takes place, she brings to class a "deep, deep red" carnation and tries ensnaring Katie with its intoxicating scent, which Katie initially resists: "Oh, the scent! It floated across to Katie. It was too much. Katie turned away . . ." ("Carnation" 322–23). Mansfield suggests that once Eve catches her prey she will begin "pulling it to pieces and eating it," as she does her flowers. The story ends, however, with merely a flirtatious gesture as "she popped the carnation down the front of Katie's blouse" ("Carnation" 324).

In discussing the significance of flowers in Mansfield's work as "a barometer of feeling," Vincent O'Sullivan cites Mansfield's remark that "even 'flower pictures affect me so much that I feel an instant tremendous excitement and delight. I mean as strong as if a great band played suddenly'" (*Collected* 3: 263 qtd. in O'Sullivan 124–25). C. A. Hankin explains that Mansfield "had long associated [flowers] with the physical beauty of women" and that her unpublished poem "Scarlet Tulips" (1908) employs images of flowers to express lesbian passions (57):

Strange flower, half opened, scarlet,
So soft to feel and press
My lips upon your petals
A hated restlessness
A fever and a longing
Desire that moves in me
A violent scarlet passion
Stirs me so savagely
(qtd. in Hankin 57)

Clearly, the "petals" of the "scarlet tulips" to which the title refers represent the labia of the speaker's beloved.

In another early piece, the incomplete novel *Juliet* (1906), Mansfield uses not tulips but a carnation to denote lesbian desire. As in "Bliss," the story involves a triangular relationship among two women and a man. At one point the protagonist, Juliet, must choose between "the Suitable Appropriate Existence" that awaits her back home and "the mode bohème" in London with her best friend, Pearl ("Unpublished" 25). After accepting Pearl's proposal of a lifelong romantic union, Juliet takes to her bed with a "nervous headache":

> After an immeasurable length of time she saw Pearl standing beside her, tall and grave in her black frock with a white feather boa around her throat. . . . "I feel better for the sight of you. *Give me that pink carnation you're wearing and sit on the bed here.*" . . . They suddenly held each other's hand. "To the devil with my relations" said Juliet. "To the devil with our Past Life" said Pearl. "All the way here I have been quoting Oscar's [Wilde's] 'Relations are a very tedious set of people.' You know, it has been like a charm. I can wait no longer." ("Unpublished" 26; emphasis added)[12]

Here, as in "Carnation," the carnation signifies sexual desire between women as an irresistible temptation.

Mansfield's reworking of Genesis in "Carnation" does not end with her lesbian version of Eve's temptation and fall. For Genesis also contains the destruction of Sodom (ch. 19), commonly interpreted "as an angry God's punishment for the homosexuality of the [town's] inhabitants" (*Alyson* 11). While Mansfield avoids the "brimstone and fire" of the biblical story (19.24), she does portray same-sex passion in "Carnation" as menacing and potentially destructive. Furthermore, just as interpretations of the story of Sodom expressly allude to sex between *men,* Mansfield's story alludes to gay male coupling.

The connection between "Carnation" and another story—Robert Hichens's *The Green Carnation* (1894)—underscores the subtext of male homosexuality in Mansfield's "Carnation." Hichens's fictional spoof of Oscar Wilde describes how Mr. Esme Amarinth (Wilde) and his young "friend," Lord Reginald Hastings (Wilde's lover, Lord Alfred Douglas), set about to find "Reggie" a rich wife so that they may pursue aesthetic posing and avid young boys in their "cult of the green carnation" (Hichens 207; *Alyson* 79, 199). The green carnation symbolizes homosexuality as an unnatural, cliquish pose, antithetical to true love, and *imposed* upon young schoolchildren: "[I]n their [Amarinth's and Lord Hastings's] buttonholes large green carnations bloomed savagely" (Hichens 56)—carnations that "never bloom on walls at all" (Hichens 22) but instead are "artificially coloured" (Hichens 208). In seducing a young admirer into the "cult" of homosexuality, Reggie gives his initiate a green carnation and tells him to "worship its wonderful green" unnaturalness (Hichens 151). As an ardent admirer of Wilde, Mansfield must have heard of Hichens's ugly attack on her mentor, as well as Wilde's own habit, after the French, of wearing a green carnation as a gay signifier (Butler, *Bodies* 160).

Borrowing the carnation as a symbol of gay passions from this mocking account of Wildean aestheticism and gay hauteur, Mansfield transforms Hichens's preoccupation with pederasty into an account of lesbian seduction in which both student and teacher collude. While Eve entices Katie with her "unnatural" *red* carnation—"that looked as though it had been dipped in wine and left in the dark to dry" ("Carnation" 322)—M. Hugo suggestively recites French poetry:

> He would begin, softly and calmly, and then gradually his voice would swell and vibrate and gather itself together, then it would be pleading and imploring and entreating, and then rising, rising triumphant, until it burst into light, as it were, and then—gradually again, it ebbed, it grew soft and warm and calm and died down into nothingness.
>
> The great difficulty was, of course, if you felt at all feeble, not to get the most awful fit of giggles. Not because it was funny, really, but because it made you feel uncomfortable, queer, silly, and somehow ashamed for old Hugo-Wugo. But—oh dear—if he was going to inflict it on them in this heat! ("Carnation" 323)

Clearly, the description of the crescendo and diminuendo of M. Hugo's voice suggests the tumescence and detumescence of penile erection and ejaculation. The women's feeling of discomfort and their sense of shame underscore his sexual violation of them. His effect is not just emotional but also physical: "He began, and most of the girls fell forward, over the desks, their heads on their arms, dead at the first shot" ("Carnation" 323). When he has finished with them, he thanks the "'ladies,' . . . bobbing at his high desk, over the wreckage" ("Carnation" 324).

While M. Hugo's display is ostensibly heterosexual, it coincides with the vigorous movements of the stableman outside as if the men were engaging in a passionate homoerotic union:[13]

> Now she could hear a man clatter over the cobbles and the jing-jang of the pails he carried. And now *Hoo-hor-her! Hoo-hor-her!* as he worked the pump, and a great gush of water followed. . . .
> She *saw* him simply—in a faded shirt, his sleeves rolled up, his chest bare, all splashed with water—and as he whistled, loud and free, and as he moved, swooping and bending, Hugo-Wugo's voice began to warm, to deepen, to gather together, to swing, to rise—somehow or other to keep time with the man outside (Oh, the scent of Eve's carnation!) until they became one great rushing, rising, triumphant thing, bursting into light, and then—
> The whole room broke into pieces. ("Carnation" 324)

This climax—suggesting a gay male couple's simultaneous orgasms under a female and lesbian gaze—complicates any univocal reading of "Carnation" as the story of a man sexually exploiting his women students. M. Hugo's performance awakens Katie physically, if unconsciously, to the possibility of sexual fulfillment in same-sex relations. M. Hugo functions as a gay role model. By watching her teacher "keep time with the man outside," Katie lets herself be aroused by "the scent of Eve's carnation."

Of course, this does not diminish the story's disturbing implications: that a woman's awakening to her desire for another woman requires entrapment, and that such entrapment involves not only unwanted lesbian advances but also forced participation in an all-pervasive and threatening male sexual display. Mansfield's choice of words at the figurative and literal climax of the story—the *"Hoo-hor-her!"* of the pump during the men's eroticized synchronism ("Carnation" 324)—underscores this entrapment. The onomatopoeic phrasing suggests the exclamation (or, perhaps, interrogation) "Who whore her," i.e., who "corrupted" her.

Who or what corrupted Mansfield, we may ask, for her to represent lesbian eroticism as something sinister and feared? In a letter to her friend Dorothy Brett, Mansfield describes "Carnation" as "just a sort of glimpse of adolescent emotion," and to her husband, John Middleton Murry, she writes, "I meant it to be 'delicate . . .'" (*Collected* 2: 260, 203). Mansfield's "delicacy" refers, perhaps, to her handling of her Queen's College years, the time spent between 1903 and 1906 as a teenager at school in London developing her literary skills and imagination, as well as several intimate emotional and physical attachments to women.[14] One of these relationships, her complicated friendship with Ida Baker, to whom she later referred as her "wife," would prove to be the longest, most enduring bond in Mansfield's life and one of the most important.[15] Another woman, Vere Bartrick-Baker—with whom, evidence suggests, Mansfield was emotionally as well as sexually involved[16]—served as the model for Eve in "Carnation" (Tomalin 25; L. Moore 26).

According to several biographers, it was Bartrick-Baker (also known as Mimi or Eve) (Crone 26) with whom Mansfield "sat in the dark shadowy niches of the Hall [at Queen's College], holding hands," discussing writers, such as the Decadents, and with whom she was "suspected of immorality" (Mantz and Murry 198).[17] And, significantly, it was she who "first lent Kathleen the book [Oscar Wilde's *The Picture of Dorian Gray*]" (Mantz and Murry 211) "in its original, unexpurgated form" (Alpers 35). Together Mansfield and Bartrick-Baker developed a sexually imbued mentorship with their German professor, Walter Rippmann. He invited them, along with other of the College's attractive and inspiring young women, to intellectual soirées at his home and "encouraged them to read modern writers, the Symbolists and Decadents and social reformers," including Wilde, "advis[ing] the girls on the necessity of . . . avoidance of the Seven Deadly Virtues" (Tomalin 25).[18] In Mansfield's "A Fairy Story," Rippmann gives just such advice, appearing as "the Wanderer who woke her [the Girl] from her sweet child's dream, to give her the key to the book of knowledge" (Mantz and Murry 209–10).

By introducing Mansfield to Wilde's writing, both Bartrick-Baker and Rippmann would be forever linked with Wilde in Mansfield's imagination and with Wilde's influence on her life and work. Sydney Janet Kaplan describes this influence as both stylistic and sexual (*Katherine Mansfield* 25): "Obviously, Wilde did not *influence* her desires [for women], but his ideas allowed her a space in which such desires might be recognized and named" (*Katherine Mansfield* 22–23). Because of Mansfield's own awareness and internalization of homophobia, however, Wilde served as both "model and terror, her impetus toward the idolization of art as a means of *controlling* the forbidden while allowing it, nonetheless, oblique expression" (Kaplan, *Katherine Mansfield* 26, 35). In describing this "difficult influence," Kaplan quips: "If 'Dorian Gray had been poisoned by a book'

. . . there must have been times when Mansfield felt she had been poisoned also" (*Katherine Mansfield* 32).

In Wilde's *The Picture of Dorian Gray,* the protagonist, Dorian, is fascinated with a book, written in the style of the Symbolists (116), in which "the sins of the world were passing in dumb show before him. Things that he had dimly dreamed of were suddenly made real to him. Things of which he had never dreamed were gradually revealed" (115). Dorian "could not free himself from the influence of this book" (117) and indeed feels compelled to live out the "sins" represented in it, including his own implicit homosexuality.

To be "poisoned by a book" à la Wilde resembles Katie's situation in "Carnation." While M. Hugo reads aloud from a book of French poetry, Katie cannot stop herself from fantasizing about gay sex or resist becoming intoxicated by the scent of Eve's carnation. Clearly, Mansfield's mentor Rippmann—who introduced her to Paul Verlaine[19] and Wilde—was a model for the overly expressive M. Hugo.[20] In underscoring the influence reading has on Katie's awareness of homoeroticism, Mansfield pays tribute to her mentors—Rippmann, Bartrick-Baker, and Wilde—who, in differing ways, influenced her sexually, intellectually, and aesthetically.

Yet, this tribute is mixed. As Kaplan observes, such influences relied on a Decadent male model of art and sexuality, whose views of women were less than flattering (*Katherine Mansfield* 28–31). Noting the problematic picture of women in *Dorian Gray,* Kaplan explains:

> [T]he call to burn oneself out for experience, to destroy the body in service to art, and all those other exaggerated aesthetic poses were intended rather to suggest a certain kind of *masculine* initiation into art. The physical beauty of Dorian was a lure for male sexual desire, his insatiable lust for experience a male prerogative. Wilde's focus is on men with the freedom of men; women are only the objects of their intermittent attention—and of their scorn. (*Katherine Mansfield* 28)

Kaplan's comments offer an important, if incomplete, feminist gloss on Wilde's influence on Mansfield. For how did Wilde's Decadent values specifically affect Mansfield's lesbianism? What sort of Wildean legacy do we find in Mansfield's portrayal of desire between women?

Perhaps it was this Decadent emphasis on momentary sensual experiences—what Dorian Gray calls "a new Hedonism" (120)—that disturbed Virginia Woolf about "Bliss." Certainly "Carnation" shares this volatile sensuality; and, more so than "Bliss," it models lesbian desire on the

Decadents' view of homosexuality as something delightfully dangerous and exciting because it is unnatural and unwholesome (Beckson and Ganz 56). However, Woolf was probably more troubled by Mansfield's depiction of a lesbian eroticism intimately tied to men and to male sexual expression. For in her own life, Woolf experienced sexual relations with women as passionate and satisfying, whereas those with men were unfulfilling or abusive (Cook; DeSalvo, "Cave"; McNaron, "Albanians"). And while in 1925 Woolf marveled that "[t]hese Sapphists *love* women; friendship is never untinged with amorosity" (*D* 3: 51; emphasis in original), she viewed male homosexuality with distaste, comparing a "Buggery Poke party" of her gay male friends to a "male urinal; a wet, smelly, trivial kind of place" (*L* 4: 200).

Certainly their misogyny fueled much of Woolf's disdain for her gay male friends, as Jane Marcus argues convincingly: "for women like Virginia Woolf, the homosexual men of Cambridge and Bloomsbury appeared to be, not the suffering victims of heterosexual social prejudice, but the 'intellectual aristocracy' itself, an elite with virtual hegemony over British culture" ("Sapphistry" 177). These men, Marcus reminds us, rejected feminist and lesbian causes in favor of maintaining their patriarchal privilege at women's expense ("Liberty" 76; "Sapphistry" 164, 177–78).

However, Woolf's disparaging remarks about homosexuals were not limited to gay men; she had ambivalent feelings about lesbians as well. For example, in a letter dated 1925, she denigratingly describes gay men and then moves on to women, proclaiming: "I can't take either of these aberrations seriously" (*L* 3: 155–56). Yet, significantly, Woolf then confesses to wanting Vita Sackville-West, who is "violently Sapphic," "to elope with me next" (*L* 3: 155–56). And Woolf was indeed happy when she did. At the height of this passionate love affair, Woolf wrote "Moments of Being: 'Slater's Pins Have No Points'" (Olano, "Women" 164; DeSalvo, "Cave" 197).

I mention earlier that we might think of "Slater's Pins" as Woolf's revision of "Carnation." In place of Mansfield's reluctant pupil coerced into desiring women, Woolf creates a protagonist whose sexual awakening is a private mental journey inspired by a beloved teacher. Whereas "Carnation" revises Genesis, maintaining its tone of seduction and violation, "Slater's Pins" rewrites heterosexual myths of Sappho, climaxing in lesbian ecstatic wonderment.

Several narrative details in "Slater's Pins," as well as Woolf's references to it as "Sapphist" in letters to Sackville-West, support my reading of the story as both lesbian and Sapphist—that is, participating in the lesbian-feminist reclamation of the much mythologized poet.[21] The classroom setting and the intrigue between student and teacher conform to the "Sappho model" that Marks elucidates; Woolf's choice of discipline—music—as the story's focus underscores her feminist intentions. According to Perry Meisel, the schoolteacher protagonist, Miss Julia Craye, is modeled after Woolf's first Greek and Latin tutor, Clara Pater (22–24). By making Julia a musician, then, Woolf transforms the languages literally taught her by her tutor—the classics, that bulwark of the patriarchal British educational system—into a musical language evocative of Sappho's poetic songs. As the speaker of Sappho's *Fragment 160 V.* says, in what Jane McIntosh Snyder contends is "a programmatic statement of Sappho's poetic mission," "Now I will sing beautifully / to delight my women companions . . ." (94–95). Of course, the connection between Woolf's story and Sappho's poetry goes beyond the musical focus and the intended female audience. As Gillian Spraggs notes, "Sappho, time and again, took up her lyre to sing . . . about the physical attraction she felt for some of her women friends and about their attachments to each other . . ." (54).

Such rewriting of patriarchal "truths" through woman-centered fantasies informs both theme and structure in "Slater's Pins." As James Hafley notes in an early critique, "[t]he 'action' of the short story—what it imitates—is not at all the past life of Julia Craye, but the mind of [her pupil] Fanny Wilmot engaged in the composition of that life . . ." (13). Unfortunately, patriarchal notions of reality cloud Fanny's mind (and, alas, Hafley's too), obscuring an awareness of Julia's lesbianism (Baldanza; Clements 17–18, 20–21). Thus, Fanny initially reads Julia's spinsterhood as a pitiful "problem" ("Slater's Pins" 217, 219); attempting to explain it, Fanny invents a heterosexual seduction scenario in which a supposedly staid and frigid Julia rebuffs a male suitor:

> They [Julia and Mr. Sherman] looked at the Serpentine. He may have rowed her across. . . . She sat hunched a little, a little angular, though she was graceful then, steering. At the critical moment, for he had determined that he must speak now—it was his only chance of getting her alone—he was speaking with his head turned at an absurd angle, in his great nervousness, over his shoulder—at that very moment she interrupted fiercely. He would have them into the Bridge, she cried. It was a moment of horror, of disillusionment, of revelation for both of them. I can't have it, I can't possess it, she thought. He could not see why she had come then. With a great splash of his oar he pulled the boat round. Merely to snub him? He rowed her back and said good-bye to her. ("Slater's Pins" 218)

Seen from the man's point of view, the only perspective afforded Fanny at this point, this sexually laden scene—a kind of verbal "intercourse interruptus"—represents Julia's failure to respond appropriately to the man's desire to propose marriage. Julia's imagined thoughts, "I can't have it, I can't possess it," echo earlier lines, all of which suggest, until the conclusion, Fanny's belief in her teacher's inability to connect physically and passionately with another person.

Yet, Woolf offers her readers another perspective if—following the example of Julia, who steers clear of the bridge and the marriage proposal—they circumvent the monolith of compulsory heterosexuality. Both Jane Marcus and Joan DeJean describe Woolf's familiarity with fallacious histories of Sappho that represent the poet as chaste or heterosexual (Marcus, "Liberty" 88–89, 92; DeJean 278, 308–11, 357 n. 6). One centuries-old story claims that Sappho was in love with a man whose desertion of her for a younger woman prompted her anguished suicide (DeJean 51–52). As DeJean explains, contemporary Sappho scholars believe that this story was concocted from an allusion to a mythical male figure in one of Sappho's poems: either Phaon or Phaethon (52). According to Greek legend, Phaon is the boatman who ferries Aphrodite free of charge while she is disguised as an old woman. After rewarding him with youth and good looks, she develops a possessive love for him (DeJean 52; Harvey 320). Phaethon is Helios's reckless son, who, after losing control of the sun's chariot, is struck by Zeus's thunderbolt and falls to his death into the river Eridanus (DeJean 52; Harvey 319).

The boating scene in "Slater's Pins" uncannily resonates with both of these legends. Mr. Sherman is Phaon and Phaethon: he offers his services as boatman for free (actually, he expects to be rewarded, but Julia refuses his marriage proposal), and he loses control of his craft (albeit narrowly avoiding falling into the river). Yet, in rewriting these classical myths, Julia and Woolf, following Sappho's lead, "[refuse] to legitimate androcentric erotic scenarios . . ." (DeJean 52): Julia, by rejecting the boatman's marriage proposal; Woolf, by repudiating the myths of Aphrodite and Sappho as scorned women. The fact that Fanny constructs a heterocentric biomythography[22] about Julia to explain her unmarried status underscores Woolf's attack on a tradition of Sappho scholarship aimed at inventing biographies for the poet in order to deny the lesbian content of her lyrics.

In the tradition of Sapphic scholars, Mr. Sherman, and Phaethon before her, Fanny—musing on her teacher's life—veers off course (DeJean 52).[23] Yet, another Sapphic moment in the story alters Fanny's perspective:

Fanny Wilmot saw the pin on the carpet; she picked it up. She looked at Miss Craye. Was Miss Craye so lonely? No, Miss Craye was steadily, blissfully, if only for a moment, a happy woman. Fanny had surprised her in a moment of ecstasy. She sat there, half turned away from the piano, with her hands clasped in her lap holding the carnation upright, while behind her was the sharp square window, *uncurtained purple in the evening, intensely purple* after the brilliant electric lights which burnt unshaded in the bare music room. *Julia Craye sitting hunched and compact holding her flower seemed to emerge out of the London night, seemed to fling it like a cloak behind her.* It seemed in its bareness and intensity the effluence of her spirit, something she had made which surrounded her, which was her. Fanny stared. ("Slater's Pins" 220; emphasis added)

According to Avrom Fleishman, Fanny's finding the pin—which, along with a carnation, falls to the floor in the story's opening—is the catalyst for her changed perception of Julia: the recovery of the phallic object facilitates an unconscious understanding of her teacher's lesbianism ("Forms" 61–62).[24] Yet, more striking than this pin is the image of Julia flinging the purple cloak of night behind her—"the effluence of her spirit," Woolf informs us.

Discussing the significance of the color purple to lesbian and gay culture, Judy Grahn notes that in the "precious remnants [of Sappho's poems] she made seven references to the color purple, five to violets or 'violet-colored,' and two to purple hyacinths. Love, she said, wore a purple mantle" (*Mother* 10). According to the Greek rhetorician Pollux, in a translation by David A. Campbell, "They say that Sappho was the first to use the word [. . .] 'mantle,' when she said of Eros [in *Fragment* 54]: . . . 'who had come from heaven clad in a purple mantle.'"[25] Gillian Spraggs translates this line as "having come from heaven wearing a purple cloak" (58).

Fanny's radical revisioning of her teacher's life when she sees her wearing her "purple cloak" corresponds to Woolf's reanimation of Sappho's spirit in the fictional body of her work, specifically in the character of Julia Craye. The scene inscribes the presence of the Greek poet, who sang songs of women's desire for women to her female audience and wrote of love personified in a purple cloak. It is this presence—of Sappho's spirit, of lesbian love—that awakens Fanny to the possibilities for happiness in her teacher's life (and, indeed, in her own).

The cloak also appears in an earlier scene, which is filtered through Fanny's memory: "Julia Craye had said, 'It's the use of men, surely, to protect us,' smiling at her that same odd smile, as she stood *fastening her cloak,* which made her, like the flower, conscious to her finger tips of youth and brilliance, but, like the flower too, Fanny suspected, inhibited" ("Slater's Pins" 217; emphasis added). The intentionally vague use of personal pronouns here, *she* and *her* referring to Julia and Fanny, serves to confuse and conflate the characters.[26] This passage signals Fanny's awareness of her own attractiveness, as seen through Julia's eyes, and both her and her teacher's restraint in openly acknowledging such attraction. Is it Julia's smile or her cloak "which made her" conscious of this attraction?

When read with this slippage of pronouns intact, the passage suggests that Fanny and Julia identify with the flower and actually see their emotional states reflected in it. A diary entry underscores Woolf's concern with the woman and the flower (rather than with the pin, as is Fleishman's concern): "I am now & then haunted by some semi mystic [*sic*] very profound life of a woman, which shall all be told on one occasion; & time shall be utterly obliterated; future shall somehow blossom out of the past. One incident—say the fall of a flower—might contain it" (*D* 3: 118). This notion of collapsing the future into the past through the process of telling the life of one woman evokes the images of Sappho with her lyre, Mansfield on her couch, and Judith Shakespeare in her unmarked grave (*AROO* 46–51). According to Catharine Stimpson, "the lesbian writer calls on myth[s]: prehistorical matriarchies; the Amazons; Sappho and her school" because of "their ability to evoke atemporal resonances within narratives that are separate from such patriarchal religious structures as the Catholic Church . . . ." ("Zero Degree" 310). Yet what kind of power does a flower hold for Woolf and for the reader of her story so that its blossoming might obliterate time?

As Stimpson explains, images of nature, such as flowers, serve as "standard tropes [of lesbian passion] carry[ing] the implicit burden of dissolving the taint of 'unnatural' actions through the cleansing power of natural language" ("Zero Degree" 306). In their writings on Mansfield and Woolf respectively, Sydney Janet Kaplan and Patricia Cramer read images of flowers as explicit references to the female body and lesbian lovemaking (Kaplan, *Katherine Mansfield* 49–50; Cramer, "Underground" 184–86).

Both "Slater's Pins" and "Carnation" employ flower imagery to represent their female characters' underlying sexual feelings for other women. The symbol of flowering passion is specifically a carnation, which passes from the hands of one woman (the woman who is sexually aware) to the breasts of the other. The eroticized descriptions of the women handling the carnations—the movement of their fingers and mouths, and their delight in pressure, taste, and scent—suggest forms of lesbian lovemaking (Levy 89; Clements 16–17). In Woolf's story, upon finding the flower that has fallen from Fanny's dress, Julia "crushed it . . . voluptuously in her smooth, veined hands. . . . The pressure of her fingers seemed to increase all that was most brilliant in the flower; to set it off; to make it more frilled, fresh, immaculate" ("Slater's Pins" 217). Later, during the scene in which Fanny recognizes Julia's happiness and ecstatic love, her teacher is holding the carnation upright in her lap ("Slater's Pins" 220).

Underscoring the emblematic eroticism in Woolf's descriptions, the carnation itself (according to the *Oxford English Dictionary*) is tied to several (obsolete) meanings and etymological forms—"the colour of human flesh," "incarnation," and "coronation"—which suggest carnality, embodiment, and ritual. In both stories, the carnation *embodies* the women's mutual *carnal* desires, while the *ritual* of exchanging the flower signifies the protagonists' awakened sexual feelings. At the end of "Slater's Pins,"

> She [Fanny] saw Julia open her arms; saw her blaze; saw her kindle. Out of the night she burnt like a dead white star. Julia kissed her. Julia possessed her.[27]
>
> "Slater's pins have no points," Miss Craye said, laughing queerly and relaxing her arms, as Fanny Wilmot pinned the flower to her breast with trembling fingers. (220).

The conclusion reverses Fanny Wilmot's unwillingness (Fanny "Will not") to see her teacher's lesbianism and with it Fanny's own desire for her. Where she once saw "perpetual frustration" in Julia, who "did not possess it [the carnation], enjoy it, not altogether" ("Slater's Pins" 217), she now sees sexual consummation, imagining herself as Julia's willing partner. Fanny's returning the newly consecrated carnation to her breast with trembling fingers suggests fear, excitement, and specifically lesbian desire.

"Slater's Pins" depicts metaphorically what "Carnation" represents literally: from reading comes knowledge; from teaching, influence. Katie discovers her passions as a result of being seduced by her teacher's reading;[28] Fanny learns to read the narrative of her teacher's life and thereby gains insight into her own desires.

The point of "Slater's Pins" seems to be, as the title tells us, that there is no point: that is, no phallic presence. In "choosing her pleasures for herself" ("Slater's Pins" 220), Julia forgoes marriage and elects to serve instead as a Sapphic model of lesbian passion and female artistic accomplishment for other women, such as her "favourite pupil," Fanny ("Slater's

Pins" 216)—a mentoring role Woolf advocates in much of her work (Marcus, "Liberty" 92; "Taking the Bull" 144; "Sapphistry" 164, 172).

In "A Woman's College from Outside," for example, women teachers and students spiritually bond at night by means of a vaporous, erotically charged laughter that pervades their beds so that while "reposing deeply, they [*Elderly women* . . . who would on waking immediately clasp the ivory rod of office] *lay surrounded, lay supported, by the bodies of youth* recumbent or grouped at the window; pouring forth into the garden this bubbling laughter, this irresponsible laughter: this laughter of mind and body floating away rules, hours, discipline: *immensely fertilising* . . ." ("Woman's College" 147; emphasis added). Here and in "Slater's Pins," Woolf celebrates cross-generational bonding among women as a mystical and erotic force that nurtures women's intellectual and emotional growth (Marcus, "Sapphistry" 172). As a component of the pedagogical relationship, such bonding through admiration and desire enables Fanny to see "back and back into the past behind her" ("Slater's Pins" 220)—from Fanny through Julia to Sappho—to see her own place in the generations of inspired and inspiring women who love and sustain each other.

I began this essay by recounting Woolf's dreams about Mansfield and my own dream about Woolf—unconscious connections with mentors forged in sleep akin to the bonding in "A Woman's College from Outside." Mansfield, too, had this type of dream. In a 1920 letter to her husband, she recounts two dreams: In the first, her friend Beatrice Hastings accuses Mansfield of being a "*femme marquée*," presumably for her flirtations with lesbianism,[29] and later in the dream a group of women from the Salvation Army ask her if she is corrupted (*Letters and Journals* 196–97). In the second dream, after meeting Oscar Wilde in a cafe, Mansfield invites him to her parents' home for a late night chat. Both repelled by and attracted to him "as a curiosity"—"He was fatuous *and* brilliant!"—Mansfield lives in fear that her parents will discover his presence "in one of the chintz armchairs" (*Letters and Journals* 197). In the rest of the dream, Wilde describes his shame at being haunted by a vision of a creme-filled pastry while in prison for homosexuality (197–98). Clearly, the two dreams encode Mansfield's terror of having her own homosexual proclivities exposed.[30]

Given the Decadent legacy that Mansfield inherited from Wilde, as well as her fears about her desire for women, it is not surprising that "Carnation" forgoes the celebratory Sapphic model of lesbian passion embraced by Julia and by Woolf herself. Yet, just as Fanny looks "back and back into the past behind her" in order to read her mentor's and thus her own lesbianism, so too Woolf and I look back on Mansfield—admiring her artistry, noting her place in a lesbian tradition, reshaping her vision to fit our own.

NOTES

This essay is dedicated to my sapphic mentors, especially Eileen.

1. I want to thank Eileen Barrett for alerting me to Woolf's dreams about Mansfield.

2. See Alpers; Banks, "Mansfield"; Q. Bell; DeSalvo, "Cave"; Gubar; Kaplan, *Katherine Mansfield*; McLaughlin; Angela Smith; Tomalin.

3. Alpers; Q. Bell; Kaplan, *Katherine Mansfield*; McLaughlin; Tomalin; Mansfield, *Collected* 1: 313, 324; 2: 311, 315–16, 347; *D* 2: 45, 225–27; *L* 4: 365–66.

4. See Grindea as a case in point (8–9).

5. *L* 2: 168, 196, 248; Mansfield, *Collected* 1: 301, 330–31; 2: 311, 347; Banks, "Mansfield" 77; *D* 2: 317–18.

6. For a discussion of how class dynamics affect women's relationships in this story, see Levy 88.

7. The relationship between Clarissa Dalloway and Sally Seton in *Mrs. Dalloway* is one example (Cramer, "Underground" 177–78; Olano, "'Women Alone'" 164).

8. See, for example, "Leves Amores" (*Poems*), "Bains Turcs" (*Short Stories*), and "Summer Idylle. 1906" ("Unpublished").

9. I am indebted to Eileen Barrett for suggesting this to me.

10. Judith Neaman has discussed the role of Genesis in "Bliss," noting Mansfield's extensive Bible reading (243).

11. Significantly, in a 1918 letter to her husband, Mansfield describes her longtime female companion, Ida Baker, as having "pecked her way into my wing . . ." (*Collected* 2: 83).

12. *Juliet*'s Pearl is modeled after Mansfield's college friend Vere Bartrick-Baker, who also served as the inspiration for Eve in "Carnation."

13. Commenting on the girls' discomfort, Mary Rohrberger also reads the above passage as sexual, emphasizing the seductive Eve's erotic handling and kissing of the (eventually "languid") carnation while Hugo reads. She notes that the simultaneity of sounds, odors, and sights at the climax of "Carnation" suggests the sex act, although she does not discuss the story's homoerotic implications (52).

14. Mansfield's sexual life, like that of many of her female contemporaries, is often misrepresented and obscured. Regrettably, Mansfield instigated the destruction of many of her personal papers, including her "early letters to Ida [Baker]" (Brown 161; Hankin 211–12). Furthermore, in editing her letters and journals, John Middleton Murry omitted details of Mansfield's intimate relationships with

women (O'Sullivan 117–18; Waldron 12–13; I. Gordon 16). Not surprisingly, critics and biographers differ in their assessments of these relationships. Mansfield's explicit descriptions of her sexual feelings for and behavior with Edith Bendall and Maata Mahupuku in her unexpurgated journals convince most scholars of her lesbian relations. Some, however, offer a skeptical gloss on these writings (Tomalin 36), focus on "evidence" and chronology (McEldowney 114), or resort to condescension and flippancy (Grindea 17–18). Several critics appropriately label Mansfield's sexual feelings, behavior, and sense of herself throughout her lifetime as bisexual (Kaplan, *Katherine Mansfield*; Hankin; Hanscombe; O'Sullivan; Tomalin).

15. For discussions of this relationship, see Hanscombe; Berkman; Boddy; Brown; Tomalin; Kaplan, *Katherine Mansfield*; Hankin; Foster; and L. Moore.

16. I base my assertions about their relationship on Tomalin's and Hankin's discussions of it, as well as on the many lesbian narratives Mansfield wrote about, and in some cases for, Bartrick-Baker: "Carnation"; *Juliet* ("Unpublished"); and "Vignettes III," "Vignette—Westminster Cathedral," and "Leves Amores" (*Poems*).

17. Tomalin 25; Alpers 35; Crone 34.

18. Alpers 25, 119, 128; Kaye 127, 135; Crone 31–32; Mantz and Murry 205–8; Kaplan, *Katherine Mansfield* 71; Mansfield, *Collected* 1: 10.

19. Alpers 25, 32. Verlaine was a French Symbolist poet (along with his lover, Rimbaud) and a leader of the Decadents (Appelbaum 121–22; *Alyson* 183, 195–96; MacIntyre 120–21).

20. Mantz and Murry argue that M. Hugo is modeled after both M. Huguenot and John Adam Cramb, Queen's College professors of French and history, respectively (191). Though critics associate "Carnation" with Queens, they elide the connection with Rippmann (Kaye 137; Meyers, *Katherine Mansfield* 15; Tomalin 25).

21. For this distinction between lesbian and Sapphist, as well as my understanding of the history of Sapphist narration, I am indebted to Joan DeJean's brilliant book *Fictions of Sappho: 1546–1937* (see, in particular, 9). Both DeJean and Jane Marcus discuss Woolf's interest in reclaiming Sappho in their readings of her short story "A Society" (DeJean 308–11; Marcus, "Liberty" 88–89, 91–92, 95).

22. Audre Lorde introduces this term to describe her "fictionalized memoir," *Zami: A New Spelling of My Name* (Gilbert and Gubar 2249).

23. Susan Clements argues that Fanny fails to recognize her teacher's and her own lesbianism due to her lack of lesbian "narrative models," such as those offered by Sappho, whose lesbianism has been erased by a homophobic society (21). Yet, as I argue below, it is precisely this lesbian literary tradition and role model (Sappho) that Fanny eventually recognizes and that Woolf's story reclaims.

24. For other discussions of the pin as phallus, see Clements 18, 22; Baldwin 53–54.

25. See Campbell 99 qtd. in Grahn, *Mother* 304 n. 13.

26. For other discussions of the use of ambiguous pronouns in this story, see Fleishman, "Forms"; Clements; Hafley.

27. Susan Dick cites the original typescript version of these lines: "Julia blazed. Julia kindled. Out of the night she burnt like a dead white star. Julia opened her arms. Julia kissed her on the lips. Julia possessed it" (10).

28. According to Linda Dowling, the notion of reading as (often homoerotic) seduction is part of "that central *topos* of Victorian literary Decadence, the motif I have called the 'fatal book'" (168; Kaplan, *Katherine Mansfield* 29 n. 23).

29. In a letter to Murry, Mansfield describes an incident at a party in which she danced with a "lovely young woman—married & *curious*—blonde—passionate" and later fought with Hastings over refusing to spend the night with her. In Murry's reply, he suggests that Hastings is a lesbian and that that fact explains her bad behavior toward Mansfield *(Letters Between* 43–45).

30. For a detailed analysis of this dream, see Kaplan, *Katherine Mansfield* (33–35).

SIX

Lesbian Modernism in the Shorter Fiction of Virginia Woolf and Gertrude Stein

CORINNE E. BLACKMER

To the extent that lesbians have been associated with the obscure, the neglected, and the marginal, there is something quintessentially "lesbian" about bringing the shorter fictions of Virginia Woolf and Gertrude Stein into critical focus. Although her accomplishment in this genre equals that of her contemporary James Joyce, Woolf has not been highly appreciated for her short stories. The standard format for a critical study of Woolf remains, as Avrom Fleishman notes, "a series of chapters on the nine longer fictions, one after another" ("Forms" 44). When mentioned at all, her short stories tend to be regarded not as innovative achievements in themselves, but rather as experiments in themes and techniques developed more fully in the novels. Her short stories occupy, in the hierarchy of Woolfian genres, a marginalized lesbian position analogous to that held by her treatment of desire between women in mainstream Woolf criticism.

In her lesbian-themed short stories, Woolf conducts a comprehensive analysis of the psychological experience of attraction among women. In "The Mysterious Case of Miss V." (1908) and "The Lady in the Looking-Glass" (1928), she uses the images of the apparitional spinster, the double personality, and the mirrored self-portrait to explore the disavowed lesbian desire that simmers beneath the surface of ostensibly conventional lives. The signal importance of these stories and, in particular, "Memoirs of a Novelist" (1909) and "A Society" (1920) lies, however, in their fiercely intimate and impassioned engagement with earlier traditions of sublimated or censored literatures of lesbianism.[1] Woolf turns specifically to the short story, rather than the review essay or literary manifesto, because this form enables her to express herself with imaginative latitude and, given the need in her historical moment for discretion in handling this explosive topic, indirection. Woolf combines critical analysis and fictional narration to fashion what are among the first examples of lesbian feminist historical criticism.

Because Stein worked extensively in all the major forms, critics have been less inclined than they have with Woolf to privilege one genre over another in her vast, multifaceted, intentionally decentered *oeuvre*. Her concise, poetic evocations of lesbian subjectivity in her short story "Melanctha" (1909) and her verbal portraits "Ada" (1908), "As a Wife Has a Cow" (1926), and "Miss Furr and Miss Skeene" (1922) achieve an aesthetic power not equaled in her more diffuse lesbian-themed writings, with the exception of her equally poetic collection of object portraits *Tender Buttons* and her erotic dialogue poem *Lifting Belly*.

Differing critical receptions of their shorter fiction cannot, however, account for the general absence of comparative commentary on Woolf and Stein, an absence all the more striking given their stature as major lesbian modernists. An analysis of their lesbian-themed short stories provides an excellent context for examining the larger implications of their distinctive approaches to creating lesbian modernist literature. For Woolf and Stein, lesbian modernism signifies a historical break with the nineteenth-century ideology of separate spheres, which, as represented in Victorian realist literature, reflected the belief that men and women have different but complementary biological traits, social roles, and sexual natures. In lesbian modernism, the lesbian enters the public domain as an autonomous, artistically creative, self-directed being whose conscious desire for women contradicts dominant assumptions regarding women's innate sexual passivity. More radically, her very existence implies the eventual elimination of gender as a significant force in cultural and social relations.

While Woolf and Stein share this broad understanding of lesbian modernism, their shorter fictions elaborate different significations around the homosexual closet, constructed by separating private from public knowledge of homosexual identity. According to Eve Sedgwick's influential paradigm, the defining feature of gay and lesbian modernism is the production of a homosexual code that restricts information about homosexuality to contexts in which its legibility depends on shared minority identification (*Epistemology* 71–73). Hence, textual occlusions, including those that ostensibly have nothing to do with sexuality, point obliquely toward individual or cultural instances of sexual identity crisis. In her lesbian-themed shorter fictions, Woolf invites her homosexual readership to identify with her lesbian subject position. Through encoded language, she reveals the repressed lesbian identities within earlier literatures of homosexuality. Concomitantly, she treats conscious acknowledgment of homosexual identity as the ethical truth of modern lesbian subjectivity by critiquing the self-ignorance and self-repressiveness informing earlier authors like Marie Corelli and Vernon Lee, Sappho scholars, and her self-portrait as the apparitional Miss V(irginia).

Because Stein occludes her gender by substituting "he" or "one" for "she," she can also be read as a lesbian modernist who, like Woolf, uses coded language. However, since readers of Gertrude Stein remain aware of her gender, these transparent sex reversals can be interpreted as sites of disruption designed not to conceal but to call attention to the fictive status of all gender constructs. Moreover, her notorious textual opacity does not disguise lesbian identity because Stein, anticipating the queer theorizations of Judith Butler, does not believe that sexuality can remain sexuality if it submits to linguistic acts of naming that promise to transform intrinsically opaque psychic processes into transparent facts (Butler "Imitation and Gender Insubordination" 15). For Stein, sexual subjectivity signifies an inner movement of self-contained being that resists capture through definitions, categorizations, or other information about persons. Since Stein based her lesbian-themed verbal portraits on her autobiographical experiences, it makes sense that she approaches lesbianism as an embodied form of desire related immediately and casually to dramatized being. In her lesbian-themed shorter fictions, she reconfigures the ontological relationship between inessential attributes that describe habitual acts and essential definitions that name persons in order to represent lesbian subjectivity as an embodied process of experience that is neither speakable nor unspeakable.

Woolf's early story "The Mysterious Case of Miss V." concerns an anonymous narrator who becomes obsessed with Miss V., an elderly spinster who haunts London society without anyone's taking notice of her existence. This narrative illustrates what Terry Castle calls the "lesbian ghost story," in which the metaphor of ghosting represents the culturally mandated specter of disavowed lesbian desire that returns to haunt another woman (28–65). The connection between the narrator and

Miss V. also recalls the covert male homoeroticism in late Victorian doppelganger stories such as Robert Louis Stevenson's *The Strange Case of Dr. Jekyll and Mr. Hyde* (1886). In her diary, Woolf noted that she wanted to study Stevenson, "not to copy . . . but to see how the trick's done" (*PA* 251). Published the year that the Labouchere Amendment outlawing male homosexuality in England went into effect, Stevenson's novella explores the double life of daytime social propriety and nighttime sexual liaisons forced upon male homosexuals. Henry Jekyll, an ostensibly respectable and celibate bachelor, mates with his double, Edward Hyde, a disreputable young man who arouses suspicion among his all-male circle of acquaintances, who fear being sexually blackmailed by working-class blackguards. The narrator of this study of male homosexual panic is Gabriel John Utterson, who, like Woolf's narrator, fills the void in his uneventful existence with an elaborate fantasy life based on vicarious identification with "downgoing men," for whom "it was frequently his fortune to be the last reputable acquaintance" (1). Just as Woolf's narrator becomes fixated on Miss V., Utterson becomes "enslaved" (13) by the mystery of Hyde, vowing that "If he be Mr. Hyde . . . I shall be Mr. Seek" (15).

Woolf represents herself, as Dean R. Baldwin notes, in the character of Miss V. (Miss Virginia) and explores her fears of becoming an isolated spinster whose personal identity has shrunk to an initial and who has no more substance than a shadow (8). Through this fictionalized self-portrait, Woolf examines how the fear of losing social acceptance makes her reluctant to embrace her desire for women. Moreover, Elaine Showalter remarks that unlike Victorian gentlemen, who "had the prerogative of moving freely through the zones of the city," Victorian ladies were not permitted "access to a nighttime world of bars, clubs, brothels, and illicit sexuality as an alternative to their public life of decorum and restraint" (118–19). In contrast to Gabriel Utterson, Woolf's narrator relates little information about her unanchored, solitary life that secretly mirrors that of the mysterious Miss V.

The sudden death of Miss V. plunges the narrator into apprehensions concerning her own anonymity: "The ease with which such a fate befalls you suggests that it is really necessary to assert yourself in order to prevent yourself from being skipped . . . It is a terrible fate" ("Miss V" 30). Although she refers to the "sister" of Miss V., she also notes that "it is characteristic that in writing of them one name seems instinctively to do for both—indeed one might mention a dozen such sisters in one breath"

("Miss V" 30). She both erases Miss V. as an individual and implies that a covert sisterly bond exists between them. While the strength of this bond makes her afraid to acknowledge her desire for intimacy with Miss V. lest she share in her insignificance, her disavowal of this connection will result in the same end.

Significantly, the narrator first notices Miss V. through her absence, which causes her a "nameless dissatisfaction" ("Miss V" 31). One morning she calls aloud her name: "Mary V! Mary V!" ("Miss V" 31). But this attempt at communication fails to raise the ghost. She conceives the "fantastic plan" of visiting Miss V. and treating her "as though she were a person like the rest of us!" ("Miss V" 31). When she arrives, she discovers that Miss V. has died "at the very moment when I called her name" ("Miss V" 32). This melodramatic ending spells out the doom of urban isolation foretold in the opening: "It is a commonplace that there is no loneliness like that of one who finds himself alone in a crowd; novelists repeat it; the pathos is undeniable; and now, since the case of Miss V., I at least have come to believe it" ("Miss V" 30). The narrator arrives too late to create an actual bond with the woman revealed, at last, not as Miss Virginia but rather her apparitional double, Mary V. The story leaves the narrator with the choice of repeating the patterns that have ghosted women like Mary V. or, alternately, of becoming intimate with and acknowledging herself, Miss Virginia.

Woolf's "Memoirs of a Novelist" reveals that in the negative anxieties over ghostly spinsterhood that characterize "The Mysterious Case of Miss V." lie the positive possibilities of recovery and rematerialization. Woolf frames this quasi-fictional, quasi-critical story as a review article that outs two late Victorian romantic friends as repressed lesbians in the process of critiquing Miss Linsett's tedious memoirs of her lifelong companion, Miss Willatt, a once popular author of insipid romances. This groundbreaking fiction should be read in conjunction with Woolf's two manifestos of literary modernism, "Mr. Bennett and Mrs. Brown" (1924) and "Modern Fiction" (1925). Years before declaring that their materialist world view prevented her Edwardian literary forbears from apprehending modern character as an "unknown and uncircumscribed spirit, whatever aberration and complexity it may display" ("Modern Fiction" 150), this story reveals how the ideology of separate spheres governing Victorian culture systemically suppressed lesbianism. Woolf accomplishes this task by exploring the difference between the official Miss Willatt, as portrayed by her Victorian biographer Miss Linsatt, and the real Miss Willatt, as revealed by the narrator.

Woolf appears to have modeled Miss Willatt on the immensely popular Edwardian novelist Marie Corelli. Her melodramas, which combined anti-sex polemics with occultism and science fiction, were often set in biblical or otherwise remote locales and rapidly fell into obscurity after her death. Corelli had a longtime romantic friendship with Bertha Vyver, a union complete with the consolations of traditional marriage except for sexual expression, which Corelli regarded as legitimate only for procreation. Viewing their female-female love as free from any "taint" of male lust, the women were openly affectionate in public. Ironically, Corelli's belief in women's natural moral superiority accompanied her staunch opposition to women's suffrage.[2] Woolf, who regarded Corelli as a model of bad writing and compared her unfavorably to Sappho (D 2: 340), treats the Corelli-like Miss Willatt as the archetype of the censorious and morally self-righteous lesbian author who regards public adulation as a personal right but cannot identify with feminists or homosexual men lest she come to recognize her sinful lesbian desires.

The story opens with the death of Miss Willatt. After considering whether anyone can or should know the truth about someone's private life, the narrator concludes that both women have, as writers, exposed themselves to historical scrutiny. Miss Linsatt, however, uses writing to mask rather than reveal truth, and since she never explains why she wrote her memoirs of Miss Willatt or who either of them was, the narrator reinterprets the official story. Miss Linsatt, she surmises, wrote the memoirs because she "felt uneasy" after her companion's death since the people on the street looked remarkably "indifferent" ("Memoirs" 69). While Miss Willatt's fate as a forgotten novelist mirrors the existential anomie of Miss Linsatt, she reinforces her predicament by excising from her memoirs the psychological conflict that would have made her and her friend fascinating and instructive to future homosexual readers. Woolf rescues Miss Willatt from oblivion but also emphasizes that authors who live by dictates of conventional opinion will die by them as well.

From the narrator's sleuth-like skill in reading between the lines of the official memoirs, we learn that Miss Willatt became alienated from society because her male relatives belittled her intellectual abilities. Expected to marry to establish her "relationship to the world," she experiences "a terrible depression" ("Memoirs" 72). To avoid institutional heterosexuality, she takes up religion. Her moral seriousness cannot, however, eliminate her persistent desires. She confesses to her best friend, Ellen Buckle, that she oscillates between feeling superior to the sexual sinfulness that surrounds her and regarding herself as an anomalous "blot upon the face of nature" ("Memoirs" 73):

> A terrible self-consciousness possessed her, and she writes to Miss Buckle as though she watched her shadow trembling over the entire world, beneath the critical eyes of the angels. . . . "What would I not give to help you?" writes Miss Buckle. Our difficulty as we read now is to understand what their aim was; for it is clear that they imagined a state in which the soul lay tranquil and in bliss, and that if one could reach it one was perfect. . . . But the only pleasure that they allowed themselves to feel was the pleasure of submission. ("Memoirs" 73)

In this crisis, however, Miss Buckle deserts her friend by marrying an engineer "by whom her doubts were set at rest for ever" ("Memoirs" 73) and leaves Miss Willatt to suffer her suspected sinfulness alone. Not surprisingly, Miss Linsatt ruthlessly censors this portion of her memoir, shrinking "the word love and whole passages polluted by it . . . into asterisks" ("Memoirs" 73) and substituting dull catalogues of virtues for the complicated truth of Miss Willatt's romantic grief. Judging that Miss Linsatt has abandoned Miss Willatt by refusing to disclose why Miss Buckle ended her friendship with Miss Willatt, the narrator, in turn, dismisses Miss Linsatt and her memoirs. The narrator surmises that Miss Willatt, having suffered rejection for revealing her anomalous character to another woman, learned to mask herself and deceive the adoring Miss Linsatt. In reality, Miss Willatt was a "restless and discontented person" ("Memoirs" 75) who doubted religion and used charity to mask her ambitions. But rather than acknowledge her lesbian desires or critique Victorian gender ideology, she turns, in a gesture common to sublimated literatures of lesbianism, to the realm of fantasy, producing romantic fables of imaginary lovers in faraway locales that transport her readers into places remote from their own constricted lives. Miss Willatt becomes a failed Sappho, a woman whose cynical failure of nerve constitutes her essential tragedy as a writer and a leader of women:

> She had thoughts of emigrating, and founding a society, in which she saw herself . . . reading wisdom from a book to a circle of industrious disciples. . . . Miss Willatt was far too clever to believe that anyone could answer anything; but the sight of these queer little trembling women, who looked up

at her, prepared for beating or caress, like spaniels, appealed to a mass of emotions, and they were not all of them bad. What such women wanted, she saw, was to be told that they were parts of a whole. ("Memoirs" 77)

Miss Linsatt lavishly describes Miss Willatt's death, but her homage does not succeed in immortalizing her friend. In "Memoirs of a Novelist," Woolf doubly inverts the traditional love story. Victorian mores result in the denial of lesbian passion and an amorous fixation on death. Miss Linsatt loves her dead companion because "[i]t was an end undisturbed by the chance of a fresh beginning" ("Memoirs" 79). But Woolf destabilizes this closure, showing the intensely lonely Miss Linsatt remembering how she and her friend "had been in the habit of going to Kew Gardens together on Sundays" ("Memoirs" 79).

In "The Lady in the Looking-Glass: A Reflection," Woolf portrays a disquieting, compelling woman modeled partly on her influential contemporary, the lesbian art critic Vernon Lee (Violet Paget).[3] The narrative begins with the statement that "People should not leave open cheque books or letters confessing some hideous crime" ("Lady" 221) and ends with "People should not leave looking-glasses hanging in their rooms" ("Lady" 225). This story reveals that the elderly spinster Isabella Tyson does not hide behind her façade a terrible crime or financial indiscretion. Rather, Isabella's reflection in the looking-glass exposes her to the narrator as an "empty" old woman who has "no thoughts," "no friends," and "cared for nobody" ("Lady" 225). This story never reveals the actual connection between the narrator and Isabella, or explains why the former observes Isabella so intently, as if determined to uncover "the truth about Isabella . . . after knowing her all these years" ("Lady" 222).

The anonymous narrator relates several facts about her friend while Isabella tends her opulent flower garden. A wealthy woman with a home furnished with Oriental antiques she has accumulated in her travels to "the most obscure corners of the world" ("Lady" 222), Isabella in her worldliness contrasts sharply with Woolf's earlier portraits of restricted, impoverished lesbian lives. Although she had "known many people, had had many friends," her intimacies have led to "nothing" ("Lady" 222), either because she has never married or has never shared the story of her personal relationships with others. Nevertheless, the narrator speculates that to judge "from the mask-like indifference of her face, she had gone through twenty times more of passion and experience than those whose loves are trumpeted forth for all the world to hear" ("Lady" 223). The narrator implies that Isabella's hermetically sealed private life protects her lesbianism from public disclosure.

Both the voyeuristic narrator and Isabella Tyson bear a striking resemblance to Vernon Lee. Woolf composed a portrait of Lee, whom she had visited in Florence and, as the ending of "Mrs. Dalloway in Bond Street" indicates, originally intended to make Lee's longtime female companion, C. Anstruther-Thomas, a character in *Mrs. Dalloway* (*MD* 159). Like Isabella Tyson, Lee was a widely traveled aesthete who collected art and antique furnishings. An enigmatic and strikingly beautiful woman, Lee forbade inquiries into her personal life. While Lee was reluctant to acknowledge her lesbianism even to her close friends, her writings on aesthetics, which influenced Woolf, were replete with encoded homosexual references.

Woolf treats Lee as a transitional figure who embodies the struggle between cultural tradition and innovation. Regarding art as the vehicle for sublimating homoeroticism, Lee's aesthetic theory combines an obsessive focus on women as the ideal object of art with a universalizing masculine gaze that causes her to construct an airtight homosexual closet. While Woolf shared Lee's contrary impulses to worship unattainable women and penetrate the enigma of their seductive allure, Woolf's aesthetic objectification was modified by her feminist valorization of female experience. In "The Lady in the Looking-Glass: A Reflection," Woolf uses the metaphor of the mirror to explore how Vernon Lee would look to Vernon Lee if she held up the reflection of her aesthetic philosophy to herself. That the narrator discovers nothingness as the secret of Isabella's life reveals Woolf's critique of the consequences of Lee's divorce of aesthetic pleasure from empathic identification. Art, like the aesthetic contemplation of human beings, exists to forbid rather than to create intimacy. Yet the very force of the forbidden creates a desire to uncover a hidden truth that the denial of female experience has already rendered not only inaccessible but also, more alarmingly, perhaps *nonexistent*.

In "A Society," Woolf turns to Sappho, the preeminent lesbian poet of Western culture. Gillian Spraggs argues that in the early twentieth century, when medical sexologists and apologists for same-sex love were adopting the names "lesbian" and "Sapphist" for a distinct psychological type, lesbian authors were identifying Sappho as an exemplary foremother. In response to these developments, "eminent scholars of ancient Greek were covering pages with passionately expressed assertions as to the 'moral purity' and generally conventional character of the poet" (51). Woolf shows how male scholars' pathologizing misinterpretations of her poetry contribute to the most egregious features of British patriarchy: fatalistic warmongering among men and compulsive childbearing among women. Cassandra, the central narrator, reports on the doings of six complaisant young women who have been taught to disparage women and praise male achievements. Their assumptions are challenged by Polly, who has been given a paternal legacy on the condition that she read all the books in the British Library. Polly "bursts into tears" when she can no longer suppress her knowledge that most books written by men are "unutterably bad" ("A Society" 124). Deciding that the object of life is to "produce good people and good books" ("A Society" 128), the women form themselves into a Society for judging the worth of patriarchal culture. They venture out to investigate what men do in the navy, the law courts, the arts, and the university. Until they receive satisfactory answers, they vow to remain chaste: "Before we bring another child into the world we must swear that we will find out what the world is like" ("A Society" 125).

As Jane Marcus notes, "A Society" represents Woolf's effort to penetrate cloistered male scholarly societies such as the Cambridge Apostles, whose members were ostensibly heterosexual even though they idealized male homosexuality and Greek culture, and "to offer a parallel sisterhood of intellectual inquiry and social conscience" ("Liberty" 91). Sappho connects this closeted male society of scholars, who live in sterile isolation without "children or animals" ("A Society" 127), to the feminist society of modern sapphists who infiltrate their domains. Castalia travels to Oxbridge to investigate the intellectual contributions of Professor Hobkin, whose scholarly life has been dedicated to an edition of Sappho. When Castalia returns, her contempt for his arid life mingles with her puzzlement over what useful knowledge his work means to convey.

> "It's a queer looking book, six or seven inches thick, not all by Sappho. Oh, no. Most of it is a defense of Sappho's chastity, which some German has denied, and I can assure you the passion with which these two gentlemen argued, the learning they displayed, the prodigious ingenuity with which they disputed the use of some implement which looked to me for all the world like a hairpin astounded me." ("A Society" 128)

Another woman speculates that Professor Hobkin must be a "gynae-cologist" since no serious literary scholar could waste so much time, in a work supposedly dedicated to a great lyric poet, over minor issues like

hairpins and disputes over chastity. But Professor Hobkin typifies a tradition of male scholars who refused, with few exceptions, to accept
Sappho's love for women as an unproblematic aspect of her being related
to her appreciation of female beauty, celebration of nature, and criticism
of warfare. Rather, they projected their compulsion to control women
onto Sappho by isolating her sexuality from its social and artistic context.
This fanatical obsession with Sapphic sexuality serves to deflect attention
from the serious issues raised by feminist reinterpretations of chastity and
to mask profound fears that women's *politically motivated* feminist bonding threatens male dominance and the patriarchal family. For the Society,
chastity means the refusal to reproduce a culture that perpetuates waste,
aggression, and mediocrity by barring women from making vitally
needed contributions.

Woolf underscores the point that productive feminist community depends on common political goals. Castalia ventures again to Oxbridge to
uncover more information about male notions of chastity. She decides to
conceive a child out of wedlock and raise it in the female world of the
Society. Although she has broken her vow of chastity, her companions do
not reject her since her pregnancy registers her protest to the life-denying
world of male scholarship. Both Cassandra and Castalia realize that they
are not chaste according to the male definition of the term, for, as
Castalia remarks, "If you'd been a chaste woman yourself you would
have screamed at the sight of me—instead of which you rushed across
the room and took me in your arms" ("A Society" 129).

In the end, however, Woolf undercuts this epiphanic moment of feminist solidarity in two ways. She reveals the tragic political consequences
of male scholars' bowdlerizations of Sappho and suggests the challenges
the women will face in coping with their new insights. The sudden arrival
of World War I represents the literalization of the disputes over Sappho's
chastity among European scholars. Masculine culture has failed to learn
anything valuable from Sappho, who linked her love for women—as
friends, students, lovers, and mothers—to her critique of the Homeric
epic that glorified violence and nationalistic warfare.[4] In a desperate
effort to protect her child from this destructive culture, Castalia wants to
prevent her daughter Ann "from learning to read" ("A Society" 134). But
Ann cannot return to the child-like ignorance of Victorian womanhood
any more than she can handle the adult responsibilities thrust upon her.
Hence, just as Polly creates the Society by bursting into tears, Ann concludes this phase of feminist inquiry by crying when the women elect her

the president of the Society of the Future. "A Society" allegorizes how the ideology of separate spheres imposed limits on the groundbreaking cultural achievements of lesbian-feminist modernism. The Society gains sapphic insight into the systemic failures of masculine civilization but still lacks the political and economic power to transform their world.

In her lesbian-themed shorter fictions, Woolf transforms lesbianism from a repressed cultural phantasm into a form of modern sexual subjectivity through encoded acts of critical reinterpretation. Identification with this textually generated lesbian subject position not only fosters awareness of the historical repression of lesbianism but also serves as a site of political resistance to sexual un-self-consciousness and complicity in patriarchal domination. While Stein, like Woolf, alludes to earlier literatures of homosexuality in her writing, her distinctive contribution to lesbian modernism resides in her use of autobiographical experience to resignify sexuality as an opaque psychic process and, concomitantly, to transform the relationships among literary representation, autobiographical narrative, and sexual subjectivity.

Stein makes the transition from Victorian realism to lesbian modernism in her short story "Melanctha." This story represents her second attempt, after her posthumously published autobiographical novella *Q.E.D.* to understand the failure of her first lesbian relationship with May Bookstaver, a student she met during medical school and on whom she based her bisexual, biracial protagonist Melanctha Herbert in "Melanctha." By applying the logic of the homosexual closet to Stein's mature writing, however, influential critics such as Richard Bridgman conclude that Stein merely covered her lesbian self-portrait in *Q.E.D.* with a heterosexual ethnic mask in "Melanctha," thereby using race to encode lesbianism (52). This interpretation not only erases the lesbianism represented legibly in the relationship between Melanctha and Jane Harden but also elides how Stein uses race to foreground how the body and sexual life are governed by arbitrary convention. While distinctions based on race, color, gender, and sexuality dominate the text's social landscape and make Melanctha "blue" about "how all her world was made" ("Melanctha" 87), these presumptively stable and discrete properties are combined and recombined through permutating contexts with such dizzying complexity that they become self-contradictory and lose their authority to enunciate any singular truth about human nature.

Stein employs "black" language as the verbal landscape of this text not to represent actual African American dialect but rather, as Michael North observes, to dramatize the conflict between realist and modernist conceptions of linguistic meaning (74). This conflict informs the central relationship between Melanctha and Jefferson Campbell, a middle-class black doctor who wants "colored people" to avoid "excitements" and "live regular" ("Melanctha" 117). While Stein's self-portrait as Jefferson encodes her gender, she masculinizes herself to parody an earlier version of herself as a naive medical student who believed in bourgeois morality and, subscribing to medical sexology, regarded "real" lesbianism as the assumption of a socially defined masculine role. Melanctha, exposed by Jane Harden's scandalous revelations to Jefferson about their sexual "wanderings" that identify her as a biracial lesbian prostitute who has sex with black and white men alike ("Melanctha" 143–44), treats language as an inessential attribute that describes immediate, self-contained experiences without reference to past or future. She insists that her words mean no more than what she is "just saying" ("Melanctha" 172) in any given moment or context. Jefferson, in contrast, in anguished conflict over the seeming contradiction between Melanctha's "sweet nature" ("Melanctha" 160) and her experiences as a "bad one" ("Melanctha" 144), wants language that commits the speaker, that links past and present selves, and that reveals the consistent inner "truth" of being. His need to "have it all clear out in words always, what everybody is always feeling" ("Melanctha" 171) not only destroys his relationship with Melanctha but also sets the stage for Stein's subsequent representations of lesbian subjectivity as a form of dynamic experience knowable only in reference to itself.

In "Melanctha," Stein masters her painful loss of May Bookstaver by relinquishing claims to linguistic mastery. Melanctha, who is neither black nor white nor homosexual nor heterosexual, explodes the claims to knowledge and ownership of selves that ground stable racial and sexual identities. Oscillating between her incompatible desires for an expansive "world wisdom" ("Melanctha" 103) on the one hand and a socially approved "right position" ("Melanctha" 212) on the other, Melanctha frustrates the will of the persons she encounters to dominate or contain her by naming her essence. Although Melanctha ultimately dies alone of "consumption" ("Melanctha" 236), exhausted by her inability to gain social acceptance, the responsibility for her tragic end rests not with Melanctha herself but with the limits her world imposes on the meaning of a woman's quest for "world wisdom" ("Melanctha" 212).

Melanctha begins her journey toward "world wisdom" through her relationship with her teacher and first lover, Jane Harden. An educated, "reckless," and hard-drinking woman, Jane was forced to leave her position at a colored college because of her "bad conduct" ("Melanctha" 103)—an allusion to the drinking habits that, unlike her lesbianism and prostitution, "can never really be covered over" ("Melanctha" 105). Melanctha becomes enamored of Jane because, as an experienced preceptor, Jane makes her "understand what everybody wanted, and what one did with power when one had it" ("Melanctha" 106). Once Melanctha gains equal footing with Jane, however, she begins to quarrel with her and forgets "how much she owed to Jane's teaching" ("Melanctha" 107). Her desertion of Jane propels Melanctha on her self-destructive quest to become "regular" by discovering her "right position" ("Melanctha" 210) through her relationship with Jefferson, the gambler Jem Richards, and Rose Johnson, a shrewdly practical woman who, near the end of the story, ejects Melanctha from her house because she threatens the stability of her heterosexual marriage. On the other hand, the breakdown of Melanctha's friendship with Jane stems from her implicit recognition that, for working-class black women leading lesbian lives, the meanings of "world wisdom" extend no further than the domains of hard drinking, prostitution, and informal relations with other women located similarly on the margins of respectable society.

Conversely, "Ada" celebrates Stein's union with Alice Toklas, whom she nicknamed Ada. This encapsulated history narrates the story of Ada's life from her subordinate position as a daughter in a conventional patriarchal household to her equal status as an adult lesbian who tells and listens to stories that have a satisfying "beginning and a middle and an ending" ("Ada" 16). Stein delineates lesbian modernism as a contextual shift from the heterosexual family to "telling stories" with "one," namely Gertrude Stein, in an open context of lesbian creativity.

As in her later relationship with "one," Ada and her mother tell stories to each another. But in this case, the people around them do not like Ada as well as her mother, for while "the daughter was charming inside in her, it did not show outside in her to every one" ("Ada" 15). In other words, in this implicitly homophobic setting, Ada's creativity remains unappreciated and inexpressible. After her mother dies, moreover, Ada becomes a servant to the "many relations who lived with them." When she tells her father "that she did not like it at all being one being living then" ("Ada" 15), he says nothing, since he cannot imagine an alternative to the unequal relations that make his daughter unhappy. Serendipitously, Ada receives an inheritance and moves away. Her father, who learns to value Ada because she leaves, eventually becomes "quite tender." Once liberated from her family, Ada does not become the proverbially frustrated or outcast spinster; rather, her capacity for "living" and "loving" liberates a *jouissance* that results in a rewriting of literary conventions of lesbianism.

In "As a Wife Has a Cow: A Love Story," Stein represents lesbian sexuality explicitly to subvert conventional notions of plot structured around conflict, rising action, crisis, falling action, and denouement or climax. While "wife" encodes a private reference to Alice Toklas, having a "cow" is a slang term for orgasm. This activity of female sexual pleasure leading to orgasm is the subject, plot, and climax of this story in which form literally becomes content. The circular story begins by describing the central action and its genre: "Nearly all of it to be as a wife has a cow, a love story" ("Wife Has a Cow" 543). This story concludes, appropriately enough, with the completed action or female "climax":

> Happening and have it as happening and having it happen as happening and having to have it happen as happening, and my wife has a cow as now, my wife having a cow as now, my wife having a cow as now and having a cow as now and having a cow and having a cow now, my wife has a cow and now. ("Wife Has a Cow" 545)

These verbal clusters indicate the rising action of sexual activity ("came in there . . . come out of there" and "feeling for it . . . feel") and the voluntary withholding of premature orgasm to increase the suspense and pleasure of the climactic close ("not and now . . . just as soon as now," "expect . . . expected," "prepare . . . preparation," and "happening . . . having").

As in her other lesbian-themed verbal portraits, Stein drew the inspiration for her most famous portrait of lesbian life, "Miss Furr and Miss Skeene," from her actual experiences—in this case, from her and Toklas's acquaintance with a lesbian couple named Miss Mars and Miss Squires. Her repetitive use of the verbal motif "gay" performs a verbal mimesis of the self-contained forces that are related immediately, dynamically, and casually to the thing signified. Stein expands the grammatical function of the adjective "gay," which signifies happy and carefree, and universalizes the attribute of "gayness," a slang term for an emerging subcultural attitude toward being homosexual that countered dominant stereotypes of the "third sex" as tragically maladjusted inverts. On the threshold between an inessential attribute and an essential name, "gay" operates as both an adjective denoting a general quality of being ("happy") and a noun designating a specific class of persons ("homosexuals"). Stein renders the contextual meanings of the "gay" relationship between Misses Furr and Skeene so transparent that only the ingrained habit of the closet, which makes readers notice lesbians only as unspeakable presences lurking behind veiled references to "the love that dare not speak its name," could prevent anyone from perceiving this story as a coming-out narrative that assumes the existence of an articulate homosexual community.

Stein presents two distinct types of gay women: the one whose restlessness and sense of adventure impels her to travel and the other whose memories of a stable home life motivate her to discover a secure community. Although their different responses to their "gayness" finally drive them apart, both women develop themselves by "cultivating" their "voices" and "other things needing cultivating" ("Furr and Skeene" 17). Stein connects singing with lesbianism because the female voice, as a form of cultivated artistic expression, can only be generated through the female body. Hence, "cultivating voices" signifies learning how to express oneself by nurturing lesbian artistic sensibility within the context of a community where they can speak gay language and live regular (rather than abnormal) gay lives.

While Woolf's "A Society" and Stein's "Melanctha" offer trenchant critiques of the ideology of separate spheres, their lesbian-themed shorter fictions signify lesbian subjectivity differently. Woolf uses encoding to reveal and *re*conceal her lesbian subject position, fashioning an enclosed, protected site of self-articulation that is constitutive of modern lesbian identity as an ethical domain. In contrast, Stein's experiences impelled her to discard the epistemological distinctions between public and private and literal and encoded knowledge of (homo)sexual identities. For Stein, conscious actors cannot articulate their sexualities as stable identities because sexuality remains occluded by subconscious process. Like Melanctha, who resists Jefferson's/Stein's attempts to commit her to consistency, when it comes to disclosing the truth about sexuality, we can never mean more than what we are "just saying" in any given moment.

NOTES

1. I am drawing a historical distinction between "lesbian literature" (literature about lesbianism written by women who identify as lesbians) and "the literature of lesbianism" (literature about lesbianism regardless of the sexual orientation or gender of the author).

2. See Patricia Smith, "Marie Corelli."

3. Vernon Lee is not the sole model for the woman in this story. In her diary, Woolf noted that "One of these days, though I shall sketch here, like a grand historical picture, the outlines of all my friends. . . . How many little stories come into my head. For instance: Ethel Sands not looking at her letters. What this implies" (*D* 3: 156–57). While Woolf was thinking of her friend Ethel Sands as someone who, like the woman in this story, does not open her letters, this portrait represents a *composite* character study. I would argue that this story's prevailing artistic influence derived from Woolf's intense engagement with Vernon Lee as the closeted lesbian embodiment of *fin-de-siècle* homosexual aestheticism.

4. In Fragments 40, 41, and 42 of Mary Barnard's translation of Sappho's lyrics, the narrator addresses her friend Anactoria, exiled from the community of women by her marriage to an army officer. Sappho bids her to remember Lesbos, where "delicious dew pours down to freshen / roses, delicate thyme" and beautiful girls lay on "soft mats" with "all that they most wished for beside them." In Fragment 41, she elevates the personal love lyric above the masculine ethos of Homeric epic: "So Anactoria, although you / being far away forget us, the dear sound of your footstep / and light glancing in your eyes / would move me more than glitter / of Lydian horse or armored / tread of mainland infantry."

SEVEN

The Death of Sex and the Soul
in **Mrs. Dalloway** and
Nella Larsen's **Passing**

TUZYLINE JITA ALLAN

Nothing is more spiritual than female sexuality.
—Luce Irigaray, *Ethique de la différence sexuelle* (57)

[W]e know that Du Bois had a perception that black
folk have "souls" that not only understand the problems
of the Veil, but also embody peculiarly transcending sensibilities that enhance their humanity. We also know that
he was aware that the folk were not all men. If anything
can be said about his views on the souls of black women
folk, it is that he felt that they had struggled through to
an even higher plane than black men had.
—Nellie Y. McKay, "The Souls of Black Women Folk
in the Writings of W. E. B. Du Bois" (229)

At first glance, Virginia Woolf and Nella Larsen might strike many critics
as too distant for the comfort of comparative analysis. On the surface,
Larsen's slender corpus and all too recent critical recovery would create a
fragile balance with Woolf's stellar writing career, prodigious *oeuvre,* and
transatlantic literary ascendancy. Linking these two writers, however,
accords with the loud challenge of current feminist practice to both
acknowledge and defy the divisions of race, class, and sexuality that
threatened feminist comity a decade or so ago. But beyond the good faith
effort to keep the ethnocentric genie locked up in the bottle, I aim to
construct a narrative of these writers' distinct yet overlapping personal

and intellectual histories and to tease out the similarities in their novel approaches to female sexuality.

The connections I make between the lives of Woolf and Larsen and their fictional representations of female sexual desire follow and simultaneously broaden the track of revisionist modernism laid out by feminist and African-Americanist critics in response to canonic orthodoxy.[1] "Modernism as caught in the mesh of gender," Bonnie Kime Scott rightly asserts, "is polyphonic, mobile, interactive, sexually charged" (4). The lengthening of modernism's reach into racial, gender, and sexual interchange, besides raising compelling questions about (white) male hegemony, calls for the re-engagement of seemingly dissimilar writers such as Larsen and Woolf. Beneath the surface realities that have sequestered Woolf from Larsen in the universe of feminist criticism—white/black, high modernism/the Harlem Renaissance, family pedigree/half-breed, woman-loving/heterosexual—lies a core of shared experiences, artistic and sexual sensibilities that is revealed to the critical eye through the subtexts of *Mrs. Dalloway* and *Passing*. Both novels inscribe a strong, spiritually charged critique of the patriarchal institution of marriage and its attendant repression of female same-sex desire in strikingly similar ways.

While the wealth of research on Woolf has opened up many paths to understanding her life and her works, Nella Larsen, as Mary Helen Washington accurately states, was "out of print for many years and was not until recently considered a major Harlem Renaissance writer" (xx). A "darkened eye [partly] restored" by Washington and other critics (xxvii), Larsen has finally been rescued from "the shadows" and brought into the brilliant sunshine of Thadious Davis's biographical study, *Nella Larsen, Novelist of the Harlem Renaissance*.[2] This tough and thoughtful work has proved to be as enabling to my essay as Deborah McDowell's evocative and groundbreaking reading of *Passing*'s lesbian subtext. Davis recounts in painstaking detail Larsen's traumatic childhood enacted as a painful drama of parental loss; her conscious efforts at self-recreation; her battle with self-doubt; her face-saving marriage; her outsider status in the Harlem Renaissance; her racial and class ambivalence; her large appetite for books and even bigger craving for writerly respectability; and her bouts with sickness and depression, culminating in suicide attempts. The striking resemblance the profile bears to the one drawn by Woolfian scholars rekindled an earlier desire of mine—following the reading of *Mrs. Dalloway* and *Passing* in an undergraduate women's literature course I had taught just before Davis's book came out—to explore the relationship between the two texts.

As expected, in this class *Mrs. Dalloway* elicited the traditional student response to unconventional narratives: frustration, more frustration, extreme frustration. Where is the plot? What is the setting? Who are these characters? Surely, they are not normal (that is, realistic) people. How do they relate to one another? Who is the narrator? What is the narrative point of view? In search of answers to these questions we descended into the novel's psychic tunnels, and with pencils in hand we wound our way through twists and turns, breaks and continuities, mergings and beginnings, collapsing on the way past, present, and future, the spiritual and the material, the body and the mind, arriving finally at sunset at the place where we began. Memories of Peter, Richard, Rezia, Elizabeth, Doris, Septimus, Sally, and Clarissa lingered for a day or two, but students seemed eager to move on to a clearing in *Passing*. But it, too, was not the sprawling drama they had come to expect from the novel based on their knowledge of, say, naturalist fiction, such as Richard Wright's *Native Son,* Ann Petry's *The Street,* or Theodore Dreiser's *Sister Carrie.* Yet *Passing,* according to this urban, ethnically diverse, black-majority group of students, was, they confessed, "more digestible." However, even as Larsen's novel engaged them on its own terms, it rekindled interest in *Mrs. Dalloway.* Unaware of my reason for coupling the texts, they talked about resonances, similarities, and parallels, confirming at every point my own thoughts about the novels' intertextual relationship. Clare's deathly jump or fall was paired with Septimus's suicide; Irene's tea and dinner parties, with servants to boot, recalled Clarissa's life as "the perfect hostess," and the final party in each novel, it was noted, was marred by death. Irene, the discussion continued, went shopping for Ted's books in Chicago and Clarissa for flowers in London. Then there were the two Hughs: Clarissa's "old friend," the "admirable" Hugh Whitbread and Irene's "dear" and "generous" friend, Hugh Wentworth.

The intertextual exercise began to heat up as attention shifted to the subject of sexuality. Suddenly, this hitherto unilluminated area in *Mrs. Dalloway* lit up, assisted in part by what students thought to be clearer cues from *Passing.* The heterosexual roles of the women characters in both novels unsettled those with staunchly traditional views of marriage (about two-thirds of a total of twenty-five students). Hardly a kind word was said about Irene, described by one student as "too uppity for my taste." The consensus on Irene was that she had bartered sexual pleasure for a bourgeois lifestyle replete with maid service, private schools for the children, frequent travel, a mansion-styled home, fine clothes, leisure, and a respectable marriage. Clarissa shared this scathing spotlight. Hers, too, was a loveless marriage, shielded by the accoutrements of social privilege. Both women, one person insisted, were merely using their husbands to maintain their lavish lifestyles. Opinion on Clare Kendry was split between those who saw her as a ruthless social climber who had sold her body and soul to the highest bidder (John Bellow being equated with the devil) and a sympathetic few too taken in by her beauty, charm, and love of life to condemn her racial passing or imagine her as a homewrecker.

On the question of the novels' lesbian subtexts, several students at first demurred, noting that, Deborah McDowell's interpretation notwithstanding, Larsen's sole aim was to uncover the ugly truth about racial passing. The politics of race threatened to bog down the investigation of female sexuality. To return to the latter, I asked, "If, as you say, Irene is emotionally detached from her husband, is there anyone else that she is attracted to?" A young woman yelled out, "Clare, of course—Irene's absent lover." She elaborated by citing and paraphrasing McDowell's conclusions but also underscoring the fear factor I had mentioned earlier— Irene's fear of the consequences of homoerotic arousal. *Mrs. Dalloway* was brought back into the discussion by someone referring to "the only kiss that Clarissa remembered." Sally Seton's relationship with Clarissa, however, baffled many, who could not understand how a lesbian woman would end up having six sons! My point that Clarissa, too, was a wife and mother (as were Irene and Clare) made little difference, and so we returned to the text (as we had done with *Passing*) to examine the context and language of lesbian sexual desire.

The students in my "Writing by and about Women" course in the spring of 1994 had confirmed my thinking that *Mrs. Dalloway* and *Passing* do cohere, particularly on the issue of female sexuality. The next step was to explore the idea more fully in an attempt to cast light on the specific aspects of this hitherto unacknowledged relationship. With the publication of the Larsen biography, the limits to my research disappeared, making it possible to locate crucial information about Larsen. First, let me tackle head on the matter of close correspondences between the two novels. There is absolutely no hard evidence that Larsen, whose novel was published in 1929, four years after *Mrs. Dalloway,* had read or was influenced by Woolf's book. However, Larsen, according to her biographer Thadious Davis, was an avid reader and a librarian, a combination that equipped her with intimate knowledge of a broad range of writers and their works, especially her contemporaries, the moderns. Davis cites the example of Larsen's spirited defense of Walter White's magazine, in which she wrote: "To my mind, warped as I have confessed by the European and American moderns, 'Flight' is a far superior piece of work than 'The Fire in the Flint.' Less dramatic, it is more fastidious and required more understanding, keener insight. Actions and words count less and the poetic conception of the character, the psychology of the scene more than in the earlier work" (204–5).

In addition, part of what Davis describes as the "main paragraph of her confession . . . [that] had not found its way into the printed letter" (205) reads as follows:

> [N]ow to your reviewer's complaints about the author's style. He grumbles about the lack of "clarity," "confusion of characters," "faulty sentence structure." These sins escape me in my two readings, and even after they have been so publicly pointed out, I failed to find [them]. Even the opening sentence, so particularly cited, still seems to me all right. But then, I have been recently reading Huysmans, Conrad, Proust, and Thomas Mann. Naturally these things would not irritate me as they would an admirer of Louis Hemon and [Edith] Wharton. Too, there's Galsworthy who opens his latest novel [*The White Monkey*] with a sentence of some thirty-odd words. (205)

Both the published and unpublished parts of Larsen's letter confess a great deal, not the least of which is the existence of fluid boundaries between British, Anglo- and African-American modernisms. As George Hutchinson points out in his revisionist reading of the Harlem Renaissance, "[b]uried relations emerge" among modernist writers if we "interrogate exclusions built into the politics of identity" (26). Several cues to the "buried relations" between Woolf and Larsen, for example, "emerge" from the excerpts from Larsen's letter quoted above: their shared disdain for the obtuse realism of John Galsworthy, who, along with Arnold Bennett, Woolf chastised in her essay "Modern Fiction" and their strong commitment to what Malcolm Bradbury, referring to Woolf's poetics, describes as "making a new poetry of prose" (239), for example. It is the buried texts in *Passing* and *Mrs. Dalloway,* however, that reveal most tellingly the bond between Larsen and Woolf.

Reflecting on the relationship between Larsen's passion for books and her writing, Davis provides a list of literary influences that seeped into *Passing*:

> [T]he novel evidenced [Larsen's] sophisticated readings and the permeation of popularized psychoanalytic thought. Clare Kendry, for instance, owes her passive nature in part to Gertrude Stein's Melanctha in *Three Lives* and the conflict between the parts of a divided self, realized in the opposition between Melanctha Herbert and Jeff Campbell, becomes one basis for the bipolar relationship between Clare and Irene Redfield, but another basis is the psychological concept of the double. The treatment of the environment and its impact in shaping the lives of individuals owes much to Theodore Dreiser's *Sister Carrie* and Sinclair Lewis' *Main Street.* ... Irene's narrated monologues and stream of consciousness reflect Larsen's reading of Joyce's *Ulysses* and her understanding of William James's explanations of the human thought process, though Larsen depended, too, on the modernist concept of the unreliable observer as represented by Joseph Conrad in *Heart of Darkness*. (311)

Woolf's absence from this honor roll, coupled with the lack of factual evidence to indicate that Larsen read Woolf's novel, complicates the effort to link *Passing* and *Mrs. Dalloway*.[3] Compared to Gertrude Stein, whose "Melanctha" Larsen admits in a letter (to Stein) to "have read many times" and with whom she shared the intimate friendship of Carl Van Vechten, a principal promoter of the Harlem Renaissance, Woolf may have proved too distant, culturally and socially, to be publicly embraced by Larsen or other black female modernists. At the same time, one can expect the facts about Woolf's burgeoning creative imagination to have been swept into the grasp of an ambitious young writer and avid reader like Larsen. Moreover, in spite of the obvious racial and cultural differences between Woolf and Larsen, they shared stunningly similar artistic and private sensibilities, as evidenced in their expression of female sexuality in *Passing* and *Mrs. Dalloway*. The latter posits the view that the social murder of female (homo)sexuality is tantamount to the death of the soul. That the idea resonates resoundingly in *Passing* has little to do with whether or not Larsen read Woolf's novel and a great deal with the authors' linked sensibilities and life experiences across boundaries of race, culture, and nationality. Larsen's announced "thesis" for White's novel *Flight*—namely, "what shall it profit a man if he gains the whole world and loses his own soul?"—serves as a locus of thematic interpretation for the sexual subtexts of both her novel and Woolf's. The texts' repressed model of female sexuality calls for a close look at the signposts and impulses that guided these two women writers toward its anguishing lure.

Woolf and Larsen moved along parallel emotional tracks as they ventured into the male-dominated world of modernism. To start, both writers sharpened their instincts for survival on books, heading off the backlash of an uneven, gender-determined educational system. "Schooled in self-education," a Woolf biographer writes, "she went on devouring books." Even at the early age of fifteen the range of her reading was wide and diverse: "her bookish appetite . . . all the sharper for her sense that to commune with the greatest minds was a privilege" (L. Gordon 83). Louise DeSalvo, chronicler of the thresholds of pain and loss in Woolf's young life, duly notes the psychological impact of such a strong craving: "Reading in effect became her refuge, her solace in grief, her substitute for the friendships she did not have. It was the way she carved out an identity for herself as a human being, the way she secured her privacy, the way she began to determine the life she would choose for herself as a woman" (*Impact* 221–22). Larsen seems to have fared slightly better than Woolf with respect to formal education, having attended elementary and high schools, as well as Fisk University. Yet, given her fragmented and incomplete schooling, she was left largely unfulfilled. To fill in the breach, Larsen turned to books, gleaning a literary abundance from the New York Public Library (she was a trained librarian), just as Woolf had done in her father's famed library. The emotional gains were hardly different from Woolf's: "Books were essential to Larsen's material wellbeing, but they represented more than physical objects. She knew the power of words to heal and subdue and create. She relied upon books for companionship, for direction, and for affirmation" (Davis 243). And, like her older contemporary, she was alternately fond of modern writings and faithful to the classics.

Woolf and Larsen sought refuge in reading from experiences that were haunted by loss and despair. While their family backgrounds were very different, they were products of the same numbing process of separation from the mother. From the fresh facts revealed by Davis about Larsen's childhood and the welter of information on Woolf's, one can discern a common theme: the total weakening of the maternal bond and the adaptive responses of the child. "Haunted" (Woolf's term) aptly describes the way both writers felt about their mothers. When Woolf wrote in a diary entry on November 23, 1926, that in writing *To the Lighthouse* she was "now & then haunted by some semimystic very profound life of a woman" (*D* 3: 118), she had in mind the image of her mother, Julia Stephen, whom she could neither pretend linkage with nor resist absorption into. Neglected as a child by an overworked and hard-edged mother (a situation DeSalvo believes contributed to her sexual abuse by her half-brothers, Gerald and George Duckworth), Woolf suffered the full impact of the absent mother at age thirteen with the death of Julia Stephen in 1895. The event triggered an anguish of loss mingled with "a tremendous rage toward Julia, although [the latter] seems to have remained unconscious" (DeSalvo, *Impact* 118).

The "larger facts" Davis draws from her research paint Larsen as the victim of maternal rejection that shattered an already fragile sense of identity: "Nella Larsen . . . was born Nellie Walker and spent her formative years with a 'white' father (Peter Larson/Larsen) as her primary parent in a South Side immigrant household [in Chicago] composed also of her 'white' sister (Anna) and 'white' mother (Mary Hanson Walker Larson/Larsen), who denied giving birth to her" (49). Larsen's biracial parentage (her birth father was West Indian, her mother Danish) combined with her mother's rejection to produce a wrenching childhood and deep psychic scars.

Like Woolf, Larsen tried throughout her life to blunt the impact of maternal loss and betrayal, beginning with the desire for self-transformation. A battery of names created the persona of a performance artist. As Davis puts it, "[t]he Nellie Walker, Nellie Larson, and Nellye Larson who grew up in Chicago, the Nellie Marie Larsen who enrolled at Fisk, the Nella Marion Larsen who entered Lincoln and married Elmer Imes, the Nella Imes who attended the Library School and lived in Harlem, the Allen Semi who wrote romance stories, the Nella Larsen who wrote novels, and the Nella Larsen-Imes who worked as a nurse were all the same person" (443). Each name opens a window on Larsen's life, revealing the vivid recreation of a motherless child, an abandoned wife, and a frustrated artist.

Less overt about her own transformation, Woolf also sought sanctuary from the torment of pain in her childhood and adult life by assuming multiple fictional identities. At age fifteen, for example, long before she found an escape route in the charted world of her fiction, Virginia Stephen in her earliest diary entries had created Miss Jan, the imposter who "helped [her] achieve individuation and intellectual independence" (DeSalvo, *Impact* 243). Still, for both Woolf and Larsen, recovery was fraught with self-rejection, as evidenced in their flirtations with suicide and nagging bouts with illness. Woolf's protracted battle with mental and physical illness and suicidal despair culminated in her death by drowning, ending a life rendered joyless from the start by the loss of her mother. Outliving Woolf by fourteen years, Larsen lingered longer in the shadow of her own painful past. The transformative potential of her serial names may have helped her to adapt to the changing circumstances of her life, but she never weathered the emotional storm brought on by her mother's rejection. Attacks of pneumonia, influenza, and depression frequently broke up the smooth and settled surface that disguised her pain. And yet illness, like her multiple identities, was an act of self-renewal. "Frequent illness," Davis writes, "became a way of reiterating her own vulnerability as a person who needed care from others and a means of depicting her singular strength as one who routinely triumphed over great debilities" (14).

Woolf, too, managed to create a delicate balance between the desperation of ill health and the joy of recovery. "To her, illness could be an act of release," a biographer writes, "a mental advantage" in her lifelong flirtation with death (L. Gordon 53). To be clear, the details of her illness and convalescence differ significantly from Larsen's. For one, Larsen's emotional crisis was not complicated by incest and madness, Woolf's twin demons. Consequently, although Larsen frequently plunged into depressive states, she was not suicide prone. In fact, according to her biographer, her suicidal behavior during the breakup of her marriage was "feigned" to get "affection and sympathy" (Davis 407). Interestingly, one of the examples Davis cites—Larsen's fall from a first-floor window—not only anticipates Clare Kendry's fatal fall in *Passing* but also closely approximates Woolf's attempt to commit suicide by throwing herself out of a window, which, as Quentin Bell points out, "was not high enough from the ground to cause her serious harm" (90). Not to be missed is the fact that this act of self-destruction occurred during significantly different periods in the writers' lives, when Woolf was twenty-two years old and Larsen forty-two, an indication perhaps of how well each of them coped with pain and loss. For both, self-erasure was a potent antidote to suffering, but while Woolf, from start to finish, believed death to be the surest pain killer, Larsen in the end chose the solace of seclusion over the siren call of suicide.

The story of self-erasure is also one about silence, and self-censorship is the hallmark of the connection between Larsen and Woolf. In an effort

to restore the dignity lost to familial infestation, both women made a
fetish of caution and concealment. "Life is a hard business—needs a rhi-
noceros skin—that one has not got!" (qtd. in DeSalvo, *Impact* 232).
Woolf was only fifteen when she entered this life-weary thought in her
diary in 1897, at which time she had lost her mother; her oldest sister and
surrogate mother, Stella; her father to oppressive grief; and possibly her
virginity to incest. For emotional protection she reached for the more
practical and familiar mask of silence. "[I]t was a Victorian middle-class
habit, especially ingrained in women, to deny or cover over deep wells of
feeling. Virginia herself did this with practiced ease. . . . By the time [she]
reached adulthood, then, she was adept at evasion" (L. Gordon 59).
Woolf's gift of camouflage was especially well suited to her artistic representation of female sexuality, a subject she shaded with as much ambiguity as silence. Of the gamut of emotions that flooded her throughout
her life, her instinctual fear of men and unrelenting passion for women
rank at the top. As Quentin Bell has accurately noted, prior to 1907
"men, as lovers, seem to have played no role at all in [Virginia's] imagination. All her passions, her jealousies and tenderness are kept for her
own sex" (118). This sexual attitude lasted through subsequent flirtations
with various men (including Clive Bell, Vanessa's husband) and her marriage to Leonard Woolf. The latter mainly served her need for order and
rehabilitative care, given her long history of physical illness and mental
breakdowns. Theirs was a loveless, sexless marriage, and "Leonard
blamed [its] sexual failure . . . on his wife's frigidity" (DeSalvo, *Conceived*
70). By comparison, Woolf's passion for women deepened, culminating
in her celebrated romance with Vita Sackville-West, "an enterprise of the
heart . . . carried out so near the verge of archetypal feeling" (Leaska,
Introduction 11). By and large, men, like her super-intellectual father and
intellectually ambitious husband, helped in a big way to shape her creative genius, but women alone stirred her sexual imagination.[4] How to
broker the conflict between learned patriarchal language and behavior
and the utterance of same-sex desire rankles Woolf throughout her writing career.

The aching voice Woolf gives this problem in *Mrs. Dalloway* is both
echoed and problematized by Nella Larsen in *Passing*. The divergent racial, sexual, and cultural identities of the two writers deserve emphasis
but, as I have indicated, they should not be allowed to give short shrift to
the ways in which Woolf and Larsen are united in their personal histories

and, in particular, their understanding of and anxiety about male hegemony. The Harlem Renaissance, as Gloria T. Hull has accurately noted,
"was, by self-definition, race-oriented" and, in practice, male-dominated,
for "despite its veneer of equal opportunity, [it] was a time when not
only Harlem and the Negro, but men as usual were 'in vogue'" (10, 17).
Their double marginalization within modernism had a coercive impact on
black women Renaissance writers such as Larsen.

In the first place, the modern surge in interest in black art fell far short
of endorsing equal status for black artists, the most talented of whom
could not break away from negative racial stereotypes. Disputing the
notion of a symbiotic relationship between blacks and whites among the
Harlem Renaissance, a commentator asserts that the movement demonstrated once more "the one-sided and unequal relationship between
blacks and whites [that] has obliged blacks to serve as eternal footmen
holding the identity coats for whites" (Singh 32). The compromised space
of racial otherness occupied by Harlem Renaissance artists prompted
this burst of relief and joy from Jessie Fauset, one of several expatriated
American blacks in Paris in the twenties:

> I like Paris because I find something here, something of integrity, which I
> seem to have strangely lost in my own country. It is simplest of all to say
> that I like to live among people and surroundings where I am not always
> conscious of "thou shall not." I am colored and wish to be known as col-
> ored, but sometimes I have felt that my growth as a writer has been ham-
> pered in my own country. And so—but only temporarily—I have fled from
> it. (Qtd. in Benstock, *Left Bank* 13)

The rigidities of gender proved equally impregnable. The phenomenon
Gloria T. Hull describes as "Harlem Renaissance fraternization" (11)
allowed for cross-racial male alliances that helped to jump-start and fuel
the careers of black male writers and at the same time alienate their aspiring female counterparts. Indeed, the very acts of fraternal socialization,
such as drinking in bars and smoking, were social taboos for women.
Alternative self-help initiatives by women, "because of women's less-
advantaged status . . . could often only amount to consolation circles for
the disenfranchised" (Hull 11). Larsen managed to break into exclusion-
ary black male and white intellectual circles with the help of two influential friends, Walter White and Carl van Vechten, but "her resentment of
confinement into race . . . [and] feminine roles" (Davis 10) made her a
perpetual outsider in the movement.

Larsen's representational practice took place within a matrix of racial, gendered, and personal histories that set the mold for the poetics of clandestine sexuality inscribed in *Passing*. Larsen was a nonlesbian writer who, as Hazel Carby points out, "recognized that the repression of the sensual in Afro-American fiction in response to the long history of the exploitation of black sexuality led to the repression of passion and the repression or denial of female sexuality and desire." She also knew, according to Carby, that "the representation of black female sexuality meant risking its definition as primitive and exotic within a racist society" (174). The tragic and bewilderingly ambivalent portrait of black female sexuality embodied in Helga Crane in *Quicksand* is, Carby concludes, Larsen's way out of the quandary. Not really, I would say, for the problem intensifies in her second novel, *Passing,* where the hesitant pessimism about black female heterosexuality inscribed in *Quicksand* transforms into eloquent silence over black women's same-sex desire.

There is overwhelming justification for this adaptive strategy in Larsen's personal narrative of alienation captured most tellingly in the following biographical profile:

> Her ability to function in [the] social domain [of the twenties] may have affirmed her sense of self, but it also exacted a toll on her self-esteem. An outer mask disguised her anxieties about belonging. Concealing her vulnerability from the "smart set," she allowed few glimpses of a troubled private life. Although loneliness and pain would occasionally pierce her haughty façade, she was, an old friend tactfully put it, "a good pretender." (Davis 10)

The passage illustrates the strength of the bond between Larsen and Woolf: two vulnerable souls in an ostensibly male world, caught in the fault line between writing against constraint and preserving a carefully cultivated image. With homoeroticism as the subject, the psychic strain resulting from the contradictory impulse to express and rein in female desire is likened in *Mrs. Dalloway* to "'the death of the soul'" (58). The phrase's psychoanalytic resonance might be intentional if one takes into account Leonard Shengold's view that "Soul, or psychic murder involves trauma imposed from the world outside the mind that is so overwhelming that the mental apparatus is flooded with feeling. The same overstimulated state can result as a reaction to great deprivation" (24). More to the point, Shengold's historicization of the term contains some details about its meaning in the late nineteenth century that may not have been lost on Woolf:

> In 1887 Strindberg gave the title "Soul Murder" to an article on Ibsen's *Rosmersholm*. He said that instances of actual murder were decreasing in the Western world, but that soul (or psychic) murder, which he defined as taking away a person's reason for living, was on the increase. The concept obsessed Strindberg who was at that time illustrating it in his great play *The Father*. . . . Soul murder was a repetitive theme of Ibsen, who uses the term directly in his play *John Gabriel Borkman* (1896). . . . In the play Ibsen speaks of soul murder as . . . "killing the instinct for love," . . . "killing the love-live in a human soul," . . . and murdering "love in a human being." (19)

The term's applicability in late-nineteenth-century psychoanalytic discourse to a wide range of fields on the psychological map—incest, parental tyranny, and homosexuality, among them—is another reason for it to be allied with Woolf's phrase, "the death of the soul." It is my view that soul murder in *Mrs. Dalloway* and *Passing* is double-edged, killing the possibility of a lesbian love life and stifling authorial expression of lesbian desire. Enacting the drama of repressed female same-sex love, the authors seem to be aggrieved by their own complicity in the process. The sense of guilt over the squandered opportunity to affirm female desire may have been felt more keenly by the lesbian Woolf than by the heterosexual Larsen, but with the popularization of deviant black sexuality by Claude McKay's novel *Home to Harlem* (1928), Larsen must have been tempted to seize the issue and redefine black lesbianism in positive terms. To do so behind a mask must have been as painful for her as it was for Woolf.

Class considerations determine the extent to which Woolf and Larsen can tap into the vein of sexuality in the texts. Indeed, the novels' class stuffiness mediates against the full expression of an exultant female sexuality. Mired in a bourgeois lifestyle, the main characters, Clarissa Dalloway and Irene Redfield, understand that forbidden passion is a high-risk commodity capable of reducing the investor to pauperism. Thus the act of sexual repression seems to them (and to their class-conscious creators as well) a small price to pay for what Larsen calls "safety [and] security" (*Passing* 195). But there is also the sense that the textual repression of female sexuality is itself an authorial judgment on the social pressures that lead middle-class women to cave in to their anxieties about maintaining class privilege. What is happening behind the mask of the "'perfect hostess'" (*MD* 62) is the deadening of Clarissa's soul. Similarly, "the firm resolution in Irene's own soul" (*Passing* 200) to remain under the suffocating influence of bourgeois culture saps her sexual will. The subtextual theme in both novels can thus be summoned up by revising the biblical question Larsen raised concerning the life crisis in Walter White's novel *Flight*: What does it profit a woman if she gains the whole world and loses her own soul? The extent to which this Faustian dilemma bedevils both Clarissa and Irene underscores the writers' (and Irigaray's) belief in the spiritual nature of female sexuality. The profit motive, be it class privilege or money, estranges women like Irene and Clarissa from their sexual selves.

Woolf intended in *Mrs. Dalloway* "to give the slipperiness of the soul" (*D* 2: 244). That she ends up illumining "the death of the soul" points to how profoundly disturbed she was by the social constraints on women's sexual lives. True to her poetics of concealment, Woolf uses "soul" as a code for lesbian love, which in turn is distinguished from heterosexual love. Clarissa refers to the latter as "that monster" (*MD* 45) that "destroyed . . . [e]verything that was fine, every thing that was true . . ." (*MD* 127). As with heterosexual love, so too with man-made religion, the suffocating kind Doris Kilman professes; both "destroy . . . the privacy of the soul" (*MD* 126–27). To Clarissa, love and religion are "[t]he cruelest things in the world" because they are "domineering, hypocritical, eavesdropping" and would "convert anyone" (*MD* 126) who is [sexually] different. No wonder Sally Seton, at the height of her passion for Clarissa, had deemed it necessary for Clarissa to be "save[d] . . . from the Hughs and the Dalloways and all the other 'perfect gentlemen' who would 'stifle her soul'" (*MD* 75). As Peter Walsh recalls the event from their past together in Bourton, he relishes the thought that it is he Sally had handpicked, albeit "half laughing of course, to carry off Clarissa" (*MD* 75). The irony is far from faint: for one thing, Clarissa had rejected Peter, fearing that he, not Richard, would strangle her with love; and for another, Peter's egotism blinds him not only to the truth about Clarissa's homoerotic desire but also to Sally's ill-disguised taunt.

Not surprisingly, although it is Peter who diagnoses Clarissa's death-of-the-soul condition, he misses its homoerotic undertones and reads it instead as a sign of Clarissa's frigidity. Peter goes from upbraiding Clarissa for being "as cold as an icicle" to concluding that "women . . . don't know what passion is" (*MD* 80). Naturally, Woolf discredits this view in a subplot that tingles with lesbian passion. But, as the following passage illustrates, she was also aware of the prohibitive nature of sexual imperialism and the caution required to express transgressive sexuality:

> yet she could not resist sometimes yielding to the charm of a woman . . . of a woman confessing . . . some scrape, some folly. And whether it was pity, or their beauty, or that she was older, or some accident—like a faint scent, or a violin next door . . . she did undoubtedly then feel what men felt. Only for a moment; but it was enough. It was a sudden revelation, a tinge like a blush which one tried to check and then, as it spread, one yielded to its expansion, and rushed to the farthest verge and there quivered and felt the world come closer, swollen with some astonishing significance, some pressure of rapture. . . . Then, for that moment, she had seen an illumination; a match burning in a crocus; an inner bearing almost expressed. (*MD* 31–32)

At first glance, this often-cited passage suggests that Clarissa does not wear her (homo)sexuality lightly, but a close reading reveals that the repressive instinct, embodied in the sentence "she did undoubtedly then feel what men felt," threatens to neutralize the imagined moment of lesbian *jouissance* by evoking male-centered heterosexual desire. The comparison between the outlawed sexual performance and its socially sanctioned counterpart is part of a narrative strategy of containment that frustrates the author's subversive intent. Similarly, with the object of lesbian desire described as "a woman confessing . . . some scrape, some folly," and lesbian love said to be provoked by "pity," "beauty," or "some accident like a faint scent, or a violin next door," Woolf evokes an alternative sexuality different from the rigid, heterosexual ideal. Like Emily Dickinson, for whom, according to Paula Bennett, "the little could also be great, the insignificant could be meaningful and valuable" (236), Woolf is trying to subvert the exalted model of heterosexual love. Yet the mask of discretion is also apparent in the polite condescension that undergirds this portrait of female homoerotic desire.

This ambivalent expression of lesbian desire is in accord with the idea of soul death that Clarissa as Mrs. Dalloway personifies. While Peter may have missed the connection between soul death and the stranglehold on lesbian desire, he scored big by linking the former to Clarissa's class status: "she had always, even as a girl, a sort of timidity, which in middle age becomes conventionality" (*MD* 20). Clarissa's soul (spiritual and sexual) is crushed by her unflagging fidelity to convention. Take the case of her "being Mrs. Dalloway, not even Clarissa any more" (*MD* 11). On the one hand, it "fascinate[s] her," (*MD* 11) and on the other hand, it renders "herself," her woman-loving self, "invisible, unseen; unknown" (*MD* 11). As a maintainer of the status quo, Clarissa wears many hats—the "'perfect hostess'" (*MD* 62) with "perfect manners" (*MD* 61); Mrs. Dalloway; the "mistress of silver, of linen, of china" (*MD* 38). Singly and together, they cost her dearly.

Clarissa's invisibility as Mrs. Dalloway is a result of her desexing. Just as the open, vibrant spaces of Bourton, where the passion-filled Sally kissed her, have shrunk into a suffocatingly narrow attic room, so has Clarissa been transformed, from a sexually and intellectually stimulating woman into "a nun" (*MD* 31) or, worse still, the socialite who "must assemble" (*MD* 186) to stay emotionally alive. Her parties, however, do not remove the "emptiness about the heart of life" (*MD* 31). Hearing of Septimus's death during the grand party at the end of the novel, she slips out of the limelight to honor a kindred spirit, a man who had defied death and "preserved" the "thing . . . that mattered" (*MD* 184), while she, equally deprived of sexual freedom, had "lost herself in the process of living" (*MD* 185).

The menace of the bourgeois lifestyle is as potent for Irene Redfield as it is for Clarissa Dalloway. Indeed, so thorough is Irene's purchase of middle-class sensibilities that she becomes the consummate "passer," both racially and sexually. Until Deborah McDowell's penetratingly critical eyes broke beneath the affluent serenity of Irene's life, she would have continued to fool critics into believing that race alone mattered most to Larsen in *Passing*. Larsen, as Davis's biography reveals, was acutely aware of her racially "contradictory selves," but her "attempts to enter the contemporary discourses on race often backfired, in part because she never fully reconciled herself to the reality of her own past and to the compelling actuality of racial injustice" (11). Larsen's general disdain for the starkly conservative ideology of racial uplift did not prove a boon to her writing career, but the attitude allowed her to examine the debilitating complications of racial uplift in her fiction. *Quicksand* dramatizes the inherent contradictions of uplift ideology that alienated her from Tuskegee's race men—their preemptive enforcement of racial difference coupled with a spellbinding admiration of things white.

For Larsen, racial uplift ideology was also gender determined. Its affiliation with Victorian belief systems had a crippling effect on female sexuality, especially that of middle-class women. Hence, while Larsen dared on occasion to duel with the titans of race, "[w]hat she sought *surrepti-*

tiously was an escape from female powerlessness" (Davis 11; emphasis added). Larsen's depiction of female sexual powerlessness includes both the heterosexual and the lesbian zones of desire, the former evident in the poisonous sexual blossoming of Helga Crane and the latter in the bizarre dance of sexual denial by Irene and Clare. Larsen thus adds a sexual dimension to Du Bois's racial and gendered discourse on the state of black souls. If by "the souls of black folk" Du Bois meant, in Nellie McKay's eloquent phrasing, "that spiritual essence that made survival and transcendence possible for an entire race in spite of indescribable oppression" (230), then clearly Larsen is sending a distress signal in *Quicksand* and *Passing* that women's "survival and transcendence" are in jeopardy due to sexual repression.

Like Woolf, Larsen saw sex murder as soul murder and, sometimes, as physical murder. Larsen's own repressed heterosexuality ("she apparently suppressed, for the most part, sexual drives in her own life" [Davis 169]) made her vulnerable in the masculinist culture of the Harlem Renaissance and, consequently, extremely sensitive to the panic and pain of her female characters. These feelings are combined and distilled in *Passing* through an intricately coded language of female desire sealed over by the protective discourse of racial politics. McDowell's successful decoding of this language is by now familiar: the description of Clare's alluring sensuality and Irene's advance toward and retreat from it; the symbolism of the letters; and the eroticism of the smiles, kisses, and touches. If we add to these the blizzard of ellipses punctuating the text, gaps that speak the unspeakable, we have an act of "rhetorical seduction" that Jane Marcus calls "Sapphistry" (167). McDowell also links Irene's exorcism of lesbian desire to her overattachment to bourgeois values: "The more [her erotic] feelings develop, the more she fights them, for they threaten the placid surface of her middle-class existence as a doctor's wife" (xxviii).

The role class plays in Irene's soul murder finds a grim parallel in *Mrs. Dalloway,* beginning with the myriad ways Irene resembles that novel's eponymous heroine. Like Clarissa, Irene is a snob; she is trapped in a sexless, loveless marriage; she is the perfect hostess and a self-promoting mother; above all, she is woman-loving, yet intoxicated by the social prestige proffered by heterosexual marriage. The seeds of deception that lie in the last detail grow a mind morbidly circumspect and mistrustful of its own emotional priorities. To thwart her desire for the transfixingly beautiful Clare, Irene is by turns an ardent advocate of her moribund marriage to Brian (as Clarissa is of her marriage to Richard) and a serious critic of Clare's character defects. It is a portrait of self-control and organized chaos that is too shallow to survive, for although Irene, like Clarissa, is held in virtual bondage to middle-class values, she is not oblivious to the distress signals, such as her thinly disguised admiration for Clare's free spirit. Recklessly daring, Clare shares Sally Seton's "melo-dramatic love of being the centre of everything and creating scenes" (*MD* 182). Left to her own devices, Clare could avert Irene's life crisis by orchestrating the "outing" of their secret desire, but this is one scene Irene does not want Clare to create. She foils Clare, therefore, with a grand gesture of her own: the reconstruction of herself as both "race woman" and jealous wife in order to resist rather than indulge Clare. The strategy is as insincere as it is grand, but Clare should have known better than to test the limits of its insincerity. Irene would rather wrest control of her life from the remnants of Clare's body than cave in to her con-science. Though she is shaken by Clare's death enough to pass out ("Her quaking knees gave way under her . . . Then everything was dark" [*Passing* 242]), the loss of consciousness is only temporary. Like Clarissa after Septimus's death, Irene will try to pick up the pieces of her shat-tered soul and go on living a death-in-life.

"Writing lesbian," according to Lillian Faderman (*Surpassing* 392), is a high-risk enterprise for women writers in a deterministically heterosexual economy. Caught between silence and censorship (the primordial fears of the woman writer), Woolf and Larsen resorted to subterfuge to inscribe lesbian desire in *Mrs. Dalloway* and *Passing,* respectively. Their furtive-ness notwithstanding, the novels' subtexts take their impetus from the desire to communicate the urgency of (homo)sexual freedom. For Larsen and Woolf, the social mandate to exorcise same-sex desire results in the death of individual souls. Moreover, the incentives of marriage—eco-nomic security and social privilege—make the middle-class woman a prime target for soul death. Having wrestled with the disquiets of the spirit throughout their lives, both writers regard the subject of sex/soul murder as a moral imperative. On this issue these elusive women and their coded texts are perfectly clear. Their arm linking across the deep racial and cultural divide that separated them is a signpost that will guide contemporary black and white feminists through a loose alliance into a cohesive feminist firmament.

NOTES

1. See, for example, Baker; Scott; Hutchinson; and Benstock, *Women of the Left Bank*.

2. In the preface to her book, Davis writes: "Larsen became in the decades following the Harlem Renaissance a figure in the shadows" (xv).

3. This is an important assertion in light of the painful plagiarism accusation that sapped Larsen's inspiration and silenced her voice. Writing about the incident, Davis is both unequivocal and speculative. First, she confirms the resemblances between Larsen's short story "Sanctuary," published in January 1930, and "Mrs. Adis," a story by Sheila Kaye-Smith that had appeared in *Century* magazine eight years earlier: "The similarities of the two stories in language, description, setting, atmosphere, characterization, action, plot, and theme, all are too exact to be merely parallel story lines. Larsen apparently followed Kaye-Smith's work in both overall pattern and specific detail. Even a cursory reading reveals as much" (351). Davis then offers a reasonable explanation for the similarities. "Larsen," she writes,

> may well have gambled on no one's recognizing the similarities between her story and the earlier one, especially because of her use of black characters and dialect. Or, she actually may *not* have considered that using the idea and format would constitute plagiarism. During her apprenticeship she had contemplated how certain works treating white characters might be translated into "Negro" material. . . . She may well have believed that there was nothing deceptive about using "Mrs. Adis" as a storyboard for her work about black characters told in the same manner; the decade was, after all, one that accepted black adaptations of works by whites, particularly in the public world of the New York stage. (351; emphasis in original)

4. See Cook.

PART II

Lesbian Readings of Woolf's Novels

EIGHT

Introduction

PATRICIA CRAMER

When shall we be able to tell the truth Nicholas?
[Eleanor] said getting up.
In about three hundred years, said Nicholas.
—*H* 5: 129

Virginia Woolf's life and work reflect that continual negotiation between truth and secrecy characteristic of gay life. In Woolf's lifetime, taboos against homosexuality influenced the majority of women and men who preferred their own sex to construct encoded lives, carefully protecting their private selves from public knowledge. This double life of the closet sometimes took on comic forms, as when Greta Garbo perfected heterosexual love scenes on the screen while she pursued women lovers in private (Castle 1–6) or when Vita Sackville-West and her husband Harold Nicolson, both homosexual, appeared together on BBC radio giving advice on how to have a happy marriage (Glendinning 214–16).[1] Even Woolf's Bloomsbury friends carefully demarcated their private and public lives. As David Eberly notes, "while the members of Bloomsbury talked freely among themselves, they were careful about what they said, and showed, to their public." Like Duncan Grant with Vanessa Bell, Maynard Keynes with Lydia Lopokova, and Lytton Strachey with Dora Carrington, Woolf's marriage with Leonard can be viewed within this gay tradition of protective heterosexual unions among friends ("Talking" 130).

This necessary negotiation between private truths and public dissimulation carried over into Woolf's writing life as well. Throughout her career, Woolf indicated her desire to write "truthfully" (*D* 2: 320) about relations between women and about women's sexuality. In 1929, in *A Room of One's Own*, she relishes the thought of writing some day about Chloe liking Olivia. In the thirties, when she became more confident about her readiness to do so, she wrote in her diary her determination to write "a sequel to a Room of Ones Own—about the sexual life of women . . ." (*D* 4: 6). Nevertheless, when Woolf indicates her intentions to speak about women and sex, she warns her readers not to expect unreserved frankness. In the opening to *A Room of One's Own*, for example, she admits she cannot "hope to tell the truth" (*AROO* 4) when writing about such a controversial subject (*AROO* 6); and in *Three Guineas*, her sequel to *A Room of One's Own*, Woolf remains committed to disguise as a writing and political strategy: "Secrecy is essential," she writes. "We must still hide what we are doing and thinking . . . " (*TG* 120). Reading Woolf within the context of these simultaneous impulses toward self-expression and self-protection is key to decoding not only her married lesbian life, but also the complex, multilayered style for which she is so famous.

While, as Eve Sedgwick notes, the closet is still a "fundamental feature" and "shaping presence" in the lives of most gay women and men (*Epistemology* 68), Woolf's creative responses to homophobia were shaped by her particular life experiences and historical moment. Born in London in 1882, Virginia Woolf grew up at a time when tolerance of public expressions of romantic bonds between women had ended; for the first time, legal and medical authorities recognized the sexual potential in such relationships and scrutinized them for signs of "perversion." Sexologists Richard von Krafft-Ebing and Havelock Ellis propagated the stereotype of the mannish lesbian, and Sigmund Freud declared erotic attachments between women a mental illness. As Eileen Barrett's and Ruth Vanita's essays in this volume make clear, Woolf was closely familiar with the sexologists and their theories of lesbianism, and she participated in frank discussions about homosexuality with her Bloomsbury friends. The sophisticated nature of these discussions about homosexuality is suggested in a draft for *The Years*, where Woolf portrays Eleanor, Maggie, Elvira, Renny, and Nicholas discussing whether homosexuality is a matter of nature or choice; for Eleanor, it's "nature," for Renny it's "fashion," and for Maggie it's "possibility" (*H* 5: 127).

The hostility toward lesbian and gay life validated in medical circles was paralleled by new legislative moves toward repressing lesbianism. In

1921, for the first time, the British Parliament debated a law that would criminalize lesbianism, and the 1928 trial and banning of Radclyffe Hall's lesbian novel, *The Well of Loneliness*, made clear to Woolf and other women writers of her generation that any public defense of lesbianism could result in legal retaliation. As Karla Jay notes, "At the very least, the obscenity trial of *The Well of Loneliness* signaled to Barney, Woolf, Barnes, and other lesbians that the era of studied blindness to Sapphism had drawn to a close and that they were as likely as any other group to suffer the consequences of public pressures for conformity" ("Lesbian Modernism" 78).

At the same time that public institutions intensified efforts to pathologize and criminalize lesbianism, women of Woolf's generation enjoyed an unprecedented flourishing of lesbian visibility and culture in their private lives. Unlike predecessors, such as Emily Dickinson and Charlotte Brontë, who enjoyed romantic friendships with women isolated from self-conscious lesbian communities, Woolf's close familiarity with Bloomsbury homosexuals and feminist circles provided her with a range of possibilities for expressing same-sex love. Through her friendships with the prominent lesbian figures Vita Sackville-West and Dame Ethel Smyth, Virginia Woolf was privy to gossip about lesbian subcultures extending beyond her immediate circle of friends. For example, the former suffragette Dame Ethel Smyth kept her well informed about the number of lesbians who found each other within the suffrage movement: Woolf wrote Vita "in strict confidence" that "Ethel used to love Emmeline [Pankhurst]—they shared a bed" (*L* 5: 256).[2]

Thus, despite the joy and inspiration so many women writers of Woolf's generation found in loving women, it is no wonder that, as Shari Benstock notes, "Sapphic modernism . . . wore many necessary and elaborate disguises" ("Expatriate" 185). When they included homoerotic content in their published works, women writers of Woolf's generation —Willa Cather, Djuna Barnes, Gertrude Stein, and Elizabeth Bowen, among others—devised a range of strategies to express the lesbian content in their work (Benstock, "Expatriate" 185; see also Jay, "Lesbian Modernism"). Many of the most overt texts written during Woolf's lifetime were hidden away until they could be published posthumously. Vita Sackville-West's memoir of her love affair with Violet Trefusis was discovered after her death by her son, Nigel Nicolson. Even comparatively open lesbian figures like Natalie Barney and Gertrude Stein carefully guarded their lesbian writings from public scrutiny. Gertrude Stein's

Q.E.D. was published after her death, and Natalie Barney's *The One Who Is Legion,* or *A.D.'s After-Life* was privately distributed (Jay, "Lesbian Modernism" 77–78).

Throughout her career, Woolf was preoccupied with the impact of censorship on her writing—especially her ability to write openly about sexuality. In 1928, upon the publication of *A Room of One's Own,* she anticipates being "attacked for a feminist & hinted at for a Sapphist" (*D* 3: 262); and in her speech to professional women in 1931, Woolf claims that the "future of fiction" depends on to what extent men become "so civilised that they are not shocked when a woman speaks the truth about her body" (*P* xl). In 1932, the family of Lytton Strachey suggested that Woolf write his biography. According to Quentin Bell, everyone agreed that to show what Lytton was really like would require honesty about his love affairs with men. Since this was deemed "completely impossible" the project was abandoned (2: 165).

It is worthwhile to emphasize Woolf's lifelong battle with external censorship because so many readers, influenced by Quentin Bell's biography and by stereotypes about what constitutes the sexual, miss the articulations of lesbian desire that permeate the novels. External censorship —not personal inhibition—is the primary cause for Woolf's circumspect treatment of lesbian themes in her writing. As Louise DeSalvo's groundbreaking book *Virginia Woolf: The Impact of Childhood Sexual Abuse on Her Life and Work* illustrates, Woolf's traumatic experience of sexual abuse and her Victorian training exacerbated her difficulties in writing about women's sexual experiences. Yet these influences did not prevent Woolf from doing so. Her novels are passionately concerned with female sexuality: particularly the role of male sexual abuse in women's subordination and the liberating possibilities of love between women.

Woolf's impetus, when writing about the possibilities of love between women, was toward expression, not repression. As Eileen Barrett points out, letters Woolf wrote to Katharine Symonds Furse while working on *Between the Acts* reiterate her commitment to frank discussion of sexuality. Referring to the interest in John Addington Symonds expressed by male homosexuals of her acquaintance, Woolf urges Furse to be forthright about her father's homosexuality in her proposed biography: "[T]hey all wish the question openly discussed; and a woman could do it more openly" (Fowler 218). In her letters and diaries, Woolf displays a remarkable degree of self-knowledge about her sexual preferences. She praises the charms of women, discussing with Vita their differences in taste. About Vita's lover, the journalist Evelyn Irons, Woolf writes, "very natty and sporty she looks to be sure—just your style Mine is the very opposite" (L 4: 369). Her letters to Vita express sexual longing—"if I saw you would you kiss me? If I were in bed would you—" (L 3: 443)—and display her considerable knowledge about lesbian sexual practices: "I feel like a moth, with heavy scarlet eyes and a soft cape of down—a moth about to settle in a sweet, bush—Would it were—ah but thats improper" (L 3: 469). In the letters, we find more explicit evidence than in the novels of the inspirational role of lesbian sexual love for Woolf's writing practices—for example, when she confides to Vita that "it was the sight of the gaiters . . . that inspired Orlando . . . the gaiters and what lies beyond—" (L 5: 157).

Woolf's resort to metaphor and ellipses to suggest sexual activity even in the letters is a reminder to those who require more overt declarations of sexual activity or self-definition from the letters that in these more private places, Woolf still relied on indirection and subterfuge because she feared exposure even there. In 1929, for example, she worried that even a letter to Vita Sackville-West would not be safe from the censorship in England. Shortly after telling Vita that "the percentage of Lesbians is rising in the States, all because of you" (that is, the publication of *Orlando*) she writes, "Lawrences poems have been seized in ms by the police in the post. . . . [N]othing will be safe—*not this letter*" (L 4: 14; emphasis added). In this volume, Leslie Hankins suggests that Vita and Virginia developed many of the coding strategies that reappear in their novels by composing letters intended to elude their husbands as well as public censors. That Woolf and Sackville-West felt they had to be cautious even in private correspondence and at home is further suggested by the fact that four letters from Virginia were recently discovered hidden in Vita's desk (Banks, "Hidden Letters" 1–2). One of these letters, dated August 8, 1938, suggests that Woolf's sexual interest in Vita survived into the late thirties: Virginia writes, "it was nice having you . . . even in its less pronounced form" (Banks, "Hidden Letters" 2).[3]

Although not entirely frank, the letters and diaries are nevertheless important resources for tracing Woolf's lesbian metaphors. In her diary, when she considered writing more truthfully about women, Woolf claimed that diary writing "loosened the ligatures" and "greatly helped [her] style" (D 2: 320). In these more private writings, she experimented with and developed the metaphors for lesbian experiences that later reappear in the fiction. In 1926, Woolf writes to Vita: "The flowers have come, and are adorable, dusky, tortured, passionate like you" (L 3: 303); and recalling the "perfection" of Vita's body, calls up clitoral imagery as "pellets which perhaps may unfold later" (D 2: 306). Flowers appear frequently in her fiction when sexual feelings are shared between women, most familiarly in Clarissa and Sally's kiss in Mrs. Dalloway. Words like "purple shade" (L 3: 332), "lamp," and "glow" (L 5: 141) from Woolf's private writings about Vita reappear in The Waves as "luminous," "purple," and "glows" (45) in Rhoda's lesboerotic raptures over Miss Lambert. Woolf's playful elopement proposals to Vita in the letters reappear as Rhoda's escape fantasies in The Waves and as a flight of geese flying overhead in Orlando.

With so much explicit material available in the letters and diaries, how is it that so many have missed the lesbian content in the fiction? Why is it, as Terry Castle observes, that "when it comes to lesbians . . . many people have trouble seeing what's in front of them?" (2). Partly, as Blanche Cook explains, because "our dominant society so fundamentally opposes . . . women's independent access to our erotic power" (730). Even readers interested in lesbian themes have found that cultural norms and academic training have predisposed them to recognize heterosexual but not homosexual themes. For example, Nancy Topping Bazin and Sydney Kaplan have described how assumptions about what constitutes good scholarship prevented their attention to the lesbian content in Woolf's novels during the 1960s and 1970s. At the 1995 Virginia Woolf conference, Bazin remembered being "very careful in those early days not to open it up into sexuality." On the same panel, Kaplan described intuiting the lesbian sexuality in Mrs. Dalloway yet feeling inhibited by the dictates of the New Critical tradition from exploring sources that might support her intuitions (Roundtable Discussion).

Nevertheless, much of the lesbian content in Woolf's fiction has remained obscure to most readers because Woolf deliberately hid her lesbian themes from hostile readers. Woolf was clearly conscious of her own coding techniques and those of other lesbian writers. For example, in 1927, she is proud that her "little Sapphist story, 'Slater's Pins Have No Points,' has passed by the editor undetected: "the Editor has not seen the point," she boasts to Vita, "though he's been looking for it in the Adirondacks" (L 3: 431); and she once teased Vita about the lesbian content hidden in her poems: "I make up poems; something in the manner of Don Juan, that you might write. But I've only (yes I think I see some very interesting things in your poems) looked between the pages here and there" (L 5: 252). Woolf's aim was to write as clearly as she could about love between women while avoiding detection. To do so, Woolf crafted works that could "pass" within the dominant culture and at the same time communicate subversive in-group messages to savvy readers. This delicate balance between self-exposure (in order to communicate with our own kind) and disguise (to avoid recognition by those who are not) is a skill developed by generations of lesbians and gay men negotiating our various relationships to the closet. Like other closeted gay writers of her generation, Woolf hid her "homoerotic incidents . . . in plain sight" (Lehmann-Haupt);[4] her seductive and allusive style simultaneously invites and resists detection.

Thus, Woolf's novels demand from her readers the same "knowing eye" she proudly displayed to her lover Vita: about the author, Elizabeth Bowen, Woolf writes to Vita:

> [M]y Elizabeth comes to see me, alone, tomorrow. I rather think, as I told you, that her emotions sway in a certain way. . . . I'm reading her novel to find out. Whats so interesting is when one uncovers an emotion that the person themselves, I should say herself, doesn't suspect. And its a sort of duty dont you think—revealing peoples true selves to themselves? I dont like these sleeping princesses. (L 5: 111)

This "viewpoint from the closet" has been aptly described by Karla Jay: "Like their counterparts in most of the books of the period, the vast majority of lesbians led encoded lives. We found each other semiotically, spotting a telltale pinky ring, hair a bit shorter than the fashion, or a book 'real ladies wouldn't read in public'" (*Lesbian Erotics* 5). Turning this "semiotic eye" toward fiction, readers learn to read obliquely for double meanings and to search in "out of the way" places—in letters, diaries, and drafts, as well as in history and myth and in the writings of other homosexual writers.[5]

Like "all minority writers," as described by Monique Wittig, Woolf was "stirred heart and soul by [her] subject—'that which calls for a hidden name'" (62). While in the fiction language is represented as inadequate to express many experiences, Woolf is particularly concerned to find words for the "unspeakable love" of women for their own sex. Toward this end, she created a range of metaphoric substitutions for erotic exchanges between women. She uses metaphors such as flowers, and birds—pigeons, nightingales, owls, and geese—to indicate female sexual arousal or fantasy or an empty milk can to stand for lesbian heartache. At times, a woman's hand on another woman's knee or the offer of a piece of ginger adds sexual tension to an otherwise mundane conversation. Woolf's strategies demand energetic reading practices: in her densely articulated "shortest of shorthand" (*AROO* 85),[6] she frequently adopts all or most of these strategies simultaneously.

As Blanche Wiesen Cook has observed, "Virginia Woolf's entire life is reflected in her work, and demonstrates her conviction that 'the public and private worlds are inseparably connected'" (730). Although careful to separate her lesbian experiences from her public persona, Woolf reintegrates private experience into public expression in her fiction. In 1937, Woolf's reminiscent comments about her Latin teacher, Janet Case, express that merging of lesbian autobiography and fiction so characteristic of her writing: "And how I loved her, at Hyde Pk Gate; & how I went hot & cold going to Windmill Hill: & how great a visionary part she has played in my life, till the visionary became a part of the fictitious, not of the real life" (D 5: 103).

As the following essays illustrate, Woolf integrates her personal experiences with loving women, as well as the experiences of lesbian and gay men she knew, into her fiction. For example, in "Bringing Buried Things to Light: Homoerotic Alliances in *To the Lighthouse*," Ruth Vanita shows how the nurturant friendships between Woolf and her homosexual Bloomsbury friends are the model for the friendship between Lily Briscoe and William Banks. In "'Pearls and the Porpoise': *The Years*—a Lesbian Memoir," I read *The Years* as Woolf's tribute to a lifetime of loving women and an elegy and love lyric commemorating her relationship with Vita Sackville-West.

Well versed in the debates about feminism and homosexuality, Woolf challenges the religious, psychoanalytic, and sexologist stereotypes of homoerotic love of her time. Eileen Barrett's "Unmasking Lesbian Passion: The Inverted World of *Mrs. Dalloway*" interprets *Mrs. Dalloway* in light of the competing discourses of feminism and sexology, arguing that through Clarissa, Woolf attempts to express lesbian sexuality free of the distortions of the sexologists.

As Susan Wolfe and Julia Penelope have noted, "invisibility is part of the social construction of a Lesbian identity," and most lesbians spend at least part of their lives invisible to themselves as well as others (23). The essays by Patricia Juliana Smith and Annette Oxindine examine Woolf's depictions of the consequences of unacknowledged lesbian feelings. Smith develops a theory, analogous to Eve Kosofsky Sedgwick's homosexual panic, of lesbian panic to explain Rachel's death in *The Voyage Out*. Smith defines lesbian panic as the disruptive reaction that occurs when a female character or an author is unable to confront her own lesbianism. Like Rachel's death, Rhoda's suicide in *The Waves* is traceable to unrealized lesbian desire. In "Rhoda Submerged: Lesbian Suicide in *The Waves*," Annette Oxindine reads Rhoda's suicide as "a sign of the lesbian's effacement within a social and linguistic system that denies her an articulation of self."

In "Entering a Lesbian Field of Vision: *To the Lighthouse* and *Between the Acts*," Lise Weil reminds us that for Woolf, loving women was a political as well as an erotic choice. Drawing on the contemporary lesbian feminist theorists Mary Daly, Marilyn Frye, and Michèle Causse, Weil links lesbianism with a perceptual shift that a woman experiences when she begins to see through the lies of patriarchal myth, and Weil traces this shift through the eyes of Lily Briscoe and Miss La Trobe.

In "*Orlando*: 'A Precipice Marked V': Between 'A Miracle of Discretion' and 'Lovemaking Unbelievable: Indiscretions Incredible'" Leslie Hankins reads the heterosexual plot in this novel as a cover letter hiding a lesbian subtext. As Hankins points out, Woolf wrote to "keep the integrity of her message and get it by the censor without bowing." With this in mind, we might reconsider Woolf's reprimand to her lover, Vita, about the aims of her writing style: "'Lovely phrases' you say which rob things of reality. Just the opposite. Always, always, always I try to say what I feel'" (*L* 3: 231).

Woolf devised a multilayered and allusive style to tell us all that she knew about lesbian and gay life during her lifetime—leaving a more complete, though less overt, record of her lesbian experiences and politics in the fiction than in the diaries and letters. Through the readings of Woolf's fiction in Part II of *Virginia Woolf: Lesbian Readings* we enter Woolf's language system, coming out through the novels and short stories into a world in which lesbian love is central, transformative, and common.

NOTES

1. In 1929, Harold wrote to Vita in regard to their BBC discussion, "We won't be able to mention sex, I presume. We can do a long bit about men's and women's professions clashing. It will be rather fun" (Glendinning 214–15).

2. I disagree, therefore, with Ellen Bayuk Rosenman's claim that critics cannot read Woolf as a lesbian because the only lesbian identity available to her was the

sexologists' definition of the mannish lesbian, a definition incompatible with Woolf's feminist values ("Sexual Identities" 639). Characteristically undeterred by her culture's impoverished models for women, Woolf focused her considerable lesbian feminist rage and writing talents on describing and re-mythologizing love between women, based on her own experiences and the experiences of women she knew. Furthermore, reading Woolf within a lesbian context does not mean that we are encasing Woolf in a monolithic "modern idea of lesbian identity," as Rosenman claims ("Sexual Identities" 635). As Julia Penelope notes, "there is no one kind of Lesbian" (33)—now or in the past. Quite simply, I claim that Virginia Woolf's primary erotic experiences were with women; that her passionate feelings for women were central to her life and work; and that the term "lesbian" is flexible and specific enough to allow us to talk about her sexual preference in meaningful ways. For discussions of lesbian identity see Card; Castle (especially, "A Polemical Introduction"); Duggan; Farwell; Garrity; Hanscombe; Hobby and White; Jeffreys' "Does It Matter If They Did It?" and *Lesbian Heresy*; Lesbian History Group (especially, the Introduction); Sedgwick, *Epistemology*; and Zimmerman, "Lesbians Like This."

3. Readers intent to prove that Virginia was chaste even with Vita often refer to Vita's letter to her husband, Harold Nicolson, dated August 17, 1926. There, Vita tells her husband that she is "scared to death of arousing physical feelings in [Virginia], because of the madness" and that that "is a fire with which [she had] no wish to play" (qtd. in Glendinning 164–65). However, this letter was written to assure Harold that Vita's love affair with Virginia would not reenact the threat to their marriage that her recent love affair with Violet Trefusis had created. Besides, relationships change: this often quoted comment was written in 1926, and Vita's intimacy with Virginia seems to have continued into the early 1930s.

4. Lehmann-Haupt refers here to homoerotic coding in the writings of Thomas Mann. For discussions of coding by gay male writers see Annan; Heilbut; Meyers, *Homosexuality*; and Sinfield. Of course, there are many permutations to the closet and to passing—familiar to other despised groups as well as lesbians and gay men. As Nechama Tec has reminded me, there are times when one's physical survival depends on "passing" even to one's kind. See Tec, *When Light Pierced the Darkness* and *Dry Tears: The Story of a Lost Childhood*; also Klepfisz, *A Few Words in the Mother Tongue: Poems Selected and New* (especially pages 187-89) for discussions of Jews passing during the Holocaust. See also, Schoppman. Like African-American slave narratives and gospel songs, Woolf's fiction is intended to communicate subversive messages to her own kind while avoiding detection from those hostile to her point of view. For discussions of coding by African-Americans see Levine and Gates.

5. Other critics have described this lesbian reading eye in similar ways. Karla Jay calls it "magical vision" ("Lesbian Modernism" 79), and Gillian Hanscombe writes, "Sometimes being a lesbian reader is rather like being one of the favoured few in the cinemas of the 1950s who were given red and green specs so they could see the breathtaking perspectives of the new 3-D movies. Audiences viewing without the specs saw only the usual thing; and sometimes not even all of that. But with the specs, all was revealed" (111). For discussions of lesbian coding

see also Wolfe and Penelope; Wittig; Hobby and White; Lesbian History Group; Castle; and Garrity.

6. I highly recommend Diane Collecott's reading of the section in *A Room of One's Own* in which this quote appears. In this passage Woolf, with characteristic bravado, gives her readers instructions for how to locate meanings hidden in novels about love between women. As Collecott notes, "although *A Room of One's Own* is now a canonical text for women's studies, few feminists are aware that in it Woolf identifies the task of articulating lesbian desire as one that involves rereading, as well as writing in previously unknown ways" (93). In this passage Woolf recommends indirection and "shorthand" to write about what happens in a novel about Chloe liking Olivia.

NINE

"The Things People Don't Say"
Lesbian Panic in **The Voyage Out**

PATRICIA JULIANA SMITH

In *The Voyage Out*, as the boat carries a band of British tourists up a river into the heart of a South American jungle forest, Terence Hewet sits on deck and reads these enigmatic lines from Walt Whitman's *Leaves of Grass*: "Whoever you are holding me now in your hand, / Without one thing all will be useless" (267). Whitman's personified book, which reveals and celebrates the secret pleasures of homosexual love only to the percipient reader, warns its peruser, "holding me now in your hand," that without this "one thing," all efforts to unlock its meaning will be in vain. Terence Hewet, an aspiring novelist who wants "to write a novel about Silence . . . the things people don't say" (216), reads these lines as he prepares to propose marriage to Rachel Vinrace, the protagonist of Woolf's own novel about "the things people don't say." Ironically, in a narrative that superficially resembles a traditional courtship plot, Terence, whom Woolf positions as the facilitator of Rachel's incorporation into institutional heterosexuality, lacks Whitman's "one thing" and accordingly finds himself bereft of the closure such a plot promises.

Whitman's cautionary note serves as a caveat to Woolf's reader as well. If apprehended by a reader blind to the variety of homoerotic possibilities Rachel Vinrace encounters in her abbreviated process of maturation, the text will defy the conventional critical wisdom and present itself as a hopelessly incoherent—if beautiful—literary failure. *The Voyage Out* is unquestionably a problematic text: What is the purpose of a courtship plot in which the heroine dies—willingly or even willfully—before the marriage can ever occur, and what is the purpose of a bildungsroman in which the heroine has so little chance to develop to any very meaningful end, save the rejection of marriage? I would suggest that the greatest short-coming of such an interpretation is a lack of the "one thing," resulting in an assumption that Woolf privileges heteroscxuality—and heterosexual perception—in this text. Conversely, discernment of the lesbian subtext and the episodes of panic that arise therefrom provides a key to the dread-ful knowledge Rachel Vinrace derives from her voyage of development.

As I have explained elsewhere, "lesbian panic" is "the disruptive action or reaction that occurs when a character—or, conceivably, an author—is either unable or unwilling to confront or reveal her own lesbianism or lesbian desire":

> Typically, a female character, fearing discovery of her covert or unarticu-lated lesbian desires—whether by the object of her desires, by other char-acters, or even by herself—and motivated by any of the factors previously described, lashes out directly or indirectly at another woman, resulting in emotional or physical harm to herself or others. This destructive reaction may be as sensational as suicide or homicide, or as subtle and vague as a generalized neurasthenic malaise. (P. J. Smith, "Narrative Strategy" 569)[1]

Virginia Woolf was certainly aware of the restrictions facing the woman writer who would endeavor to "overcome the conventions" and "make use" of the "very queer knowledge" she possesses "about womens bodies for instance—their passions—and so on" (P xxxviii–xxxix). While she claimed to lack "the courage of a hero" required to take on the con-ventions directly, few writers have concerned themselves as extensively as she with the problems of representing lesbian desire within the para-meters of the conventions. Consequently, while staying between the lines of novelistic mores, Woolf effectively deconstructs the courtship narrative and decentralizes its primacy as a feature of female-authored texts.

In undoing the timeworn courtship plot, Woolf nevertheless employs many of its traditional features. As in earlier models of lesbian panic, the threat of lesbian desire in *The Voyage Out* is embodied not in the pro-spective bride/heroine but rather in a secondary female character. Yet unlike characters in Victorian novels whose threatening presence is both intermittent and cut short by mishap, Helen Ambrose is present through-out the narrative, appearing before Rachel and ultimately surviving her. That Helen is initially the primary focus of narration in the beginning chapters and subsequently relinquishes center stage to Rachel has been deemed a structural problem in this work; the enigmatic quality of her presentation, however, compels attention to her motives and desires.[2]

Helen first appears in a state of emotional distress, weeping, ostensibly at the thought of leaving behind her children while she embarks on a voyage many months in duration. Why her presence on this journey takes priority over her maternal duties is nonetheless unclear, and while her grief is ascribed to this separation, little subsequent reference is made to the children or to her concern for them. Here, as elsewhere in the text, Helen is characterized not by any tangible and absolute qualities but rather by the absence or indefiniteness thereof. Her emotional responses are inconsistent with her actions and thus suggest that the outward signs she presents conceal rather than reveal her motives and feelings. Similarly, her appearance of normative womanhood in marriage and maternity masks the lack of conventionality that places her in contradistinction to other women of her class and status. While most of the minor female characters disport themselves with trivial gossip and concerns, Helen, who passes her time aboard ship reading G. E. Moore's *Principia Ethica*, prefers the company and conversation of intellectual men; and while Clarissa Dalloway can proclaim that she feels for her husband "what my mother and women of her generation felt for Christ" (*VO* 52), Helen is apparently content in a companionate marriage. Given her ability to negotiate social norms through outward appearance while retaining a sense of individuality, Helen would seem to be able to present the niece entrusted to her tutelage with an acceptable alternative version of the ends of the courtship plot. Yet Helen's own sexual dysphoria, manifested in emotional vacillation, destabilizes her quasi-maternal authority over Rachel and climaxes in an otherwise inexplicable display of panic.

As part of her greater structure of elaborate self-masking, Helen's disdain for women's conversation, her preference for male companionship, and her marriage to Ridley Ambrose all give the appearance of male centeredness and heterosexuality while actually signifying neither. Her contempt for petty femininity is matched by that she feels toward the hypermasculinity of her "big and burly" brother-in-law Willoughby Vinrace (*VO* 24). Her interactions with men are primarily intellectual, and lacking in flattery and flirtation. Likewise, while her scholar husband relies almost childishly upon her for his comfort and privacy, their relationship, while devoid of any demonstrable sexual passion, is marked by affectionate friendship. Their marriage has achieved a "stage of community" that allowed them "to become unconscious of each other's bodily presence . . . and in general seem to experience all the comfort of solitude without its loneliness" (*VO* 195). Her contacts with men, then, allow

Helen a sort of privacy and life of the mind similar to that which Rachel wishes to gain through submersion in music. But while Rachel's attempts result in a reinforcement of her unsocialized conditions, Helen's more sophisticated withdrawal provides a façade of matronly privilege and propriety that allows her hidden inclinations to pass undetected, not only in society but in the perceptions of many readers.

Lyndie Brimstone speculates that the lesbianism present in Woolf's texts has, by and large, gone unnoticed because many of her fictional characters are, "like Vita Sackville-West, Violet Trefusis, Vera Brittain and Woolf herself, all seemingly 'normal' women who enjoyed lesbian attachments 'between the lines' of their respectable marriages" (94).[3] Textual evidence of Helen's lesbianism, accordingly, is concealed quite literally "between the lines" of *The Voyage Out* by means of tacit allusion or indirect representation. An indication of the otherwise unarticulated conditions of the Ambrose marriage may be discerned in one of the rare instances in which Ridley participates in a social gathering. At a tea with various other members of the English party in Santa Marina, Mrs. Thornbury, the quintessential devoted wife and mother, "sweetly" if incongruously responds to one of Ridley's philosophical observations by exclaiming, "You men! Where would you be if it weren't for women!" He "grimly" replies, "Read the Symposium" (*VO* 199). The reference to Plato's discourse on male homosexual love is, understandably, lost on this matron, yet it underscores Ridley's understanding of, if not his covert desire for participation in, an all-male world free from such "feminine" attentions.

Even more telling are the silences that surround many of Helen's conversations, particularly those with the homosexual St. John Hirst. Like Ridley Ambrose, Hirst finds most women intolerably mindless and the social intercourse of men and women revolting. Accordingly, he is relieved and gratified to discover the company of Helen, who is, significantly, "the only woman I've ever met who seems to have the faintest conception of what I mean," one to whom he "could talk quite plainly . . . as one does to a man—about the relations between the sexes" (*VO* 162). Helen's worldliness and lack of dependence on men render her like a man in Hirst's estimate; at the same time, her apparent lack of sexual interest in men frees Hirst from the burden of paying her the amorous attentions he is loath to give any woman. Encouraged by Helen's knowing response, Hirst quickly engages her in a forthright discussion of the matters perplexing him, yet the contents of their conversation are so unspeakable that they must be kept not only from the other guests in the crowded ballroom in which they sit but also from the reader. Accordingly, the whole of their "long" conversation is condensed into one paragraph of indirect discourse that remains oblique to those who fail to read "between the lines":

> Certainly a barrier which usually stands fast had fallen, and it was possible to speak of matters which are generally only alluded to between men and women when doctors are present, or the shadow of death. In five minutes he was telling her the history of his life. It was long, for it was full of extremely elaborate incidents, which led on to a discussion of the principles on which morality is founded, and thus to several very interesting matters, which even in this ballroom had to be discussed in a whisper, lest one of the pouter pigeon ladies or resplendent merchants should overhear them, and proceed to demand that they should leave the place. When they had come to an end, or, to speak more accurately, when Helen intimated by a slight slackening of her attention that they had sat there long enough, Hirst rose, exclaiming, "So there's no reason whatever for all this mystery!" (VO 162–63)

But while there may be "no reason" between Hirst and Helen for "all this mystery," obviously reasons for mystery remain between author and audience. We can only surmise that the "very interesting matters" they share, topics that, if heard, would evoke the opprobrium of the "pouter pigeon ladies" and "resplendent merchants," involve that love that truly dared not speak its name in Edwardian England.

In a strange interlude following this conversation, a vision of life without such repression is realized as social barriers and gender roles drop momentarily. Although the ballroom musicians pack their instruments and leave, the crowd, still eager to dance, call upon Rachel to play the piano. Given this opportunity to indulge in her greatest pleasure, she eschews the usual popular pieces and performs an eclectic repertory for which the usual dance steps will not suffice. Accordingly, once the traditional dance music is discarded, so are gender-based dance traditions. Terence performs "the voluptuous dreamy dance of an Indian maiden," while Helen suggestively "seizes" the spinster Miss Allan, and together the two women whirl round the dance floor (VO 166). Yet this lapse in Helen's façade is an isolated incident, and as she is rarely alone with a woman, her desires remain concealed.

When initially faced with the prospect of months of close companionship with Rachel, Helen attempts an emotional subterfuge. She represses herself emotionally and retreats into the outward display of contempt she reserves for her sex, claiming that "women of her own age usually bor[ed] her, [and] she supposed that girls would be worse" (20). But Woolf reveals elsewhere that Helen "did not like to feel herself the victim of un-classified emotions" (277), and that when under emotional duress, it was "only by scorning all she met that she kept herself from tears" (9). She therefore initially distances herself from her niece by scorning the younger woman's social ineptness; only after Rachel begins to enjoy the attentions of Clarissa Dalloway does Helen, provoked by jealousy, take an active interest in her well-being.

That Rachel is the daughter of Helen's long-dead sister-in-law Theresa makes the dynamics of their relationship all the more complex. Theresa, Ridley's sister, "had been the one woman Helen called friend"; in an erotically charged passage in the first draft of the novel, Helen, "flushing" and "with Rachel pressed to her," articulates the complexity of her feel-ings: "I've never told you, but you know I love you, my darling. . . . Sometimes, you're so like Theresa, and I loved her" (M 209). Helen's entangled desires thus encroach on numerous taboos; not only does Rachel reawaken her aunt's love for Ridley's sister, but, as Helen has assumed the role of a maternal surrogate for Rachel, her desires become quasi-incestuous, echoing the previous attachment. Moreover, through this surrogation, Helen "becomes" her beloved Theresa in a sense while transferring her desires to the daughter who is in a different sense a sur-rogate for Theresa. Thus, through this ghostly triangulation, Helen's object of desire is bifurcated, while she herself assumes a bifurcated sub-ject position in the sublimation of her desires. Her suspicion of Wil-loughby's "nameless atrocities with regard to his daughter, as indeed she had always suspected him of bullying his wife" (VO 24), while possibly accurate, may well reflect her anger at his disruption of female-female love, as well as her projection of her own sense of guilt.

As Rachel moves away from Helen's influence toward the romantic attentions of Terence Hewet, Helen's jealousy gradually turns to panic, and because this panic is unarticulable, on the part of both the author and the character, it becomes all the more potent and explosive. This ever-increas-ing tension reaches its climax at a crucial moment of the courtship plot, in what Mitchell A. Leaska has termed the "strangest [passage] . . . of any in Virginia Woolf's fiction" (*The Novels* 30)—a passage that becomes far stranger when considered in light of its earlier holograph versions.

At the first disembarkment of the boat after Rachel and Terence have agreed to marry, the couple, who have yet to announce their betrothal, wander ahead of the others into the wilderness landscape. In the pub-lished text, a pursuer suddenly rushes upon them:

> A hand dropped abrupt as iron on Rachel's shoulder; it might have been a bolt from heaven. She fell beneath it, and the grass whipped across her eyes and filled her mouth and ears. Through the waving stems she saw a figure, large and shapeless against the sky. Helen was upon her. Rolled this way and that, now seeing only forests of green, and now the high blue heaven, she was speechless and almost without sense. At last she lay still, all the grasses shaken round her and before her by her panting. Over her loomed two great heads, the heads of a man and woman, of Terence and Helen.
>
> Both were flushed, both laughing, and the lips were moving; they came together and kissed in the air above her. Broken fragments of speech came down to her on the ground. She thought she heard them speak of love and marriage. Raising herself and sitting up, she too realised Helen's soft body, the strong and hospitable arms, and happiness swelling and breaking in one vast wave. (VO 283–84)

The savage and erotic violence of Helen's actions stands in sharp contrast to the worldly and aloof demeanor she has heretofore displayed. Yet this most obvious interpretation is confounded by Terence's reaction. In "looming" along with Helen over the fallen girl, he is positioned as a copredator in a mimetic realization of Rachel's ongoing rape phobias; yet in exchanging laughter and a kiss with Helen, he presents simultaneous possibilities of both infidelity and the establishment of a triad, both of which would implicate Helen as Rachel's rival, rather than Terence as Helen's rival. Subsequently, as Terence apparently informs Helen of the engagement, the older woman's embrace of the younger becomes a motherly benediction in a *rite du passage*; yet the orgasmic images with which Woolf inscribes this embrace connote that what Rachel "realises" is nothing less than the intent of Helen's homoerotic desire.

That Woolf's characters resume their everyday, upper-middle-class propriety and sociability immediately thereafter and never speak of this incident only increases the passage's disturbing inexplicability. If, as Leaska observes, this incident had "received the least comment" from Woolf's critics, then the reasons for this lacuna are apparent. Pamela Caughie, one of the few critics addressing this challenge, examines *The Voyage Out* in terms of the problems it poses to conventional narrative expectations. Arguing that the "disturbing quality of the scene is its point, not some obscurity to be cleared up or dismissed," she posits that the "lack of satisfaction" the scene offers to the reader's "desire for consummation and confirmation" functions as a means of "keep[ing] the disturbing force of sexuality vibrating through the novel" (204). I would add, moreover, that not only does this incident confound typical narrative expectations in its lack of sexual resolution, but it also, perhaps more significantly, frustrates most conventional attempts to draw any distinction between heterosexuality and homosexuality. Yet it would follow from Caughie's argument that the confusion that results is an end in itself. An examination of Woolf's earlier drafts, however, would indicate that this is not the case; rather, they give evidence of an ongoing struggle on the author's part to articulate in a mode acceptable to her audience "the things people don't talk about."[4]

In the holograph version dated 1912, Helen's desire for Rachel is less ambiguous, as is her rivalry with Terence. The "uneasy" Helen, who has been carefully observing the "significant" interactions of the pair as they wander into the forest, advises the rest of the party that she will "fetch" them, as if they were delinquent children:

> Helen was off, sweeping over the ground at a considerable pace & leaving a trail of whitened grass behind her. The figures continuing to retreat, she broke into a run, shouting Rachel's name in the midst of great panting. Rachel heard at last; looked round, saw the figure of her aunt a hundred yards away, and at once took to her heels. Terence stopped and waited for her. But she swept past him, cantering over the waving ground like one of the deer themselves, pulling handfuls of grass and casting them at Rachel's back, abusing her roundly as she did so with the remnants of her breath. Rachel turned incautiously to look, caught her foot in a twist of grass and fell headlong. Helen was upon her. Too breathless to scold, she spent her rage in rolling the helpless body hither and thither, holding both wrists in one firm grasp, and stuffing eyes, ears, nose, and mouth with the feathery seeds of the grass. Finally she laid her flat on the ground, her arms out on either side of her, her hat off, her hair down. "Own yourself beaten!" she gasped. "Beg my pardon!" Lying thus flat, Rachel saw Helen's head pendent over her, very large against the sky. A second head loomed above it, "Help! Terence!" she cried. "No!" he exclaimed, when Helen was for driving him away. "I've a right to protect her. We're going to be married."
>
> For the next two seconds they rolled indiscriminately in a bundle, imparting handfuls of grass together with attempted kisses. Separating at last, and trying to tidy her hair, Helen managed to exclaim between her pants, "Yesterday! I guessed it!" (qtd. in Leaska, *Novels* 35–36)

The distinctions between heterosexual and homosexual desire that are absent in the published version are more clearly drawn in this earlier attempt. Terence assumes the traditional, socially prescribed role of defender, with the "right to protect" the woman he has claimed as his own. Despite this clarification, the passage is possibly more disturbing in its own manner than that which superseded it, for it would seem that the incomprehensibility of the latter is primarily a means of obscuring desires too unseemly and unspeakable to be articulated forthrightly. Helen, in plunging into pursuit, steps out of any subject position that, according to the lights of the early twentieth century, could conceivably be termed feminine and positions herself as a masculine opponent to Terence's "right." In addition, the sheer sadism evident in Helen's actions and words (particularly the demand that Rachel own herself "beaten") not only indicates a truly sinister aspect of the lesbian "threat" she poses to the courtship plot but also replicates the conditions of heterosexuality that she disdains and Rachel obsessively fears. Finally, this passage offers its own ambiguities. Helen's response to Terence's announcement of his prerogative, her engaging Rachel in erotic play that might simply be deemed kissing "under other conditions," is simultaneously a challenge to male authority and an expression of affectionate goodwill in the context of a celebratory occasion. Subsequently, the scene moves incongruously toward an attempted resolution in Helen's congratulatory remark, which is actually little more than a compliment to her own proleptic intuition.

Melymbrosia, the earliest extant complete draft of the novel, provides an insight into the original function of this scene, one in which the dynamics of subject-object relationship between the two women shift significantly. Helen, although warned by Hirst, suggestively, of the dangers of snakes in the "rich thick grass," is nonetheless "in a reckless mood" (208). Reluctantly, Hirst accompanies Helen, who uncharacteristically exclaims at the beauty and the "benevolence and goodness" of the world as she ventures into the jungle. Suddenly, Rachel appears:

> Helen felt Rachel springing beside her.
>
> She went ahead, and called back over her shoulder to Helen, "It's like wading out to sea!"
>
> She left behind her a trail of whitened grass, like a track in water. Without thinking of her forty years, Helen cried "Spring on! I'm after you!" whereupon Rachel took longer leaps and at last ran. Helen pursued her. She plucked tufts of feathery blades and cast them at her. They outdistanced the others. Suddenly Rachel stopped and opened her arms so that Helen rushed into them and tumbled her over on to the ground. "Oh Helen Helen!" she could hear Rachel gasping as she rolled her, "Don't! For God's sake! Stop! I'll tell you a secret! I'm going to be married!"
>
> Helen paused with one hand upon Rachel's throat holding her head down among the grasses.
>
> "You think I didn't know that!" she cried.
>
> For some seconds she did nothing but roll Rachel over and over, knocking her down when she tried to get up; stuffing grass into her mouth;

finally laying her absolutely flat upon the ground, her arms out on either side of her, her hat off, her hair down.

"Own yourself beaten" she panted. "Beg my pardon, and say you worship me!"

Rachel saw Helen's head hanging over her, very large against the sky.

"I love Terence better!" she exclaimed.

"Terence" Helen exclaimed.

She sat clasping her knees and looking down upon Rachel who still lay with her head on the grass staring in to [sic] the sky.

"Are you happy?" she asked.

"Infinitely!" Rachel breathed, and turning round was clasped in Helen's arms.

"I had to tell you" she murmured.

"And if you hadn't, I knew" said Helen.

"He's unlike any one I've ever seen" said Rachel. "He understands." Lost in her knowledge of Terence, which she could not impart, she said no more. (208–9)

In this version, the erotic interplay between the two women is not only considerably less violent—the threat of physical restriction and punishment is certainly subdued in comparison to that which appears in subsequent revisions and can be deemed playful—but it is also mutual. Indeed, Rachel, the pursuer in this case, invites Helen's participation. The presence of the homosexual Hirst, who is completely absent in later versions, together with Terence's absence, removes every trace of heterosexuality from the scene, giving it the ambience of a lesbian utopia in an Edenic setting. That a "snake" should appear to disrupt this brief paradise is figuratively fulfilled in Rachel's recollection of her own betrothal, which jolts her into a protest against the action she has instigated and becomes the direct causation of Helen's apparently jealous use of physical force. Yet once Helen verbalizes her jealousy and her desire for the younger woman's love, Rachel offers an almost apologetic explanation for her happiness, her engagement to a man who "understands," although precisely what Terence understands is unclear and has been effectively erased in Woolf's process of revision.

Louise DeSalvo observes that "Woolf's tendency, as she got closer to publication, was to blunt the clarity" (Introduction xiv). Given the legal restrictions and social inhibitions of time, such self-censorship, as it were, is surely understandable. Nevertheless, as Woolf obscures the precise relationship between the women, both in the particular scene and in the text in general, she evokes the more sinister possibilities of alternatives to institutional heterosexuality, especially those of sado-masochism, amazonism, and a general breakdown of social and gender hierarchy. Such possibilities are, significantly, nothing less than the outcome predicted by late-nineteenth-century medical sexologists should lesbianism be allowed to flourish unchecked.[5]

The fear of *fin-de-siècle* European society, encouraged by medical sexology, that lesbianism and its inherent refusal to submit to the "evolved" social institutions of marriage and motherhood would ultimately result in a return to "bestial primitivism" (Dijkstra 335–36), is implicit in the setting of Helen's scene of lesbian panic. In the South American jungle, away from the safeguards of upper-middle-class British culture, Helen is unrestricted in exploring and enacting the "bestial" tendencies that would otherwise remain repressed. In this sense, the text becomes a journey to a female "heart of darkness." But whereas Joseph Conrad's male protagonist discovers only "the horror" of male power and corruption instead of an idealized homosocial bond with Kurtz, both Helen and Rachel encounter the fearful depths of repressed female sexuality.[6] The visit of the British tourists to a native village immediately after the encounter between Helen and Rachel serves to underscore this social dread. In one of Woolf's rare representations of racial "others," naked native women sit passively and uninterestedly on the ground, nursing their infants and regarding their guests "with the motionless inexpressive gaze of those removed from each other far, far beyond the plunge of speech" (VO 284). Ironically, this spectacle causes neither Helen nor Rachel shame or repugnance about their covert homoerotic desires; if anything, it presents the "natural" condition of motherhood as "devolved" and static. Indeed, the village scene marks the beginning of Rachel's resistance to her own engagement, as the native women leave her with a sense of "insignificance" and "pain" in her being "in love" (285).

Woolf's revision of the lesbian encounter in the realm of "nature" from the pastoral to the pathological and, ultimately, to the incoherent, however, shifts the function of these contiguous scenes from that of a premarital homoerotic rite of female initiation to that of lesbian panic. As the ostensible rationale for Helen's reactions become more obscure, her alarm at the courtship plot she sees unfolding becomes more intense and palpable. In the final published version, her pursuit of Rachel and Terence as they seek solitude in the forest becomes an impotent, futile attempt to interfere with the seemingly inevitable heterosexual consummation, now configured as "natural" in the "primitive" setting. Yet even if it were in Helen's power to disrupt the courtship plot in more than a symbolic manner, the point becomes moot, as Woolf provides Rachel with an escape from immurement in the institution of matrimony; and if Rachel does not unambiguously embrace her means of escape, she certainly does not resist its force.

Rachel accedes to the seduction of death at the end of a narrative marked by her continual resistance to a variety of proffered sexual experiences. That a courtship plot that contains many of the archetypal elements of the quest narrative should be abruptly curtailed by the death of the bride/seeker most assuredly thwarts most highly conditioned narrative expectations. To understand *The Voyage Out* as a quest narrative, however, is to assume a search on Rachel's part; whether she actively seeks anything beyond her hermetic space in which she can dwell in art and music is certainly debatable. Contrastively, that she finds much that she does not actively seek in the world of men and women whose very identities, actions, and thoughts are controlled and preordained by socially constructed gender roles is most evident.

Woolf first presents Rachel as a completely unsocialized young woman raised in relative isolation. Exposed to little learning or culture save that which she fancies, she has scarce knowledge of sexuality and desire. Thus, "at the age of twenty-four she scarcely knew that men desired women and was terrified by a kiss" when Richard Dalloway makes his overture to her aboard the ship. Her ensuing sexual awakening, to which she responds with alternating moods of fascinated exhilaration and utter revulsion, is only the first in a series of shocks as the depth and variety of human sexuality are revealed to her. Subsequently, early in her sojourn in Santa Marina, Rachel witnesses the enactment of the traditional courtship plot by fellow tourists Susan Warrington and Arthur Venning. While on a stroll with Terence, Rachel accidentally stumbles upon Susan and Arthur lying on the ground in each other's arms. Her response is simple and telling: "I don't like that" (140). Rachel's consequent reaction is to feel so "sorry for them ... [that] I could almost burst into tears" (140–41), yet she soon discovers the social rewards for participation in such "unlikeable" actions, as Susan, who heretofore "had no self" (134), becomes the focus of her fellow travelers' attention.

Conceivably, Helen, in her roles of matron and mentor, should be able to allay Rachel's anxieties about sexuality and marriage. Yet Helen is herself in a destabilized sexual position, and her pragmatic advice does little more than reveal her own distaste for the heterosexual act: "You oughtn't to be so frightened. . . . It's the most natural thing in the world. . . . The pity is to get things out of proportion. It's like noticing the noises people make when they eat, or men spitting; or, in short, any small thing that gets on one's nerves" (91). But if this "maternal" advice has the subliminal intent of dissuading Rachel from heterosexual experience, it does not follow that it will induce her to greater susceptibility to a lesbian encounter.

Within this microcosm of British society displaced in a tropical setting, the possibilities proffered to Rachel include a number that are of an ambiguously homoerotic variety. In one visit to the hotel, preliminary to the jungle expedition, Rachel endures two panic-ridden encounters with women, both of which reveal the extent to which ignorance, feigned or otherwise, in such "unspeakable" (and thus unspoken) interchanges safeguards both parties from blame. In the first, the sexually opportunistic Evelyn Murgatroyd, thwarted in the execution of her heterosexual adventures, seizes Rachel, who "had no wish to go or to stay," and leads her upstairs to her room, "two stairs at a time" (246). The domineering Evelyn alternately emotes over the brutality of men and attempts to enlist Rachel in her proposed schemes for the promotion of social causes and women's rights; all the while, Rachel, scarcely listening, sits "vacant and unhappy" (248). This impasse is broken when Evelyn sits beside Rachel on the floor and, asserting the importance of being human and "real," places her hand on Rachel's knee. Rachel displays no reaction yet feels "that Evelyn was too close to her, and that there was something exciting in this closeness, although it was also disagreeable" (249). Evelyn, for her part, continues to rant uninterruptedly about her beliefs, the illegitimacy of her birth, and the meaning of "being in love" (250), until, wanting "intimacy," she discerns that "Rachel was not thinking about her. . . . Evelyn was tormented . . . always being rebuffed" (251). Silence overtakes both women, and Rachel grows visibly uneasy. At this point Evelyn, who has clearly played the aggressor in this exchange, switches subject positions and feigns victimage; as her erstwhile captive creeps toward the door, she cries out, "What is it you want? . . . You make me feel as if you were always thinking of something you don't say. . . . Do say it!" (251). Rachel, in turn, rather incoherently expresses her hopes that Evelyn will marry one of her many suitors and leaves to wander without direction.

In this mutual rhetoric of silence, neither woman expresses her desires or anxieties directly, allowing both to feel innocent of blame if nonetheless distressed in the aftermath. Evelyn sets a tone of seduction by speaking continuously on a wide variety of topics, all of which have sex or sexuality as a common thread. Simultaneously, she avoids any direct reference to desire between women, allowing her hand on Rachel's knee, a gesture that could just as easily signify close friendship, to communicate this possibility. Rachel, in turn, maintains complete passivity. In this manner, she avoids the responsibility inherent in either acceptance or rejection—until Evelyn, growing impatient, evokes discomfort and the potential for panic. Thus, Rachel departs in order to forestall any emotionally or socially disastrous consequences. Finally, as if to absolve herself from culpable participation in forbidden activities, she leaves, invoking the now decontextualized concept of institutional heterosexuality in order to erase what has and what has not transpired.

Rachel's unreflecting flight nevertheless fails to save her from the dangers posed by other women. Wandering into a courtyard, she is transfixed by the almost surrealistic spectacle of an elderly native woman decapitating a chicken with "vindictive energy and triumph," a metaphorical representation of her own imagined victimage at the hands of her elders. While Rachel gazes with fascination at "the blood and ugly wriggling," she is approached by the schoolmistress Miss Allan, who in the same breath comments wryly on the carnage and invites the young woman to her room. As in the previous episode, Rachel complies without resistance, "for it seemed possible that each new person might remove the mystery which burdened her" (252); yet what ensues is no less "mysterious" than her contretemps with Evelyn. Miss Allan "liked young women, for she had taught many of them" (253), yet she is hard pressed to "entertain" the recalcitrantly unresponsive Rachel. In a symbolically charged attempt to break this social stalemate, Miss Allan offers her guest a piece of ginger. Before the gift can be retrieved, however, Rachel demurs, certain that she would not like it. To this refusal, presented in much the same language as Rachel's reaction to Susan and Arthur's coupling, Miss Allan launches into a disjointed and didactic, if nonetheless suggestive, disquisition on experience that needs little explication:

> You've never tried? . . . Then I consider that it is your duty to try now. Why, you may add a new pleasure to life, and as you are still young— . . . I make it a rule to try everything. . . . Don't you think it would be very annoying if you tasted ginger for the first time on your deathbed, and found you never liked anything so much? I should be so exceedingly annoyed that I think I should get well on that account alone. (254)

Rachel accepts the ginger, only to be so distressed that she must "spit it out." Miss Allen wonders if Rachel is sure she has "really tasted it," but

Rachel answers by throwing the offending sweet out the window. Unperturbed, Miss Allan rules, with pedagogical authority, that it was "an experience anyway" (254).

Although Rachel is as resistant to the enjoyment of ginger as she is to other, more dangerous pleasures, she remains in the teacher's room, filled with an ineffable longing:

> Surely there must be balm for all anguish in her words, could one induce her to have recourse to them. But Miss Allan . . . showed no signs of breaking the reticence which had snowed her under for years. An uncomfortable sensation kept Rachel silent; on the one hand, she wished to whirl high and strike a spark out of the cool pink flesh; on the other she perceived there was nothing to be done but to drift past each other in silence. (255)

Rachel envisions the realization of surcease from her distress in terms that are remarkably and simultaneously physical, erotic, and violent. But Rachel can no more articulate her anguish than she or Miss Allan can define the cause of the older woman's reticence, and thus no spark can ever be struck. Instead, Miss Allan offers aphorisms about age and the difficulties of life, as well as droll stories about a talismanic bottle of crème de menthe she has continued to exchange with a woman friend for twenty-six years, about a female colleague who overcame the "unsatisfactory" nature of her life by breeding guinea pigs, and about "a yellow guinea-pig [that] has had a black baby" (256). Like Evelyn, she discourses endlessly on indirectly sexual themes, all of which are constructed in a manner that appears innocent of erotic intent. Simultaneously, in an elaborate display of passive-aggressive behavior, she removes her coat, skirt, and blouse and, citing her need to arrange her hair and change clothing, she enlists Rachel's help in dressing for dinner with the seemingly rational explanation that "I should be particularly glad of your assistance, because there is a tiresome set of hooks which I can fasten for myself, but it takes from ten to fifteen minutes; whereas with your help—" (256). Rachel says nothing but cooperates, while Miss Allan continues her discussion of guinea pigs, for Miss Allan "was not an impulsive woman, and her life had schooled her to restrain her tongue" (257). They descend to dinner, where the plan for the fateful jungle expedition is put in motion.

That Woolf should juxtapose these two scenes, in which two vastly dissimilar women employ parallel strategies to stimulate homoerotic interest while impeding its actualization, indicates that desire between women, far from being an extreme or isolated phenomenon, is, in reality, quite commonplace. The apparently self-defeating mechanisms of this suggestive rhetoric are an end in themselves. Because no clearly defined sexual action can occur under the circumstances, the participants are allowed the frisson arising from potential danger without the guilt or responsibility its realization would entail. Thus Rachel, immediately after fleeing from one encounter she finds both "exciting" and "disagreeable," does not hesitate to allow herself to be coerced into experiencing a second.

Because Rachel's sexual reactions are mitigated to a very great extent by dread and resistance, any attempt to define sexual preference in her case must ultimately be frustrated. What can be ascertained, via negativa, is her lack of differentiation between male- and female-inspired sexual dread. Her response to Evelyn is merely an encapsulation of the "physical pain of emotion," succeeded first by "strange exultation" and then by a feeling of being "merely uncomfortable," she undergoes in the wake of Richard Dalloway's kiss (76, 77). This vision of "something . . . which is hidden in ordinary life" culminates in a nightmare fraught with sexual symbolism:

> She was walking down a long tunnel, which grew so narrow by degrees that she could touch the damp bricks on either side. At length the tunnel opened and became a vault; she found herself trapped in it . . . with a deformed man. . . . His face was pitted and like the face of an animal. The wall behind him oozed with damp. . . .
> She felt herself pursued. . . . A voice moaned for her; eyes desired her. All night long barbarian men . . . stopped to snuffle at her door. (77)

For Rachel, the physical "violation" of the kiss resonates as rape, and male sexuality is signified as bestial and grotesque. Still, the unsubtle vaginal symbolism (the wall that "oozed with damp") can only indicate that this pursuit arouses desire as well as dread.

The threat of female sexuality produces remarkably similar results in her subconscious. In the aftermath of her encounter with Helen, Rachel grows increasingly querulous in her relationship with Terence; and, returning from the jungle to the structures of British society in Santa Marina, she sickens and dies. In a fevered deathbed hallucination, Helen and the bedside nurse displace the "barbarian men" of the earlier dream:

> [She] found herself walking through a tunnel under the Thames, where there were little deformed women sitting in archways playing cards, while the bricks of which the wall was made oozed with damp, which collected into drops and slid down the wall. But the little women became Helen and Nurse McInnis after a time, standing in the window together whispering, whispering incessantly. (331)

The most singular difference between the two dreams is in the pursuers' mode of vocal expression. Whereas the men "moan" and "snuffle," the women whisper, as befits the actual and rhetorical silences that surround their desires.

Shirley Neuman posits that the orgasmic description of Rachel's "happiness" in Helen's embrace, occurring at the moment of the announcement of her engagement, suggests on Rachel's part "not only an unwillingness to face the sexual implications of marriage but an unresolved ambiguity about her sexual choice"; and that "in making the socially acceptable female choice—marriage," she has ultimately "ventured too far" (63). If so, as Rachel is given no viable mode in which she could potentially articulate or resolve this ambiguity, death would seem the only acceptable alternative to marriage for her, much as it did for the numerous "unmarriageable" female protagonists of eighteenth-century and Victorian novels. If the panic afflicting Rachel is somewhat less clearly lesbian than that which Helen undergoes, a less specific form of panic arising from the prospect of being permanently subsumed into institutional heterosexuality is surely an active agent in Rachel's retreat from life and its possibilities. Consequently Rachel, in her very unwillingness or inability to attempt a resolution of her sexual dilemma, becomes an inviable, indeed, a non-narratable character.

Rachel Blau DuPlessis argues that "Rachel's death may accordingly be interpreted as the death of a person who evaded constitutive components of her Bildung," and "that Woolf meted out death as Rachel's punishment for her being insufficiently critical and vocal" (51). In this case, the self-reassurance of Mrs. Thornbury, the pious advocate of marriage, motherhood, and Empire, in the wake of Rachel's death, that "surely order did prevail" (360), possesses an ironic truth. In form, if not in content, *The Voyage Out* remains a traditional novel; and the restoration of order prerequisite for closure in the form can prevail only through the removal of the embodied sign of contradiction. Yet, as Duplessis points out, its ending is "the aggressive act of the author against the hegemonic power of the narrative conventions with which the novel is, in fact, engaged—love and quest" (50). By aborting the mechanisms of the courtship plot, Woolf begins the process by which she subsequently undermines the narrative and social ideologies that configure desire between women as the ultimate agent of disorder.

NOTES

1. The narrative strategy of lesbian panic is the subject of my forthcoming book, *Lesbian Panic: The Homoerotics of Narrative in Modern British Women's Fiction*. This paradigm is, quite obviously, analogous in many ways to Eve Kosofsky Sedgwick's "axiom" of homosexual panic delineated in *Epistemology of the Closet*. But, as I have noted in "And I Wondered If She Might Kiss Me," there can be no "systematic transferal [of Sedgwick's theory] across sexual boundaries because of the substantial historical differences in the social regulation of male and female sexual expression" (571). Sedgwick bases her concept in great part on the writings of Gayle Rubin and Luce Irigaray (*This Sex*), who see male homosociality as a system of exchange of women between men. Traditionally disempowered and dispossessed of any significant proprietary status, women, the objects of exchange, have generally lacked the wherewithal to create an analogous exchange of men among or between themselves. The stakes of survival are, quite obviously, very different for an object than for a subject. Consequently, women have had to concern themselves with maintaining their "exchange value" as marriageable/sexual commodities. Lesbianism or the suspicion thereof would undoubtedly obviate such an exchange value and thus threaten a woman's very means of survival (i.e., the economic support of men).

2. James Naremore, in analyzing the aesthetic shortcomings of the novel, cites Helen's shift from foreground to background as a primary example of the manner in which "the novel tends to frustrate conventional expectations" (6).

3. Brimstone also notes that although Woolf feared exposure and attack on account of her "Sapphism" as a result of her writings, her articulation of lesbian subject matter was nevertheless so subtle that "it is not until recent years that the lesbian implications have been noted" (93). According to Edward de Grazia, Woolf's sexual preference and practices were so little known to the public during her lifetime that she was thought an appropriate witness to testify on behalf of the merits of Radclyffe Hall's *The Well of Loneliness* at that book's obscenity trial (178–79).

4. As no critic has offered more than a cursory explanation of these enigmatic and crucial passages, and because these three different versions do not appear together in any one published text, I am reproducing them here in toto despite their considerable length.

5. For a comprehensive examination of the medical sexologists' perceptions of lesbianism and its presumed threat to the very fabric of civilization, see Dijkstra (119–59).

6. For a thoughtful discussion of the analogies between *The Voyage Out* and *Heart of Darkness*, see Neuman. Fleischman, *Critical Reading* (1); Naremore (45); and Zwerdling (*Real World* 306) also address this issue.

TEN

Unmasking Lesbian Passion: The Inverted World of **Mrs. Dalloway**

EILEEN BARRETT

I came out in the early 1970s, when, as for many other women my lesbianism was inseparable from my feminism. I came out as a "woman-identified woman" who agreed with the Radicalesbians that lesbianism "is the primacy of women relating to women, of creating a new consciousness of and with each other, which is at the heart of women's liberation, and the basis for the cultural revolutions" (245). Perhaps I was naive, but I was thrilled by my own and other women's potential to transform the world. Protected by a community of lesbian feminists, I came out at a time and in a place when the sheer exuberance of feminism enabled me—at least temporarily—to disregard the social condemnation of lesbianism.[1]

Sheila Jeffreys suggests that a similar energy infused the nineteenth-century and early-twentieth-century feminist movement, many of whose leaders had relationships with other women.[2] In *The Cause*, Virginia Woolf's friend Ray Strachey captures how feminist ideas spread across classes of women and persuaded women like Woolf to join suffrage organizations, which she did in 1910. Strachey writes of "The Great Days" (303) between 1906 and 1911, when "women who had never before given a thought to public questions began to be roused" (305). According to Strachey, these women "read into the Cause not only what lay upon the surface, but all the discontents which they, as women, were suffering" (305).[3] During the last decade of her life, Woolf immersed herself in the history of this movement, its political militancy, and its critique of marriage and compulsory heterosexuality. In *Three Guineas* she summarizes the movement's feminist analysis: "It was with a view to marriage that her mind was taught. . . . It was with a view to marriage that her body was educated . . . all that was enforced upon her in order that she might preserve her body intact for her husband" (38).

Many feminists Woolf knew rejected marriage, instead choosing to live with other women. In the 1920s, the playwright Beatrice Mayor introduced Woolf to such lesbians as Chris St. John and Edith Craig (D 1: 174). Through her suffrage work, Woolf probably would have known that during the first decades of the century St. John and Craig collaborated with others to write and direct numerous feminist plays—*How the Vote Was Won, A Pageant of Great Women,* and *Trifles,* to mention a few—that both critique the social and sexual repression of marriage and celebrate bonds between women.[4] As the work of Lillian Faderman and Paula Bennett demonstrates, the writing of Woolf's numerous female literary precursors is replete with erotic images of same-sex love. The scholarship of Blanche Cook, Ellen Hawkes, and Jane Marcus conveys the erotic, women-centered milieu in which Woolf thrived. In her letters, Woolf routinely responds with flirtatious innuendos when her sister, Vanessa Bell, teases her about her "Sapphist tendencies" (V. Bell 84); and by the late 1920s, Woolf was referring to herself as "the mouthpiece of Sapphism" (L 3: 530). These political, literary, and personal influences inspired Woolf to inscribe lesbianism throughout her works, including her most powerful feminist essays *A Room of One's Own* and *Three Guineas.*[5] As with many of us who came out in the 1970s and 1980s, Woolf's lesbianism is inseparable from her feminism.

At the same time, Woolf was aware of competing discourses about lesbianism and male homosexuality, and in this essay I explore how she incorporates such discourses throughout *Mrs. Dalloway.* The novel's scathing depictions of heterosexuality in marriage demonstrate Woolf's lesbian-feminist critique of this institution. Her representations of same-sex love reflect her feminist sensibility, as well as the sexologists' influence. The relationship between Sally Seton and Clarissa Dalloway exemplifies the romantic friendships between women that were thriving at the turn of the century. Her portrayal of Septimus Warren Smith exposes the consequences of the most repressive legal and medical attitude that all forms of homosexuality are crimes against nature. Doris Kilman and other minor female characters, on the other hand, embody many of the negative characteristics ascribed to lesbian feminists by sexologists such as Havelock Ellis, Edward Carpenter, and Stella Browne.

Finally, Woolf's portrayal of the ambivalent Clarissa reflects the conflict among these divergent depictions of lesbian passion. Clarissa rejects the idea that same-sex love is a crime against nature, yet she projects onto Doris all the negative, distorted stereotypes of lesbians. Clarissa's erotic fantasies reflect the ideal of romantic friendship. But by echoing the imagery of Clarissa's fantasies in her descriptions of Doris's and other characters' lesbian desires, Woolf also illustrates the power of the sexologists to pervert the erotic language of romantic friendship into the language of homophobia and self-hatred. At the same time, the repeated association of Clarissa's lesbian passion with the soul suggests Woolf's efforts to embrace a philosophy of lesbianism, however inadequate, influenced by the trapped soul theory of the sexologists. Signifying "the revelation, the religious feeling" (*MD* 36) that Clarissa identifies with her lesbianism, the image of the soul helps Clarissa shield such erotic feelings from public scrutiny. Through the relationship between Clarissa and Doris, then, Woolf not only challenges the sexologists and their stereotypes but also attempts to reconcile public and private expressions of lesbian passion and identity.

Woolf was not immune to the prevailing condemnation of homosexuality. By the late nineteenth century, the homosexual person—at least the male—had become the subject of legal, medical, social, and psychological categorization (Weeks, *Coming Out* 102). The 1885 law against sexual acts between men led to the infamous persecution of Oscar Wilde, who was convicted in 1895. Wilde was subjected not only to imprisonment but also to virulent condemnation by the popular press for his attack against "the wholesome, manly, simple ideas of English life" (Greenberg 393). Efforts to counter such commonly expressed homophobic sentiments and the violence they perpetuated were frequently censored. Woolf's friend Margaret Haig, the editor of the feminist periodical *Time and Tide*, recalled surreptitiously reading in the 1910s Havelock Ellis's *Studies in the Psychology of Sex*, which contains *Sexual Inversion*, the volume in which he discusses homosexuality. "Though I was far from accepting it all, it opened up a whole new world of thought to me" (qtd. in Spender 608). But as she noted, "one could not walk into a shop and buy 'The Psychology of Sex'; one had to produce some kind of signed certificate from a doctor or a lawyer to the effect that one was a suitable person to read it" (qtd. in Spender 608). Although the sexologists opposed overt persecution of homosexuals, the "whole new world of thought" included theories that homosexuality indicated developmental degeneration or insanity. Moreover, the scientific description of congenital female inversion and the so-called mannish lesbian that Ellis and other sexologists promoted influenced not only Woolf and her contemporaries. As Sheila Jeffreys notes, such depictions of lesbianism have "had a momentous effect on the ways in which we, as women, have seen ourselves and all our relationships with other women up until the present time" (*Spinster* 105).

Barbara Fassler suggests the extent to which Woolf read and discussed with E. M. Forster and Lytton Strachey, among other friends, many of the sexologists' evolving theories about homosexuality. Of special interest to Bloomsbury were the philosophical and social defenses of same-sex love developed by such writers as John Addington Symonds and Edward Carpenter, who were themselves homosexual. For example, E. M. Forster acknowledges that his overtly homosexual novel *Maurice* "was the direct result of a visit to Edward Carpenter ("Terminal Note" 249). In their writings, Carpenter and Symonds celebrate the historical and literary tradition of homosexuality, pointing to the acceptance of same-sex love among the Greeks and the preference for their own sex to be found in the masterpieces of such great artists as Michelangelo and Shakespeare. Woolf's continual references to Sappho in her novels, essays, and stories suggest her attempt at a parallel argument for a lesbian tradition. When she mentions this lesbian precursor in "The Intellectual Status of Women," for example, she quotes Symonds on the "case of Sappho" (*D* 2: 314). Fassler also argues that Woolf's theory of androgyny owes much to what Fassler calls the "trapped soul theory" of sexual inversion. Developed by Symonds and Carpenter, this self-concept of homosexuality was articulated by Woolf's friend Goldsworthy Dickinson, who wrote, "'It's a curious thing to have a woman's soul shut up in a man's body but that seems to be my case'" (qtd. in Fassler 241).

At least one turn-of-the-century lesbian feminist incorporated such views into her writing. In 1915, thirteen years before *The Well of Loneliness* appeared, the feminist playwright Chris St. John depicted herself as a congenital sexual invert in *Hungerheart: The Story of a Soul*, the novel based on her love relationship with Edith Craig. The novel's subtitle—the story of a soul—hints at St. John's acceptance of the trapped soul theory of homosexuality, and her preference for Christopher St. John over her birth name Christabel Marshall underscores her belief in the masculine component of what she perceived as her own congenital inversion. As Julie Holledge observes of this fictionalized version of the Craig–St. John love story, "Although *Hungerheart* challenged the Victorian assumption that women were sexually passive, it conformed to the prevalent attitude held by sex psychologists that inversion was either true and congenital or artificial and acquired through temporary influences" (117).[6]

Such beliefs in congenital inversion, along with anti-feminist ideas, infected the most ardent defenders of homosexuality as well as the Bloomsbury circle. Whereas in his 1894 essay Carpenter benignly observes among feminists "a marked development of the homogenic passion" ("Homogenic Love" 45), three years later in Love's Coming of Age, he banishes feminists from other women. "Such women," he argues, "do not altogether represent their sex; some are rather mannish in temperament; some are 'homogenic,' that is, inclined to attachments to their own sex, rather than to the opposite, sex . . . " (72). Although Forster later apologized, during a frank if inebriated discussion of sapphism and homosexuality, he admitted, as Woolf records his conversation, to thinking "Sapphism disgusting: partly from convention, partly because he disliked that women should be independent of men" (D 3: 193).

The sexologist and birth control reformer Stella Browne expressed similar antagonism towards lesbian feminism. In "Studies in Feminine Inversion," a 1923 paper presented to the British Society for the Study of Sex Psychology, Browne describes five cases of what she defines as innate female inversion.[7] Stressing that these so-called cases "are absolutely distinguishable from affectionate friendship. They have all of them in varying degrees, the element of passion" (606), she draws an artificial distinction between lesbian passion and affectionate friendship. "I am sure that much of the towering spiritual arrogance which is found . . . in the Suffrage movement . . . is really unconscious inversion" (611). With this broad stroke, she discounts the dynamic relationship between feminism and lesbianism. Feminist political convictions for Browne indicate either spiritual arrogance or repressed sexual inversion.

Despite the underlying hostility toward the political arguments of lesbian feminism, the sexologists who acknowledged the existence of the so-called congenital invert also enabled lesbian self-definition. As Faderman points out, "in Germany, where the impact of the first theorists, who were for the most part German, was felt earliest and most strongly, a new lesbian society was flourishing by the turn of the century" (250).[8] The potential for flourishing lesbianism was not lost on members of the British Parliament, who successfully argued against a 1921 law that would have criminalized sexual acts between women. Reflecting the popularly held belief in women's sexual ignorance, one opponent argued: "'You are going to tell the whole world that there is such an offence, to bring it to the notice of women who have never heard of it, never thought of it, never dreamt of it. I think this is a very great mischief'" (Weeks, *Coming Out* 106–7).

Mrs. Dalloway serves for many contemporary critics as a model text inscribing such lesbian mischief through Clarissa. In her 1956 *Sex Variant Women in Literature*, Jeannette Foster quotes the significant scenes depicting Clarissa's love for Sally Seton to praise Woolf's subtle and sensitive depiction of a lesbian (273–75). Seventeen years later, Nancy Bazin notes in her introduction to *Virginia Woolf and the Androgynous Vision* that Woolf "suggests the lesbian's experience by describing Mrs. Dalloway's sexual response to Sally Seton" (5). Two years after Bazin's book appeared, Judith McDaniel asks in her 1975 MLA paper "Why Not Sally?" why such little attention was given to Clarissa's passion for Sally. Responding to McDaniel's question, current readings of the novel decode the lesbian plot crystallized in Sally Seton's kiss, "the most exquisite moment of [Clarissa's] whole life" (*MD* 35). Lyndie Brimstone sees *Mrs. Dalloway* as "the most lesbian specific piece of writing Woolf ever published" (103); Patricia Cramer describes the novel as Woolf's gift "to lesbians seeking historical models and explanations for their sexual attractions for women" ("Underground" 181).[9]

Numerous critics notice that Woolf modeled the relationship between Clarissa and Sally Seton upon her own love for Madge Symonds Vaughan, the oldest daughter of John Addington Symonds.[10] In a biography full of evasions about his aunt's lesbianism, Quentin Bell nonetheless writes of Madge Vaughan:

> Virginia was in fact in love with her. She was the first woman—and in those early years Virginia fled altogether from anything male—the first to capture her heart, to make it beat faster, indeed to make it almost stand still as, her hand gripping the handle of the water-jug in the top room at Hyde Park Gate, she exclaimed to herself: "Madge is here; at this moment she is actually under this roof." Virginia once declared that she had never felt a more poignant emotion for anyone than she did at that moment for Madge. (60–61)

In the passionate friendship of Sally and Clarissa, Woolf captures the intermingling of the intellectual and erotic, the personal and the political that she experienced in her own feminist friendships. From their first meeting, Clarissa "could not take her eyes off Sally" (*MD* 33). Together they discuss "women's rights" (73), "how they were to reform the world ... to found a society to abolish private property" (33). They read Plato and, challenging the censorship of the period, Sally gives Clarissa the socialist writings of William Morris "wrapped in brown paper" (33). Along with her outspoken political views, Sally's direct sensuality seduces Clarissa; while Clarissa indulges in a lifetime of erotic floral fantasies, Sally gathers flowers, cuts their heads off, and makes them swim in bowls (34). "Indeed she did shock people" (34), Clarissa recalls. Yet, in language that reverberates with Woolf's passion for Madge Symonds, the narrator describes how her power to shock fills Clarissa with "excitement" and "ecstasy" when Sally is "'beneath this roof. . . . She is beneath this roof!'" (*MD* 34; ellipses in original).

This romantic friendship also contains a criticism of marriage that Woolf explores throughout the novel. Marriage, as Clarissa and Sally Seton always spoke of it, is a "catastrophe" for women (34), beginning with Evelyn Whitbread. While Hugh Whitbread maintains a "manly," "perfectly upholstered body" (6), Evelyn suffers from "some internal ailment" (6) that suggests the toll marriage takes on the female body. Whereas Clarissa's impatience with Evelyn—"that indescribably dried-up little woman"—and her interminable female ailments (10) distances her from the Whitbread catastrophe, Peter Walsh, who believes "there's nothing in the world so bad for some women as marriage" (41), observes that Evelyn "sometimes gave the show away" (74). "She was almost negligible," he thinks. "Then suddenly she would say something quite unexpected—something sharp" (74). A similar tragedy befalls Lady Bradshaw, the wife of Sir William Bradshaw. The burden that marriage places on her to minister "to the craving which lit her husband's eye so oilily for dominion" diminishes Lady Bradshaw, who "cramped, squeezed, pared, pruned" to make room for the "great doctor" (101). Fifteen years ago, the narrator informs us, Lady Bradshaw, "had gone under. It was nothing you could put your finger on; there had been no scene, no snap; only the slow sinking, water-logged, of her will into his" (100).

Marriage can also be a catastrophe for men such as Septimus, who sinks like a "drowned sailor" (97) beneath the will of Bradshaw. Throughout the novel Woolf depicts his painful struggle to stay afloat. Described by the narrator as "on the whole, a border case" (84), Septimus is haunted by his love for his comrade Evans. In moments of bitterness, Septimus accepts Shakespeare's decree that love between men and women is repulsive and considers "[t]he business of copulation filth" (89). He rebuffs his wife's plea for children—"One cannot bring children into a world like this. One cannot perpetuate suffering, or increase the breed of these lustful animals" (89)—and he sneers at heterosexual couples, "drawing pictures of them naked at their antics in his notebook" (90). Still, like many of the conflicted homosexuals the sexologists describe, Septimus agonizes over the deception his marriage to Rezia has wrought: "he had married his wife without loving her; had lied to her; seduced her; . . . and was so pocked and marked with vice that women shuddered when they saw him in the street. The verdict of human nature on such a wretch was death" (91).

At times of euphoria Septimus delays the verdict of human nature. As Carpenter and Symonds had done, he associates his love for Evans with the Greeks, imagining that in death his fallen comrade returns to Thessaly (70). In his prophetic moment in Regent Park, in fact, Septimus's revelation echoes Walt Whitman's poetic pledge that Carpenter quotes in "Homogenic Love": "'I will make,'" Carpenter quotes Whitman, "'the most splendid race the sun ever shone upon, I will make divine magnetic lands . . . I will make inseparable cities with their arms about each other's necks, by the love of comrades'" (345; ellipses in original). Similarly, when Septimus "sees light on the desert's edge" with "legions of men prostrate behind him," he promises "[h]e would turn round, he would tell them in a few moments, only a few moments more, of this relief, of this joy, of this astonishing revelation—" (70).[11]

Bereft of the love of comrades, Septimus accepts the prevailing homophobia, envisioning his homosexuality not as an "astonishing revelation" but as a crime against human nature: "He had committed an appalling crime and been condemned to death by human nature" (96). At the same time, the longing "to speak out" (67) occasionally breaks through Septimus's shell-shocked madness. "But if he confessed? If he communicated?," he wonders, "Would they let him off then, his torturers?" (98). He yearns to disclose his love for Evans, his supreme secret. "The supreme secret must be told . . . there is no crime . . . love, universal love, he muttered, gasping, trembling, painfully drawing out these profound truths which needed, so deep were they, so difficult, an immense effort to speak out . . ." (67).

Unfortunately, Septimus is incapable of the immense effort—"the trembling, painfully drawing out"—that truthful disclosure requires. His faltering attempts, however, continue until his suicide—"'Communication is health; communication is happiness, communication—' he muttered" (93). Dr. Holmes brushes aside the concerns of Septimus, prescribing golf and cricket (90). Complacently married, with four children, Holmes stresses "duty to one's wife" (92); "health," he pontificates, "is largely a matter in our own control" (91). Septimus knows better: "Once you stumble, Septimus wrote on the back of a postcard, human nature is on you. Holmes is on you" (92). Denied a sympathetic listener, confronted instead by Dr. Holmes, who embodies the heterosexuality human nature requires, Septimus flings himself "vigorously, violently" upon the railings (149). The verdict of human nature is swift and definitive: "'The coward!' cried Dr. Holmes" (149).

Woolf's critique of marriage uncovers how this institution buries women's spirits under the domination of men. It also reveals how it destroys men whose passion is for their own sex. Her poignant description of Rezia's suffering discloses the hidden pain of women married to homosexual men. With Septimus's tragic suicide, Woolf condemns her culture's silencing of homosexuality and its insistence on heterosexuality. In this sense, her narrative echoes the compassion found in some work of the sexologists.

Between the time of the exquisite moment when Sally Seton kisses Clarissa (1890) and the present time of the novel (1923), the major works of the sexologists appeared. Previously acceptable romantic friendships such as the one between Sally and Clarissa were now scrutinized by sexologists for their deviance. In the October 1884 *Journal of Mental Science*, for example, Sir George Savage, Virginia Woolf's own physician, described a case of female homosexuality, questioning whether "'this perversion is as rare as it appears" (391).[12] Thirteen years later, Havelock Ellis opened his chapter "Sexual Inversion in Women" from his book *Sexual Inversion* with a partial answer to Savage's question. "Homosexuality," Ellis acknowledges, "is not less common in women than in men" (195).[13] Havelock Ellis knew from personal experience. After all, his own wife, Edith Ellis, was a lesbian, who maintained intimate relationships with women both before and throughout her marriage.[14]

The most famous nineteenth-century English work on lesbianism, Ellis's *Sexual Inversion*, is full of incongruities. While professing tolerance for congenital inversion, which he believes cannot be helped or cured, he emphasizes remote or extreme examples of lesbian life. He uncovers evidence of lesbianism everywhere from New Zealand to South America to China to Africa. He describes lesbian activity among women in Muslim as well as American Indian cultures, with relish for the graphic detail. When he discusses European women, he finds lesbianism predominantly among women already designated as deviant: transvestites, prostitutes, suicides, and murderers. As he informs his reader, "Inverted women, who may retain their feminine emotionality combined with some degree of infantile impulsiveness and masculine energy, present a favorable soil for the seeds of passional crime, under those conditions of jealousy and allied emotions which must so often enter into the invert's life" (201).

Yet, the case studies he includes belie his efforts to categorize lesbians as remote or criminal others. Written to Ellis by the mostly English women themselves, the case study narratives poignantly describe the writers' efforts to contain their sexual longings.[15] In his analysis of the cases, Ellis, like Browne after him, tries to demarcate the boundaries between friendship and female inversion. He claims that the former attachments generally end when, in his words, "a man brings the normal impulse into permanent play, or the steadying of the emotions . . . leads to a knowledge of the real nature of such feelings and a consequent distaste for them" (219). He advises female inverts to avoid overt sexual experiences. Thus, coupled with descriptions of longing for other women, these narratives include depictions of acute sexual repression. I quote from one woman's writing to illustrate:

> For some time it satisfied us fully to be in bed together. One night, however, when she had had a cruelly trying day and I wanted to find all ways of comforting her, I bared [m]y breast for her to lie on. Afterward it was clear that neither of us could be satisfied without this. She groped for it like a child, and it excited me much more to feel that than to uncover my breast and arms altogether at once.
>
>   Much of this excitement was sexually localized, and I was haunted in the daytime by images of holding this woman in my arms. I noticed also that my inclination to caress my other women friends was not diminished, but increased. All this disturbed me a good deal. The homosexual practices of which I had read lately struck me as merely nasty; I could not imagine myself tempted to them;—at the same time the whole matter was new to me, for I had never wanted anyone even to share my bed before; I had read that sex instinct was mysterious and unexpected, and I felt that I did not know what might come next. (220)

On one level, this narrative illustrates the seamless quality of sexuality in lesbian friendship. These women's erotic desires mingle with their longing for compassionate friendship, and the narrator's sexual closeness with her significant friend enhances her pleasure in the company of other women. Yet the discourse of the sexologists that she reads perverts her mysterious, unexpected lesbian attractions into disturbing temptations to so-called nastiness. What comes next for this woman is a warning from a male (presumably Ellis) advisor. "I was to be very wary of going further," she reports him as cautioning; "there was fire about" (221). Ellis includes what she writes after receiving this advice:

> We love each other warmly, but no temptation to nastiness has ever come, and I cannot see now that it is at all likely to come. With custom, the localized physical excitement has practically disappeared, and I am no longer obsessed by imagined embraces. The spiritual side of our affection seems to have grown steadily stronger and more profitable since the physical side has been allowed to take its natural place. (221–22)

A number of female characters in *Mrs. Dalloway* live with other women in similar situations. Throughout Clarissa's party, Ellie Henderson makes mental notes of everything to tell her companion, Edith (*MD* 169, 194). Although Clarissa sees only the "taper[ing] and dwindl[ing] of Ellie, the narrator detects in this wispy creature of fifty "some mild beam" shining through (168), perhaps due to her friendship with Edith. Ellis might interpret Ellie's friendship with Edith, as well as the relationship between Lady Bruton and Milly Brush, as being "on the borderland of true sexual inversion" (219). Described as "deficient . . . in every attribute of female charm" (103), Milly Brush is at the same time "capable of everlasting devotion, to her own sex in particular" (106). Lady Bruton, the recipient of Milly's devotion, exemplifies what Ellis terms the "able women inverts, whose masculine qualities render it comparatively easy for them to adopt masculine avocations" (196). "She should have been a general of dragoons herself" (105), Woolf's narrator tells us. When Hugh Whitbread arrives bearing carnations, Lady Bruton ignores his attentions, thinking "the difference between one man and another does not amount to much" (104). The dominant invert in this couple, she is "more interested in politics than people; of talking like a man" (105).[16]

With such excessive dedication to her "masculine avocations," Lady Bruton, the narrator warns, "had perhaps lost her sense of proportion" (109). The erotic description of her avocation, however, suggests that she sublimates her lesbian desire: "this object around which the essence of her soul is daily secreted, becomes inevitably prismatic, lustrous, half-looking glass, half precious stone; now carefully hidden in case people should sneer at it; now proudly displayed" (109). The imagery Woolf uses to describe Lady Bruton's devotion mirrors that which she associates with Clarissa's lesbian identity, her "infinitely precious" "diamond" (52–53), the privacy of her soul. Ultimately, as we shall see, both characters reveal as they conceal the essence of their souls that their precious stones represent. The "half-looking glass," after all, reflects only the partial truth.

Ironically, the cause to which Lady Bruton sublimates her inversion is emigration, one among many solutions of the period devised to rid England of sexual inverts. Although she attempts a letter to the *Times* on this topic, her battle to write—"beginning, tearing up, beginning again"— suggests her inner turmoil about this so-called remedy. She summons Hugh Whitbread, "[a] being so differently constituted from herself" "who possessed—no one could doubt it—the art of writing letters to the *Times*" (109). Hugh's discussion of "superfluous youth" (110) echoes homophobic sentiments from a 1909 *British Medical Journal* essay that urges homosexuals to emigrate to "some land where their presence might be welcome" and hence to spare England from hearing of "the culture of unnatural and criminal practices" (Porter and Hall 162).

Ellis accepts the idea of congenital inversion, for which "prevention can have but small influence." Rather than advocate such draconian measures as emigration, he advises using, in his words, "direct and indirect methods to reduce the sexual hyperesthesia which frequently exists" (338). He also recommends "psychic methods to refine and spiritualize the inverted impulse, so that the invert's natural perversion may not become a cause of acquired perversity in others" (338). Ellis opposes forcing a heterosexual relation on an invert; instead, he advocates a kind of proportion. At the same time, he suggests methods to spiritualize the inverted impulse, to redirect the interests in a kind of conversion. We, of course, remember Woolf's commentary on a prescription similar to Ellis's from Sir William Bradshaw in *Mrs. Dalloway*:

> Proportion, divine proportion, Sir William's goddess . . . Worshipping proportion, Sir William not only prospered himself but made England prosper, secluded her lunatics, forbade childbirth, penalised despair, made it impossible for the unfit to propagate their views until they, too, shared his sense of proportion. . . . But Proportion has a sister. . . . Conversion is her name and she feasts on the wills of the weakly, loving to impress, to impose, adoring her own features stamped on the face of the populace. (99–100)

Clarissa dislikes Sir William Bradshaw. "Why did the sight of him, talking to Richard, curl her up?" (*MD* 182), she wonders. "For think what cases came before him—people in the uttermost depths of misery; people on the verge of sanity; husbands and wives" (182). "She had once gone with some one to ask his advice. He had been perfectly right; extremely sensible." "Yet—what she felt was, one wouldn't like Sir William to see one unhappy" (182).[17]

Despite this disdain, Clarissa cultivates the proportion and control Sir William and the sexologists recommend. She rejects Peter Walsh's marriage proposal, fearing the heterosexual passion a life with him would require, choosing Richard, who grants her "a little license, a little independence" (7). She accepts responsibility for the lack of a sexual component in their marriage, acknowledging what Peter refers to as her "coldness," her "woodenness," her "impenetrability" (60). She remembers "when, through some contradiction of this cold spirit, she had failed [Richard]" (31). She admits that "she resented [sex], had a scruple picked up Heaven knows where, or, as she felt, sent by Nature (who is invariably wise)" (31). Whereas Septimus sees his homosexuality as a crime against nature, Clarissa accepts hers as a gift bestowed by nature in her wisdom. These beliefs allow Clarissa to withdraw into a chaste, impenetrable, nun-like existence where she feels "blessed and purified" (29), with "a virginity preserved through childbirth" (31).

Clarissa's proportion of marriage and chastity enables her both to maintain the appearance of conventionality and to acknowledge her attractions to women. "But this question of love (she thought, putting her coat away), this falling in love with women" (32). In Miss Pym's flower shop, she compares sweet peas and roses to young women, thinking "every flower seems to burn by itself, softly, purely in the misty beds" (13). This hot yet pure image helps Clarissa overcome her disgust for the overt sexuality she associates with Doris Kilman. It also opens her to her own lesbian sensuality: "a wave which she let flow over her and surmount that hatred, that monster, surmount it all; and it lifted her up and up" (13). Later, in the privacy of her own misty bed, she too burns "softly" and "purely": "[S]he could not resist sometimes yielding to the charm of a woman, not a girl, of a woman confessing, as to her they often did, some scrape, some folly. . . . [S]he did undoubtedly then feel what men felt. Only for a moment; but it was enough" (31–32).

To purify and spiritualize her own lesbianism, Clarissa relies on the trapped soul theory of same-sex love developed by Carpenter, Symonds, and Dickinson. Whereas Dickinson acknowledges his woman's soul, Clarissa associates her lesbianism with the privacy of the soul, the place where she can feel what men felt, where she can recognize women as the source of the central, erotic feelings that permeate,

> like a blush which one tried to check and then, as it spread, one yielded to
> its expansion, and rushed to the farthest verge and there quivered and felt
> the world come closer, swollen with some astonishing significance, some
> pressure of rapture, which split its thin skin and gushed and poured with
> an extraordinary alleviation over the cracks and sores! (32).

This orgasmic moment, this "match burning in a crocus," illuminates "an inner meaning almost expressed" (32). Moments like this, along with the memory of Sally's kiss, alleviate the cracks and sores of her sexless marriage. More significantly, they define the privacy of Clarissa's soul. Still, in her efforts to protect "the purity, the integrity, of her feeling for Sally" (34), Clarissa vacillates between self-deception and self-revelation about her own sexual preferences. This inner meaning, after all, is *almost* expressed.

Several critics note that Doris Kilman functions as Clarissa's alter ego. Kenneth Moon, for example, writes that Kilman "both provokes the fierce hatred from Clarissa and becomes at the same time the externalizing and informing image of what Clarissa detests and fears in herself" (149). Indeed, Moon calls Kilman Clarissa's "sexual alter ego" (150). Jane Marcus points out that Clarissa prefers to deny her desire rather than live Doris's life ("Niece" 10). Emily Jensen argues that Clarissa's feelings for Doris Kilman reveal her self-destructive rejection of her own lesbianism. "Kilman reminds Clarissa," Jensen writes, "of the choice she made to deny her love for women and marry respectably" (174). Lyndie Brimstone contends that Clarissa's disdain for Doris reflects in part her culture's abhorrence of spinsters. At the same time, Doris Kilman represents for Clarissa "the 'brutal monster' of culturally repressed desire that 'rasps' throughout the novel . . . " (101).

Doris Kilman's German origin associates her with the early German sexologists, and her name reflects the popular belief that all lesbians were man haters. At the same time, she conveys the message of feminism: "And every profession," Elizabeth recalls Doris telling her, "is open to the women of your generation. So she might be a doctor. She might be a farmer" (136). Indeed, Doris is a model of professional achievement: "She had her degree. She was a woman who had made her way in the world. Her knowledge of modern history was more than respectable" (132). Much like Ellis, who places such "girlish devotions" "on the borderland between friendship and sexual passion" (218), Richard Dalloway considers the relationship between Elizabeth and Doris "a phase . . . such as all girls go through" (11). Recognizing in Doris a reflection of her own lesbian desires, Clarissa intuits that this attachment "might be falling in love" (11); in fact, she envisions Doris as "Elizabeth's seducer" (175).

Unlike Clarissa, Doris Kilman is incapable of masking her own lesbian passion. On her shopping trip with Elizabeth, she desperately searches for feminine disguise, rummaging through a display of petticoats: "There were the petticoats, brown, decorous, striped, frivolous, solid, flimsy; and she chose, in her abstraction, portentously, and the girl serving thought her mad" (130). Although she tries to sublimate her desire with food—"The pleasure of eating was almost the only pure pleasure left her" (130)—the éclair she fingers and devours cannot compensate for losing Elizabeth: "Ah, but she must not go! Miss Kilman could not let her go! this youth, that was so beautiful, this girl, whom she genuinely loved! Her large hand opened and shut on the table" (131). Deserted by Elizabeth, Doris lurches about in a public display of her suffering; ultimately, she confronts her lesbian self "full length in a looking-glass" (133).

Doris chooses Ellis's prescription of spiritualizing the inverted impulse, converting her sexual desire into religious devotion. "The Lord had shown her the way. So now, whenever the hot and painful feelings boiled within her . . . she thought of God" (124). Conversion requires a constant battle against her passions, as Doris reminds herself. "It was the flesh that she must control," "the fleshly desires" (128). But conversion, as Woolf's narrator warns, "feasts on the wills" (100) of women such as Doris Kilman, miring her in self-hatred. Her body is to her an "infliction" (128). "She could not help being ugly" (128), Doris thinks, and this helplessness inspires in her a "violent grudge against the world which had scorned her, sneered at her, cast her off" (129). Describing Doris's attempts at conversion, the narrator concludes: "(it was so rough the approach to her God—so tough her desires)" (134). Her efforts at conversion ultimately fail since she cannot overcome her desire for Elizabeth.

As Clarissa recognizes Doris's lesbian desires, on some level Doris too perceives Clarissa's lesbian identity. "Clarissa Dalloway . . . had revived the fleshly desires. . . . But why wish to resemble her? Why?" (128). Doris resents Clarissa for her reserve and her seeming ability to control her own lesbian passion: "But why should she have to suffer," Doris ponders to herself, "when other women, like Clarissa Dalloway, escaped?" (129). Whereas Clarissa's lesbian feelings gush, pour, and alleviate her desire, Doris remains trapped by the "hot and turbulent feelings" for Elizabeth that boil and surge within her (124).

> She was about to split asunder, she felt. The agony was so terrific. If she could grasp her, if she could clasp her, if she could make her hers absolutely and forever and then die; that was all she wanted. But to sit here, unable to think of anything to say; to see Elizabeth turning against her; to be felt repulsive even by her—it was too much; she could not stand it. The thick fingers curled inwards. (132)

Like the woman in Ellis's case study, Doris is haunted by so-called disturbing temptations to nastiness. Incapable of repressing or sublimating these desires, she, like Septimus, is tormented by the agony of inextinguishable longings. Clarissa's erotic lesbian feelings leave her, as we have seen, "swollen with some astonishing significance, some pressure of rapture, which split its thin skin" (32). In contrast, the agony of unrequited lesbian love splits Doris asunder. Woolf illustrates how Doris internalizes the case studies of the sexologists and their perversions of lesbian desire. Tragically, she sees herself as repulsive; her fingers have indeed "curled inwards."

Confronted with the intensity and public display of Doris's lesbian passion, Clarissa loses her sense of proportion. To contain her own sexuality within acceptable private boundaries, she constructs the other, just as the sexologists do. Doris Kilman as lesbian thus becomes the object of her disdain. "Horrible passion! she thought. Degrading passion! she thought, thinking of Kilman and her Elizabeth walking to the Army and Navy Stores" (127). To preserve the purity, integrity, and privacy of her sapphic moments, Clarissa categorizes Doris Kilman, the "prehistoric monster" (126), with her public passion, as lesbian, as deviant, as other. For Clarissa, Doris Kilman embodies the sexologists' perversion of lesbian passion and desire.

At the same time, Clarissa half acknowledges what she is doing, realizing that the monstrous lesbianism she associates with Doris "had gathered in to itself a great deal that was not Miss Kilman" (12). "For it was not her one hated but the idea of her" (16). The idea of Doris as lesbian coincides with Clarissa's idea of her own lesbian passion and becomes "one of those spectres with which one battles in the night; one of those spectres who stand astride us and suck up half our life-blood" (12). Failing to project this distortion of lesbianism completely onto the other forces Clarissa to recognize the so-called monstrous lesbian within:

> It rasped her, though, to have stirring about in her this brutal monster! to hear twigs cracking and feel hooves planted down in the depths of that leaf-encumbered forest, the *soul*; never to be content quite, or quite secure, for at any moment the brute would be stirring, . . . as if indeed there were a monster grubbing at the roots. (12; emphasis added)

Throughout the years, Sally's kiss embodies the private treasure of her soul, "a diamond, something infinitely precious, wrapped up" (35). This hidden, "wrapped up" "diamond" represents the core of Clarissa's self, the inner meaning almost expressed: "That was her self when some effort, some call on her to be her self, drew the parts together, she alone knew how different, how incompatible and composed so for the world only into one centre, one diamond" (37). Clarissa recognizes her difference, her inner incompatibility with the public identity "Mrs. Dalloway" that she composes for the world. Despite her outward composure, the lesbian within threatens to stir the tranquility of that "leaf-encumbered forest, the soul."

She admires Septimus for dying with his secret intact. "Suppose he had had that passion?" she wonders. Sir William, who she recognizes as "without sex or lust," was capable "of some indescribable outrage—forcing your soul," insisting that Septimus reveal the secret of his own trapped soul (184). Rather than disclose the truth of his homosexuality, Clarissa rightly imagines that Septimus "plunged holding his treasure" (184). On some level, Clarissa perceives Septimus's failure to speak out as protecting her private lesbian passion.

But if Septimus's suicide somehow preserves "the privacy of the soul," Clarissa fears that "The odious Kilman would destroy it" (126–27). In fact, the narrator suggests that Doris might locate and expose the secret of Clarissa's lesbian desires. "[I]t was not the body," Doris realizes, "it was [Clarissa's] *soul*" (125). Thus, as the narrator puts it, "there rose in [Doris] an overmastering desire . . . *to unmask her*" (125; emphasis added).

Yet on another level, Clarissa longs for someone to unmask her secret lesbian passions. She, too, tires "of being herself invisible, unseen; unknown" (11). At the height of her party, she sees its "hollowness" (174) and thinks instead of Doris Kilman: "That was satisfying; that was real" (174–75). Indeed, the reality of Doris's lesbian existence enables Clarissa to release the lesbian trapped within her soul. Doris inspires Clarissa to name—at least to herself—her lesbian desires, and to recognize as positive and satisfying the lesbianism of other women. Clarissa is too insightful to fail to see that "with another throw of the dice, had the black been uppermost and not the white, she would have loved Miss Kilman!" (17). After all, Clarissa knows that it is in this inverted world that Sally's kiss lingers— ". . . the most exquisite moment of her whole life . . . Sally stopped; picked a flower; kissed her on the lips. The whole world might have turned upside down!" (35). And, as contemporary lesbians would tell her, those exquisite moments, along with the mischief they inspire, can last a lifetime.

NOTES

1. See Barry; Daly, *Gyn/Ecology*; Dworkin; and Raymond, among others, for discussions of sexual politics that influenced lesbian feminists like myself in the 1970s and 1980s.

2. See Jeffreys, *Spinster*. Her chapters titled "Feminism and Social Purity" and "Women's Friendships and Lesbianism" have been especially helpful to me.

3. Ray Strachey's *The Cause* was Woolf's main source in *Three Guineas*.

4. In 1922, Edith Craig produced two plays by Beatrice Mayor. Woolf attended the rehearsal; in her diary she describes Edith Craig as "a rosy, ruddy 'personage' in white waistcoat, with black bow tie & gold chain loosely knotted" (*D* 2: 174). See Holledge on Edy Craig and Christabel Marshall, and on their work with the Actresses' Franchise League and the Pioneer Players.

5. See Marcus's "Sapphistry"; Rosenman's "Sexual Identities"; and Zimmerman"s "Chloe" for discussion of *A Room of One's Own* as lesbian narratives.

6. In the 1930s, Chris St. John, friend as well as biographer of Ethel Smyth, had a brief affair with Vita Sackville-West. This affair caught Woolf in a snafu with Smyth, the defender of the distraught St. John, and Sackville-West, the thoughtless though never malicious flirt (Glendinning 263–64).

7. Founded in July 1914, the British Society for the Study of Sex Psychology established its headquarters in Bloomsbury in the 1920s. According to Porter and Hall, "The Society attracted a cross-section of individuals interested in the open study of sexual phenomena: as well as those who desired greater understanding of the problems of the homosexual" (182). In 1918, Lytton Strachey provided Woolf with "an amazing account of the British Sex Society." The sound, she wrote in her diary, "would suggest a third variety of human being . . . I think of being a member" *(D* 1: 110).

8. The lesbian characters in Aimée Duc's 1903 German novel *Are These Women?*, for example, advocate dissuading their lesbian sisters from marriage: "[I]t is the duty," one character exhorts the others, "the sacred duty of each one of us who belongs to the third sex to warn our undecided sisters against marriage, those whose conditions we easily recognize with knowing eyes and the feeling of solidarity . . . " (qtd. in Faderman and Erikssons 6).

9. See also McNaron, "'Albanians'"; Olano, "'Women Alone'"; and Roof for lesbian readings of *Mrs. Dalloway*.

10. Margaret Symonds collaborated with her father on a series of essays, *Our Life in the Swiss Highlands*, published in 1891. According to Wayne Koestenbaum, the essays J. A. Symonds contributed to this volume were "explicitly homoerotic—racier than most of his published work" (64). In 1925, Woolf reviewed *Out of the Past*, Margaret Symonds Vaughan's memoir about her father (*CE* 4: 12–13). In her introduction to previously unpublished letters between Woolf and Katharine Furse, Symonds's youngest daughter, Fowler notes that "All Symonds's daughters seem to have been well aware of their father's homosexuality" (201). Moreover, the letters reveal Woolf's keen interest in discussing "the forbidden topics" of sexual preferences; "I'm glad to think that now we needn't hush up so much" (207). Woolf urges Furse to be forthright in her proposed biography about her

father's homosexuality. Referring to male homosexuals of her acquaintance, Woolf writes "how much interest there is among them about him," concluding that "they all wish the question openly discussed; and a woman could do it more openly" (218). John Addington Symonds's memoirs, to which these letters refer, remained unpublished until 1984.

11. See Tyler for a discussion of Whitman's influence on Woolf's depiction of lesbianism.

12. Anne Olivier Bell describes Sir George Savage (1842–1921) as "a distinguished physician who specialised in the treatment of mental diseases" (D 1: 31). An old friend and medical advisor of the Stephen family, he treated Woolf from as early as 1904. Savage served as at least a partial model for Sir William Bradshaw.

13. J. A. Symonds collaborated with Ellis on *Sexual Inversion*, which included Symonds's case study. After Symonds's death in 1893, at the request of family representatives, his name was removed from the book. See Grosskurth; Koestenbaum; and Weeks, *Sex, Politics, and Society*. In her letters to Furse, Woolf refers to the account of his homosexuality, case XVII, that Symonds supplied to Ellis (Fowler 218).

14. For discussion of Edith Ellis and her relationships with women, see White and Grosskurth. One anecdote about Edith Ellis's lesbian relationships resonates for me. At the turn of the century, while staying in St. Ives, Edith had a love affair with a woman artist named Lily (Grosskurth 211). See Grosskurth for a 1902 photograph of Lily.

15. Edith Oldham Ellis asked her friends to contribute the lesbian case studies. One case is based on her own sexual experiences with women. Grosskurth quotes a letter from Havelock Ellis to Symonds on this topic: "'Many thanks for congratulations on my marriage. My wife—I may say—is most anxious I should collaborate and can supply cases of inversion in women from among her friends'" (178).

16. Brimstone analyzes Lady Bruton, Milly Brush, and Doris Kilman in the context of cultural attitudes toward spinsterhood and lesbianism in the 1920s. She too notes the masculine qualities of "the indomitable army general's daughter, Lady Bruton (brute one)" (102). This pun further associates Lady Bruton with lesbianism. Clarissa envisions her lesbianism as "this brutal monster," "the brute . . . stirring" (MD 17).

17. Poole compares Sir William Bradshaw to Dr. Henry Head, a physician with whom the Woolfs consulted in 1913. As numerous biographers note, Woolf's depression and suicide attempt during this time indicated, among other things, her unhappiness in her first year of married life. In 1930, Woolf summed up the experience to Ethel Smyth: "I married Leonard Woolf in 1912, I think, and almost immediately was ill for 3 years" (L 4: 151). Head was also known, as Woolf remarks years later in her diary, for his so-called ability to convert homosexuals (D 3: 193).

ELEVEN

Bringing Buried Things to Light
Homoerotic Alliances in
To the Lighthouse

RUTH VANITA

Bloomsbury inherited from such literary forebears as the Romantics and Wilde's circle the aspiration to a chosen community of friends and lovers —an aspiration visible in the lives and work of E. M. Forster, Lytton Strachey, Vanessa Bell, and Virginia Woolf. Crucial to this chosen community was the sharing of unsanctioned and unconventional sexual preferences, especially homosexual preferences. I see Woolf's alliances with her male homosexual friends, and her writing of such alliances and supportive community into her fictions, as of vital importance to her construction of relationships between women.[1] Feminist and lesbian criticism has tended to downplay the significance of these alliances in favor of Woolf's alliances with women. For instance, Phyllis Rose refers to "the masculine exclusivity of Bloomsbury, what Noel Annan has called 'the homosexual conspiracy'" (46), and Madeline Moore terms Lytton Strachey's homosexuality, as distinct from that of Duncan Grant and Maynard Keynes, "unquestionably misogynist" (19), apparently using this term synonymously with an exclusive sexual preference for men. Living in a society where homosexuality tends to be relatively invisible and unspoken, and where feminist activism has been wary of acknowledging lesbian presence, I have found the friendship and support of homosexual men crucial to survival and to the building of an identity, even when political differences exist (as they exist even among lesbians). I have a particular interest, therefore, in Woolf's ongoing dialogue with her male homosexual friends.

These friends who constituted Bloomsbury and its fringes shared a sense of being not so much outcasts—although that too was a word they used—as outsiders. In one real sense an elite, they were, in another equally real sense, threatened and embattled, suffering too from continuing exclusion, even oppression. The dominant note in the love lives of such men as Lytton Strachey, G. L. Dickinson, and E. M. Forster was one of anguish induced by unrequited or partially requited, and often unexpressed, love. These men's acceptance of their homosexuality was a key factor in their easy acceptance of women as equals and confidantes. It is surely not accidental that Bloomsbury was perhaps the first literary constellation in England to have been presided over and represented to the world by two women.

Woolf was conscious of the importance of shared homosexuality in these friendships. On the death of G. L. Dickinson, she remarked that she had with him "the same sort of intimacy I had with Lytton and some others; though of course not nearly so close as with Lytton" (L 5: 85). In 1921, she had written to Roger Fry about G. L. Dickinson:

> I do my best to make him jump the rails. He has written a dialogue upon homosexuality which he won't publish, for fear of the effect upon parents who might send their sons to Kings: and he is writing his autobiography which he won't publish for the same reason. So you see what dominates English literature is the parents of the young men who might be sent to Kings. (L 2: 485)

In 1928, Woolf and Forster co-authored a letter to the editor of *The Nation* protesting the banning of *The Well of Loneliness*: "The subject matter of the book exists as a fact. . . . [Yet] novelists in England have now been forbidden to mention it. . . . Although it is forbidden as a main theme, may it be alluded to . . . ? Perhaps the Home Secretary will issue further orders on this point" (qtd. in Furbank 2: 154). In one of her many appreciative comments in her diary on the nature of her intimacy with Strachey, she wrote: "On Sunday Lytton came to tea. I was alone, for L. went to Margaret. I enjoyed it very much. Intimacy seems to me possible with him as with scarcely anyone; for, besides tastes in common, I like & think I understand his feelings" (D 1: 89).

On the one hand, Woolf found distasteful the deliberately cultivated effeminate mannerisms of the younger generation of male homosexuals like Eddy Sackville-West, remarking fastidiously: "They paint and powder, which wasn't the style in our day at Cambridge" (L 3: 155). Here she identifies herself with an older generation of homosexuals: "our day," an identification that, in this homosexual space, overrides her sense of exclusion from Cambridge as a woman. Despite her repudiation here of what she seems to see as effeminacy in men, the qualities she appreciated and praised in men were those normally associated with women—gentleness, shyness, modesty. To these qualities she was prepared to give unconditional praise: "But why not let oneself be content in the thought of Lytton—so true, gentle, infinitely nimble, & humane? I seldom rest long in complete agreement with anyone. But here I think one's feelings should be unqualified" (D 2: 243). It was not for nothing that she paid Strachey the compliment of calling him "a female friend" (L 1: 492); repeatedly, over the years, she stressed the uniqueness of their intimacy and noted how she hoarded up thoughts to share with him. He too had a strong desire for a life with her. Although the idea of marriage caused him to panic and withdraw his proposal to her (which she had accepted), he wrote, when she was on her honeymoon: "I saw you for such a short time the other day: it was tantalizing. I should like to see you every day for hours. I have always wanted to. Why is it impossible? Why is everything that is satisfactory in this life impregnated with unsatisfactoriness?" (Woolf and Strachey 42). Woolf's initial ridicule of Eddy and his friends gave way to liking and appreciation: "I like Eddy: I like the sharpness of his spine; his odd indivualities [sic] and angles" (L 3: 248). Their friendship developed to the point where she could tease and argue the question with him, even acknowledging herself to be irrationally prejudiced (L 4: 200).

Both in her life and in her work, talking about the relatively more visible phenomenon of male homosexuality was the route whereby Woolf was able to express her own anxieties and finally her own desire for a Sapphic relationship. Not only was talk of "buggery" and of Plato's *Symposium* the first spoken language of homosexuality that she encountered and used as a girl, but in a January 1924 letter to Jacques Raverat, she first expressed her desire for Vita Sackville-West via comments on male homosexuality and a sudden *volte-face*:

> Have you any views on loving one's own sex? All the young men are so inclined, and I can't help finding it mildly foolish. . . . Then the ladies, either in self-protection, or imitation or genuinely, are given to their sex too. My aristocrat . . . is violently Sapphic, and contracted such a passion for a woman cousin, that they fled to the Tyrol . . . I can't take either of these aberrations seriously. To tell you a secret, I want to incite my lady to elope with me next. (L 3: 155–56)

The disowning of "these aberrations" is clearly a blind for her own strong feelings. In her fictions, Woolf poses homosexual love against marriage, which is the symbol of the social order that thwarts individuality. In this specific kind of reworking of the mainstream English novel, Woolf works in a tradition that includes Pater, Wilde, Samuel Butler, and E. M. Forster. She is the first major woman writer to integrate herself into this homo-erotic literary tradition and mold it to her own ends, blending it with her concern for women's position in society.

Phyllis Rose suggests that St. John Hirst in *The Voyage Out* is modeled on Lytton Strachey; he has a more definite literary ancestor in Forster's Ansell in *The Longest Journey*.[2] The first half of the novel oscillates between presenting Hirst as a pompous misogynist and understanding his hostility to Rachel and to women in the context of his emotional isola-tion. The initial unsympathetic portrayal of Hirst gives way to an almost wholly internalized and sympathetic depiction in the second half. Hirst emerges as a rebel who breaks social codes to which Hewet conforms. In his rebellion Hirst finds allies in unconventional women—a pattern that recurs in Woolf's last novels. It is to Helen, not to Hewet, that Hirst con-fides the story of his life. The narrator's tone is detached, as if describing a fact that is neither to be blamed nor praised, when Hirst acknowledges that he is emotionally centered in his university friends: "When he began to consider them he found himself soothed and strengthened. . . . They gave him, certainly, what no woman could give him, not Helen even" (*VO* 208). In a less serious way, he also finds an ally in Mrs. Flushing, a sym-bol of aristocratic freedom of spirit. When he surreptitiously reads in church Swinburne's translation of Sappho's "Ode to Aphrodite" (a signif-icantly chosen constellation), she eagerly joins him. Hewet, however, objects to this and even quarrels with Hirst about it (*VO* 230).

The development of the friendship between Helen and Hirst parallels the mutual gravitation of Rachel and Hewet. Both Helen and Hirst are depressed, fearing an impending emotional loss. Helen's feelings are con-veyed through a striking image, which suggests the phallic entrance of Hewet into her Edenic love for Rachel: "Her sense of safety was shaken, as if beneath twigs and dead leaves she had seen the movement of a snake" (*VO* 263). The image is repeated a few pages later, this time by Hirst, when Helen tries to dissuade Rachel and Hewet from taking the walk in the for-est that is to decide their future: "'Good-bye!' cried Rachel.'Good-bye. Beware of snakes,' Hirst replied" (*VO* 270). Rachel's last words in the novel are a vehement protest against being displayed as an engaged woman, and her last conscious wish is for aloneness. Hewet's desire for oneness, which is in fact a desire to absorb Rachel into himself, stands in contrast to Hirst's desire for the sight of Helen, which revives him despite, even because of, distance: "It was asking a good deal of Hirst to tell him to go without waiting for a sight of Helen. These little glimpses of Helen were the only respites from strain and boredom, and very often they seemed to make up for the discomfort of the day . . ." (VO 336).

The novel ends with Hirst's vision, and this figure looks forward to much that is significant in Woolf's work. In *Jacob's Room*, the depiction of Bonamy's love for Jacob comes closest to a romantic depiction. As Ian Young has suggested, "Gay novels . . . have been among the last remaining examples of Romantic literature" because they deal with "the struggle to discover, create or sustain personal values in the face of social hostility" (160). In her depiction of this love rooted in a Forsterian university-based friendship, Woolf uses the image of the spaniel that was to recur in her work, at greatest length in *Flush*, as an image of unrequited homosexual love.[3] Words and images that were heavily encoded in the late nineteenth and early twentieth centuries surround this love and extend beyond it when the narrator muses on what is valuable in life: "A strange thing— when you come to think of it—this love of Greek, flourishing in such obscurity, distorted, discouraged, yet leaping out, all of a sudden . . . always a miracle" (*JR* 76). And again: "Plato and Shakespeare continue" (*JR* 109). "Greek love" was, in the writings of such men as J. A. Symonds, G. L. Dickinson, and Edward Carpenter, virtually the equivalent of the term "gay love" today, and was well enough known outside of these circles for Robert Browning to apply it to the two women lovers who wrote under the pseudonym "Michael Field."[4] "Strange" was similarly encoded in the writings of Pater and Wilde. Plato and Shakespeare were repeatedly invoked in tandem by all of these writers as homoerotic ancestors.[5]

Woolf had connections, through family or friends, with these "other Victorians." One of the first women she fell in love with, Madge Vaughan, was the daughter of J. A. Symonds. Symonds, an early researcher on homosexuality, was a friend of Leslie Stephen. Roger Fry was a friend of Symonds, and of Ricketts and Shannon, the homosexual artist couple who were close friends of "Michael Field." Woolf's father, a contemporary of these flourishing circles of highly influential homosexuals, was himself a resolute exemplar of rigidly patriarchal heterosexuality. Or was he so rigid, after all? *To the Lighthouse* suggests the fascinating possibility that he too may have had "university friendships" of the kind Jacob had, although he may have refused to acknowledge their significance.

Mr. Bankes and Mr. Carmichael visit the Ramsay household, much as

Symonds (and other homoerotically inclined men—Henry James, for example) visited the Stephen household. Mr. Bankes makes his first appearance in chapter four, through Lily's consciousness, at a moment when she is reflecting on the "absurdity" and "impossibility" of revealing to Mrs. Ramsay her feelings for her. She feels under immense stress, compelled as she is to "control her impulse to fling herself . . . at Mrs. Ramsay's knee" and declare these feelings for which, however, she cannot find appropriate names (*TTL* 19). At this moment, William Bankes enters her consciousness as a person with whom she can wordlessly share her suppressed feelings:

> So now she laid her brushes neatly in the box, side by side, and said to William Bankes:
> "It suddenly gets cold. The sun seems to give less heat," she said, looking about her, for it was bright enough, the grass still a soft deep green, the house starred in its greenery with purple passion flowers and rooks dropping cool cries from the high blue. But something moved, flashed, turned a silver wing in the air. It was September, after all, the middle of September, and past six in the evening. (*TTL* 19)

The imagery here suggests the passing of life and a sense of passion missed; the alluring green, purple, blue, and silver are countered by the growing cold and by the sun losing its heat on an autumn evening. As Lily and William Bankes set out for their walk, the imagery more and more strongly suggests a guarded and suppressed erotic desire they cannot express:

> So off they strolled down the garden in the usual direction, past the tennis lawn, past the pampas grass, to *that break in the thick hedge, guarded by red-hot pokers* like braziers of clear burning coal. . . .
> They came there regularly every evening *drawn by some need*. It was as if the water floated off and set sailing *thoughts which had grown stagnant* on dry land, and gave to their *bodies even some sort of physical relief.* (*TTL* 19–20; emphasis added)

The sight they "watch" and "wait for" as a "delight" is a "fountain of white water" that "spurted irregularly" (*TTL* 20). The fountain in *To the Lighthouse* is an erotically charged image, appearing most famously when Mrs. Ramsay's "fountain and spray of life" is aggressively "plunged" into by Mr. Ramsay's phallic "beak of brass, the arid scimitar" (*TTL* 38). Here its orgasmic quality does not link Lily and Bankes or even emanate from them; they stand apart from one another and at a distance from the fountain. What they share is a vision. They are observers, and their "common hilarity" gives way to "some sadness—because the thing was completed partly" (*TTL* 20).

The sense of distance and of unfulfillment or partial fulfillment is linked not with heterosexual but with homosexual feeling, as is evident from the narrative's immediately sliding into Mr. Bankes' memories of his youthful relationship with Mr. Ramsay, which was broken off by the latter's marriage:

> Looking at the far sand hills, William Bankes thought of Ramsay: thought of a road in Westmorland, thought of Ramsay striding along a road by himself hung round with that solitude which seemed to be his natural air. But this was suddenly interrupted, William Bankes remembered . . . by a hen, straddling her wings out in protection of a covey of little chicks, upon which Ramsay, stopping, pointed his stick and said "Pretty—pretty," an odd illumination into his heart, Bankes had thought it, which showed his simplicity, his sympathy with humble things; but it seemed to him as if their friendship had ceased, there, on that stretch of road. After that, Ramsay had married. After that, what with one thing and another, the pulp had gone out of their friendship. (*TTL* 20–21)

Bankes feels let down by Mr. Ramsay's unexpected appreciation of domesticity and parenthood; however, his own feelings remain unchanged, and the characterization of these feelings reveals them as not merely intellectual but as erotically charged:

> But in this dumb colloquy with the sand dunes he maintained that his affection for Ramsay had in no way diminished; but there, like the body of a young man laid up in peat for a century, with the red fresh on his lips, was his friendship, in its acuteness and reality, laid up across the bay among the sandhills. (*TTL* 21)

The language emphasizes the physicality of his feeling for Ramsay and its untimely but only partial death occasioned by the latter's marriage. This metaphorical death recalls many similar moments in Woolf's work: for instance, the death of Evans associated with Septimus Smith's marriage and the death of Clarissa's erotic self with her marriage.[6] The death here is troped as a burial alive, rather like the mock deaths of such figures as Snow White and Shakespeare's Imogen. Although buried, the young man's body remains "fresh," "acute," and "real." The terms in which it is conceived recall such celebrations of male beauty as Shakespeare's *Sonnets,* and the poet's promise that his verse will keep the beloved ever young and fair even after physical death and entombment have taken place. The *Sonnets* were an underground password among turn-of-the-century English homosexuals, their significance elaborated in such texts as Wilde's "The Portrait of Mr. W. H."

At stake here is the evaluation of homoerotic emotion. Bankes' own deepest feeling is that his attraction to Ramsay is alive and beautiful, although buried, and that, by marrying, Ramsay betrayed both their friendship and his own potential: "as if he had seen him divest himself of all those glories of isolation and austerity which crowned him in youth to cumber himself definitely with fluttering wings and clucking domesticities" (*TTL* 22). Remembering the past, Bankes is forced to acknowledge the stagnancy of the friendship in the present: "repetition had taken the place of newness. It was to repeat that they met" (TTL 21).[7] He also feels acutely sensitive to his own exclusion from the world of passion conventionally symbolized by flowers:

> Mr. Bankes was alive to things which would not have struck him had not those sandhills revealed to him the body of his friendship lying with the red on its lips laid up in peat—for instance, Cam . . . would not "give a flower to the gentleman" as the nursemaid told her. (*TTL* 21)

Cam (who bears the name of the river flowing through Cambridge, site of so many homosexual attachments among men in Woolf's circle), by her refusal, triggers in Bankes an awareness of society's condemnation of him, its stigmatization of his "wrong" loyalty to the buried friendship: "And Mr. Bankes felt aged and saddened and somehow put into the wrong by her about his friendship. He must have dried and shrunk" (*TTL* 22).

Describing the sensibility of the woman artist in *A Room of One's Own*, Woolf had used the image of burial: "it ranged too, very subtly and curiously, among almost unknown or unrecorded things: it lighted on small things and showed that perhaps they were not small after all. It brought buried things to light and made one wonder what need there had been to bury them" (92). She figures the woman artist here as one who retrieves the past. Bankes' friendship, buried in the landscape of his mind, is described in an odd phrase as "laid up in peat for a century" (*TTL* 21). The mention of a century suggests that more is involved than one lifetime or one relationship. If Woolf is rewriting her father's youth, this goes back to the mid-nineteenth century; however, from the perspective of Bankes himself, a century would take the phenomenon back to at least the beginning of the nineteenth century. I would like to suggest here a possible historical source for the figure of William Bankes, a source that Woolf certainly came across, and that she may consciously or unconsciously have drawn upon.

William Bankes, who died in 1855, appears in *The Dictionary of National Biography*, edited by Leslie Stephen and Sydney Lee, as "the eldest surviving son of Henry Bankes of Kingston Hall, Dorsetshire . . . educated at Trinity College, Cambridge. . . . Byron, his contemporary, describes him as the leader of the set of college friends which included C. S. Matthews and Hobhouse. Bankes was Byron's friend through life" (1: 1044). Woolf would have come across Bankes in *Lord Byron's Correspondence*, a collection of about 350 formerly unpublished letters, which arrived from Mudie's on February 18, 1922 and which she declared herself eager to read immediately.[8] She was also familiar enough with Thomas Moore's *Life, Letters, and Journals of Lord Byron* (published in two volumes in 1830 and reprinted in 1832) to refer to it in a reading note on Beau Brummell.[9]

Moore's collection contains several admiring references by Byron to Bankes. Byron describes Bankes as "my collegiate pastor, and master, and patron" (60). There are a total of nine letters to Bankes here, spanning a period of well over a decade. Byron confides his sorrow for two deceased male lovers: "the only beings I ever loved, females excepted; I am therefore a solitary animal, miserable enough" (42). Bankes, in turn, makes claims on Byron's affection, complains of neglect on account of Byron's "superabundance of friends," and bids Byron "farewell" since the latter does not write frequently enough (173). Byron responds with reassurances. The letters are pervaded by a tone of deep intimacy. For instance, in a highly flirtatious letter of February 19, 1820, inviting Bankes to Ravenna, Byron writes: "Neither dangers nor tropical heats have ever prevented your penetrating wherever you had a mind to it, and why should the snow now? . . . all your evenings, and as much as you can give me of your nights, will be mine" (435).

What *The Dictionary of National Biography* carefully refrains from mentioning in its entry on William Bankes is that this Dorset Member of Parliament and lifelong friend of Byron was twice arrested for homosexual offences—once on June 7, 1833, and again in 1841. On the first occasion he was with a soldier, Private Flower, in a public lavatory in Westminster, at ten at night, and the soldier's breeches were unbuttoned. The Duke of Wellington, the Earl of Ripon, and the Master of Harrow stood as character witnesses at Bankes' trial, and he raised three thousand pounds bail and was acquitted. The second arrest was for the same kind of offence.[10] Whether or not Woolf was aware, from Bloomsbury's

active interest in the history of homosexuality, of these incidents, so reminiscent of episodes in Forster's stories such as "Arthur Snatchfold," she
would certainly have decoded the Bankes-Byron letters, whose language
is not substantially different from that of Strachey's or Forster's letters.[11]

William Bankes' case, then, was a signal case of the status of male
homosexuality in Victorian England. His class position rescued him from
the final disgrace that Private Flower and, later, Wilde suffered (difference
in class accounting for differential treatment of homosexuals is com-
mented on by Forster in his Terminal Note to *Maurice*, where he perceives
it as a continuing phenomenon).[12] However, the primary emotional reality of Bankes' life remained invisible in literary history, as monumentalized
by such commentators as Woolf's father. He was included in *The
Dictionary of National Biography* as an intellectual, a writer, and an ama-
teur archaeologist "known to the literary world by his travels to the East.
He . . . translated from the Italian in 1830 an autobiographical memoir of
Giovanni Finati, with whom he travelled in Egypt and the East. In 1815 he
discovered an ancient Egyptian obelisk in the island of Philae . . . "
(Stephen and Lee 1044). Bankes' travels to Italy, Egypt and "the East," like
those of A. E. Housman, Forster, and Ackerley, had much to do with a
search for freer homosexual adventure. Byron's letter, quoted earlier, alludes to this; the *Dictionary*, of course, does not. The *Dictionary* reduces
Bankes' choice of singleness to sterility, noting that (like Woolf's Bankes,
who is a childless widower) he died (interestingly, in Venice!) "leaving no
issue" (Stephen and Lee 1044).

The unusual spelling of the surname "Bankes" (instead of "Banks")
strengthens the possibility that Woolf commemorates and rewrites a chosen ancestor in *To the Lighthouse*.[13] Her rewritten fictional Bankes stands
in relation to Mr. Ramsay (her father rewritten) somewhat as men like
the historical William Bankes stood in relation to Leslie Stephen. If Leslie
Stephen rewrote Bankes by suppressing his homosexuality, Bankes has
his revenge in Stephen's Sapphic daughter's book, where he collaborates
with Lily Briscoe to critique Mr. Ramsay's intellectual dishonesty, characterized by Lily as "blindness" and "narrowness" and by Bankes, less
charitably, as "hypocrisy" and "concealment":

> [H]is little dodges deceived nobody. What she disliked was his narrowness,
> his blindness, she said, looking after him.
>   "A bit of a hypocrite?" Mr. Bankes suggested, looking, too, at Mr.
> Ramsay's back, for was he not thinking of his friendship, and of Cam refus-
> ing to give him a flower? (*TTL* 46)

If Cam turns out to be her father's daughter at the end of the book, her refusal of the flower to Mr. Bankes connects in his mind with Ramsay's denial of the full meaning of their friendship, his killing of it before it could flower.[14]

In the *Dictionary*, the loves of William Bankes could not be mentioned because homosexuality was a nameless abomination; in *To the Lighthouse*, it is Mr. Ramsay who literally and metaphorically has no name. We are never told the first name of either Mr. or Mrs. Ramsay—their personal identity is swallowed up by their conjugal identity. In his philosophical explorations of the nature of reality, Mr. Ramsay reaches "Q" but is at that point interrupted by the sight of "his wife and son, together, in the window. They needed his protection; he gave it them. But after Q? What comes next?" "A shutter, like the leathern eyelid of a lizard, flickered over the intensity of his gaze and obscured the letter R. . . . He would never reach R" (*TTL* 33–34). One irony here is that his wife and son are in no need of his protection and in fact experience his presence as an intrusion; the other irony is that R is his own initial. Domesticity and patriarchal imperatives prevent self-knowledge.

Later, we are told that "even his own name was forgotten by him" (*TTL* 44). This forgetfulness, contrasting as it does with Bankes' acute memory of the past, is ascribed to emotional fearfulness:

> [H]e had not done the thing he might have done. It was a disguise; it was the refuge of a man afraid to own his own feelings, who could not say, This is what I like—this is what I am; and rather pitiable and distasteful to William Bankes and Lily Briscoe, who wondered why such concealment should be necessary. (*TTL* 45)

In a remarkable maneuver, Woolf reverses the idea of the homosexual as one who fears, conceals, and disguises the self, suggesting instead that it is the respectably married who fearfully hide from themselves. Her parents' tragedy is that they could not do what they might have done. Conversely, tropes of concealment and revelation operate to suggest that the homoerotically inclined Lily and Bankes, pitied by the Ramsays, are able to reveal their buried selves to each other.

Lily has mixed feelings about both Mr. Bankes and Mr. Ramsay, and is critical of both for very different reasons, yet it is with the former that she enters into an alliance, sharing as she does with him the condition of singleness and solitude. It is with him that she chooses to share the painting containing her hidden love, her "vision" of Mrs. Ramsay:

[I]f it must be seen, Mr. Bankes was less alarming than another. But that any other eyes should see the residue of her thirty-three years, the deposit of each day's living, mixed with something more secret than she had ever spoken or shown in the course of all those days was an agony. At the same time it was immensely exciting. (*TTL* 52)

The language here strongly suggests the sharing of homoerotic feeling. At first, Mr. Bankes is not a perceptive viewer, but he takes in "complete good faith" her explanation, and she concludes: "This man had shared with her something profoundly intimate" (*TTL* 53). Lily thanks Mr. and Mrs. Ramsay's "world" for making possible this sharing, yet the sharing is not with either of them but with William Bankes. In a heterosexually defined world, the homosexually inclined man and woman share their buried secrets and develop a lifelong alliance. In the closing section of the book, Lily reflects: "Indeed, his friendship had been one of the pleasures of her life. She loved William Bankes" (*TTL* 176).

Lytton Strachey and E. M. Forster were among the readers of most importance to Woolf; she always anxiously awaited their reactions to her new books.[15] To Strachey, she wrote in 1919: "I don't suppose there's anything in the way of praise that means more to me than yours" (*L* 2: 394). Despite her moments of aversion to male homosexuality and Forster's to lesbianism, she and he continued to talk "of sodomy, & Sapphism, with emotion" (*D* 3: 193).[16] It is important that the conversation continued, with an acknowledgment of the irrational nature of each one's aversion. In 1925, she counted Strachey and Forster among the half-dozen most important people in her life: "But then if 6 people died, it is true that my life would cease. . . . Imagine Leonard, Nessa, Duncan, Lytton, Clive, Morgan all dead" (*D* 3: 48).

The idea of this kind of sharing is repeated in "The Lighthouse" section, where Mr. Carmichael takes Mr. Bankes' place as Lily's secret sharer. At this point, unlike Mr. Ramsay, who is overwhelmed with sympathy from all quarters when he loses his wife, and demands such sympathy, Lily is not even perceived by others as a mourner: "No one had seen her step off her strip of board into the waters of annihilation. She remained a skimpy old maid, holding a paint-brush on the lawn" (*TTL* 181). She conquers her pain and absorbs it into her "ordinary experience," but it recurs (as did Mr. Bankes' pain over his lost friendship) since it is part of that experience, both past and present: "'Mrs. Ramsay! Mrs. Ramsay!' she cried, feeling the old horror come back—to want and want and not to have. Could she inflict that still?" (*TTL* 202). The phrasing indicates that Mrs. Ramsay inflicted this pain on Lily during her lifetime too. The pain of mourning a death merges with the pain of mourning a love made impossible and, as it were, killed by marriage.

Lily organizes her anguish and also completes her understanding of Mrs. Ramsay through the painting. It is therefore appropriate that she shares the completed painting with Mr. Carmichael, as she had shared the half-finished painting with Mr. Bankes. As Bankes' half-complete friendship with Mr. Ramsay paralleled Lily's incompletely realized relationship with Mrs. Ramsay, so Carmichael's transmutation of his loss of Andrew Ramsay parallels Lily's transmutation of her loss of Mrs. Ramsay.

The Carmichael–Andrew relationship is an exquisite little cameo traced as if with invisible ink beneath the surface of the text.[17] It is first indicated by Mrs. Ramsay, who, feeling that Carmichael disapproves of and shrinks from her, notices "how devoted he was to Andrew, and would call him into his room and, Andrew said,'show him things'" (*TTL* 96). The other meaning of the word "thing" would be familiar to any reader of Shakespeare's *Sonnets*, its most famous use being in the master–mistress sonnet where Nature, framing the beloved, tries to frustrate his male lover "By adding one thing to my purpose nothing." In "The Lighthouse" section, Lily recalls

> that when he had heard of Andrew Ramsay's death (he was killed in a second by a shell . . .) Mr. Carmichael had "lost all interest in life." What did it mean—that? she wondered. . . . She did not know what he had done, when he heard that Andrew was killed, but she felt it in him all the same. (*TTL* 194)

What Mr. Carmichael "had done" is revealed in the "Time Passes" section. Chapter six of that section has four parenthetic insertions, of which the first two relate to Prue Ramsay's marriage and death. The third and fourth tell of Andrew's death and suggest Carmichael's response, respectively:

> [A shell exploded. Twenty or thirty young men were blown up in France, among them Andrew Ramsay, whose death, mercifully, was instantaneous.] . . . [Mr. Carmichael brought out a volume of poems that spring, which had an unexpected success. The war, people said, had revived their interest in poetry.] (*TTL* 133–34)

The process of mourning, loss, and recuperation through art is viewed externally and from a distance in the case of Carmichael, and in Lily's case with excruciating inwardness, but they go through a similar experience: "They had not needed to speak. They had been thinking the same things and he had answered her without her asking him anything" (*TTL* 208), we are told.

Two years after *To the Lighthouse*, Woolf wrote *A Room of One's Own*, in which she chose to name the woman author of sapphic fiction Mary Carmichael. "Mary" is the name of the virgin who creates without the intervention of a man; it is also the name of the feminist who chooses not to marry in *Night and Day*. The unusual surname, however, must link to Woolf's earlier use of it.[18] If *To the Lighthouse* is about chosen ancestors, spiritual and literary, as much as about biological ancestors, is Augustus Carmichael, author of elegiac love poems for a man, the "parent" of Mary Carmichael, author of a novel about Chloe, who likes Olivia?

NOTES

This essay is dedicated to Sanju Mahale and Saleem Kidwai, whose friendship has been one of the pleasures of my life.

1. In this formulation, I follow such theorists as Christine Downing. The present essay is part of my book *Sappho and the Virgin Mary: Same-Sex Love and the English Literary Imagination*, which examines the shared languages, tropes, and literary ancestries of homoeroticism in texts by both men and women from the Romantic period to Bloomsbury.

2. Bernard Blackstone points this out: "St. John Hirst is an E. M. Forster character. He reminds us irresistibly of Ansell in *The Longest Journey* (26).

3. See my essay "Love Unspeakable" for a fuller exposition.

4. A letter from Edith Cooper to Alice Trusted, dated May 1888, reports a visit by herself and Katharine Bradley to Browning and his addressing them as "my two dear Greek women" (qtd. in Sturgeon 40). For one use of the term "Greek love," see Symonds, *A Problem in Greek Ethics*: "I shall use the term *Greek Love*, understanding thereby a passionate and enthusiastic attachment subsisting between man and youth" (173; emphasis in original).

5. The openly homosexual poet Neville in *The Waves* invokes the same ancestry when he reflects on the intellectual tradition constructed by him and his friends: "Thus we spin round us infinitely fine filaments and construct a system. Plato and Shakespeare are included, also quite obscure people, people of no importance whatsoever. . . . To follow the dark paths of the mind and enter the past . . ." (TW 179–80). Notice the use in both passages of the word "obscure," which literally means "hidden."

6. See Jensen.

7. Bankes here articulates the feeling many gay people have about the kind of limited friendship that ensues when ex-lovers get married. Compare Rickie's

wish, in Forster's *The Longest Journey*, that there were a registry office where friendships could be registered and thus given the status of marriage.

8. See Murray for *Lord Byron's Correspondence*. See Woolf's comment, "the sight of the new Byron letters just come from Mudie's," and the editorial footnote (*D* 2: 160).

9. See Silver, *Virginia Woolf's Reading Notebooks*, for the reference to Woolf's note in the Holograph Reading Notes, Vol. 20, in the Berg Collection (113).

10. These details are from Bartlett (58–59) and Crompton.

11. In "Arthur Snatchfold," a prosperous elderly widower has a brief encounter with a young milkman; the latter, when arrested, goes to prison without betraying the former, who, when he later learns of this, notes the young man's name, Arthur Snatchfold, as that of "his lover, yes, his lover."

12. "Clive on the bench will continue to sentence Alec in the dock. Maurice may get off" (Forster, "Terminal Note" 255).

13. There is also a "William Banks" (1820–1872) in the *Dictionary*. He was famous for his manuals on walks in Yorkshire. Interestingly, Woolf also gave the name "William" to the homosexual Dodge in *Between the Acts*. Dodge reveals his first name to the two women who befriend him; toward the end of *To the Lighthouse*, Lily, after a lifetime's friendship with Bankes, thinks of him as "William" (as did Mrs. Ramsay) rather than as "Mr. Bankes." "William" was also the name of the most famous chosen ancestor of nineteenth-century English homosexuals, the Shakespeare of the *Sonnets*.

14. Eileen Barrett, in her comments on this essay, made the delightful suggestion that the private flower refused by Cam recalls Private Flower, whose encounter with the historical Bankes was rudely interrupted by the official representatives of Victorian society.

15. Thus, "the only judgment on Mrs. D. I await with trepidation (but thats too strong) is Morgan's. He will say something enlightening" (*D* 3: 22) and "Well, Morgan admires. This is a weight off my mind . . . kissed my hand and on going said he was awfully pleased" (*D* 3: 24). She declared herself more invigorated by Lytton's dislike of *Mrs. Dalloway* than by the praise of Clive and others (*D* 3: 32).

16. On this occasion, Forster acknowledged that "he thought Sapphism disgusting: partly from convention, partly because he disliked that women should be independent of men" (*D* 3: 193). That he realized this feeling was not rational, and did not base his political stance on it, is clear from the fact that a month later, he wrote the letter with Woolf, protesting the banning of *The Well*. Woolf made equally phobic remarks, comparing the atmosphere of what she termed a "Buggery Poke" party to that of a male urinal.

17. Hermione Lee notices in passing that Mr. Carmichael is "probably homosexual" but does not elaborate (172).

18. Suggestion made by Eileen Barrett, private communication.

TWELVE

Orlando: "A Precipice Marked V" Between "A Miracle of Discretion" and "Lovemaking Unbelievable: Indiscretions Incredible"

LESLIE KATHLEEN HANKINS

[19 November 1926]

You are *a miracle of discretion*—one letter in another. I never thought of that. I'll answer when I see you—the invitation, I mean.

> —*L* 3: 302; emphasis added

9th Oct. [1927]

Look, dearest what a lovely page this is, and think how, were it not for the screen and the [Mary] Campbell, it might all be filled to the brim with *lovemaking unbeliev- able: indiscretions incredible*: instead of which, nothing shall be said but what a Campbell behind the screen might hear.

> Yr V. W. (thats because of Campbell)
> —*L* 3: 427; emphasis added

March 23rd, 1927

Dearest Honey,

   Talking to Lytton the other night he suddenly asked me to advise him in love—whether to go on, over the precipice, or stop short at the top. Stop, stop! I cried, thinking instantly of you. Now what would happen if I

let myself go over? Answer me that. Over what? you'll
say. *A precipice marked V.*

Yr

Virginia

—*L* 3: 352; emphasis added

Orlando came out of the closet as a lesbian text in the 1970s and remains
out as critics continue to discover and celebrate its subversive, pervasive,
and persuasive lesbian strategies.[1] The complex and witty lesbian text
plays an elaborate game of hide and seek with the reader and the censor,
teasing with taunts: "What can we suppose that women do when they
seek out each other's society?" (*O* 220). Woolf's lesbian narrative in
Orlando suggests love and erotics between women, mocks compulsory
heterosexuality, challenges homophobia, and slips coded lesbian signatures and subplots into the novel. In the pivotal moment of the lesbian
narrative, after Orlando changes sex, the novel brilliantly outmaneuvers
the censor:

> "Love," said Orlando. Instantly—such is its impetuosity—love took a
> human shape—such is its pride. For where other thoughts are content to
> remain abstract nothing will satisfy this one but to put on flesh and blood,
> mantilla and petticoats, hose and jerkin. And as all Orlando's loves had
> been women, now, through the culpable laggardry of the human frame to
> adapt itself to convention, though she herself was a woman, it was still a
> woman she loved; and if the consciousness of being of the same sex had
> any effect at all, it was to quicken and deepen those feelings which she had
> had as a man. (160–61)

With this simple, understated passage, Woolf pulls a fast one on the censor, crafting a radical text that enables readers to repudiate homophobia
and experience lesbian desire. Because *Orlando* plays such complex games
with the censor, it is wise to enlist Vita and Virginia as decoders; their
crafty epistolary theory and practice help us to read between the lines of
their published intertexts, *Passenger to Teheran* and *Orlando*. Virginia and
Vita share their delight, writing letters as erotic exchanges, coding lesbian
elopement proposals and filling texts with flights of lesbian fancy.

But *Orlando* is not solely a lesbian text; it is a lesbian *feminist* one.
Reading *Orlando* as a lesbian feminist novel opens up fascinating net-

works of artistry and agency in the novel. Current bisexual, androgynous, or pansensual camp theories that relegate lesbian feminism to the
recycling bin of literary history[2] may direct our attention to Woolf's original agenda for the novel, which included her assertion of lesbian feminism in the face of opposition. The 1990s did not invent conflicts
between lesbian feminism and other voices in gay and lesbian culture;
they were there for Woolf in the 1920s. In *Orlando*, Woolf addresses
other Bloomsbury figures who seem vivid precursors of Queer theory
and performative camp—Lytton Strachey leaps to mind—and Sapphists
such as Vita who distanced themselves from feminism.[3] *Orlando* reminds
us that a queer theory into which feminism disappears without a trace
cannot contain Woolf's texts, for she refused gay male Bloomsbury's
misogyny, protesting against the views of E. M. Forster, who found
Sapphism disgusting; male bisexuals such as Maynard Keynes, who
basked in male privilege; and Sapphists who were not feminist. Subtly
addressing this vexing gay family, *Orlando* inextricably ties gay and lesbian issues with feminist ones through Woolf's fusion of perverse[4] sexualities with feminist consciousness. Throughout the novel, Woolf brings
feminism squarely into the queer realm by confronting the sexually
ambiguous protagonist with his/her own complicity in the misogynist
sex/gender system and by encouraging a feminist conversion experience.
In *Orlando*, as in *A Room of One's Own*, she educates the pre-feminist
Vita (as Orlando, captive audience on the deck of the *Enamoured Lady*)
by tutoring her in the facts of being female in a patriarchal culture.[5] By
tying lesbian erotics to feminist politics, Woolf seduces non-feminist lesbianism. We may reclaim *Orlando* as the longest and most charming *lesbian feminist* love letter in literature,[6] recognizing its narrative strategies
as specific responses to the heterosexist censorship and non-feminist gay
and lesbian cultures of Woolf's day.

Censorship and Seduction

The complex text of *Orlando* is a letter with multiple dueling addressees,
addressed not only to Woolf's "common reader" but lovingly to Vita (the
lesbian lover), mockingly to the censor (intent on banning lesbian love),
and polemically to straight, gay, and lesbian readers—and the tension
between the addressees provides much of the wit, delight, and power of
the novel. Woolf's lesbian signatures, messages, and strategies were
shaped by the brooding presence of the censor, for no lesbian writer in

1928 was immune from the perils of censorship. Woolf confronted censorship through political activism (attempting to testify in the Hall trial) and subversive artistry—incorporating protests against censorship in *Orlando*, as subject and strategy, and foregrounding the games censors require. She lampoons the censors and censorship trials in her outrageous mock masque trial and sex change at the centerpiece of *Orlando*. For her guerrilla attacks against the censors, Virginia used all the resources of her own fancy and appropriated tactics from allies. Vita's crafty "miracle of discretion" that hid a letter within a letter to pass an invitation to Virginia behind the back of her husband (the Censor in the House) offered one intriguing model.

Placing Woolf's strategies in *Orlando* within the censoring climate of her day reveals the text as both an accommodation to censorship and a profoundly witty and powerful critique of censorship.[7] Always aware of the looming figure of the Beadle-like censor waiting and watching, Woolf addressed *Orlando* to the censor as well as to Vita. The mocking, teasing tone she adopts serves both of her purposes—to taunt and to seduce.[8] If Woolf chose to laugh at the censor, however, it was her tactical choice, not a sign that censorship was a laughing matter for lesbian writers who had to decide how to cope with the specter of the censor. Some chose to publish privately. Some (such as Radclyffe Hall) braved censorship trials. Vita was confronted with these options when she planned to publish her 1924 lesbian text *Challenge*, a thinly veiled autobiographical novel about her lesbian elopement with Violet Trefusis. She decided to comply with the censor, rewriting the novel to change the sex of one of the lesbian lovers to provide the required heterosexual couple, and also chose to suppress the novel in England.

What, then, were Woolf's choices? Censorship trial? Suppression? Interrupting the lesbian relationship? Sex change? She could have published an overtly lesbian novel and faced a certain censorship trial, written but suppressed the lesbian novel, or altered the novel via a sex change to fit the compulsory heterosexuality demanded by the censor. But none of these choices suited Woolf. How could she keep the integrity of her message and get it by the censor without bowing? In a brilliant rhetorical coup, Woolf chose to spotlight the various strategies for avoiding the censor, making these options and strategies the topic and the focal point of her book. Was it necessary to hide lesbian love? Well then, turn the novel into a rollicking game of hide and seek! Did censorship require that lesbian love be interrupted? Well then, turn the tables and make a game of interrupting heterosexual love throughout the book! Was a sex change necessary to provide the appropriate heterosexual coupling of boy girl boy girl? Well then, make that compulsory sex change the centerpiece of the novel! Turning compulsory heterosexuality into a carnival of Eros, Woolf toys with the options by using the sex change subversively rather than for protective coloration. She draws attention to the constructed nature of the sexuality and gender of her protagonist and torments the censor with daring suggestions of cross-sex desire—all the while demurely obeying the dictates of censorship. In cheeky defiance of the censor, Woolf complies with the letter of the law while outrageously demolishing the spirit of the law. Her deft targeting and teasing of the censor seems to me the most radical and daring choice because it renders farcical—and thereby critiques and disrupts—compulsory heterosexuality and censorship per se.

The Trials of Censorship: The Angel in the House and Queer Spirits

> [T]he Angel in the House stole behind me and said "You have got yourself into a very queer position. You are young and unmarried. But you are writing for a paper owned by men, edited by men. . . . Therefore whatever you say let it be pleasing to men."
>
> —*P* xxxi

Woolf's mock-theatrical skirmishes with censors throughout her essays shed light on some puzzling moments in *Orlando*. In the draft of the speech that became "Professions for Women," Woolf, in self-defense against censorship, melodramatically murders the allegorical figure of the Angel in the House and encourages women to abandon heterosexual institutions and align themselves with another allegorical figure, "a spirit in the house <not by any means an Angel>—a very queer spirit—I don't know how to define it—it is the sort of spirit that is in Dame Ethel Smyth" (*P* xlii). The centerpiece of *Orlando* where the allegorical figures of the Ladies of Modesty, Chastity, and Purity (with Curiosity guffawing in the wings) cavort and insist upon hiding the naked truth makes sense if the scene is read as a mocking allegory of the melodramatic and farcical frenzy of a censorship trial. We may then recognize the trio of Ladies not as queer spirits or Sapphic goddesses[9] but as censors who must be mocked and eliminated. As the Angel urges the woman writer to censor herself, the Ladies of Purity, Modesty, and Chastity argue for Censorship, whitewashing or covering up: "I cover vice and poverty. On all things frail or dark or doubtful, my veil descends. Wherefore, speak not, reveal not. Spare, O spare!" and the three do their dance of the veils, singing: "Truth, come not out from your horrid den. Hide deeper, fearful Truth" (O 135). In a passage reminiscent of the Proportion and Conversion diatribes in *Mrs. Dalloway*, the Ladies claim as allies a vile coterie of censors:

> [T]hose who honour us, virgins and city men; lawyers and doctors; those who prohibit; those who deny; those who reverence without knowing why; those who praise without understanding; the still very numerous (Heaven be praised) tribe of the respectable; who prefer to see not; desire to know not; love the darkness; those still worship us, and with reason; for we have given them Wealth, Prosperity, Comfort, Ease. (O 137)

Thus, Woolf links the Ladies and censorship not only with ignorance but with self-interest and the state, just as in *Mrs. Dalloway* she links the psychologist, Dr. Bradshaw, with institutions such as empire and patriarchy. The text further indicts censorship by suggesting that censorship trials breed hypocritical voyeurs,[10] as "Chastity, Purity, and Modesty, inspired, no doubt, by Curiosity, peeped in at the door and threw a garment like a towel at the naked form" (138). With a mocking laugh, Woolf stops the trial and evicts the prurient censors.

The Censor in the House and "A Miracle of Discretion"

> Long Barn, Weald
> Sevenoaks.
> Thursday, 17th June [1926]
>
> Dear Mrs Woolf
>   I must tell you how much I enjoyed my weekend with you. . . . Darling Virginia, you don't know how happy I was.
>   I am sorry you should think me crafty. I don't think I am half crafty enough.   —Sackville-West, *Letters* 128

> [19 November 1926]
>
> You are *a miracle of discretion*—one letter in another. I never thought of that.

I'll answer when I see you—the invitation, I mean.
—*L* 3: 302; emphasis added

18th July 1927

My dear Mrs Nicolson,
    I cant tell you how I enjoyed myself on Sunday. It was
so good of you and your husband to let me come. And
what a lovely garden! . . . And I still have some of your
lovely flowers to remind me of the happy time I had
with you, and your husband, to whom please give my
best thanks and remembrances, and with much love to
you both, I am. There, you ramshackle old Corkscrew,
is that the kind of thing you like? I suppose so.
    . . . Honey dearest, don't go to Egypt please. Stay in
England. Love Virginia. Take her in your arms.
                                                —*L* 3: 397–98

The letters of Virginia and Vita acknowledging censorship on the home
front challenge the prevailing fiction that the husbands were divinely benign and sympathetic. But the letters also witness Woolf's learning from
and critiquing Vita's impressive strategies for circumventing the domestic
censor, and provide innovative ways to consider Woolf's narrative strategies in *Orlando*. Alas, we do not have a copy of the secret letter-invita-
tion Vita tucked within her cover letter—her "miracle of discretion" yet
these lines offer a fascinating glimpse into the coding of lesbian love letters and lesbian literature. Compact, suggestive, compelling, these three
short lines beg for a close reading. What specific material occasioned
these lines? Was there a letter tucked inside the letter she had received
from Vita? Why? Was that secret note an invitation? To what? What sort
of letters must be discreet? I assume that Vita sent Virginia a letter she
could read aloud or show Leonard, a letter that would not compromise
her. Then, within the safe letter, Vita included a private letter—one that
seems to have included an invitation. Virginia elsewhere mocks Vita as a
slow learner, but here she is quite genuinely delighted with what Vita has
taught her: "one letter in another. I never thought of that." It is clear that
the lesson took, and that Woolf applied that lesson not only to her love
letters but also to her fiction.
    What does this all tell us? First, it raises questions. The strategy links
husbands with censors—a provocative concept. Is the husband the Cen-

sor in the House? Woolf's irritation at the need to bow to the husbands and the conventions surfaces in the very suggestive "ramshackle old Corkscrew" letter. The first part of the letter reads like the "miracle of discretion." That portion of the letter bows repeatedly to the institution of marriage, ostentatiously including the husband and overstating gratitude to the husband for permission to come. But Virginia rudely interrupts and repudiates this tissue of clichés, while accusing Vita of liking that sort of conventional behavior, and then launches into a passionate, imperative love letter. Woolf's impatience with the hackneyed form and content is palpable.

Even as the letters address strategies for outwitting censors that might prove of use beyond the domestic sphere, they also suggest problems with such strategies. A discreet cover letter, addressed to the censor and intended to dupe that censor in order to get around the silencing or punishing authority, still bows to the censor. Such a cover letter, then, is complicit with censorship, at least on the surface, though it may have a secret agenda to pass along some contraband, to evade the censor. It does, however, present one way to "have your cake and eat it too," something, evidently, that Virginia had not explored before. Now that she thinks of it, what will she do with it? She is obviously impressed. Were she to put this new insight into practice in fiction, she might write an artfully coded text—say, a lesbian text—so carefully enclosed in a safe cover that it would pass the censor and still get to her addressees, her intended readers. But is Woolf content to tiptoe by the censor? Was there any other way? The "Corkscrew" letter suggests that Woolf might rebel and burst through constructions and conventions, regardless of how much she might admire the finesse initially.

The Semi-Transparent Envelope of Heterosexuality

In *Orlando*, heterosexuality operates as a cover letter, an outer envelope that Woolf presents as her own "miracle of discretion" (for example, in her pointedly farcical narration of Orlando's courtship and marriage of convenience with Shelmerdine). Akin to Vita's letter within the letter meant to deceive the controlling husband, the enveloping heterosexual text protects the lesbian note and allows it to be transmitted under the nose of the censor. However, by drawing our attention to the packaging of compulsory heterosexuality within which we find the hidden lesbian text, Woolf undermines social norms and literary conventions, challenging and critiquing heterosexuality. Heterosexuality is interrupted, side-lined, and undercut throughout the novel. Woolf's Orlando never finds men sexy. Once Orlando is a woman, heterosexuality loses ground; the odd courtship between the Archduke and Orlando, using dead flies on sugar cubes for foreplay and clammy toads to say "no," is singularly repulsive. With this version of female heterosexuality, Orlando has rea-son to be grateful for androgynous camaraderie rather than physical pas-sion when she marries Shelmerdine. Marriage,[11] the hackneyed happy ending of the heterosexual narrative, plays a significantly different role in Woolf's lesbian fantasy, where it is presented as a compromise requiring suspect complicity or undercut as the merely penultimate ending. The contrived courtship and marriage remind readers by default of the more convincing passionate relationship with Sasha. Regardless of Orlando's marriage and despite the fact that Sasha has become "a fat, furred woman, marvellously well preserved" (303), Sasha remains so "seductive" that Orlando (now a woman too) "bowed her head over the linen so that this apparition of a grey woman in fur, and a girl in Russian trousers with all these smells of wax candles, white flowers and Russian sailors that it brought with it might pass behind her back unseen" (303). Sasha still dis-orients Orlando so she can barely collect her wits in the department store of the twentieth century, reminding the reader of Woolf's words: "Women alone stir my imagination" (L 4: 203). Woolf's lesbian text reveals the most ardent stirrings of that imagination, as it embodies pas-sionate, delightful "lovemaking unbelievable: indiscretions incredible" for her lesbian lover.

"Indiscretions Incredible": How to Read a Lesbian Love Letter (or Text)

> The art of reading letters, too, is at least as great as the art of writing them, and possessed by as few. The read-er's co-operation is essential. There is always more to be extracted from a letter than at first sight appears, as indeed is true of all good literature, and letters certainly deserve to be approached as good literature, for they share this with good literature: that they are made out of the intimate experience of the writer, begotten of something personally endured.
>
> —Sackville-West, *Passenger* 11

Recently, we learned of the discovery of a hidden drawer in Vita Sackville-West's tower study—and of its cache of previously unknown letters from Virginia Woolf.[12] We should have been prepared for the hidden treasures by the earlier discovery of Vita's lesbian confessions, hidden in "a locked Gladstone bag lying in the corner of the little turret room that opens off it" (Nicolson, *Portrait* vii). As Vita left traces and secret texts, so did Woolf. The hidden treasures in letters and texts, as well as the actual hidden letters, challenge critics to a game of hide and seek. In their letters and texts, Virginia and Vita direct each other (and other readers) how to read between the lines or between the sheets. We must pay close attention to the complex instructions on how to read letters that fill their correspondence, lest their scoldings for misreadings apply to us as well. Their instructions suggest that the writings are coded, closed texts that will open up when teased patiently by a careful, desiring reader. One such coded text, Vita's *Passenger to Teheran*, was culled from letters Vita wrote Virginia during her trip to visit Harold in Persia. The love portions were edited out for the travel book, but Vita instructed Virginia to re-read between the lines of *Passenger to Teheran* for the omitted love letters, filling in the blanks. Virginia and Vita discussed the complex coded structure of the text in a series of letters a year later when Vita was repeating the trip:

> [28 January 1927]
>
> My darling, it's so shaky I can hardly write, we are tearing through my Weald—(see Passenger to Teheran, Chap. 2 passim.) So odd to have all the same emotions repeated after a year's interval—but oh *worse* where you are concerned. I really curse and damn at the pain of it—and yet I wouldn't be without it for anything—I shall remember you standing in your blue apron and waving. Oh damn it, Virginia, I wish I didn't love you so much. No I don't though; that's not true. I am glad I do. (Sackville-West, *Letters* 164; emphasis in original)

> Sunday, Feb 28th 1927
>
> Write again, as soon as you can.
> I did like your letter. And, following your orders (P to T) I read it so as to elicit every grain, and could write an exposition of its meanings and submeanings in 20 volumes. (*L* 3: 337)

Vita's introduction to *Passenger to Teheran* theorizes about epistolary desire, telling what is wrong with letters and how to write and read them, focusing on their role in stimulating and fulfilling desire. Arguing that "there is something intrinsically wrong about letters," she notes that "they are not instantaneous" and that "they do not arrive often enough" (*Passenger* 9). Her descriptions of letters teasingly suggest lovemaking and multiple orgasms: "A letter which has been passionately awaited should be immediately supplemented by another one, to counteract the feeling of flatness that comes upon us when the agonising delights of anticipation have been replaced by the colder flood of fulfillment" (*Passenger* 9–10). The long building period of desire, endless foreplay, and hunger that cannot be satisfied even when the text is devoured describe passion:

> For weeks we have waited; every day has dawned in hope (except Sunday, and that is a day to be blacked out of the calendar); it may have waned in disappointment, but the morrow will soon be here, and who knows what to-morrow's post may not bring? Then at last it comes; is torn open; devoured;—and all is over. It is gone in a flash, and it has not sufficed to feed our hunger. (*Passenger* 10)

Any lover, any letter, is doomed to failure:

> For a letter, by its arrival, defrauds us of a whole secret region of our existence, the only region indeed in which the true pleasure of life may be tasted, the region of imagination, creative and protean, the clouds and beautiful shapes of whose heaven are destroyed by the wind of reality. For observe, that to hope for Paradise is to live in Paradise, a very different thing from actually getting there. (*Passenger* 10)

Suggesting ever-cresting desire as the ideal role of the letter, the writer mourns the inevitable failure to balance on that teasing threshold. Desire then, according to Vita, might best be embodied in the trope of the letter in transit, or figures in elopement or flight, rather than settling, which may account for Woolf's decision to end *Orlando* with the image of the wild goose in flight.

Vita's narrator excuses the poor letter, pities the lover-writer, and introduces a fascinating vignette that subtly plays with gender expectations:

> The poor letter is not so much in itself to blame,—and there is, I think, a peculiar pathos in the thought of the writer of that letter, taking pains, pouring on to his page so much desire to please, so human a wish to communicate something of himself, in his exile—not so much to blame in the

inadequacy of its content, as in the fact that it has committed the error of arriving, of turning up. "Le rôle d'une femme," said an astute Frenchman once," est non de se donner, mais de se laisser désirer." ["The role of a woman is not to give herself, but to let herself be desired."] (*Passenger* 11)

The association of the letter with the woman is especially intriguing from a lesbian writer. Her use of such a clichéd and masculinist quotation about the role of woman takes on a different spin, offering a conspiratorial glimpse of the teasing lesbian in drag.

Intertexts on Passing and the Customs-House of Censorship

Not only in the letters, but also in the texts, we witness Vita and Virginia wrestling with issues of complicity, subversion, rebellion, and critique. In *Passenger to Teheran* and Virginia's response in *Orlando*, the two writers and lovers consider ways of presenting "indiscretions incredible" while negotiating with the censor. In her travel book, V. Sackville-West, adopting the generic male author pose and employing subtle cues such as the masculinist quote about the role of women, used the ruse of the ostensibly male-gendered narrator rather than identifying herself as female. The narrator does not claim to be a man but goes in drag, just as Vita sometimes went in drag as Julian.[13] It is only on the last page of the travel book that she discloses her gender; in a line that seems oddly gratuitous, the narrator comments, "The customs-house officer at the Dutch frontier made me an offer of marriage" (*Passenger* 181). Why the sudden disclosure? What difference does the disclosure make? Does it startle and disrupt the reader? Is this, in other words, on the level of narrative, a model for the sex change in *Orlando*? The main protagonist, with whom we have identified, whose adventures have been our focus throughout, suddenly (from the reader's point of view) changes into a woman. What purpose does this sex change and display serve? I think it provides the same thrill as the subtle difference that marks butch from man (Case 293–95). It flashes the butch identity, exposing the secret in a daring way. Some readers interpret the abrupt disclosure as Vita's anxious gesture to placate critics, to claim the narrator's status within the heterosexual economy, but if Vita had intended to claim heterosexual privilege, why wouldn't she have claimed it at the outset? Vita seems to be mocking the reader who may have been duped and winking at the lesbian reader who may have delighted in the drag disclosure.

The vignette concerning the customs-house agent allows the reader to assume that the narrator is female and was not interested in the proposal of marriage. What kind of woman would be most likely to treat so dismissively a proposal of marriage? Obvious possibilities would be a married woman or a lesbian. So, what is Vita signaling here? She signals to multiple addressees—indicating that she is perhaps married and/or interested in women. If she wished to claim heterosexual privilege, this would be a logical textual site to disclose her marital status. That she does not is significant. Why does the flash of contraband identity take place at the customs-house, where contraband must be declared and where undesirables are turned away?

The startling gender switch with which Vita turns the tables on the reader shows up again in *Orlando*, but Woolf also responded in other ways to the customs-house passage, incorporating the vignette in her discussion of the transaction between Orlando as a writer and the censor:

> At this point she felt that power (remember we are dealing with the most obscure manifestations of the human spirit) which had been reading over her shoulder, tell her to stop. . . . but—girls? Are girls necessary? You have a husband at the Cape, you say? Ah, well, that'll do.
>
> And so the spirit passed on.
>
> Orlando now performed in spirit (for all this took place in spirit) a deep obeisance to the spirit of her age, such as—to compare great things with small—a traveller, conscious that he has a bundle of cigars in the corner of his suit case, makes to the customs officer who has obligingly made a scribble of white chalk on the lid. For she was extremely doubtful whether, if the spirit had examined the contents of her mind carefully, it would not have found something highly contraband for which she would have had to pay the full fine. (O 265–66)

Woolf's intertextual reference to the customs-house passage in Vita's *Passenger to Teheran* may be double-edged. She may be signaling her recognition of Vita's subversive drag gesture and winking back at that strategy. Or Woolf may be critiquing Vita's timidity before the censors, reminding Vita that she hid her lesbian contraband and compromised her lesbian novel by turning it into yet another heterosexual romance. The holograph draft indicates that Woolf wrestled with this passage, drafting and re-drafting the scene, paying special attention to the tone. The argumentative quality of the draft is considerably tamed in the published version.[14] Woolf's strongest questioning of compliance would come in the later essays, where her hypothetical figures claim their writing and kill or laugh at the censoring Angels, spirits of the age, or patriarchal police.

Yet, even in 1928, Woolf was not completely reconciled to genuflecting to the customs-house censor. In *Orlando*, Woolf figures out a way to stride rather than tiptoe past the censor—flaunting the contraband and making gestures toward the censor that undermine his authority.

Lesbian Feminist Pedagogy and Non-Feminist Sapphism: Woolf's Lesson Plan of "Lovemaking Unbelievable"

Woolf's audacious and artful engagements with the censor are matched by the innovative lesson plan she designed for Vita. Woolf pulls out all her pedagogical tricks to teach lesbian feminism to Vita. The text is full of teaching tools: teasing, seducing, rewarding, punishing, repeating, quizzing, and demonstrating with apt examples. Woolf's text doesn't choose between lesbian and feminist discourse; she uses desire to seduce Vita into the feminist text, and the most lesbian moments in *Orlando* are made richer, wiser, and more delightful by the feminist energy. Woolf slyly suggests that Orlando/Vita is a slow learner: "Nobody, indeed, ever accused her of being one of those quick wits, who run to the end of things in a minute" (*O* 154) and paces the lesson plan accordingly. The scene on the *Enamoured Lady* subtly chastises Vita for her refusal to engage feminism: "It is a strange fact, but a true one that up to this moment she had scarcely given her sex a thought" (*O* 153). Woolf painstakingly stages the feminist conversion scene for Orlando. When Orlando finally does her homework and sits down for this long, hard feminist consciousness-raising session, she is rewarded with multiple orgasms during the sensual reverie on deck. The reward for recognizing the social construction of gender and identifying the inequities of patriarchy is the lusty recognition of desire and fulfillment: "At last, she cried, she knew Sasha as she was, and in the ardour of this discovery, and in the pursuit of all those treasures which were now revealed, she was so rapt and enchanted . . . " (161). Feminist insight wins the prize: *jouissance*!

Orlando is promptly punished when she allows the male to intrude into the sexual fantasy. When she plays the heterosexual female, the orgasm is interrupted and she is mocked by the ghost of Sasha; Orlando on the arm of the sea-captain "felt, scampering up and down within her, like some derisive ghost who, in another instant will pick up her skirts and flaunt out of sight, Sasha the lost, Sasha the memory" (163). Orlando bemoans the price of heterosexual privilege (reigning as a consort): "If it meant conventionality, meant slavery, meant deceit, meant denying her love, fettering her limbs, pursing her lips, and *restraining her tongue*" (163; emphasis added).[15] This complex system of narrative rewards and punishments ties lesbian and feminist impulses together. *Orlando* and *A Room of One's Own* attempt to seduce Vita, her lover, to initiate her into feminism. Vita, as Virginia's guest at her feminist lectures and the recipient of the gift book and manuscript of *Orlando*, is the student Woolf most wishes to enlighten.

Drafting Lesbian Desire

> On the day of publication I received a parcel containing the printed book—which, as you may imagine, I read with unparalleled avidity and curiosity—and also containing the manuscript of Orlando which is today amongst my most treasured possessions. I might add here that Virginia had gone to the trouble of getting them both specially bound for me in niger leather with the additional detail of my initials on the spine.
> —Sackville-West, "Virginia Woolf" 158

Though Woolf censored some of the most explicit lesbian proposals from the published text, she carefully bound the holograph draft for Vita: she meant it to be read as a key. Looking at the draft and the final versions of *Orlando* side by side gives us some idea of her secret message to Vita and tells us about Virginia's self-censorship for the public. We find subtle censorship in Woolf's passages on the appropriately named *Enamoured Lady* when Orlando daydreams erotically about Sasha and fills in the gaps in her knowledge of that lady by considering her own sensuality. The draft passages are more sensual and explicit than the published passages. In the draft Orlando indulges herself in "[a long] rhapsody about her lost Sasha" (*H* 127), while the published version dilutes the reference. Orlando's sexual fantasy about Sasha is much more erotic, with its repeated starts or multiple orgasms. The passage—"she could understand a thousand things that had been dark to her; now the old wound ceased to ache & began to tingle" (*H* 127)—suggests sexual pleasure. The sexual slang for the female "castrated" genitals ("the old wound") no longer is a wound that "aches" but a site of pleasure that "began to tingle." The draft undercuts heterosexuality through disturbing descriptions hinting at interrupting heterosexual violence as the "rough resolute hand of a Sea Captain burst through her dreams" (*H* 128). The draft's clear assertion that entering England means abandoning loving women— "once Orlando set foot there, adieu ladies!" (*H* 128)—is muted in the published version to sailors singing the farewell to ladies while "the words echoed in Orlando's sad heart" (*O* 163). The sexual fantasy aboard the *Enamoured Lady* is a strongly lesbian text in the draft, and traces remain encoded in the published version.

Likewise, in the near miss with Sasha in the department store of the twentieth century, the draft plays with close encounters of two women lovers. Woolf drafted and redrafted the vignette, at one point alternating the shopkeeper's discussion of the bed sheets with Orlando's memories of Sasha, emphasizing Orlando's efforts to repress the memories of that sensuality, desire, and pain. One draft reads, "It was strange how she [?] the memory of that woman whom she could never forget!" (*H* 262); and "How much, How much? she repeated sharply, to ward off the memory, which all the same—would the man never have done groping at those figures on the label? bore down at her, on the scent of wax candles blown from the Fancy Goods department next door. Faithless! Faithless! she cried" (*H* 262–63). The second draft mutes the jarring juxtapositions but includes interesting passages Woolf eliminated before the published version. The scene bows to the censor (as Orlando bows to the shopman who has gone to fetch sheets) by avoiding the encounter between the two women lovers, but as Orlando bows over the sheets (how aptly and wittily coding the love!) her eyes fill with tears. The published passage shifts the emphasis to Sasha's aging and gaining weight, muting Orlando's confession in the draft version that the passion was still alive, seductive and dangerous: "yet she still desired her & cried for her & thought of her at night as one thinks of some dangerous white wolf very . . . seductive . . . " (*H* 264). It is worth noting that Woolf may be subtly signing herself in the draft as the "dangerous white wolf," a signature conspicuously absent in the published version.

"A Precipice marked V" Coding a Lesbian Enveloping: Signature and Proposal

> Dear V and V, I feel empty when I write one without the other. Even the letter V—one side an obverse mirroring of the other, only connected at that precise swelling point. There must be a name for this effect—V. In

any case, it reads like a lesbian effect; a lesbian can claim it as her own. (Y)ours is, after all, "a captivating image."

V V V V V V V V V V V V V V V V V V V

> Taking flight,
> Love,
> L.
> —Meese, *(Sem)erotics* 41–42

I forgot to say that I thought your [Vanessa's] cover most attractive—but what a stir you'll cause by the hands of the clock at that precise hour! People will say —but theres no room.

> —*L* 4: 81

Wild geese, when on the wing together for any distance, are frequently observed to assume some particular figure. If there are only three or four birds, they mostly fly in a straight line one right after the other; when more numerous they assume a wedge-shaped form like the letter < placed horizontally, the angle in advance.

> —Yarrell, *A History of British Birds* 63

Ce [Orlando] sont les aventures imaginaires d'un être bisexué, ou plutôt, tour à tour, homme et femme, depuis le règne d'Elisabeth jusqu' à nous; fort vivant encore puisqu'il survola nos hêtraies en compagnie d'un autre oiseau de passage: son biographe. Nous avons aperçu des photographies d'Orlando en costume de dame 1840, ou en jupe courte, cheveux courts, telle que nous le ou la voyions hier sur les côtes de la Manche, se reposant à peine une heure avant de reprendre son vol vers le Nord. Les hôtes chez qui les deux voyageuses ont suspendu leur course aérienne vous trouverez leurs noms dans la préface dédicatoire de ce livre étrange.

[These are the imaginary adventures of a bisexual being, or rather, alternately a man and a woman, from the reign of Elizabeth up to us; still very much alive since he flies over our beech groves in the company of another bird of passage: his/her biographer. We have seen photographs of Orlando in the costume of an 1840s lady, or in a short skirt with short hair such as we have seen him or her yesterday on the shores of the English Channel, resting barely an hour before taking off again on his/her

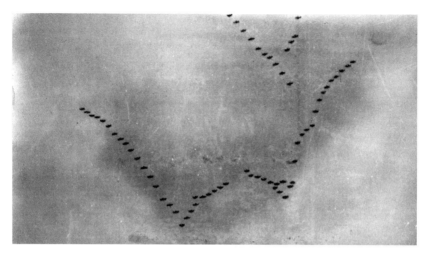

Multiple "Vs" of wild geese in flight replicate the "VW" signature. 1934 Photograph by George Shiras III, © National Geographic Society Image Collection.

flight toward the North [of France]. You will find the names of the hosts at whose home the two [feminine] travelers suspended their aerial outing in the dedicatory preface of this strange book.][16]
  —Blanche, *"Un nouveau roman de* Virginia Woolf"

19 February 1929

Blanche has written a long, very sugary, very acid, article on O——o; with so many hits [hints?] and double meanings that one cant see the wood for the trees; something very arch about two birds flying together to France and alighting at Dieppe last autumn.
  —*L* 4: 27

Because Woolf coded some of her love signatures, we may read the holograph draft to clarify ways to read riddles in the published text as lesbian signatures, especially the letter "V," so richly endowed with multiple references for both Virginia and Vita. The "V" signatures appear in their letters to each other and, as Elizabeth Meese demonstrates, may be read as Sapphist signatures.[17] Diane Gillespie first drew attention to the playful, artful use of the "V" as a signal in Vanessa Bell's cover painting for Woolf's *A Room of One's Own*, which encodes the "V" as the time registered (11:05) on the clock face on the mantle (Gillespie 70–72).[18] Virginia suggests that there is something scandalous in that "V" in a letter to Vanessa, a letter that interrupts and thus censors its message: "but what a stir you'll cause by the hands of the clock at that precise hour! People will say—but theres no room" (*L* 4: 81). What would there be to gossip about in the "V" signature? What makes the letter "V" so exciting? Does the thrill come from the suggestion of Vita or the lesbian "V"? or both? Years earlier, Woolf played with the "V" signature or sign for Vita as lover in her letter to Vita about love: "Now what would happen if I let myself go over? Answer me that. Over what? you'll say. A precipice marked V" (*L* 3: 351–52).

In the draft she had bound for Vita, we find keys (not in the final version) that suggest one explanation for the "wild goose" that so perplexes critics. My argument depends upon Danell Jones's superb essay "*The Chase of the Wild Goose*: The Ladies of Llangollen and *Orlando*," which links "the chase of the wild goose" with the lesbian couple. Jones explores connections between *Orlando* and Hogarth Press's 1936 publication, Mary Gordon's fictionalized biography of the Ladies of Llangollen, *The Chase of the Wild Goose*. Jones uncovers the "wild goose" image in the exchange of vows between Sarah and Eleanor on their elopement when Sarah responds to Eleanor's proposal with the lines "I want to hear you say I may chase the wild goose with you" (Jones 188). Jones points out the significance of the wild goose image for the relationship of Vita and Virginia and convincingly argues for the lesbian subtext.

But we might ask how Woolf claims the wild goose lesbian signature in *Orlando* and makes it her own. Are we missing clues about the "wild goose chase"? Perhaps we should be looking for wild *geese* instead of the solo wild *goose*. Woolf's drafts personalize and claim the lesbian wild goose signature through her drafting of the wild geese image as the "V" image of the geese flying overhead:

> She looked into grey air now; & by came flying, *in the shape of a v*, each with a long neck outstretched, wild geese. As they passed over her she . . . heard their wings creak melodiously; harshly yet with a wild music, & they flew very fast, very high,—They were gone. (*H* 284–85; emphasis added)

In this draft passage, the "wild geese" signal Virginia, signing herself (and/or Vita) with a "V," identifying lesbian love and Virginia with the cryptic, compelling vision that ends the novel. In the draft, the wild geese "V" suggests lesbian elopement, flying away like migrating wild geese, voyagers in the "V" formation.[19] The published version, by changing the "geese" to "goose" and erasing the telltale "V" signature, reduces the wild bird image to a cipher that appears inexplicably in the text:

> And as Shelmerdine, now grown a fine sea captain, hale, fresh-coloured, and alert, leapt to the ground, there sprang up over his head a single wild bird.
> "It is the goose!" Orlando cried. "The wild goose." (O 329)

With elaborate care, Woolf coded her love for Vita between the lines of the text and in the spaces between the draft and the published version. The final vignette in the published version is packed with innuendo. Woolf's coded protest against marriage is apparent in her faintly dismissive portrayal of Shelmerdine; in the penultimate ending, the grand reunion is far from reassuring. Shelmerdine "now grown a fine sea captain, hale, fresh-coloured, and alert" is less sexy than sinister because he signifies the return of the sea captain, Captain Bartolus, who interrupted the multi-orgasmic lesbian reverie earlier on the *Enamoured Lady*. What does it mean that Shel descends in an aeroplane while Orlando cries out for the wild goose in flight?[20] Orlando loses interest in Shelmerdine to cry out for the wild goose, which is, significantly, over Shelmerdine's head. Does this suggest that Virginia wafts the lesbian elopement proposal over Harold's head in her own "miracle of discretion" to Vita? The "V" and Woolf's careful manipulation, flaunting and hiding that image and signature, from the drafts to the published version indicate that she may have wished to get her message across to Vita, and to veil it from others. Virginia gave Vita the published version and the holograph version that had hidden within it the "V" signatures. Whether or not Vita got the message, Virginia delivered it.[21]

And did Vita get the message? If she did, she did not tell Harold; to him she wrote: "The more I think about it, the weaker I think the end is. I simply cannot make out what was in her mind. What does the wild goose stand for? Fame? Love? Death? Marriage? Obviously a person of V.'s intellect has had some object in view, but what was it? The symbolism doesn't come off" (qtd. in Glendinning 204). Was Vita a slow learner or hiding the lesbian love note and signature from her husband? That we don't know. But if the wild goose is a sign, as Jones suggests, of a lesbian elopement proposal and, as I argue, Virginia's claiming of the lesbian signature, *Orlando* opens up a new letter within a letter to readers decoding lesbian literary history—and new flights of fancy.

NOTES

1. See Cook; Stimpson, "Zero Degree"; DeSalvo, "Cave"; DuPlessis; Brimstone; Jones; Knopp; McNaron, "Mirrors"; Meese, *(Sem)erotics*; Marcus, "Sapphistry"; Olano, "Reading"; and Zimmerman, "Chloe."

2. See Gaard for an example of an articulate and theoretically current argument for pansensuality. Isolating the queer bits—the polysexuality, pansensuality, androgyny, or drag elements—and often bracketing the feminism, some attempts to fit Woolf into queer theory drag are vexed because her queer texts are inextricable from her feminist ones.

3. Marcus and others have noted the misogyny of the male homosexual coterie surrounding Woolf. See the section "Cock-a-doodle-dum" in "Sapphistry" (177–86).

4. My use of "perverse" follows Bonnie Zimmerman's efforts to reclaim that term, expressed in her 1993 essay "Perverse Reading: The Lesbian Appropriation of Literature."

5. See Marcus, who notes, "Much of *A Room* was meant simply to convert her beloved Vita to feminism, its seductive tone an extension of her love letters" ("Sapphistry" 166). Louise DeSalvo, in "Lighting the Cave," also argues that Vita's fiction shows Woolf's feminist influence (208ff.).

6. The Virginia Woolf Conferences have been stages for excellent lesbian readings of Virginia Woolf, including those by Patricia Cramer, Annette Oxindine, Eileen Barrett, Janet Winston, Elizabeth Lambert, Danell Jones, Pamela Olano, Laura Doan, and Deborah Wilson. See Hussey and Neverow-Turk, *Emerging Perspectives.*

7. For discussions of the divergent fates of two lesbian novels—Woolf's *Orlando* and Hall's *The Well of Loneliness*—see Marcus, "Sapphistry"; Benstock, "Expatriate"; Brimstone; Cook; DeSalvo, "Cave"; McNaron, "Journey"; Parks; Newton; Knopp; and Stimpson, "Zero Degree."

8. Marcus is persuasive: "An earnest feminist appeal to political solidarity would not be half as effective as shameless flirtation, Woolf seems to feel" ("Sapphistry" 169).

9. The trios of women call up the "Maiden-Trinities" in Jane Harrison's *Prolegomena to the Study of Greek Religion* (286ff.) or the sentimental Victorian "Angel in the House" trios from the patriarchal photographs of Julia Margaret Cameron, but it is significant that Woolf turns those icons into caricatures here while exploiting their iconic status and making gestures toward those works.

10. I refer readers to Marcus' careful excavation of references to the Hall trial in *A Room of One's Own*, where she notes Woolf's overt references to Sir Chartres Biron or Sir Archibald Bodkin for evidence of Woolf's attention to the censorship trial and her well-honed response: to diminish the authority of such figures by mockery ("Sapphistry" 166).

11. Marriage and bisexuality were much more complex issues in the lives and writings (including other letters) of Virginia Woolf and Vita Sackville-West than Woolf's farcical treatment of marriage in *Orlando* suggests. But here Woolf side-

lines the tragic, melodramatic, and poignant aspects, emphasizing the caricature value of the institution to celebrate more fully the lesbian fantasy.

12. See Banks, "Four Hidden Letters." Banks speculates that these letters were hidden not from Harold but from Vita's secretary, another jealous lesbian lover. Likewise, Woolf self-censored her "indiscretions incredible" letter because she was angry and jealous that Vita may have read her letters to Vita's lover Mary Campbell.

13. Vita's unusual gestures that draw attention to the disguise suggest the heady delight of drag rather than the anxious effort of attempting to pass as a male. Though space limits our exploration here, for intriguing discussions of the theoretical subtle differences between drag and passing, I recommend Sue-Ellen Case and Judith Butler, *Gender.*

14. The drafts are more dismissive of Orlando's writing, debate more extensively whether she was "an authentically married woman," and, interestingly enough, describe the "spirit of the age" as "the old woman" (*H* 225–27).

15. It is interesting that in the draft this reads "restraining her language" (*H* 129) and that Woolf, for the published version, chooses the more suggestive "tongue."

16. Thanks to Diane Griffin Crowder for the translation and for a stimulating conversation about lesbian codes and symbols.

17. See Wilson for a thoughtful paper exploring the fin in Woolf's work as the inverted "V" sapphist signature.

18. Though Gillespie links the "V" with Vanessa and Virginia, she does not draw the connection with Vita.

19. In my efforts to chase the wild goose symbolism, I explored Jane Harrison's fascinating writings about mantic and oracular birds in *Themis* (98ff.). Her references led me to W. R. Halliday's *Greek Divination*, with its chapter on "Augury," which probes the historical fascination with the hermeneutics of reading the flight of birds as signs of deeper truths and to D'Arcy Wentworth Thompson, *A Glossary of Greek Birds* which decodes the goose as "an erotic bird" and "a lover's gift" (194). William Yarrell's *A History of British Birds* (from Woolf's library) describes the "V" figure in flight.

20. If the wild geese signal lesbian flight, does the aeroplane signal male interruption of that flight and the heterosexist interruption and threat of the "brace of husbands" who descended in a plane to stop the elopement of Vita and Violet? Woolf aligns the figure of the husband with the posse rounding up lesbian runaways from the institution of marriage: "My aristocrat (oh, but I have now 2 or 3, whom I'll tell you about—they interest me) is violently Sapphic, and contracted such a passion for a woman cousin, that they fled to the Tyrol, or some mountainous retreat together, to be followed in an aeroplane by a brace of husbands" (*L* 3: 155–56). Evidence in her letters and diaries and in *Orlando* challenge the two-dimensional longstanding depictions of Leonard and Harold as benign, indulgent, long-suffering, loyal spouses. Remembering how "a brace of husbands" thwarted Vita's earlier lesbian elopement, Woolf in *Orlando* encodes that threat. And when Orlando responds by "curtseying deeply" (328) (as she did to the cus-

toms officer) and telling the dead Queen that "Nothing has been changed. The dead Lord, my Father, shall lead you in" (328), is this scene mocking Orlando's capitulation to the whole patriarchal and heterosexual imperative?

At the Fifth Annual Woolf Conference, we brainstormed about the significance of the aeroplanes in V formations as a negative V, the positive V turned into its nightmare self. Would the replacement of the V as a wild geese image (signifying lesbian love and elopement) with the V bombers (signifying masculine violence) hit Woolf especially hard? Vita's 1940 description (published by Hogarth Press) of the V bombers and the dying goose-plane is chilling:

> We do not pay much attention to the cyrene in the country. It is just "that thing" to which we have become accustomed. Then the planes arrive. They fly overhead in a great flight like geese, and people looking up from the fields wonder vaguely whether they are Germans or ours. We then observe that one goose has become detached from the flight and that two fighters are tumbling round it in the summer sky. Machine-guns cackle. The goose wavers in its flight; it banks; it sinks; it is wounded; its great wings flag; we hear later that it has come down at Appledore, ten miles away. (Sackville-West, *Country Notes in Wartime* 79)

If Woolf read the skies and tied the wild goose image with lesbian elopement, how would she have read this passage of Vita's, where the bombers kill off the solitary wild goose?

21. In an interview, Vita makes it plain that she must not have read the draft as carefully as Woolf would have wished, because some passages seemed new to her years later: "I was looking idly through the manuscript one day when something struck me as unfamiliar and I realised that I had lit upon an entirely unpublished passage" (Sackville-West, "Virginia Woolf" 158).

THIRTEEN

Rhoda Submerged: Lesbian Suicide in
The Waves

ANNETTE OXINDINE

I am a woman
who understands
the necessity of an impulse whose goal or origin
still lie beyond me. . . .
like amnesiacs
in a ward on fire, we must
find words
or burn.

—Olga Broumas, "Artemis," 1977

Although it is Shakespeare's "incandescent," androgynous mind that Virginia Woolf reveres in *A Room of One's Own*, it is Shakespeare's silenced sister, a victim of suicide, who haunts that essay and impels Woolf's passionate peroration on "the dead poet who . . . will put on the body which she has so often laid down" (*AROO* 118). Why, then, in Woolf's next book, *The Waves*, does she lay down the body of the "incandescent" Rhoda, also a victim of suicide, and create in her male counterpart, Bernard, a figure many critics have come to revere as the ideal androgynous artist? Answering this question involves exploring one of the eeriest suicides in modern fiction—eerie because Rhoda disappears from the novel instead of dying "in" it. Her death occurs outside the narrative space created by the novel's soliloquies; as Rhoda herself laments, she is "not composed enough" (*TW* 107).[1]

While heralding Rhoda as "the most extravagant avatar of discontinuity in modern fiction," Garrett Stewart's poststructuralist reading of *The Waves* denies the importance of gender in Rhoda's "recoil from language as a system" (453, 439). Recent feminist scholarship, however, attempts to situate Rhoda's silence within a distinctly feminine discourse. In *Virginia Woolf and the Problem of the Subject*, Makiko Minow-Pinkney, evoking Kristeva, contends that "Rhoda marks out the locus of a feminine space, that non-symbolisable Other that must be repressed but none the less exists for a normative discourse to be installed" (183). Rhoda's feminine discourse, maintains Minow-Pinkney, is "impossible except as silence" (183). Taking issue with Minow-Pinkney, Patricia Ondek Laurence argues that Rhoda's silence is in fact a triumphant reaction against what Minow-Pinkney would designate as "normative discourse": Rhoda's silence, she argues, "subverts . . . the claim-making 'phrases' of Bernard . . . who dominates the end of the novel" (*Reading* 169). In *The Reading of Silence*, Laurence goes further than any critic to date in her attempt to "de-pathologize" Rhoda and instead celebrate her "feminine way of knowing, imagining and being"—which, Laurence suggests, creates a "new meta-physical space" (169). But even though Laurence invests Rhoda's "dreaming body" with potent energy, she contends that the space Rhoda engenders is "a poetic correlative of mind, the dream state," rather than an erotic space (169).

It is, however, precisely the erotic space that Rhoda occupies in *The Waves* that necessitates analysis, for her sexuality is crucial to understanding her silence and ultimately her suicide. That Rhoda's sexuality continues to be evaded by feminist critics is not altogether surprising, however, given that Woolf was complicit in de-sexualizing one of her most enigmatic characters, as an investigation of her revisions of Rhoda's speeches will suggest. Through close readings of significant elisions and revisions in Rhoda's speeches in the two holograph drafts of *The Waves*, I will argue that Rhoda's eroticism is overtly lesbian in the first draft of the novel and implicitly so in the final text, and analyze what I contend to be Woolf's most heavily coded treatment of both patriarchal resistance and lesbian desire. Finally, I will advance a reading of Rhoda's suicide as a sign of the lesbian's effacement within a social and linguistic system that denies her an articulation of self.

That Rhoda's death seems to vanish from the text or to exist so curiously beyond its margins befits a character who in some sense also does not "exist" within the text. Her presence in *The Waves* is spectral from the beginning. As a young girl, Rhoda is unable to confirm her own existence in a looking glass: "for I am not here. I have no face. Other people have faces; Susan and Jinny have faces; they are here. Their world is the real world" (43). Although Rhoda makes this declaration of self-negation while an adolescent enrolled in an all-girl's school, the "real world" depicted episodically before and after adolescence is very clearly a heterosexual world, one from which Rhoda excludes herself in the novel's opening panorama of childhood and again in the episode that explores each female character's awareness of her own adult sexuality.

In the novel's first episode, an Edenic atmosphere pervades the sentient discoveries of the children, most of whose emotions are directly or indirectly stirred by an unexpected kiss: Bernard's overwhelming passion is to comfort Susan, who is shocked and alienated when she sees Jinny kiss Louis, a "strike" that "shatters" "all" for Louis. Meanwhile, Rhoda is creating her own world: she rocks her fleet of white-petal ships in an oceanic basin; while many ships founder, only hers sails on alone. Louis is drawn to Rhoda because he doesn't fear her as he fears Jinny, for Rhoda has "no body as the others have" (22). Rhoda's solitary avoidance of heterosexual passion is later confirmed in Bernard's final monologue. Recalling the adolescent girls who "had grown long pigtails and acquired the look of startled foals," Bernard depicts Rhoda as a rebellious non-initiate into the heterosexual courtship ritual:

> Jinny was the first to come sidling up to the gate to eat sugar. She nipped it off the palms of one's hand very cleverly, but her ears were laid back as if she might bite. Rhoda was wild—Rhoda one never could catch. She was both frightened and clumsy. It was Susan who first became wholly woman, purely feminine. (247–48)

Because Rhoda runs from heterosexual romance—"I left Louis; I feared embraces" (204–5)—critics, like Bernard in the speech above, focus on her fear and awkwardness instead of on the erotic dimensions of her wildness. Thus, Rhoda's fear of heterosexuality is often conflated with a fear of sexuality, even a fear of her own body. Pamela Transue's interpretation is typical in its intimation of Rhoda's asexuality: "Rhoda's body both imprisons and frightens her, so that she finds a necessary solace in moments of escape in which her physical being dissolves and she has a sense of merging with the universe" (130). Rhoda's desires, however, are not as amorphous or as metasexual as Transue suggests. Rhoda is replete with sexual yearning; she just cannot find someone to whom she can give "all that . . . flows through" her "warm," her "porous body" (57). "Oh! to whom?" becomes Rhoda's longing refrain after she discovers "The Question," Shelley's "poem about a hedge" (56). Unable to find confirmation of her sensual self in the world she inhabits, Rhoda exiles her desires to another world: "She gazed over the slate roofs—the nymph of the fountain always wet, obsessed with visions, with dreaming," recalls Bernard (274).

Rhoda's visions and dreams are exiled to an imaginary world within the text; and they are significantly elided from the published novel, appearing primarily in Woolf's earlier drafts of *The Waves*. In the published novel, the "dark pools" in Rhoda's dream world are suggestive of the subconscious: "Pools lie on the other side of the world reflecting marble columns. The swallow dips her wing in dark pools" (105). The submerged sexuality in the image of "dark pools" is manifest in Woolf's evocation of women's sexuality in "Professions for Women" when she describes herself, then "a girl," "writing a novel in a trance":[2]

> She was letting her imagination sweep unchecked round every rock and cranny of the world that lies submerged in the depths of our unconscious being. Now came the experience, the experience that I believe to be far commoner with women writers than with men. . . . Her imagination had rushed away. It had sought the pools, the depths, the dark places where the largest fish slumber. And then there was a smash. . . . The imagination had dashed itself against something hard. The girl was roused from her dream. To speak without figure she had thought of something, something about the body, about the passions which it was unfitting for her as a woman to say. . . . The consciousness of what men will say of a woman who speaks the truth about her passions had roused her from her artist's state of unconsciousness. She could write no more. The trance was over. (240)

In this essay, delivered on January 21, 1931, to the Women's Service League, Woolf admits she has not yet "solved" the problem of "telling the truth about [her] own experiences as a body" (241). It is telling that Woolf gave this speech when she was within weeks of finishing the second draft of *The Waves*,[3] and the idea of "an entire new book—a sequel to a Room of Ones Own—about the sexual life of women" (*D* 4: 6) so enthused her that she had trouble returning to her novel. Two days after reading her paper, Woolf writes, "Too much excited, alas, to get on with The Waves. One goes on making up The Open Door, or whatever it is to be called. . . . I find it hard to get back inside Bernard again" (*D* 4: 6).[4]

Almost a year before Woolf's declaration that a woman writing of her bodily passions could be silenced by "the consciousness of what men would say," she records in her diary a triumphant morning of writing "what Rhoda said," a morning in which her "trance" was apparently uninterrupted by such a consciousness. On March 17, 1930, Woolf writes:

> The test of a book (to a writer) [is] if it makes a space in which, quite naturally, you can say what you want to say. As this morning I could say what Rhoda said. This proves that the book itself is alive: because it has not crushed the thing I wanted to say, but allowed me to slip it in, without any compression or alteration. (D 3: 297–98)

How revealing that Woolf feels she has to "slip in" what she wants to say in her own novel, afraid that the very thing she is creating will "crush" what she wants most to express. While it is impossible to determine exactly what Woolf felt she "slipped in" while composing the speech on March 17, it is possible to locate and examine Rhoda's speeches that appear between the holograph pages Woolf dated March 9 and March 25, 1930. Midway between those approximately thirty pages is a three-page monologue, Rhoda's longest and most impassioned within these pages, which seems most likely to be the one referred to in the diary entry. In this speech, which remains largely unaltered in the published novel, Rhoda dines with her friends at Hampton Court for the last time and expresses her resentment toward their aggressive quotidian refrains: "I wish to stretch my mind wider & wider, & you are always plucking at me, with your children or your poems or your chilblain, or whatever it is you do [or] <& suffer> & wish to press on my attention" (H1 297). In both the published version and the rough draft, Rhoda describes her vision of another world to which she escapes to render life more bearable. In the published text, Rhoda conjures up the recurrent image of the dark pools alluded to earlier—"The swallow dips her wings in midnight pools"—as well as imagines "fishermen on the verge of the world [who] are drawing in nets and casting them" (TW 223), an image Woolf retains from the first draft. What Woolf does *not* retain in the published version, however, is an allusion to "a grove in a Greek island," which Rhoda will "lie awake and look at" to replenish her dreams after she leaves her friends (H1 297). This island—referred to earlier in the holograph as the island of Artemis—is one of several things Woolf "allowed" to "slip" out of that particular soliloquy.

To ascertain what Rhoda is seeking and what she is fleeing, especially with regard to her sexuality, it is crucial to return to the "Greek island" Woolf omits from the published novel. In the passage discussed above, Woolf writes no more about the island; but earlier in the same draft, it is clear that the Greek island that nourishes Rhoda's dreams is inhabited by Artemis' hunters. In the published novel, Rhoda dreams of marble columns and pools for the first time when, "not yet twenty-one," she attends a dance at which she is expected to take a man's hand:

> I must take his hand; I must answer. But what answer shall I give? I am thrust back to stand burning in this clumsy, this ill-fitting body, to receive the shafts of his indifference, and his scorn, I who long for marble columns and pools on the other side of the world where the swallow dips her wings. (*TW* 105)

The marble columns for which Rhoda yearns, while indistinct throughout the published novel, are highly suggestive in Woolf's first draft: Rhoda seeks "a statue of [*Aphro*] Artemis in the glade," "the pillar of Artemis among the dark green laurels" (*H1* 202). A close reading of the first draft's version of this particular episode suggests that Rhoda's attribution of "indifference" and "scorn" to the man whose hand she must take is both a projection of the scorn and indifference she feels toward him and a projection of the scorn she feels toward herself for being unable to feel anything but indifference about the possibility of a heterosexual union; she longs instead to be left alone in the glades where Artemis' statuesque reign sanctions women's love of their own and each other's self-defined sexuality.

In order to examine why Rhoda seeks out the image of Artemis to steel herself against feelings of worthlessness, it will be necessary to discuss in some depth the scene at the dance that Woolf alters considerably in the novel's published version. These unpublished passages offer a significant delineation of what is much more vague in the published passages: Rhoda's acute awareness that she is somehow unreal, that she does not exist because she is unable sincerely to feel heterosexual desire. In the holograph, Woolf initially stresses Rhoda's painful sense of difference from other people, especially Jinny, who knows how to be sincere with men: "And at once her sense of being unlike other people, & shut out from some simple piece of knowledge which Jinny had, thus making her real[,] effective, able to be quite sincere with that man she was talking to, overcame her" (*H1* 199). As Rhoda is convinced that others would hate her if her private deficiencies were made public, her inadequacies engender fervent self-hatred, emphasized by Woolf's uncharacteristic use of repeated exclamation marks: "I am detached, dishonest, somehow not right. If people could see me as I am how they would [*disli*] despise me!

What a vile nature I have been given! [*What a deception I am!*] How . . . despicable I am!" (*H1* 200).

Rhoda's feeling detached and "somehow not right" can be attributed to her inability to feel what she thinks she is supposed to feel—namely, desire—when she sees heterosexual "couples assuming the rapt look of dancers" (*H1* 200). Unable herself to feel enraptured when she watches men and women dancing, Rhoda's conception of herself as "a complete globe, universal, comprehending everything, vanished; was burst" (*H1* 200). She feels "that all the things one had collected & believed in & tethered oneself to [*were*] proved false. [*And she was false*]" (*H1* 200). Rhoda does not want to dance with the men at the party because "she hated being asked to do what would at once reveal her [*str*] incompetency in the supreme art of being a real person" (*H1* 201). For Rhoda to be a "real person" as she is defining "real" in the context of this passage would certainly require "supreme art," that is, supreme artifice; for Rhoda senses that what is natural to her will not suffice to make her part of the "real world": her "nature," she has determined, is "vile." Rhoda realizes that only through self-deception could she assume the "rapt look" of a woman dancing with a man. Rapture, for Rhoda, lies elsewhere.

Rhoda's self-abasement is tempered and her sense of inadequacy subsides when she seeks a "perfectly sincere" relation, when she thinks that perhaps "the battle was not worth while, for her at least, towards reality" (*H1* 201)—reality being a concept that is deeply ironic for Rhoda. Reaching beyond images that foster self-effacement, which are so abundant at the dance, Rhoda attempts to restore herself to her own body:

> The [*thing that was*] to make for what was out, beyond, hard, real: something intimate, her own. . . . There [*was*] it was beyond those people, & she walked . . . to the window, to the balcony, to the sight of the sky . . . she was here quit of all that obligation, absolved, & let be herself, alone; part of the sky; so curiously barred with black. (*H1* 201)

In the sky Rhoda finds "a relation that was perfectly sincere," "a relation ringing like metal, very pure, unmitigated, without alloy, no question of adapting oneself, only of letting mix, of being" (*H1* 201). Though Rhoda's unmitigated mixing with the sky is ostensibly a very asexual coalescence, her "sincere relation" opens her up to erotic self-discovery.

Relieved of having to "adapt" herself to heterosexual expectations and having been consequently restored to her own body, Rhoda makes a very cryptic discovery about herself—"I'm that; I'm not this" (*H1* 202). This ambiguous revelation is powerfully informed by the fact that it spurs Rhoda's descent "down the dark laurel groves" where "there is a statue of Artemis in the glade"—a descent that, as will be shown in the passage below, culminates in autoerotic rapture of the "livid foam."

After Rhoda's essentially passive, "pure" mixture with the sky, she becomes uninhibited enough to formulate a self-revelatory apostrophe; she then achieves a more aggressive, sexually suggestive union with waves breaking on a shore:

> But you know what I think, she said addressing herself very hurriedly in case she should be interrupted, I'm that; I'm not this. [*Cant be helped.*] \<Thats\> One of those things to be noted. . . . It was \<a\> great relief after being so inadequate . . . to be calm up here entire, alone. Regardless as I am, pure as I am, let us away then, down the dark laurel groves, where the hunters go, & there is a statue of [*Aphro*] Artemis in the glade. . . . Shall I go with the fishing fleet? Shall I see the rippled waves? [*I shall*] Now I shall see the waves break on the shore—The \<livid\> white [*brilli*] foam was herself. The white, the swift, the coursing, the unimpeded, the free was her. She was [*galloping with*] sweeping the shores of the world; yet steadfast; high uplifted, piercing, aloof. (*H1* 201–2)[5]

Rhoda's enigmatic "I'm that; I'm not this" obviously obscures her meaning; but given that her realization follows the rejection of heterosocial imperatives, there are substantial grounds for reading the statement as a declaration, if not of her lesbianism, at least of her rejection of heterosexuality. In *Mrs. Dalloway*, Clarissa—who, like Rhoda, feels "invisible; unseen; unknown" (*MD* 11)—also uses "this" and "that" ambiguously: "she would not say of herself, I am this, I am that" (*MD* 9). In a later passage Woolf uses "that" to refer to the warm contact of women together. Clarissa thinks she lacks "something warm which broke up surfaces and rippled the cold contact of man and woman, or of women together. For *that* she could dimly perceive" (*MD* 31; emphasis in original). That "*that*" refers to Clarissa's ability to perceive the warmth women felt together is reinforced by her confession that "she could not resist sometimes yielding to the charm of a woman" and that "she did undoubtedly then feel what men felt" (*MD* 31–32). The "stylistic, syntactic and grammatic ambiguity" present in Woolf's use of "this" and "that" is often practiced when women writers "want to entice their Reader without incurring the social censure . . . that would inevitably arise if they were to reveal the truth" about their own or other women's desires, Barbara Mossberg observes in her study of evasions in texts by Emily Dickinson and Gertrude Stein (242).

Reading Rhoda's self-identifying statement as a declaration of her sexual autonomy is further supported by Woolf's crossed-out line "Cant be helped," a statement that absolves Rhoda of any blame or guilt for rejecting heterosexuality and that advances her sense of "great relief" after "being so inadequate" at the dance. Furthermore, Woolf's description of Rhoda's becoming the foam of a wave parallels her description of a woman discovering her sexuality in "Professions for Women," discussed earlier. In the margins of the draft of Rhoda's speech, opposite the description of Rhoda's sea change, Woolf writes that the foam of the wave was "racing into the crannies of the rocks"—an image very similar to the one used to convey the awakening of sexual self-knowledge in "Professions for Women": "She was letting her imagination sweep unchecked around every rock and cranny of the world that lies submerged in the depths of our unconscious being" (152).

As with the writer in "Professions for Women," Rhoda's trance is interrupted: she "fell off from the edge of the moon; could not any longer see the pillar of Artemis among the dark green laurels; missed the next beat of the <stride> idea. . . ." (*H1* 202). Though much less explicitly than the girl in Woolf's essay, Rhoda feels mocked by an awareness of what "men [would] say of a woman who speaks the truth about her passions." After Rhoda loses hold of her vision and begins to feel foolish, "left standing, rather weak, rather vulnerable," "she become[s] suddenly aware of the comfortable laughter, or whatever it might be" of a group of "boasting boys." The laughter, it turns out, is really singing: the boys "burst into chorus . . . trolling out something very unanimous, very wholeheartedly; so that everybody's heart inclined to it" (*H1* 203–4). Their unanimity impinges upon, almost seems to declare prohibitive, Rhoda's solitary quest for self-definition. Their collective, unanimous voice "was like a roar of flame when the doors of an oven in a smithy are flung open. It was like the parting wind. . . . It swept one into its own sweet lusty tide" (204). And so Rhoda, who longs to crest on the waves of her own *jouissance*, is subsumed by the chorus of male voices.

Although Woolf omits from *The Waves* the scene of the singing boys, the image of flames pursuing Rhoda is among the most recurrent and powerful in the corresponding published speech. The image is transformed and made more sinister by its association with "flicker[ing]" tongues (106) and a leaping tiger whose presence terrifies Rhoda to the point of speechlessness: "I am not composed enough, standing on tiptoe on the verge of fire, still scorched by the hot breath, afraid of the door opening and the leap of the tiger, to make even one sentence. . . . Each time the door opens I am interrupted" (107). The terror Rhoda associates with a tiger leaping through an open door—"the door opens; the tiger leaps ... terror rushes in; terror upon terror, pursuing me" (105)— becomes less oblique when we recall the image in its incipience: "The very unanimous" voice of the singing boys "was like a *roar* of flame when the doors of an oven in a smithy are flung open" (emphasis added). Could this male "roar" have suggested to Woolf an aggressive animal?[6] If the image of the tiger is contextualized by the image that seems to have engendered it—the powerful, united male voices that invade Rhoda's thoughts— Rhoda's inability to speak, to "compose" herself, can be intertextually read as her reaction to the overpowering choric roar of patriarchal song, made all the more derisive by its initial resemblance to laughter.

Just as the boasting boys are not altogether expunged but rather transformed into an animal aggressor in Woolf's final draft, so too is the image of Artemis metamorphosed into more oblique representations of her power. Having expressed a longing for "marble columns and pools on the other side of the world," Rhoda looks out a window, craving respite from the tiger's pursuit, and espies "some unembarrassed cat, not drowned in light, not trapped in silk, free to pause, to stretch, and to move again" (105). In Ovid's *Metamorphoses*, Phoebe, also a name for Artemis, turns herself into a cat in order to escape the "earth-born" monster Typhon (109)—who, like Rhoda's pursuer, is associated with fire: Typhon is described by Hesiod as a "flaming monster" whose "eyes flashed glaring fire" (qtd. in Hamilton 67). The moon goddess Artemis is also evoked by Rhoda's calming connection with the moon: "I see the sky, softly feathered with its sudden effulgence of moon" (*TW* 106). Telling of Woolf's overall strategy of evasion is the fact that in her first draft, which is much longer and more descriptive, she makes no reference to a cat, nor does she mention the moon when Rhoda looks to the sky for her "sincere relation." But when she excises her direct allusions to that powerful goddess worshipped by Amazons and frequently associated with lesbianism, Woolf inserts what may be regarded as coded references to Artemis. These allusions to Artemis add a crucial dimension to the image of Rhoda as the "wild" one who could never be caught. Another reference to Artemis is suggested by the image of Rhoda as "the nymph of the fountain always wet." The myth of Arethusa, whom Artemis turns into a fountain to escape the river god Alpheus, "is an apt analogue to Rhoda's own flight from Louis and her suicide by drowning," as Beverly Schlack has observed (124).

While the image of Rhoda as a fountain in relation to the Arethusa myth suggests sexual avoidance and/or violation, Woolf also uses the image of pulsating water to suggest Rhoda's sexual gratification. Once again, in order to discern fully Woolf's conception of Rhoda as an erotic being, we must turn to what Woolf excised from her own text. Rhoda's orgasmic ecstasy while reading Shelley's poem "The Question" is much more overt in Woolf's unpublished passages. The homoerotic component of Rhoda's experience will also be much more discernible when we examine passages Woolf excised both during and after their initial composition. Throughout the two holograph drafts and the published version of *The Waves*, Rhoda asks, "Oh, to whom?" to give of herself, give the flowers she has "gathered" while reading Shelley's poem. Rhoda first asks *her* question during a sensual awakening brought on by reading the poem:

> I will bind flowers in one garland and clasp them and present them—Oh! to whom? There is some check in the flow of my being; a deep stream presses on some obstacle. . . . Now my body thaws; I am unsealed, I am incandescent. Now the stream pours in a deep tide fertilising, opening the shut, forcing the tight-folded, flooding free. To whom shall I give all that now flows through me, from my warm, my porous body? (*TW* 57)

While this passage is erotic in its own right, Woolf's first draft is substantially more sensual and more explicit. Woolf's earlier draft describes sensations in Rhoda's thighs and, though she crosses it out, Woolf refers to Rhoda's moistness as well as the wetness of the flowers—water lilies with "broad green leaves," which in this early draft are also intensely eroticized. Moreover, there is in this version the suggestion that Rhoda is aroused by the flowers themselves and that her flowing occurs simultaneously with the flowing of the water lilies' sweet scent: Rhoda laid the "floating water lilies"—"soft [*damp wet*]"—beside her, and "her body felt like them"; she felt "her sense of the overpowering sweetness of life, & its terror, in her thighs, which seemed full, [*lit*] laden like . . . bees with honey"; she let the "burden" in her thighs "flow, along with all the flow [*& sweetness & mystery of something hidden*], of the sweet smelling flowers, . . . of deep . . . sweet waters, with white lilies floating on them" (*H1* 128). And even more so than in the published version, Rhoda's "flooding" suggests orgasm, even ejaculation: "The sweet stream . . . went flowing out in a [*delicious*] <deep> tide fertilizing [*&*] thick & sweet, leaving her [*moist*], white, <in the pale—languid> exhausted, but relieved of some oppression, having overcome some vast obstacle & impediment. . . . "

(*H1* 129). Therefore, the image of Rhoda as "nymph of the fountain always wet" resonates not only with her connection to Arethusa and Artemis but also with her erotic experience of water lilies—Nymphaecea being their botanical family name.

Rhoda's *jouissance*, her "overcom[ing] of some vast obstacle," occurs while she is away at an all-girl's school, a section of the novel Woolf labeled in her notebook "Love for other girls" (*H* "Notebook" 750). In this part of the novel, Rhoda had tried unsuccessfully to "<seize the heart>" of a homoerotic "<adventure>," but it "<slipped, & escaped her>" (*H1* 123). The adventure, almost completely edited out of the published novel and even out of the second draft of *The Waves*, is one of the first imaginary worlds to which Rhoda retreats: "lying alone safe in the dark," "deep into the night," she invented "dream by dream, the wondrous story" of herself and Alice, whose lips faded as Rhoda was about to kiss her (*H1* 123). During the day "sometimes, [Rhoda] dared cast a look at [Alice]; & then quickly looked away; so as to gather that wonderful material from which to build, . . . in chapel, . . . sitting over a book, or in bed at night, those pagodas, those dreams" (*H1* 123). When Rhoda saw her during the day, her "whole being washed <rocked> from side to side and stopped," and she found it difficult to "sit still & draw breath . . . while Alice looked at her" (*H1* 122), for the "fact of her presence was staggering" (*H1* 123). At a young age, Rhoda understands that her desire to live out a "wondrous story" with another girl must be relegated to another world, must be knocked down during the day; and even in her dreams, she is aware of the need for concealment, for when an imaginary tree fails to provide shade from the censure of light, the lips she is about to kiss fade:

> How beautiful when night came, to let the great tower, that one has always to knock down by day, build itself over one. . . . The day . . . was too hard for the perfect unfolding, complete and entire, of what was in her <all those pagodas>; but in the emptiness of night these giant trees grew, these unreal & beautiful trees; & she lay awake [*long*] deep into the night, going with agility among their [*gr*] glistening leaves; but always as she was about to kiss [*her*], the lips faded. The tree was light; it had no roots; its leaves cast no shadow. (*H1* 123)

In the published novel, these dreams center on "nameless," "immaculate people" and suggest that Rhoda desires their admiration more than their affection: "At night, in bed, I excite their complete wonder. I often die pierced with arrows to win their tears" (44)—perhaps another coded reference to Artemis. Some of what Rhoda feels for Alice is transferred in the published novel to Rhoda's feelings for Miss Lambert, who makes Rhoda feel literally lambent and whose flame melts Rhoda's spine into softness: "things are changed under her eyes. . . . even my body now lets the light through; my spine is soft like wax near the flame of the candle. I dream; I dream" (45). Miss Lambert's standing "like a statue in a grove" also resonates with Woolf's excised reference to Artemis—"there is a statue of Artemis in the glade" (*H1* 202). While Rhoda's feelings for Miss Lambert comprise the most overtly lesbian text in the published novel, they allow a resisting reader to posit that admiration rather than sexual longing fuels Rhoda's affection—a reading nearly impossible to sustain in the story of Rhoda and Alice.

The haunting quality of the imaginary world Rhoda inhabits with Alice, where lips fade and trees cast no shadow, is also present in Woolf's narration of Rhoda's death. With each revision of *The Waves*, Rhoda's death is further elided: fewer details are given about how she dies, and the revelation of her death becomes less dramatically situated in the novel. In the first holograph draft, Rhoda drowns: "<This air will fill my throat with bubbles>" (*H1* 320), an unsettling foreshadowing of Woolf's own suicide. In the second holograph Rhoda "fall[s] by accident it was said, from a window" (*H2* 720) (eerily, Woolf tried to commit suicide by throwing herself out of a window in 1904). In the published novel, however, the way Rhoda kills herself remains vague. Her suicide is first mentioned in Bernard's final soliloquy at the end of a long sentence of which Rhoda is not even the primary subject: the revelation that "she had killed herself" follows a semicolon (281). However, in the novel's first draft, Rhoda's death is revealed before Bernard's final soliloquy and is mourned in the soliloquies of Jinny and especially Louis (*H1* 321–28). In the published novel, her suicide receives much less narrative attention. Rhoda—who lives in the white spaces between hour and hour, who comes "from nowhere" to greet her friends (120), and who as a child cries, "Oh, save me, from being blown for ever outside the loop of time!" (22)—fittingly seems to disappear from the novel. Even the phrase that alludes to the act of suicide decenters Rhoda as subject: says Bernard, "I . . . feel the rush of the wind of her flight when she leapt" (289).

In an intricate linguistic analysis of the phrase that "stands in" for Rhoda's suicide, Garrett Stewart concludes that "[d]ying by elision, Rhoda is mourned by it" (454). Moreover, Stewart introduces the linguistic possibility of a "spectral" murderer who "shoves" Rhoda to her death:

> Beyond the precipitant cadence charted by those doubled "of's" ("the rush of the wind of her flight"), what is so grueling and at the same time so elusive about the phrasing is the flickering displacement between the "rush" and the preposition that places it, that ascribes it to Rhoda. . . . Between "rush" and "of," in other words, in quite another word, flashes in eclipse the very "shoving" off that brings her to her death. Overheard, that is, in the interstice, flung between monosyllables, is the phantom reshuffling: "*rush of.*" Though the verb "shove" can be intransitive, it usually takes an object; yet the ghostly hint of some unspoken external agency here—someone shoving *her*—remains just that, phantasmal. (453–54)

Stewart contends that because Rhoda's "own death scene" is "syncopated out of plot altogether," she "leaves the novel as the most extravagant avatar of discontinuity in modern fiction" (452–53). The "spectral assault" that occurs as a result of the syncopation vanishes in a "phonemic schism," notes Stewart, for "[i]t is immediately *internalized* by the fact of self-murder" (454; emphasis added).

But what transpires linguistically in the phrase that represents Rhoda's death can be said to occur to her throughout *The Waves*: she internalizes the assaults of others against her. In an apostrophe addressed to "human beings"—"how I have hated you" (203)—Rhoda summarizes the lifelong self-effacement demanded of her:

> What dissolution of the soul you demanded in order to get through one day, what lies, bowings, scrapings, fluency and servility! How you chained me to one spot, one hour, one chair, and sat yourselves down opposite! How you snatched from me the white spaces that lie between hour and hour and rolled them into dirty pellets and tossed them into the wastepaper basket with your greasy paws. Yet those were my life. But I yielded. . . . I did not go out into the street and break a bottle in the gutter as a sign of rage. (204)

Rhoda is not only made to conform to the desires of others, she is destroyed by them. By "yield[ing]" to their demands instead of raging against them, she finishes the "murder" they have begun. This is more literally the case in an earlier draft of the speech in which Rhoda completes the disposal of her life that others have incited. While in the published monologue others roll her life into dirty pellets *and* throw them away, in the earlier manuscript Rhoda says, "I have tossed [the pellets/ my life] into the wastepaper basket directly you were gone" (*H2* 624), making more explicit the reciprocity between symbolic murder and symbolic suicide.[7]

Garrett Stewart attributes Rhoda's destructive self-erasure to a pervasive semiotic crisis: "Otherness, massed before her, is a theft of self-presence, a robbery by the mob of symbol-using peers" (434). Stewart's brilliant analysis of Rhoda's trauma concludes that her "recoil from language as a system, from writing as a sequence, is only a measure of her expulsion from it at its point of origin" (439–40). Therefore, he credits Woolf with creating "one of the first characters in the modern novel to recognize in this way the self's native effacement" (440). However, in the margins of Stewart's analysis of Rhoda's crisis is another "specter," toward which he occasionally glances—often with thinly veiled irritation—but that he invariably dismisses: the politics of gender and sexuality. Invoking Kristeva's deconstruction of the opposition between the masculine and the feminine when addressing gender, Stewart does not explore the political implications inherent in the fact that Bernard's semiotic crisis is much less detrimental to him than Rhoda's is to her. Stewart maintains that for Bernard, Rhoda's "counterpart" (449), "this dispersal across the weft of language" is "most explicitly a metaphysical crisis" because he "has all along had the greatest faith in the easing and healing power of language," while for Rhoda this dispersal "is most piercing a grief" (426). Stewart's reliance on Kristevan theory obscures the sexual politics of Rhoda's semiotic crisis, for he encounters the very limitations that Toril Moi warns against when positing the "considerable promise" of a "combination of Derridean and Kristevan theory" for feminist readings of Woolf: "[Kristeva's] belief that the revolution within the subject somehow prefigures a later social revolution poses severe problems for any materialist analysis of society" (15).

In a sentence that was completely excised from the published novel, Bernard reveals his own acute consciousness of the sexual politics inherent in his ability to adjust to a world Rhoda must finally flee:

> No *woman* can ever know that feeling of perfect [*adjustment*]; of well being; of power; of absolute adjustment to a [*perfectly*] satisfactory universe (think of Rhoda) . . . [and] waifs & strays of our civilization, outside always, flying through the world to some other end, intolerant & scornful & always ridiculing my [*trophies, my succeses*], measured tread, . . . & the *trophies* which I could show her. (*H2* 685; emphasis added)

But Stewart's heralding of Rhoda as an "avatar of discontinuity" and as a *universal* symbol of the individual's break with language as a system of meaning overlooks Rhoda's unique position in Woolf's novel: she is the only character in *The Waves* whose sexuality creates itself outside a phallocentric universe, who rejects and scorns the "trophies" such a universe could show her.

Outwardly disdainful of "trophies" herself, Woolf was nonetheless aware of the importance of not appearing too disdainful of patriarchy, as she made playfully apparent in *A Room of One's Own*. It was perhaps Woolf's fear of censure that caused her to excise and encode references to Rhoda's lesbianism in *The Waves*, a novel that Woolf deemed to be "serious" and that she very much wanted taken seriously. In 1929, the same year Woolf began writing *The Waves*, she was worried that even a letter to Vita Sackville-West would not be safe from the tyrannical censorship that was spreading across England. In the same letter in which she tells Vita that "The percentage of Lesbians is rising in the States, all because of you"—that is, the publication of *Orlando*—she writes, "Lawrences poems have been seized in ms by the police in the post. . . . nothing will be safe—not this letter" (*L* 4: 14). It was also only one year since obscenity charges had been brought against Radclyffe Hall's *The Well of Loneliness*. So it is not surprising that in her first draft of *The Waves*, Woolf draws a line through the name of the girl Rhoda loves: "the wondrous story of [Alice] & herself"; "as [Rhoda] was about to kiss [*her*], the lips faded" (*H1* 123).[8] Interestingly, the title page of the manuscript book that directly precedes this excised passage about Rhoda and Alice is dated October 29, 1929, only six days after Woolf writes in her diary that upon the publication of *A Room of One's Own* she anticipates being "attacked for a feminist & hinted at for a sapphist," adding, "I am afraid it will not be taken seriously" (*D* 3: 262).

Woolf was very likely anxious that hints of sapphism, playfully negotiated in *Orlando*, would be virulently attacked (perhaps even prosecuted) in her self-described "very serious, mystical, poetical work," and that such content would further alienate friends like E. M. Forster, who wouldn't review *A Room of One's Own* and who was recorded in Woolf's diary as saying that "he thought Sapphism disgusting: partly from convention, partly because he disliked that women should be independent of men" (*D* 3: 193). Not surprisingly, Woolf is direct about Neville's homosexuality and his love for Percival in *The Waves*; for male homosexuality, at least as Woolf witnessed it in her circle of friends, cemented rather than weakened patriarchy. Furthermore, Woolf's depiction of same-sex desire between men often serves to reinforce more subtle evocations of same-sex desire between women, as Septimus Smith's homosexuality in *Mrs. Dalloway* underscores the more oblique lesbianism of Clarissa Dalloway.

While Rhoda's lesbianism is even more obliquely depicted by Woolf than Clarissa Dalloway's, Rhoda's invisibility is much more profoundly rendered. Rhoda remains invisible, as she is unable to conjure a self that will conform to patriarchal standards. Rhoda's world, her face, her body, even her language, are still inchoate—as is a way of writing the truth about a woman's experiences as a body, as Woolf reminds us in "Professions for Women." In the meantime, others create Rhoda and destroy her: they chain her "to one spot" so that they may sit themselves "down opposite" (204); they print her mind with their faces and "stain" and "corrupt" her (203); even Louis acknowledges this destruction, for he thinks of Rhoda "when the old men come with pointed sticks and pierce little bits of paper as we pierced her" (203). At the six characters' last meeting, Rhoda feels she must "undergo the *penance* of Hampton Court" (223; emphasis added), where she imagines her death as aided by her friends:

> After all these callings hither and thither, these pluckings and searchings, I shall fall alone through this thin sheet into gulfs of fire. And you will not help me. More cruel than the old torturers you will let me fall, and will tear me to pieces when I am fallen. (224)

The "old torturers" may be those who leap at Rhoda like tigers through the open doors of drawing rooms, whose "tongues" flicker over her like flames, making her "prevaricate and fence them off with lies" (106).

But Woolf may also be evoking those "old torturers" who burned women they called witches—women, who like Rhoda, do not contribute to, and thereby threaten, the patriarchal economies of production and desire. Even without Woolf's expurgated hints of Rhoda's lesbianism, there is much to recommend Rhoda as a "witch." Fatherless, husbandless, manless, childless, and "wild"—Rhoda is a "conspirator" (227), who seemingly comes from "nowhere" to meet her friends; who conjures up dark pools on the other side of this world where a swallow can dip her wings at midnight; who dreams of "falling off the edge of the earth at night when [her] bed floats suspended" (223); who seems to vanish from the novel; and "who flies with her neck outstretched and blind fanatic eyes, past us" (198).

With a bewitching incantation of her own, Virginia Woolf conjures up Shakespeare's sister in *A Room of One's Own* in order to prove to us that "any woman born with a great gift in the sixteenth century would certainly have gone crazed, shot herself, or ended her days in some lonely cottage outside the village, half witch, half wizard, feared and mocked at"

(51). Rhoda reminds us that in the twentieth century, women still must live on the margins, must exile their dreams to another world. Though centuries apart, Judith Shakespeare and Rhoda share the same silencer: the choric roar of patriarchal rite that drums its way into women's dreams and sends them to their deaths or exiles them to invisible spaces that edge over into madness. That such a roar echoed in Woolf's brain is evidenced in nearly everything she wrote. Locating even its most faint reverberations can help us hear what melodies it altered, maybe even what melodies it silenced altogether.

NOTES

1. The pagination of J. W. Graham, editor of the holographs, is used throughout my citations. *H1* indicates the first holograph draft and *H2* the second. "Notebook" indicates looseleaf notes included in Graham's edition. However, I have checked every citation of Graham's for accuracy against those in Woolf's seven holograph notebooks of *The Waves* in the Berg Collection at the New York City Public Library. Having found only minor discrepancies, I have decided, for the sake of uniformity, to refer to them in the "Notes," in which case I use the pagination of the Berg Collection.

2. Jane Marcus suggests that the submerged sexuality in "Professions for Women" is lesbian: "the underwater world of the woman artist's imagination suggests a submarine lesbian utopia where desire and writing are intimately connected" ("Taking the Bull" 155).

3. According to Woolf's diary and the research of J. W. Graham, Woolf completed her second draft and her second typescript on February 7, 1931 (*H* 39).

4. As Anne Olivier Bell points out, what emerged from Woolf's plans to write a sequel to *A Room of One's Own* were actually two books, *The Years* and *Three Guineas* (*D* 4, fn. 6).

5. That Aphrodite briefly entered Woolf's mind, as is indicated by the crossed-out "~~Aphro~~," is significant given the goddess of love's emergence from sea foam. It also suggests that the statue Rhoda seeks is imbued with eroticism. In Woolf's holograph notebook 2 at the Berg Collection, page 165, the line is drawn through only part of the word: "A~~phro~~" (*H1* 202).

6. Louise DeSalvo has observed that Woolf frequently used animal imagery to convey male aggression, especially sexual violence. When Woolf referred to her own sexual abuse, she wrote about "her feeling of being pursued by something animal, of being locked in a cage from which she cannot escape the bestial attention of her animal pursuers" (DeSalvo, *Impact* 159).

7. In *A Rhetoric of Motives*, Kenneth Burke offers a useful method of analysis for poetry that symbolizes suicide by murder imagery and vice versa: "You need to look for a *motive that can serve as ground for both these choices* [murder and

suicide], a motive that while not being exactly one or the other, can ambiguously contain them both" (10).

8. In Woolf's holograph draft, the word "Alice" does not have a line drawn through it, as J. W. Graham indicates in his transcription. Woolf drew a light, squiggly vertical line (slightly on an axis) through the ampersand: "Alice & herself" (H2 7). Graham's mark, however, is in keeping with editorial practices surrounding the transcription of Woolf's holographs, as she often crossed out only part of what she wished to delete.

FOURTEEN

"Pearls and the Porpoise": **The Years—** A Lesbian Memoir

PATRICIA CRAMER

Virginia Woolf began writing *The Years* in her fiftieth year—an apt time for recollection and reassessment. Woolf's reminiscent mood during the thirties is apparent in the letters and diaries as well as in the novel. During her trip to Greece in April 1932, for example, Woolf considers the passage of time: "but what can I say about the Parthenon—that my own ghost met me, the girl of 23, with all her life to come" (*D* 4: 90). That Woolf's nostalgia during the thirties carried over into the writing of the novel is suggested by the end to the holograph when Eleanor similarly looks back on a younger self: "And then she must have been young, almost a girl; and that girl was dead; had vanished; But that the sleeping street seemed for a moment the grave; & the pigeons were crooning a requiem, for her past; for all of the selves that had been here" (*H* 8: 956). Between 1931 and 1937, as she composed this novel, the deaths of valued friends—Lytton Strachey, Dora Carrington, and Roger Fry—and the rise of fascism seemed to portend "the end of everything [she] cared for" (*TY* 332). At the same time, Woolf was reluctantly accepting the end of her romantic intimacy with Vita Sackville-West, which had begun in 1925. In 1935, Woolf writes, "I could here analyse my state of mind these past 4 months, & account for the human emptiness by the defection of Vita; Roger's death; & no-one springing up to take their place" (*D* 4: 287).

However, as Carolyn Heilbrun points out, Woolf responded to the challenges of age and loss with a vigorous self-confidence. Woolf declared herself in 1932 "free to define my attitude with a vigour & certainty I have never known before" (*D* 4: 135). This well-earned self-confidence and the urgency of the times inspired Woolf's grandiose plans for *The Years*: that it be a "terrific affair"; "give the whole of the present society—nothing less" (*D* 4: 151); "a summing up of all [she] knew" (*D* 4: 152). A confluence of these influences—the nostalgia and self-assurance of middle age and the loss of Vita—seem to have motivated Woolf to encode a lesbian memoir into her seemingly conventional chronicle, *The Years*.[1]

Virginia Woolf's intentions to write a lesbian memoir of epic proportions are perhaps best indicated by *The Years'* carefully constructed kinship with Marcel Proust's *Remembrance of Things Past*. Early in her writing career, Woolf considered Proust as a possible influence. In 1922 she writes to Roger Fry:

> But Proust so titillates my own desire for expression that I can hardly set out the sentence. Oh if I could write like that! I cry. And at the moment such is the astonishing vibration and saturation and intensification that he procures—theres something sexual in it—that I feel I *can* write like that, and seize my pen and then I *can't* write like that. Scarcely anyone so stimulates the nerves of language in me: it becomes an obsession. But I must return to Swann. (*L* 2: 525; emphasis in original)

The parallels between *The Years* and *Remembrance of Things Past* are numerous and easily identified. Both works follow the changes within the middle and upper classes within a generation; adopt composite characters based on people the authors knew; focus on parties and dinners as keys to personal and political mores; and code homosexual content into familiar life stories. Thematically, both works are preoccupied with the associative logic of memory; the ways in which the past encroaches on the present; the role of childhood in the formation of adult sexual desire; the search for the objects that will release buried emotions; and—most important for the focus of this essay—the joys and anguish of unrequited homoerotic love.

In *The Years* Woolf writes a lesbian-based "remembrance of things past," a retrospective memoir of her own sexual history and an elegy and love lyric commemorating her relationship with her lover, Vita Sackville-West. During the composition of this novel, memoirs by homosexual authors were very much on Virginia Woolf's mind. In 1933 she praised Ethel Smyth's autobiography *Female Pipings in Eden* (*L* 5: 249), and in 1934 she read André Gide's journal, which she found "full of startling recollection—things I cd have said myself" (*D*: 4: 241). In her early draft of *The Years*, *The Pargiters*, she makes explicit her intention to imitate memoirs: "It is based upon some scores—I might boldly say thousands—of old memoirs" (*P* 9). Like Proust, Woolf integrates fragmented memories from her own life into a fictionalized autobiography and weaves a lament for lost homoerotic love into a seemingly conventional literary chronicle.[2]

Typically, Woolf integrates her lesbian themes into a multilayered narrative and metaphoric structure. Thus *The Years* is simultaneously a "threnody for the dying Victorian patriarchal family" (Marcus, *The Years* 36), and for the demise of the British empire (Phillips 26–51) and the patriarchal state (Cramer, "Matriarchal")—as well as an elegy for her love affair with Vita Sackville-West. However, the passing of patriarchal norms is celebrated in this novel, while the losses of lesbian love—the unacted desires and the love that has ended—are tinged with regret. As she reviews her lifetime of passionate attachments to women, Woolf makes use of the elegy's capacity to commemorate the value of what was and the tragedy of what possibilities remain unfulfilled.[3]

The emphasis on loss and memory in *The Years* was inspired in large part by Vita's "defection" due to her preoccupation with her sister-in-law Gwen St. Aubyn (Glendinning 265). Vita's love was very important to Virginia's personal happiness and to her work. Vanessa Bell, who probably knew Virginia best, once described Vita as "the person Virginia loved most . . . outside her own family" (474). In her letters and diaries, Woolf repeatedly attests to the sensuous joy she found only with Vita. In 1926, Virginia tells Vita, "I was wholly and entirely happy. If you could have uncored me—you would have seen every nerve running fire—intense, but calm" (*L* 3: 306). In 1928, she describes to Vita "*a sensation I get only from you* . . . physically stimulating, restful at the same time I feel supple and anointed" (*L* 3: 540; emphasis added). Woolf frequently speaks of Vita's inspirational influence on her writing. For example, shortly after a visit from Vita, Woolf writes: "I felt the spring beginning, & Vita's life so full & flush; & all the doors opening; . . . I then begin to make up my story whatever it is; ideas rush in me" (*D* 3: 287). As late as January 1933, Woolf complains that when Vita is gone, "a whole patch of my internal globe [becomes] extinct" (*L* 5: 148). In 1927, Woolf could confidently tease Vita—"Never will you shake me off, try as you may" (*L* 3: 453)—but by 1934, Woolf found that Vita was, tactfully but inexorably, doing just that. As she wrote *The Years*, Virginia Woolf was reluctantly accepting that the woman who had been her lover, confidante, and muse for nearly ten years had left her for another woman.

Woolf complained to Ethel Smyth: "I've never a word from V which rather hurts me, save that I know what is to be has to be" (*L* 5: 435). To

Vita, Virginia described herself as "hardened and battered" by love (*L* 6: 194). Despite Woolf's characteristic humor, her pain at Vita's defection was real, and so, too, her need to reconcile herself to this loss. In 1935, Woolf writes to Ethel, "I'm pained, rather, to use my grandmother's language, about Vita and Gwen" (*L* 5: 362). But as Woolf reluctantly began to accept her loss of intimacy with Vita as unavoidable, her letters, as well as Vita's, began to focus on fond remembrances of their former passion. In 1935, Virginia asks to see Vita, adding, "Mere affection—to the memory of the porpoise in the pink window" (*L* 5: 370). In 1937, Woolf writes to Vita, "Dont you remember offering me Thackerays wine cooler or ash tray or something in the days of the fishmonger and how I said: Unhand me Sirrah?" (*L* 6: 195). In 1935, Virginia writes to Vita, "My mind is filled with dreams of romantic meetings. D'you remember once sitting at Kew in a purple storm?" (*L* 5: 370).

Woolf has "filled [*The Years*] with dreams of romantic meetings" by integrating references to her most cherished memories of Vita throughout the novel. Although Woolf attaches reminiscences of Vita to other women characters—for example, Peggy and Eleanor—Kitty most often enacts Woolf's favorite recollections. Kitty embodies the "commanding presence" (*L* 3: 153), the "dash & courage of the aristocracy" (*D* 2: 313) Virginia typically associated with Vita,[4] and other parallels between them are numerous and easy to find. Both drive huge motor cars; both garden; both appear frequently accompanied by dogs; and Kitty, like Vita, loses an estate because, as a woman, she cannot inherit the land she loves. Like Vita and Virginia, Kitty chooses a marriage that in her mother's words, "could give her what she wants . . . scope" (83).

Woolf's first recorded fantasy is of Vita striding through the woods: "If I were she, I should merely stride, with 11 Elk hounds, behind me, through my ancestral woods" (*L* 3: 150). In the 1930s, Woolf is still asking Vita, "And are you tramping the hills?" (*L* 4: 19). Kitty's most ecstatic moment is in tramping the hills of her ancestral woods in northern England. In the orgasmic imagery describing Kitty's climb to the top of the hill, we find that a significant source of Kitty's arousal is her unconscious response to scenery associated with her early crush on Miss Craddock: "spring was sad always, she thought; *it brought back memories*" (277; emphasis added). Like Proust, Woolf locates the stimulus for accessing buried emotion in objects reminiscent of a past experience. In *Remembrance of Things Past*, Marcel explains that material objects linked with the past can release profound emotions, whether or not the actual memory becomes conscious: "and so it is with our own past. It is a la-bour in vain to attempt to recapture it: all the efforts of our intellect must prove futile. The past is hidden somewhere outside the realm beyond the reach of intellect in some material object (in the sensation which that material object will give us)" (47–48).

Like Swann's famous madeleine, the flowers Kitty encounters on the moors release emotions linked with past memories. When Kitty kisses a flower, she unconsciously recalls her adolescent love for Miss Craddock "brought back" by the sight of the "blue and white flowers, trembling on the cushions of green moss" (277). This memory suggests a sequence of gynelineal associations. Miss Craddock had given Kitty "wild flowers, blue and white, stuck into a cushion of wet green moss" (65); Miss Craddock is from the northern moors; the flowers are a present from Miss Craddock's sister from the moors; Kitty's mother is from the moors, and also the family of her friend, Nelly Robson. Swann's made-leine resurrects feelings of "exquisite pleasure" and "all-powerful joy" (Proust 48) associated with childhood memories of eating a madeleine on Sundays with his aunt, and Kitty's flowers cause her to feel "vigorous," "strong," and "happy" (277–78)—just as her tutoring sessions with Miss Craddock had invigorated and inspired her in her youth.

Proust's method of isolating small pieces of a past experience—such as the tea-soaked madeleine and Vinteuil's "little phrase" (Proust 379)—to access powerful feelings locked in memory is also Woolf's strategy for coding lesbian autobiography in *The Years*. For example, the alpine flow-ers are avatars of Woolf's own lesbian past, as well as Kitty's, because Vita once gave Virginia a miniature garden similar to the one Miss Crad-dock gave to Kitty: "an earthenware pan containing several rocks and small alpine plants" (*L* 3: 210). By weaving reminiscences of her love affair with Vita throughout this novel, Woolf is able to resurrect, grieve, and pay tribute to those passionate lesbian feelings associated with her mem-ories of Vita. Just as Woolf's characters in *The Years* are repeatedly per-plexed by emotions called up by objects or fragmented memories linked with the past, involved readers not privy to Woolf's lesbian codes unwit-tingly participate in Woolf's work of mourning by sharing ecstasies like Kitty's hilltop epiphany that are autobiographical and lesbian-based.

Woolf's autobiographical intentions for Kitty's journey to the moors are even more evident once we recognize that Kitty's journey replicates one of Virginia's favorite memories of Vita—a train ride to the north that they took together on June 29, 1927, to watch an eclipse at dawn. The details of Virginia and Vita's holiday are recorded in "The Sun and the Fish" published in *Time and Tide* on February 3, 1928. On February 8, Vita wrote to Virginia, "I can't tell you how much I like the Sun and the Fish (all the more because it is all about things we did together) . . ." (Sackville-West, *Letters* 255).

Kitty's overnight train ride closely imitates Virginia's memory of her journey to Yorkshire with Vita. Both journeys begin in London late at night and end in Yorkshire at dawn at approximately the same time of year: May (Kitty) and June (Virginia and Vita). In the "cold raw air" (272) and "chill early morning" ("Sun and Fish" 212), all three find themselves on high ground overlooking the moors. In "The Sun and the Fish," Woolf describes the moors "as a high fell where the hills stretched their limbs out over the flowing brown moorland below" (213). In *The Years*, Kitty looks "over the billowing land that went rising and falling, away and away" (277). In both the essay and the novel, Woolf describes the trip as a journey out of time and as a moment of transformation: "we were no longer in the same relation to people, houses and trees" ("Sun and Fish" 213) and "she seemed to be passing from one world to another; this was the moment of transition" (*TY* 267).

Woolf summarizes the emotional transition that the eclipse suggested to her: "after destruction calm; after ruin steadfastness" ("Sun and Fish" 216), apparently suggested to Woolf by the "defeat [and return] of the sun" ("Sun and Fish" 215). Time seems to stop: "the flesh and blood of the world was dead and only the skeleton was left" ("Sun and Fish" 215), until suddenly the sun "rose again elsewhere" ("Sun and Fish" 215–16). Although Kitty does not see an eclipse, as she looks over the moors, cloud movements imitate the dappling effects of the eclipse from 1927: "light and shadow went traveling over the hills and over the valleys" (*TY* 278). Both of these memoirs of Virginia and Vita's journey to the eclipse conclude on a note of triumph. "The Sun and the Fish" finishes with "a sense of rejuvenescence and recovery" (215–16), and Kitty's hike up the hill ends with "the land itself, singing to itself, a chorus, alone" (*TY* 278).

There are many other references in *The Years* to memories from the heyday of Vita and Virginia's courtship besides this midnight train ride to see the eclipse. For example, Vita frequently picked Virginia up in her "sweeping black car" (*L* 6: 232) or sent presents through her chauffeur. Kitty's arrival at the suffragette meeting is heralded by the cooing of pigeons and the "rush of a car outside" (176). Whenever Kitty offers Eleanor a lift in her "magnificent car" (179), she reenacts one of Virginia and Vita's favorite dating rituals. The incident Woolf recalls most often in the letters and diaries occurred in December 1925 when Virginia unexpectedly came upon Vita standing in the doorway of a fishmonger's shop in Sevenoaks. In 1925, Woolf imagines Vita "hung with grapes, pink with pearls, lustrous, candle lit, in the door of a Sevenoaks draper" (*L* 3: 224); and in 1926, she compares Vita to "that festal light . . . which stands in the door of the Sevenoaks fishmonger" (*L* 3: 309). Such dramatic doorway stances seem characteristic of Woolf's fondest memories with Vita, so that the mysterious "well dressed lady" "vibrating, in the door" whom Nicholas compares to "a ball on the top of a fishmonger's fountain" (369) is likely another apparition of Vita.

Recollections of Virginia and Vita's week alone in France in 1928 appear, significantly, during Peggy's scornful thoughts about heterosexual love and marriage. Thinking of North, Peggy sneers, "he'll tie himself up with a red-lipped girl, and become a drudge. He must, and I can't" (396). Peggy's comments could simply mean she doesn't want to marry, but "can't" simultaneously suggests that she envies Martin's socially approved sexual access to women.[5] Thoughts of love and marriage stir up old memories in Peggy: "I've a sense of guilt always. I shall pay for it, I shall pay for it. I kept saying to myself even in the Roman camp" (396). At the literal level, Peggy probably refers to the night when she broke family rules to hear owls singing at midnight when she was still a young girl at home. At the same time, Woolf has again "slipped in" another reference to a rendezvous with Vita. In 1928, as Woolf anticipated a trip to France with Vita, Woolf was ambivalent about leaving Leonard: "I am melancholy and excited in turn. You see, I would not have married Leonard had I not preferred living with him to saying good-bye to him. But at the same time, the Roman ruins in Auxerre excite my interest" (*L* 3: 531). Apparently, guilt over Leonard did not entirely ruin their vacation, for in 1939, Vita includes their trip to France among her fondest memories with Virginia: "Well, dig in your memory and perhaps you will remember a porpoise on a marble slab—You remember a thunderstorm at Vezaley [France] . . . ?" (Sackville-West, *Letters* 422). Woolf often "slips" lesbian content into her fiction as she does in Peggy's reference to the Roman ruins, even when the autobiographical allusion has no obvious relevance to the narrative. In this way, she is able to include lesbian meanings without disturbing the non-lesbian narrative or metaphoric intentions of a passage.

In *The Years*, Woolf even manages to pay homage to Vita's aging beauty by slipping comments about Vita's appearance into Eleanor's admiring thoughts about Mrs. Levy's daughter. Eleanor finds Mrs. Levy's daughter, with her "red cheeks and white pearls," "extraordinarily hand-some" (31) even though "she had taken to painting her face" (30). Char-acteristically, the parallels between Woolf's life and the novel are close. In the novel, Mrs. Levy's daughters "wore pearls as big as hen's eggs" (30); in her diary, Woolf recalls "knotting [Vita's] pearls into heaps of great lustrous eggs" (D 3: 117). Vita's use of paint was on Woolf's mind when she composed *The Years*: she complained in 1934 that Vita had "grown opulent & bold & red, tomatoe coloured, & paints her fingers & lips which need no paint" (D 4: 226).

The pigeons, nightingales (TY 319; L 4: 29), and porpoises (TY 62) scattered throughout the novel also have associations with Vita. During the thirties, Vita became increasingly preoccupied not only with Gwen St. Aubyn, but with gardening at her estate, Sissinghurst. One of Woolf's favorite jokes during Vita's thirties retreat to Sissinghurst are of Vita alone, writing in her tower, surrounded by pigeons. In 1933, Woolf writes about Vita, "do let her come down from her rose-red tower where she sits with thousands of pigeons cooing over her head" (L 5: 266). Pigeons fre-quently accompany Kitty in the novel and appear in passages suggestive of lesbian meanings. Following her visit to Miss Craddock, Kitty cannot identify the object of her restless desire, so she merely articulates to her-self—"I want. . . ." When she glances at a nearby jug, Kitty's mind leaps to thoughts of Eleanor: "What would Nel think of this" (75).[6] As Kitty unconsciously locates the object of her interest in Eleanor, we find "far away pigeons were cooing. . ." (75). Pigeons herald Kitty's typically dra-matic arrival at the meeting that Sara reports to Maggie: "there were pigeons cooing . . . and in came Kitty clothed in starlight" (187). At the end of the novel, Kitty, still trying to get Eleanor into her car, asks, "Can't I give you a lift back, Nel? I've a car waiting." Eleanor does not answer, but "pigeons begin shuffling on the tree tops." "I've a car," Kitty repeats, hopefully. Then Eleanor, like Miss Craddock before her, resorts to the metaphoric shorthand Woolf developed for lesbian feelings: "Listen," Eleanor answers: then we are told, "it was the pigeons she meant" (433).

In *The Years* metaphors with lesbian connotations are invariably associ-ated with images of freedom and fertility—like the "slow porpoises [turn-ing] in a sea of oil" (48) linked with the revivifying rain. ("Porpoise" was one of Virginia's nicknames for Vita, probably linked in her imagination with Vita's appearance in the fishmonger's shop [L 5: 177].) Even the dap-pled lighting that recurs in the novel during visionary moments originates in romantic memories with Vita. In March 1941, Woolf writes to Vita, "I suppose your orchard is beginning to dapple as it did the day I came there. One of the sights I shall see on my death bed" (*L* 6: 476). When Martin views Sara "netted with floating lights from between the leaves," "a primal innocence seemed to brood over the scene" (242). The metaphors linking creative and visionary forces with lesbianism that permeate this novel are not limited to Vita. Laura Gottlieb identifies the red and gold images so prevalent in *The Years* with Sappho (224). This background mosaic of idyllic lesbian imagery, together with the romanticized reminiscences of her love affair with Vita that permeate this novel, can be read as expressions of the idealization of the beloved characteristic of elegiac nostalgia.

However, we can account for this utopian impulse in Woolf's representations of lesbian desire by reference to lesbian as well as elegiac literary conventions. As Terry Castle writes, lesbian fiction typically exhibits

> a profoundly attenuated relationship with what we think of, stereotypically, as narrative verisimilitude, plausibility, or "truth to life." Precisely because it is motivated by a yearning for that which is, in a cultural sense, implausible—the subversion of male homosocial desire—lesbian fiction characteristically exhibits, even as it masquerades as 'realistic' in surface detail, a strongly fantastical, allegorical, or utopian tendency. (88)

Nevertheless, throughout *The Years*, Woolf balances idealized portraits of lesbian love with realistic memories of betrayal, loss, and "defection." We can see this pattern most clearly in her autobiographical references to Vanessa, Janet Case, Madge Symonds Vaughan, and Ethel Smyth. As Woolf reviews her love life from the perspective of her sadness over losing Vita, she discovers a lifelong pattern of unrealized possibilities and recurrent lesbian heartache.

For example, in her recollections of Vanessa, Woolf recalls the life-affirming delights of their childhood "conspiracy" and lifelong friendship, as well as her anguish when Vanessa married. Woolf often referred to her love for her sister as one of the most important "romances" of her life: "But with you," she once wrote to Vanessa, "I am deeply passionately, unrequitedly in love" (*L* 3: 546). In *Moments of Being*, Woolf recalls the "private nucleus" and "instantaneous sympathy" she and her sister formed as little girls growing up in a "world of many men, coming and going" (*MOB* 143). "Together we shaped our own angle," Woolf writes, "and from it looked out at a world that seemed to both of us much the same" (*MOB* 143). Woolf associates the development of this sisterly point of view with their "continuous romance" conducted "under the nursery table" (*MOB* 28).

In *The Years*, Woolf imitates that childhood world "peopled with legs and skirts" (*MOB* 29) in the air raid shelter, where Eleanor "saw people's legs and skirts as they went past the area railings" (289), and in the Present Day chapter when Peggy, sitting at Eleanor's feet, gets a "queer view of people's feet" (385). In *The Years*, this "queer" viewpoint from below is Woolf's metaphor for the political and creative potential of lesbians' and other outsiders' points of view. For example, working-class women are included in this underworld of outsiders when the opening pages of the novel describe "servant girls in cap and apron . . . deviously ascending from the basement" (4). From the basement during the air raid, Eleanor imagines a world without war; at Eleanor's feet, Peggy imagines "real happiness" and "a world in which people were whole . . . free" (390). Despite these euphoric tributes to her relationship with Vanessa, Woolf suggests that this childhood promise of mutual love and common purpose was truncated by her sister's shift of her primary loyalties from Virginia to her husband, Clive Bell. In Sara's tearful disappointment when she faces her sister Maggie's impending marriage and motherhood (190), Woolf recalls her own jealousy and rage when Vanessa married.

When she recalls her adolescent crush on her tutor Janet Case in Kitty's history lesson with Miss Craddock, Woolf creates a scene tense with unacknowledged lesboerotic desires. Despite the mutual admiration between them, Miss Craddock rejects Kitty's attempt to become more confidential—partly out of loyalty to Kitty's father, who pays the tutoring fees. Instead, Miss Craddock diverts Kitty's attention with, "Look at my flowers . . . wild flowers, blue and white" (65). Woolf commonly uses flowers to suggest erotic feelings between women; the draft makes the unacknowledged lesbian desire between teacher and student even more obvious when Woolf writes that Kitty then "put her hand on the damp moss" (*H* 2: 114).

Woolf's youthful passion for Madge Symonds ended in disappointment when Madge married William Vaughan.[7] In a 1904 letter to Violet Dickinson written during a visit with Madge, Virginia describes the Vaughan marriage in terms nearly identical to her description of Eugenie's marriage to Digby:

> So I dont get much talk with Madge, and whenever we are alone for a minute in blunders Will, like George, and begs me not to let Madge talk morbidly. . . . Madge only longs for amusing unconventional people— artists and writers—and as she says—only Madge says many things without meaning them—Will is a Philistine and thinks there's something wrong

in cleverness. . . . The children are delightful; very healthy independent little animals. . . . Madge is always trying to make them go their own way,
and have their own ideas—and Will wants to "discipline" them in true ped-
agogic manner. (L 1: 156–57)

All of this is recognizable in *The Years*. Eugenie, though charming, "exag-
gerate[s]" (151), and she is "silenced the moment [Digby] comes into the
room" (L 4: 157). Eugenie encourages her daughters' wild dance around
the fire, and Digby is "lame and rather pompous" when he talks to the
children (127).

Just as Madge Vaughan's loyalty to her husband inhibited honest dialogue between her and Virginia, Eugenie's subservience to Digby limits
her intimacy with her daughters. When Eugenie's dance for her daughters is interrupted as soon as Digby calls her away, Sara responds to her
mother's abandonment by retreating into a chrysalis-like ball and falling
asleep. In the holograph draft, Sara's rage at her mother's defection is
more overt: "Whats the use of anything Maggie . . . tears stood in her
eyes. . . . She had no feeling of shame that her sister should see them roll
down her cheek. The woman's a liar. She spoke with . . . extraordinary
bitterness. . . . And why cant she tell the truth? Because of that little man
. . . the man's a shell; corrupt" (H 3: 148–49).

In the 1910 section, Rose reiterates Sara's angry and tearful response
to a woman's marriage. In depicting Rose's militant posturing and suffragette commitments, Woolf pays tribute to her lively relationship with
the lesbian Dame Ethel Smyth. In the draft, Rose's lesbian life is overtly
identified: we are told that "Rose flung herself into the arms of Mildred
in a greenhouse" (H 4: 70); the published version alludes merely to her
roommate. On her way to visit Maggie and Sara, Rose pauses on a
bridge and "remember[s] how she had stood there on the night of a certain engagement, crying." Rose concludes her reminiscence of lost love
by yelling, "Damn humbugs!" (161–62)—likely intended for those who
made lesbian love in her lifetime nearly impossible and lesbian heartache
almost inevitable.

Virginia Woolf's preoccupation during the thirties with the topic of
unrequited homosexual love is the probable reason that in *The Years* she
self-consciously imitates Marcel Proust's *Remembrance of Things Past*.
During the thirties, as Virginia Woolf reluctantly adjusted to Vita's
estrangement, she probably found in Proust's painstaking depiction of
Swann's disappointed love of Odette many "things she could have said
herself." When Swann begins to feel, with Odette, "the insinuation of a

possible undercurrent of falsehood which rendered ignoble all that had remained most precious to him" (Proust 404), Woolf may have recognized her own growing realization that Vita had lied to her on several occasions. In October 1932, for example, she writes to Vita, "Oh I was in such a rage of jealousy the other night, thinking you had been in love with Hilda that summer you went to the Alps together! Because you said you werent. Now were you?" (L 5: 111). Like Swann, Woolf was eventually forced to accept that her "hopes for happiness would not be realized now" (Proust 384), and in Remembrance of Things Past she recognized an author familiar with the heartache of the closet and of unrequited homosexual love.

The emotional center of Remembrance of Things Past (and of The Years) is aptly expressed in the "Overture" chapter of Swann's Way: "the anguish that comes from knowing that the creature one adores is in some place of enjoyment where oneself is not and cannot follow" (Proust 32). Woolf's letters to Ethel Smyth during the composition of The Years repeatedly express this longing for the absent lover: "Theres only one person I want to see, and she has no burning wish for anything but a rose red tower and a view of hop gardens and oats" (L 5: 66). In Proust's novel, this theme is represented most prominently in the stories of Swann's unrequited passion for Odette and Marcel's similarly frustrated love first for Gilbertte and then Albertine—but also by the reiteration of broken-hearted lovers in every volume. For example, in Swann's Way, figures such as M. Vinteuil, "dying of a broken heart" (Proust 161); the young woman secluded from society to avoid "him whose heart she had once held but had been unable to keep" (Proust 186); and even the parodied Legrandin, whose "wounded heart" longs for "silence and shadow" (Proust 138) compose a backdrop of loss out of which the dominant stories of disappointed love emerge.

In The Years, Woolf establishes kinship with Proust by constructing her novel in a similar reiterative pattern. In Eleanor's confused responses to Kitty's overtures, Miss Craddock's denial of Kitty's unconscious lesbian desires, Rose and Sarah's tears, and Peggy's regrets we find that lesbian love in The Years is passionate and unrequited. Like the broken-hearted lovers in the background of Remembrance of Things Past, this litany of lesbian heartbreak in The Years amplifies the emotional focus of the novel on mourning, memory, and Vita Sackville-West. With a writer's eye for what is common in personal experiences, both Proust and Woolf have identified in their novels what Terry Castle has defined as an archetype of homoerotic literature: "the pattern of rhapsody and betrayal"—

caused by the "sort of erotic misfortune to which the 'inverted' woman [and man] is prone and must somehow strive to transcend" (179, 180).[8]

The conversation between *The Years* and *Remembrance of Things Past* is so intimate that we can actually turn to Proust's novel to complete meanings in *The Years* that are otherwise inaccessible. For example, both novels portray characters leading double lives—particularly in regard to sexuality. The theme of the double life is introduced early in *Remembrance of Things Past*, where we find that Swann "had another almost secret existence of a wholly different kind ... when he left our house in Paris" (Proust 18); later, Swann finds that Odette's secret life had included lesbian affairs—sometimes contracted while he was present. As David R. Ellison points out, "The importance of homosexuality as one of the *Recherche's* major themes is obvious to all readers who have completed all six volumes of *Remembrance of Things Past*: by the end of the story many of the characters who had been (or appeared to be) heterosexual turn into *invertis*; the Proustian world becomes a homosexual haven" (659).

Through such close ties to *Remembrance of Things Past*, Woolf calls into question the presumed heterosexual fronts of all of her characters. If the six volumes of *Remembrance of Things Past* expose the closeted homosexual lives of so many seemingly straight characters, what would subsequent volumes of *The Years* tell us about— Rose's roommates? Eleanor and Miriam Parrish? Kitty and Margaret Marrable? Martin's late night rendezvous with the man from the nearby ranch? Edward's fondness for undergraduates?[9] I don't mean here to suggest anything so simple as that all the characters in *The Years* are gay or lesbian, but rather that the uncertainty of "who is and who isn't" is an ambiance deliberately created by Woolf in this novel. In *The Years*, not everyone is homosexual, but anyone *could be*. This atmosphere of tantalizing uncertainty and ubiquitous possibility is, of course, the world seen from the perspective of the lesbian and gay closet—the same angle of vision from which *Remembrance of Things Past* is cast. When we recall that in *The Pargiters* Woolf declared her "intention ... to represent English life at its most normal, most typical, and most representative" (9), we find that through this deliberately created ambiguity Woolf reflects a version of British history in which lesbians and gay men are commonplace and omnipresent, or in Terry Castle's words, "as familiar and crucial as an old friend" (2).

In *The Years*, the best example of Woolf's sharing of metaphors from *Remembrance of Things Past* is Eleanor's otherwise enigmatic memory of the milk can at the end of the novel.[10] Appropriately, for a novel so preoccupied with sex and romance, *The Years* concludes with a summing up of the aging Pargiters' love life. Just after Patrick and Delia have recalled romances from their youth, Eleanor adds: "And I . . . She saw an empty milk jug and leaves falling" (433). In *The Years*, autumn and an empty milk jug refer back to 1891, when Eleanor went to Delia's rundown apartment to speak about Parnell's recent death. Eleanor anxiously paces in the street below in a "horribly poor" neighborhood; looks up at the closed windows; "mounts the wooden stairs"; knocks on a closed door; sees the empty milk can. Eleanor's ruminations as she glances anxiously up at the window express her desire to speak with Delia and her upper-middle-class discomfort with working-class poverty. However, with pigeons "croon[ing] on the tree tops" nearby, we can be sure Woolf intends a simultaneous lesbian dimension to this scene. If we recall Woolf's depictions of Vita as inaccessibly shut away in her "rose-red" tower, Eleanor's anxious pacing in the street below seems to act out Woolf's fantasy scenario for her relationship with Vita during the thirties. In keeping with the simultaneity of meaning Woolf sustains throughout the novel, the "paper-boys crying death . . . death . . . death" certainly refer to Parnell but also, perhaps, to the death of love (114–15).

We can also turn for clues to Eleanor's mysterious love story to the companion piece to Woolf's novel, *Remembrance of Things Past*, where the figure of the distraught lover pacing outside the closed door of the recalcitrant beloved is overtly linked with the anguish of unrequited love—in language nearly identical to that used by Woolf. In the Overture chapter to *Swann's Way*, we find the young Marcel longing to meet his uncle's mistress, "thinking of the weary and fruitless novitiate eminent men would go through, perhaps for years on end, on the doorstep of some such lady who refused to answer their letters and had them sent packing by the hall porter" (Proust 81).

The culmination of Swann's romantic enthrallment to Odette occurs during Saint-Euverte's party, and here, again, the fantasy of the rejected lover pacing outside a closed door reappears. While climbing the elegant staircase at Saint-Euverte's, Swann imagines climbing "that pestilential but longed-for staircase to the old dressmaker's," where Odette had told him she would be that evening; he further pictures "an empty, unwashed milk-can set out upon the door-mat in readiness for the morning round" (Proust 354). The empty milk jug as emblem of "the anguish that comes from knowing that the creature one adores is in some place of enjoyment where oneself is not and cannot follow" is underlined when Swann returns in his imagination to the "house in which at that very moment he might have been if Odette had only permitted it, and the remembered glimpse of an empty milk-can upon a door-mat wrung his heart" (Proust 355). Even in happier days, while Odette is pampering him with rose-colored lights and cushions of Japanese silk, Swann's mind remains fixed on the solitary, outcast lover he will become: he imagines the colored lights "filling, perhaps with romantic wonder the thoughts of some solitary lover wandering in the street below and brought to a standstill before the mystery of the human presence which those lighted windows at once revealed and screened from sight" (Proust 241). Like Swann, Eleanor climbs dilapidated stairs to find a closed door and an empty milk jug. Like the solitary lover peering longingly up at Odette's windows, Eleanor, gazing up from the street, "guessed at the life that went on behind those thick yellow curtains" (115).

In *Swann's Way*, the feelings called up by the pain of unrequited love—joy, longing, hope, and despair—are expressed most succinctly for Swann by Vinteul's sonata. This musical phrase, associated in Swann's mind with his love for Odette, recalls for him the "volatile essence of that lost happiness" (Proust 376), as well as "the possibility of a sort of rejuvenation" (Proust 229). At Saint-Euverte's party, the "slow and rhythmical movement" (Proust 228) of this musical phrase takes Swann through a "vast, unfathomed and forbidding night of [the] soul" (Proust 380) wherein he relives the happiness he has lost: "all his memories of the days when Odette had been in love with him . . . had taken wing and risen to sing maddeningly in his ears, without pity for his present desolation" (Proust 375). In Swann's movement through memory toward liberation from his romantic thralldom to Odette, Proust portrays the same pattern of loss and consolation Woolf identified in "The Sun and the Fish" and rewrote into Kitty's train ride and Yorkshire hike: "after destruction: calm; after ruin: steadfastness." Swann's mourning in consort with Vinteul's sonata returns to him the possibility of finding pleasure in a life without Odette: "that the sufferings through which he had passed that evening, and the pleasures, as yet unsuspected, which were already germinating there—the exact balance between which was too difficult to establish— were linked by a sort of concatenation of necessity" (Proust 415).

Historically, as John Mepham notes, "what is discovered, and woven into the fabric of lament, are fragments of memory, snatches of conversation, haunting images, little tags of poetry and song" (155). Though painful, such repetition affirms the value of what has been lost and makes real to the mourner the irrevocability of the loss. It is this "exact balance between suffering [recognition of loss] and pleasure [in remembrance of past joys]" (Proust 415) that Swann discovered in Vinteul's sonata and Woolf re-creates in *The Years*. By integrating "fragments of memory" and "haunting images" of Vita within an elegiac metaphoric and narrative structure, Woolf's work of mourning in *The Years* moves toward the reconciliation promised by elegy and eventually achieved in her private life. *The Years*, for example, begins in spring and ends with the dawn: moving from the cloudy skies of the "uncertain spring" (3) of the first paragraph to the skies of "extraordinary beauty, simplicity, and peace" (435) cleared by the risen sun at the very end. Thus the overall structure of the novel reiterates the movement from "destruction [to] calm"; from "ruin [to] steadfastness" characteristic of mourning rituals. In the body of the text, the work of mourning for lost love is further taken up by the alternating rhythm of light and dark, together with the "slow and rhythmical" (Proust 228) "Take Too Coos" of the pigeons that reappears throughout the novel.[11] Like the Overture in *Swann's Way*, the first paragraph of *The Years* introduces the core images that reiterate the theme of mourning and consolation throughout the novel.[12] Here we find that despite the gas lights, "broad stretches of darkness were left on the pavement" and that the moon is "obscured now and then by wisps of cloud" (4). Not only over Kitty's moors, but again and again in *The Years*, we find the "sun . . . going in and out" (12), "shining fitfully" (16), and "clouds parting and massing let[ting] the light shine and then veil[ing] it" (15).

In the Present Day chapter, Eleanor is the conduit for the culminating reenactment of the movement from darkness toward light, from sorrow to consolation characteristic of mourning rituals. Just before dawn, Eleanor dreams she is moving through a "very long dark tunnel. But thinking of the dark, something baffled her; in fact it was growing light" (428). Readers privy to Woolf's lesbian codes can discern in Eleanor's summary thoughts Woolf's intentions to link her own farewells to her love affair with Vita to this elegiac pattern. In the final pages, the rhythm and structure of requiem are abbreviated to "pigeons . . . crooning" (433) (memories of past happiness); "an empty milk jug" (433) (anguish of loss); and the dawn (434) ("rejuvenescence and recovery") ("Sun and Fish" 216).

As usual, Woolf's intentions are clearer in the holograph. In the following passage from Woolf's draft for the conclusion to *The Years*, Woolf's elegiac allusions to her love affair with Vita are more poignant and overt than in the published version. Here Woolf writes her requiem to past joys with Vita in the language of metaphor and memory she adopts throughout *The Years*:

> [T]he duchess . . . no longer uses fish knives. The age of fish knives is . . . over. They smiled, a curious slow smile, as if uncertain whether it were right or wrong. . . . Light starlight falling on a pool at dawn. cold, inaccessible: ice cold, remote. And the deer came down to drink. the deer came pacing through the frosted grasses, in the valleys of the moors. [A dream I dreamt. That's all]." (*H* 8: 5)

In this passage, Woolf condenses four favorite memories of Vita. "Duchess," reflects Woolf's delight in playing up Vita's aristocratic ways, and "fish knives" condenses two associations from the twenties when their love affair was just beginning and most intense. "Fish" hearkens back to the "days of the fishmonger shop," and "knife" refers to the silver paper knife Vita gave to Virginia as a gift on the night they began their love affair. The chilly dawn and frosted grasses of the moors call up, once again, Vita and Virginia's train ride to see the eclipse in northern Yorkshire.

As Margot Gayle Backus points out, canonical elegies have supported patriarchy and war by elevating violent men as suitable objects of collective mourning. By granting the pains and joys of lesbian love a central place in *The Years*, Woolf challenges traditional ideas about who is worthy of love and of grief. Thus, despite the reiteration of lesbian heartache and betrayal in her personal life and in this novel, Woolf's emphasis is on the joys of lesbian love. Woolf's 1937 letter to Vita confirms her determination not to let the differences that separated them overshadow the happy memories of their former love: "Why, 'once' Virginia?" Virginia wrote to Vita. "Just because you choose to sit in the mud in Kent and I on the flags of London, thats no reason why love should fade is it? Why the pearls and the porpoise should vanish?" (*L* 6: 186). In 1940, Virginia wrote to Vita, "You have given me such happiness" (*L* 6: 424); and Vita to Virginia, "Darling, thank you for my many happy hours with you. You mean more to me than you will ever know" (Sackville-West, *Letters* 437). Like Djuna Barnes' *Nightwood* (1937), "with its lament for a lost relationship and its invocation of Nora Flood, and of lesbian identity, into being" (Backus 820), *The Years* transforms personal loss into historical gain by adopting the public lament as "a way of conjuring up, or bringing back into view, that which has been denied" (Castle 7). By saturating her literary chronicle with reminiscences of the "many happy hours" she spent with the woman she loved, Woolf has written a memorial not merely to her beloved Vita, but to the continuing possibilities of lesbian love.

NOTES

I would like to thank Krystyna Colburn, Mary Cygan, Susan DeMark, Lise Low, Vara Neverow, Nechama Tec, and the anonymous New York University Press reader for helpful comments on this essay.

1. Woolf originally intended *The Years* to be about the "sexual life of women" (*D* 4: 6). Although I focus on lesbian sexuality, Woolf explores a wide range of sexual norms and emotions in this novel. See Sears for an excellent essay on sexuality in *The Years*. See DeSalvo, *Impact*; Eberly, "Incest"; and Leaska, "Virginia Woolf" for discussions of the incest theme.

2. Several critics have pointed out that in *Remembrance of Things Past*, Proust includes his own homosexual affairs in heterosexual disguise. For example, André Gide called Proust "that great master of dissimulation" (qtd. in Meyers, *Homosexuality* 58). Jeffrey Meyers claims that Marcel is a thinly disguised homosexual and that Albertine is based on Proust's lover, Alberto (Meyers, *Homosexuality* 108). See also Rivers, as well as Sedgwick, *Epistemology*, especially chapter 5. See Heacox and Mares on Woolf and Proust.

3. In 1925, Woolf wrote, "I have an idea that I will invent a new name for my books to supplant 'novel.' A new—by Virginia Woolf. But what? Elegy?'" (*D* 3: 34). See Mepham for discussions of *Jacob's Room*, *Mrs. Dalloway*, *To the Lighthouse*, and *The Waves* as elegies. See also Marcus, "Britannia," on *The Waves*.

4. Gottlieb mentions, but does not develop, the connections between Kitty and Vita Sackville-West, as well as those between Rose and Dame Ethel Smyth. Even Kitty's heterosexual experience with Alf, the farm hand whose kiss is interrupted by Mr. Carter's arrival leading a bull by a ring, has a lesbian base (71). Vita had a similar adolescent encounter with a farmer's son, Jackie, who nearly raped her (Glendinning 22). In adulthood, Kitty's memory confuses genders and introduces a woman—Margaret Marrable—into this scene of sexual initiation (271). During the thirties, Vita wrote and sent to Virginia a poem entitled "The Bull," and Woolf subsequently associated Vita with this animal (*L* 5: 153).

5. Leaska points out that the line Peggy reads, "nox est perpetua una dormienda," comes from Poem V by Catullus, an admirer and imitator of Sappho. A line preceding this passage reads: "My Lesbia, let us live and love / And forget the censorious old men" (qtd. in "Virginia Woolf" 172–210).

6. Woolf often uses juxtaposition of seemingly unrelated elements (e.g. "I want—jug—Nel") to create lesbian meaning. Eleanor's "No, never" (387) just after thinking of marriage and Renny suggests that her spinsterhood has origins other than her inability to find the "right man." See Radner for discussion of feminist codes and Phillips on Woolf's use of juxtaposition to condemn the British Empire.

7. Vita wrote that "V[irginia] told me the history of her early loves—Madge Symonds who is Sally in Mrs Dalloway" (qtd. in Q. Bell, 1: 61).

8. Terry Castle identifies this pattern of "rhapsody and betrayal" in Henry James' *Bostonians*, Dorothy Strachey's *Olivia*, and Djuna Barnes' *Nightwood*.

9. In the draft, Edward as well as Nicholas is homosexual (*H* 4: 69–70). Cited in Johnson 318.

10. See Marcus, "Sapphistry," for discussion of Woolf's intertextual allusions to *The Well of Loneliness*, and see Tyler on Woolf's intertextual relationship to Walt Whitman. Woolf's symbols are not, of course, limited to the lesbian dimensions I cite in this essay. For example, Marcus notes that "each section of the novel has a central vessel" and suggests that Woolf's vessels represent transformational symbols of the Great Goddess (*The Years* 43). Eleanor's empty milk jug also recalls the jug that reminds Kitty of Eleanor in the 1880 section.

11. Woolf adopts a conventional elegiac use of the sun as a metaphor for successful mourning. Unfortunately, she is still caught within the racist metaphors of her culture when she uses white and light for "good" and dark for "evil." The searchlight image that recurs frequently in *The Years* supports this pattern of light and dark imagery. In the holograph Woolf associates the searchlight with the sweeping expansion of the soul: "The soul repeats the same rhythm again and again and again: whereas we want the soul to sweep—round and round and round—and to expand and to expand—" (5: 112). The searchlight also has specific connections with Vita. Vita writes, "You remember your admissions as the searchlight went round and round" [in Berlin on the Funkturm on January 19]?" (Sackville-West, *Letters* 318). While associated with the liberated imagination and lesbian love, the searchlight is simultaneously a sign of war—perhaps signaling a conjunction of rapture and endangerment in Woolf's experiences of lesbian desire. Mark Hussey links this image with Woolf's short story written in 1939, "The Searchlight." Hussey notes that Woolf refers to "The Searchlight" as "The old Henry Taylor story," and says that Taylor's granddaughter, Una Troubridge, became the lover of Radclyffe Hall, author of the lesbian novel *The Well of Loneliness* (*A to Z* 251–52).

12. Marcus suggests that Woolf's discussions about music with Ethel Smyth during the thirties may account for the pervasive musical quality of this novel and for Woolf's decision to imitate Wagner (*The Years* 51).

Entering a Lesbian Field of Vision
To the Lighthouse and
Between the Acts

L I S E   W E I L

Despite the fact that *Between the Acts* boasts the only "out" lesbian in Woolf's fictional repertoire and *To the Lighthouse* abounds in female sexual imagery,[1] neither book exhibits the kind of specifically lesbian imagery that recent readings of her other novels have brought to light.[2] Yet I see these as two of the most radically lesbian texts ever written, by Woolf or any other writer. My premise here is that a narrow focus on sexual identity in Woolf's writings can actually distract us from more significantly lesbian movements of the heart and mind. This essay draws on a tradition of lesbian thinkers—among them American philosophers Mary Daly and Marilyn Frye and French writer Michèle Causse—in whose work "lesbian" is associated primarily with a certain kind of vision or attention. Briefly, what I am going to argue here is that each of these novels in its own particular way creates a lesbian field of vision—and that in its own way each moves the reader into this perceptual field.

Mary Daly claims that being a woman in patriarchy means inhabiting two simultaneous worlds: a one-dimensional, patriarchally constructed realm she calls "the foreground"—we could think of it as "patriarchal realism"—and the background: "the realm of the wild reality of women's selves" (*Gyn/Ecology* 2). For Marilyn Frye, the background is that realm of perpetual female activity on which "phallocratic reality"—her preferred term for "foreground reality"—depends for its very existence. Since the nature of foreground reality, as both these thinkers see it, is to pass itself off as reality itself—to posit itself as "all that is"[3]—attention to the background is of itself subversive and liberating. According to Michèle Causse, such attention is the hallmark of the lesbian: "[the lesbian] regards the masculine world for what it is: a peripetia, an avatar of the human world" (21).

Patriarchal myths, as Daly's work has shown, can themselves point the way out of the apparently all-encompassing foreground, for in them are congealed not only the lies of the fathers but also remnants of ancient female power. Like Mary Daly, Virginia Woolf understood that such myths can neither be taken at face value nor dismissed. *To the Lighthouse* and *Between the Acts* are virtual tapestries of patriarchal myth, both ancient and contemporary—myths that simultaneously shroud and reveal a wild female background. Each novel recapitulates the perceptual shift that a woman experiences when she begins to see the lies of patriarchal myth, to see that what she had mistaken for reality itself was only one possible version of it—a version that made it all but impossible for her to discover the truths she is now able to recognize as her own. As it happens, this perceptual shift is identical to the process that Marilyn Frye, in her essay "To See and Be Seen: The Politics of Reality," describes as characteristic of "the event of becoming a lesbian." "The event of becoming a lesbian is a reorientation of attention in a kind of ontological conversion. It is characterized by a feeling of a world dissolving, and by a feeling of disengagement and re-engagement of one's power as a perceiver" (171).

Lily Briscoe's journey in *To the Lighthouse* is above all a journey of vision; in Frye's terms, it is a journey to lesbian vision. In the course of the novel, Lily comes to see clearly and fully not only Mrs. Ramsay, but everything that had once overwhelmed her about the Ramsays and their way of life, all that had been included in the sweep of her hand at the beginning of the novel when she said, "I'm in love with this all . . ." (*TTL* 19). As Lily hews ever more strongly to her own vision, as she begins to see all that has been left out of the patriarchal version of reality, she becomes the very kind of seer Marilyn Frye defines as a lesbian: "a seer for whom the background is eventful, dramatic, compelling . . . one who, by virtue of her focus, her attention, her attachment, is disloyal to phallocratic reality" (171). As Lily moves from her marginal role in "The Window" to "The Lighthouse," where she becomes the novel's central perceiver, the reader's perceptions are increasingly drawn into her field of vision. Along with Lily, the reader begins to see like a lesbian.

"The Window," the first part of *To the Lighthouse*, is a window onto the triumphs of Western civilization, from Shakespeare and Walter Scott to Mrs. Ramsay's Boeuf en Daube. It is at the same time a window onto the most hallowed of patriarchal myths. The novel opens on a classic Oedipal drama: the blissful fantasy world of mother and son brutally shattered by the intrusion of the stern father, whose interruption inspires murderous impulses in the son. The configuration of Mrs. Ramsay reading with James at her knee is iconic in its evocation of Madonna and child; Lily's abstract rendering of such "objects of universal veneration" (*TTL* 52) as a triangular purple shadow smacks of irreverence. There is an archetypal grandeur to most of the characters and events in "The Window" that suggests their inevitability and universality. At one point, Mr. and Mrs. Ramsay are made to appear to us as "the symbols of marriage, husband and wife" (*TTL* 92). This is the airtight realm of patriarchal realism, to which no alien element is admitted.[4] From within this realm, which is utterly dominated by the majestic figure of Mrs. Ramsay, no criticism of her or her domain can be taken seriously. Like her children at the table, imagining a different life for themselves, dissenters can only "sport with infidel ideas" (*TTL* 6) in silence.

The idyll of Part One is shattered, in "Time Passes," by Mrs. Ramsay's death and the bombs of World War I. If "The Window" showed us the triumphs of Western civilization, "Time Passes" shows us the precariousness of civilized structures, their vulnerability to the forces of corrosion, decay, and disintegration. It also reveals a crucial fact that this civilization has done its best to suppress: that it is women above all who keep those forces at bay—that it is only thanks to women's unremitting labors that the civilized world holds together at all. In a very real sense, the nibbling airs, the mold and the rot that now threaten to bring down the Ramsays' summer house, were unleashed by Mrs. Ramsay's death. It was she, we are given to understand, who had held them at bay.

When the surviving members of the Ramsay clan decide to convene again in the old summer house, some ten years after their last stay there, it is Mrs. McNab and Mrs. Bast who are called in "to stay the corruption and the rot" (*TTL* 139). The phrase Mrs. McNab keeps grumbling to herself is significant: "It was beyond the strength of one woman" (*TTL* 138). The secret revealed in "Time Passes" is that the world of family bliss depicted in "The Window" required the enormous expenditure of a resource that is as non-renewable as it has been unacknowledged: the resource of female energy.[5]

The reality in the foreground, according to Frye, can continue to "hang together" only as long as the background remains invisible. "It is essential to the maintenance of foreground reality that nothing within it refer in any way to anything in the background, and yet it depends absolutely upon the existence of the background" (167–68). Just so, the family romance of "The Window" clearly hung together thanks to Mrs. Ramsay's tireless efforts to keep the barren rooms of the house filled with life, to oil the wheels of social intercourse, to perform the constant work of "merging and flowing and creating" (*TTL* 83); it also depended for its continued existence on the invisibility of her labors. In fact, a substantial portion of her labors consisted in rendering invisible—to children and to men—what foreground reality needs to exclude from its field of vision: the facts of life and death, of change, aging, growth, and decay. Charles Tansley waits discreetly outside while she pays her visit to a sick woman in town; Mr. Ramsay must be shielded from the knowledge that the bill to repair the greenhouse has come to 50 pounds.

Frye continues, "Anything which threatens the fixation of attention on the play threatens a cataclysmic dissolution of Reality into Chaos" (170). In "Time Passes," the background comes forward; the elements come flooding in. The universe now seems bereft of meaning, terrifyingly empty: "the stillness and the brightness of the day were as strange as the chaos and tumult of the night, with the trees standing there, and the flowers standing there, looking before them, looking up, yet beholding nothing, eyeless, and so terrible" (*TTL* 135). Gone is the assurance that "beauty outside mirrored beauty within"—and so "contemplation was unendurable; the mirror was broken" (*TTL* 134).

Critics have tended to assume that the perceiver behind these remarks is the author herself; time and again, they have pointed to the bleakness, the blankness, of this section.[6] Yet what has fled from the universe in "Time Passes" is no meaning inherent in the natural world, but only the meaning bestowed upon it by man himself, and, through man, by "God." The "mirror" that breaks in this section, where all fixed meanings collapse, is the mirror of patriarchal realism, of a reality that has imposed itself as "Reality." (Also evoked here is the passage in *A Room of One's Own* where Woolf describes women as reflecting men back to themselves at twice their natural size.) The events of "Time Passes" expose the reality of "The Window" as only one possible reality, a scenario that faithfully reflected man's wishes, dreams, and needs (indeed more of a mirror than a window) but one whose beauty and charm were costly, if not fatal, in terms of human and especially female life. The naked reality that is exposed here could seem bleak and meaningless only from the point of view of the male world of fixed meanings, of the "Reality" of patriarchal realism, the very point of view that "Time Passes" radically undermines.

The passage from "The Window" to "The Lighthouse" is a passage out of patriarchal realism and into a lesbian field of vision; the radical perceptual shift that occurs in this section from foreground to background reality involves exactly the kind of "reorientation of attention," "the feeling of a world dissolving . . . and . . . of disengagement and re-engagement of one's power as a perceiver" that Frye associates with "the event of becoming a lesbian." From this new vantage point, the crises of "Time Passes" can be seen not as terminal but as generative. The naked world exposed here, the shattering of preconceived meanings, creates a space where new questions and answers can take root; from this chaos, new shapes can be found and given.

The third part of *To the Lighthouse* opens with Lily's question: "What does it mean then, what can it all mean?" (*TTL* 145). Here in this space shorn of maternal mythologies and civilized conventions, Lily is able to pursue her own questions. Among other things, what she comes to perceive is the tragic wastefulness of the human economy depicted in "The Window." Her first important insight, just pages into "The Lighthouse," is that it was the direct cause of Mrs. Ramsay's death: "Giving, giving, giving, she had died . . ." (*TTL* 149). If Lily sees the price in female energy demanded by this economy, it is in part because she herself has not been spared. In "The Window" we saw her coming reluctantly to Mrs. Ramsay's rescue at the dinner table to help her feed Charles Tansley's insatiable ego. We are given to understand that this is not the first time she has been pressed into service. For the "hundred and fiftieth time," we are told, Lily has "had to renounce the experiment—what happens if one is not nice to that young man there—and be nice" (*TTL* 92).

Soon after "The Lighthouse" opens, Lily is at last able to perform her experiment. Mr. Ramsay comes bearing down on her, demanding sympathy, and instead of giving him what he wants and seems to need, she decides to give him "what she could" (*TTL* 150). She praises his boots. To her enormous surprise, it is enough. Mr. Ramsay bounds off with renewed energy, just as if she had given him the sympathy he wanted. This transaction is the first in a series of such exchanges throughout "The Lighthouse" that, taken together, suggest the outlines of an alternative human economy in which women's emotional and creative resources are not funneled into men and their projects. The envisioning and enacting of such an economy is made possible here by Lily's perceptual shift, her "reorientation of attention" from the foreground to the background, from the family romance of "the Window" to her own creative work.

In order to become free of the rigid archetypes that bind us to patriarchally ordained roles, Mary Daly writes in *Pure Lust*, women need to discover the Archimage, "the Witch within our Selves" (90). Lily's shift of
attention in Part Three of the novel can be seen precisely as a shift of focus
to this witch within, to her own muse, and it leads ultimately to a subversive revisioning of the patriarchal archetypes. If the drama pictured in "The
Window" was classically Oedipal, with its father-son rivalry and its sacri-
ficial mother, the drama of "The Lighthouse" orients itself by the relations
of mother and daughter, as these might be conceived outside the bounds
of patriarchal history and discourse, as they might have been celebrated in
the rites of Eleusis.[7] Within the framework of "The Window," Mrs. Ramsay
remains, for all intents and purposes, essentially a maternal icon, an adored
object, while Lily never fully rises above the role of old maid. In Part Three,
Lily (and, along with her, the reader) begins to see past the archetypes—
the fragmented, limiting roles in which she and Mrs. Ramsay were cast on
the stage of Part One—to a background reality in which each of them has
access to unlimited possibility. In order to do so, she needs first to learn
to see the mother beyond the filter of her own needs and desires.[8]

As the boat with Mr. Ramsay, James, and Cam sails off across the bay
toward the lighthouse, Lily, spying the boat from the shore, suddenly
recalls a scene: Mrs. Ramsay looking out to sea and asking, "Is it a boat?
Is it a cork?" and then hunting for her spectacles and looking out to sea
again, her vision restored. The sudden memory brings her into the presence of Mrs. Ramsay as never before, and Lily feels "as if a door had
opened, and one went in and stood gazing silently about in a high cathe-
dral-like place, very dark, very solemn" (*TTL* 171). The imagery is reminiscent of the scene in "The Window" where Lily sat with her arms round
Mrs. Ramsay's knees, wanting to absorb the "knowledge and wisdom . . .
stored up in Mrs. Ramsay's heart" (*TTL* 51). Pressing against her, she
wondered, "what art was there, known to love or cunning, by which one
pressed through into those secret chambers? What device for becoming,
like waters poured into one jar, inextricably the same, one with the object
one adored" (*TTL* 51)?

Now, ten years later, Lily is able to creep inside the Mrs. Ramsay who
sat beside her then, to see and feel *with* her, to see the world from behind
her eyes:

> Mrs. Ramsay sat silent. She was glad, Lily thought, to rest in silence, uncom-
> municative; to rest in the extreme obscurity of human relationships. Who
> knows what we are, what we feel? Who knows even at the moment of inti-

macy, This is knowledge? Aren't things spoilt then, Mrs. Ramsay may have asked . . . by saying them? Aren't we more expressive thus? (*TTL* 171–72)

If Lily is finally admitted into those "secret chambers," it is because she no longer approaches them with the same ravenous hunger; hers is no longer the desire of the patriarchal daughter (who, as Adrienne Rich has written, is always "wildly unmothered" (226) for the great, wise mother who will fill all her gaping holes.[9] Freed of her hunger, Lily alone is able now to begin to see her, not as an idealized, all-knowing figure but as she was. The anguished longing of the daughter for the mother yields to a longing to *see* the mother, to *know* her.[10] "One wanted fifty pairs of eyes to see with, she reflected. Fifty pairs of eyes were not enough to get round that one woman with, she thought. Among them, must be one that was stone blind to her beauty" (*TTL* 198).

If Lily no longer desires to become *one* with Mrs. Ramsay, it is also because, in a very important sense, she has already become one with her; she has incorporated the power of the mother into her own creative work. She has learned to reject the false choice of maiden and fertility goddess, the patriarchal split of mother and virgin.[11] In mythic terms, Daly writes, the Archimage corresponds to the Triple Goddess, that matriarchal divinity in whom mother, maiden, and crone were seen as three aspects of the same female self. In this sense too, Lily, by the end of the novel, can be said to have discovered the Archimage. Having doubted her womanhood when assailed by Mr. Ramsay's need ("[I] who am not a woman, but a peevish, ill-tempered, dried-up old maid, presumably" [*TTL* 151]), Lily now comes to recognize in her virginal self a fountain of wisdom and life. In Mrs. Ramsay, who was the wellspring, the source of life for her family, she comes to recognize the prodigious power of creativity.[12]

"A lesbian . . . has an excruciating pain about the destiny of women at large," says Michèle Causse.[13] Her words echo those of Quebec writer Nicole Brossard, who claims that the lesbian "rejects *mortification* as a way of life. The lesbian suffers because of the mortification of women" (121). In "The Lighthouse," the primal cry of the bereaved daughter yields to a more mature sorrow: over the fact that the enormous creative power of the mother has been dedicated exclusively to the welfare of others. Necessarily, this grief extends to the reduction and fragmentation of all female lives lived within the foreground reality of patriarchal realism. There are those, like Causse and Brossard, who would argue that such grief is the very mark and measure of the lesbian.

The perceptual shift that is forced upon the reader in Part Two of *To the Lighthouse* is elicited, gently but persistently, throughout *Between the Acts*. If the background moves forward in "Time Passes"—between the acts, so to speak—in *Between the Acts* this movement occurs most noticeably during La Trobe's play, when the natural world comes forward to participate in the action on the stage. On first reading, all the characters in the novel may seem trapped in the foreground, tyrannized by patriarchal endings. Between the warplanes flying overhead, the scars on the landscape, and the military souvenirs in Pointz Hall, all roads here seem to lead to war. Yet successive readings of the novel reveal a constant presence of the mythic background, onto which the drama in the foreground can be seen to open up again and again.[14]

Woolf's last novel is a continuous exercise in what Mary Daly calls "Anamnesia . . . unforgetting our Elemental connections" (*Pure Lust* 85). Once again, here, Woolf is working the territory of the Archimage: excavating remnants of female divinity and elemental power and "re-establishing . . . connections with natural rhythms that have been severed" (*Pure Lust* 90). Time and again, throughout the novel, the reader's attention is drawn to this forgotten territory; time and again, we are ushered from the grim circularity of the foreground into a lesbian field of vision—a place from which the background is seen as "eventful, dramatic, compelling."

On the surface of it, *Between the Acts* seems to embrace the alienated modernist vision of Woolf's male contemporaries. The novel is pervaded by a mood of inescapable doom. La Trobe's play, displaying as it does virtually every lifeless literary and dramatic convention in the English canon, implies a culture that has exhausted its resources. Most of the company gathered at Pointz Hall to view the play seem to be fighting a losing battle against drowsiness, fatigue, or ennui. In fact, as I am about to show, this last novel of Woolf's, written as the bombs of World War II were falling, bears a strong resemblance to T. S. Eliot's "The Waste Land," written in the aftermath of World War I and published by the Woolfs' own Hogarth Press in 1923.

Since Virginia Woolf had set the type for Eliot's poem with her own hands, it is only natural that her work should contain echoes of his. But the allusions to "The Waste Land" in this novel are too profound and pervasive to be explained away by unconscious influence. If we read *Between the Acts*, as I believe we must, as an attempt to invoke and restore ancient female powers, it becomes clear that far from merely echoing Eliot's poem, the novel constitutes a cry of outrage at the monstrous reversal implied in his vision. For the poem, though it exposes the hollowness of patriarchal realism, also remains true to its logic; from its point of view the entire universe is void of meaning. The novel, while sharing with "The Waste Land" its terminal diagnosis of Western civilization, also points beyond it, beyond the doomed wasteland in the foreground, to something Eliot's vision ignores: namely, the power of female and elemental creativity. If the prophet figure at the center of "The Waste Land" is a hermaphrodite, the prophet figure at the center of Woolf's novel is a lesbian, and it is she above all who is conjurer and rememberer of this power; it is Miss La Trobe who points most insistently and defiantly to the forgotten background.

The sun beats down mercilessly upon the guests at Pointz Hall on this hot June day, making Isa long for "A beaker of cold water, a beaker of cold water" (*BTA* 66). The earth is parched: "This dry summer the path was hard as brick across the fields. This dry summer the path was strewn with stones" (*BTA* 98). Isa, imagining herself intermittently as a donkey crossing a desert, encounters there "a withered tree." We are in a landscape identical to the one evoked in the opening of "The Waste Land":

> A heap of broken images, where the sun beats,
> And the dead tree gives no shelter, the cricket no relief,
> And the dry stone no sound of water. (Lines 22–24)

Both poem and novel depict a civilization in ruins. Like the poem, the novel is a mosaic of scraps from the Western canon; both seem to have been composed from the rubble itself, from the "heap of broken images." Those broken images drift through the minds of the novel's characters as bits and pieces of poetry, doggerel, and rhyme. "'Is there nothing in your head?'" asks a voice in "The Waste Land," "'But / o o o that Shakespherian rag / it's so elegant / so intelligent'" (lines 127–30). In the novel, quoting Shakespeare has become a party game: "'Shakespeare by heart!' Mrs. Manresa protested. She struck an attitude. 'To be, or not to be, that is the question. Whether 'tis nobler . . . Go on!' she nudged Giles, who sat next to her" (*BTA* 54).

In "The Waste Land," Eliot refers to "voices singing out of empty cisterns and exhausted wells" (line 385). The dining room of Pointz Hall is described by the narrator in similar terms: "Empty, empty, empty; silent, silent, silent. The room was a shell, singing of what was before time was; a vase stood in the heart of the house, alabaster, smooth, cold, holding the still, distilled essence of emptiness, silence" (*BTA* 36–37). And, just as

Eliot's barren waste land awaits relief from some fertile source, all living creatures in the novel seem to be awaiting some great deliverance from on high.

The rhythms of the poem can be heard throughout the novel, as well. The inexorable "tick tick tick" or the "Chuff Chuff Chuff" of the machine in the bushes—Miss La Trobe's way of signaling the march of time but also, presumably, the march of industry—echoes the barkeeper's refrain in "A Game of Chess": "HURRY UP PLEASE IT'S TIME." The mood of the novel recalls the fevered ennui of this section of the poem, in which a nameless character cries out:

> My nerves are bad tonight. Yes, bad. Stay with me.
> Speak to me. Why do you never speak. Speak. (Lines 111–12)

> > What shall I do now? What shall I do?
> > I shall rush out as I am, and walk the street
> > With my hair down, so. What shall we do tomorrow?
> > What shall we ever do? (Lines 131–34)

The guests awaiting their cars at Pointz Hall after the play is over send up a chorus of fragmented banalities that, like Eliot's lines, suggest the hysterical chatter of a dying civilization:[15]

> I shouldn't have expected either so many Hispano-Suizas . . . That's a Rolls . . . That's a Bentley . . That's the new type of Ford . . . To return to the meaning—Are machines the devil, or do they introduce a discord . . . Ding, dong, ding . . . by means of which we reach the final . . . Ding dong . . . Here's the car with the monkey . . . Hop in . . . And good-bye, Mrs. Parker . . . Ring us up. Next time we're down don't forget . . . Next time . . . Next time . . . (*BTA* 201)

Jane Marcus has pointed to the motif of rape and revenge embedded in the novel in the form of recurrent allusions to the myth of Procne and Philomela. According to this myth, the two sisters were turned into a swallow and a nightingale, respectively, after King Tereus raped Philomela ("Liberty"). Eliot wove this same myth into the tapestry of his poem.

> > yet there the nightingale
> > filled all the desert with inviolable voice
> > and still she cried, and still the world pursues,
> > "Jug Jug" to dirty ears. (Lines 100–3)

Marcus shows how the Swinburne lines quoted in the novel by old Bartholomew, "Oh sister swallow, O sister swallow, / How can thy heart be full of spring?" shift the burden of guilt from the rapist to his victim, erasing the feminist content of the myth.[16] Interestingly, in an earlier version of "The Waste Land," the lines that appear in "The Fire Sermon"—"Twit twit twit / Jug jug jug jug jug jug / So rudely forced / Tereu" (lines 203–6)—are followed by the words "O swallow swallow" (line 140).

Finally, and very strikingly, both works hark back to ancient myth and fertility rituals. The story of the Fisher King, whose death or impotence has brought drought and sterility to this land—a story on which Eliot avowedly based most of the symbolism of his poem—has many resonances in the novel, where fish figure prominently as a symbol of life and regeneration.

And here the more profound differences between the two works begin to emerge. Eliot's poem ends on a note of unrelieved—and apparently unrelievable—despair, with the image of a man fishing "with the arid plain behind me" (line 425), though the fish, the symbol of life, is nowhere to be seen. According to Arthurian legend, and the Fisher King story on which Jessie Weston claims that legend is based, only the questing knight is capable of restoring the land to fertility. As there is no Parzival in the world of "The Waste Land," no relief from the drought, the impotence, the sterility of that world is in sight. The point of the poem would seem to be simply to register the poet's despair—to exhibit "these fragments I have shored against my ruins."

No Parzival comes to restore fertility to the land in *Between the Acts* —but, given the performances of the would-be heroes of the novel, the clumsy, bullying Bart and his bond-trading son Giles, whose single act of valor consists in stamping on a snake that has swallowed a toad and killing them both, the reader is not inclined to hope for deliverance from a male savior here. If fertility is to be restored, it will not be through acts of male heroism. While Eliot's vision of a civilization lying in ruins, in utter exhaustion, is unmistakably incorporated into *Between the Acts*, the novel is *not* reducible to that vision. For all its ambience of repressed violence and radical ennui, this novel also contains an abundance of signs that the forces of life will prevail. To read these signs requires a kind of attention that millennia of Western civilization have made it difficult to bestow—in Frye's terms, attention that is "disloyal to phallocratic reality." It is only to the female characters in the novel (and ultimately, of course, to the reader) that these signs are made to appear.

After the guests have left Pointz Hall, Lucy Swithin wanders down to the lily pond in a dark mood. When the play ended, she had wanted to go offer her thanks to Miss La Trobe, but her brother stopped her. Now, as she stares into the water, her faith is restored to her. The movement of the fish stirs in her a memory: a deep memory of the life force, in its infinitely variegated colors and forms. "Then something moved in the water; her favorite fantail. The golden orfe followed. Then she had a glimpse of silver—the great carp himself, who came to the surface so very seldom. They slid on, in and out between the stalks, silver; pink; gold; splashed; streaked; pied" (*BTA* 205). Jessie Weston tells us that the fish is "a life symbol of immemorial antiquity" (*BTA* 125). Here the fish assumes its ancient mythic status. To Lucy, who is in the habit of "one-making," this vision is a reminder of the life force that flows through all of us. For as she sees it, the fish *are* "ourselves": "'Ourselves,' she murmured. And retrieving some glint of faith from the grey waters, hopefully, without much help from reason, she followed the fish; the speckled, streaked, and blotched; seeing in that vision beauty, power, and glory in ourselves" (*BTA* 205). Lucy Swithin, who is derided for her musings by her brother Bart, nicknamed "Old Flimsy" by the village youngsters, and accused by William Dodge of not believing in history, is often seen as escapist by Woolf critics, one of whom argues that "she makes consoling fictions out of the cosmic emptiness" (Zwerdling, "Coming of War" 230). But the version of history Lucy Swithin does not believe in is, the novel shows us, only one version. To Bartholomew, the grim realist who believes in shining his "torch of reason" into every corner, the patriarchal realist for whom foreground reality is "all there is," Lucy's faith is blind. Yet her faith brings her recurringly into the presence of a world Bart is unable to see, one where life is ever renewing itself.

If in *To the Lighthouse* elemental power was seen to pose a threat to human meaning and to civilization itself, in this novel Woolf is able to envision human/elemental relations in far less antagonistic terms. In fact, the revisioning of those relations in this book is every bit as radical as the revisioning of mother-daughter relations in *To the Lighthouse*. Once again, this revisioning involves looking back in history to a time of original wholeness, to a background reality where other possibilities can be imagined. In "Anon," an essay Woolf was working on as she wrote *Between the Acts*, she attempts to imagine the world of art and theater before the invention of the printed word. "The voice that broke the silence of the forest," Woolf writes in the essay, "was the voice of Anon" (382). Inspired by birdsong, Anon's was "the common voice, singing out of doors." "The audience was itself the singer. . . . Everybody shared in the emotion of Anon's song, and supplied the story" (382). Nora Eisenberg's perceptive reading of the novel in the light of this essay treats them as "companion pieces, sharing a single hero and theme" (253). *Between the Acts*, Eisenberg suggests, is Woolf's attempt to recreate this world of communal ritual and song.

According to Eisenberg, Miss La Trobe *is* "Anon" of the essay. In fact, Woolf suggests as much herself: one of La Trobe's nicknames is "Whatsername," and when, at the end of her play, she speaks from the bushes, her voice is "a megaphonic, anonymous, loud-speaking affirmation" (*BTA* 186). When the Reverend Streatfield entreats the author to come forth from the bushes and receive the audience's thanks, she stays where she is, as if wanting to give the play back into the hands of the audience. The Reverend remarks that the author "wishes it seems to remain anonymous" (*BTA* 194). La Trobe keeps music playing throughout the performance; it is at her insistence that the pageant is performed in the open air, and she tries to enlist the participation of the audience as well as the villagers in the play. In all these ways, she can be seen to be attempting to reforge an ancient connection to song and to the natural world—from which, Woolf reminds us in "Anon," all drama, all literature, have arisen.

Twice, in the course of the performance, Miss La Trobe feels the audience slipping from her grasp and experiences a failure that feels like death. Both times nature comes to her rescue. The first time, the cows begin suddenly to low, as if on cue, filling the silence with a primeval sound: "Then suddenly, as the illusion petered out, the cows took up the burden. One had lost her calf. In the very nick of time she lifted her great moon-eyed head and bellowed. All the great moon-eyed heads laid themselves back. From cow after cow came the same yearning bellow. The whole world was filled with dumb yearning" (*BTA* 140).

The second instance occurs when the audience, confronted with "Present Time. Ourselves," begins to grow restless, and the author fears she has miscalculated. "She wanted to expose them, as it were, to douche them, with present-time reality. But something was going wrong with the experiment. 'Reality too strong,' she muttered. 'Curse 'em'!" (*BTA* 179). Once again, she feels as if she were dying. Once again, nature proves her ally. In the very nick of time, a healing rain bursts from the sky: "No one had seen the cloud coming. There it was, black, swollen, on top of them. Down it poured like all the people in the world weeping. Tears. Tears. Tears" (*BTA* 180).

What occurs on each occasion when nature stepped in felicitously, "took up the burden" (*BTA* 140) and "continued the emotion" (*BTA* 141) of the play, is a modulation to another *voice*—as if indeed some ancient source had been tapped. The cows bring forth "the primeval voice sound-ing loud in the ear of the present moment" (*BTA* 140). And, after the rain falls, the music itself is transformed: "it was the other voice speaking, the voice that was no one's voice" (*BTA* 181). It is truly as if the playwright had initiated her audience into some ancient mystery.

Of course, on one level, she *has*. Drama has functioned here, as it did of old, as fertility ritual, invoking rain. The rain is a deliverance; it is relief from the heat and dryness that have prevailed all day. This is the deliver-ance that never comes to "The Waste Land," where the vegetation cycle has been aborted and rebirth never occurs. But there is more to this rain; not only does it fall like tears, it falls down Isa's cheeks "as if they were her own tears," and she murmurs, "O that our human pain could here have ending!" (*BTA* 180). Soon her voice merges with the anonymous, univer-sal voice, "the voice that wept for human pain unending" (*BTA* 181). The suggestion here of a ritual dirge of weeping women, a dirge that brings fer-tility to the land, is a certain allusion to the Eleusinian mysteries—in which Demeter's tears for her lost daughter Persephone bring cyclical regenera-tion to the earth.[17] In this light it is interesting to note that the opening section of *Three Guineas*, which spells out the connections between fas-cism and the war on women, first appeared as an essay titled "Women Must Weep." Acknowledged, in both instances, is the ancient and forgot-ten power of female grief. In *Between the Acts*, women's tears are the fer-tilizing agent that restores the earth.

Isa's tears and their healing power take on further mythic resonance in light of the wealth of evidence supplied in Evelyn Haller's essay "Isis Un-veiled: Virginia Woolf's Use of Egyptian Myth," which links the novel as a whole, and the figure of Isa in particular, to the myth of Isis, the ancient Egyptian goddess who was known as the source of all life. Of immediate relevance to the passage above is the fact that it was Isis' tears for her brother Osiris that were said to have caused the Nile to rise every year. In Egyptian myth, female grief was seen to be *the* fructifying agent in the cycles of life.

A central element in the myth of Isis is the goddess' power to restore life by means of literal re-membering. In gathering the pieces of her slain brother Osiris and putting them back together again, Isis manages to raise him from the dead. When we read the novel in its full mythic con-text, the contrast to Eliot's poem is thrown into even sharper relief. In place of the image of an old man "shoring fragments against my ruins" in a helpless gesture of despair, Woolf gives us the image of a goddess who gathers fragments to renew life. What is so shamelessly absent from the landscape of "The Waste Land" is invoked and embodied in the textual reality of *Between the Acts*: the power of divine female presence.

Isis' features are distributed among the three female protagonists in the novel, perhaps in subtle tribute to the Triple Goddess. All three women share an awareness of cyclical activity, of elemental regenerative power. If Isa is the grieving mother-sister whose tears restore life, Lucy is the re-memberer, restoring memory to its ancient power of integrity, of making whole. Her habit of "one-making," for which she is derided, is nothing other than the power of weaving, of *integrity*, for which Isis is noted: "She was off, they guessed, on a circular tour of the imagination—one-making. Sheep, cows, grass, trees, ourselves—all are one. If discordant, producing harmony—if not to us, to a gigantic ear attached to a gigantic head . . . and so . . . we reach the conclusion that *all* is harmony, could we hear it" (*BTA* 175).

But it is La Trobe who most potently personifies Isis as the source of life, the original creation goddess, La Trobe who "seethes wandering bodies and floating voices in a cauldron, and makes rise up from its amorphous mass a re-created world" (*BTA* 153). A lesbian and an outsider, she fits in nowhere, and yet she is *the* unifying force of the novel, performing the very role that is fulfilled by the hostesses of Woolf's earlier novels. "She was an outcast. Nature had somehow set her apart from her kind. Yet she had scribbled in the margin of her manuscript: 'I am the slave of my audience'" (*BTA* 211). By means of her play, she manages to mix gentry with villagers and, in a series of daring maneuvers, to bring members of the audience face to face with each other, with the elements—and finally, with themselves.

Utterly free of the "unreal loyalties" of patriarchal realism, La Trobe most clearly occupies the lesbian field of vision in this novel. To the patriarchal perceiver, this place is mistaken for a void. Bartholomew restrains Lucy when she sets out to thank the author of the play, saying, "She don't want our thanks, Lucy!" What she does want, he imagines, is "darkness in the mud; a whiskey and soda at the pub; and coarse words descending like maggots through the waters" (*BTA* 203). Lucy "ignored the battle in the mud," he thinks. He is both right and wrong. With these words he unwittingly evokes both Lucy's pre-historic swamp and Isa's healing tears; unwittingly, he names the very element out of which La Trobe will renew the act of creation. As La Trobe sits and drinks at the bar, "The mud became fertile. Words rose above the intolerably laden dumb oxen plodding through the mud. Words without meaning—wonderful words" (*BTA* 212). In the heart of darkness, in the primordial slime, profound transformation occurs. The void becomes a cauldron out of which La Trobe will recreate the world.

After the guests are gone, La Trobe utters one last groan of defeat and is answered one last time by the elements: a tree humming and vibrating with the sound of a flock of starlings: "A whizz, a buzz rose from the bird-buzzing, bird-vibrant, bird-blackened tree. The tree became a rhapsody, a quivering cacophony, a whizz and vibrant rapture, branches, leaves, birds syllabling discordantly life, life, life, without measure, without stop devouring the tree" (*BTA* 209). According to Haller, this tree is evocative of Isis' sistrum; it is unmistakably an image of the tree of life. It may remind us of the tree in Lily Briscoe's painting, the tree that she suddenly realizes she must move to the middle, even as she realizes she "need never marry anybody." Now, sitting at the bar with words rising from the mud, La Trobe suddenly envisions the opening scene of her next play: "There was the high ground at midnight; there the rock; and two scarcely perceptible figures. Suddenly the tree was pelted with starlings. She set down her glass. She heard the first words" (*BTA* 212).

"Elemental women," writes Mary Daly in *Pure Lust*, "heal the broken connections between words and their sources" (18). La Trobe's "first word," engendered by birdsong like the words of her forebear Anon, can be said to restore a lost connection between the human and the elemental world. In rather stark contrast to Tiresias, the prophet-sage of "The Waste Land," the visionary of this novel is not content to merely forecast, from a position of impotence and detachment, a miserable future. "Always agog to get things up," Miss La Trobe, for all her fear and stumblings, remains a figure of pure *potency*. Like the elements themselves, she will continue to create.

Moreover, there is in the structure of the novel's ending a close parallel to the end of *To the Lighthouse*, where the landing of the Ramsays at the lighthouse is juxtaposed to Lily's vision of the landing and the completion of her painting. Here Miss La Trobe's vision of her new play in the bar is juxtaposed with the evening scene taking place simultaneously at Pointz Hall, where Giles and Isa, Bart and Lucy, are settling back into their familiar routine. And here as in *To the Lighthouse*, a causal relationship is seen to exist between the two scenes. For we are given to believe that the words Giles and Isa are about to speak, as the novel ends, are also the first words of La Trobe's play—and that it is thus in her power, as the playwright, to choose those words, whatever they might be.

Just as Lily Briscoe can be said to have catalyzed the voyage to the lighthouse by virtue of her fierce attention to her own creative work, so in *Between the Acts* the potency and vision of La Trobe bring some hope of renewal to the deadly sameness of life at Pointz Hall. And like Lily's, La Trobe's vision becomes our vision; along with her, we enter a place where the forgotten background—that wild realm of elemental female creativity—can be seen, remembered, and lived. Here now at the end of *Between the Acts* the lesbian—she who has found the witch within herself and dared to see women and nature as they were never meant to be seen in her time—has come out of the bushes clutching a new script in her hands. In it are words that may yet shake her listeners free of the old plot; this time they may be stirred to play out their "unacted parts."

NOTES

1. Pointing to the wealth of erotic imagery in *To the Lighthouse*, McKenna argues that the novel is Woolf's attempt to "reclaim the language of desire and orgasm for women." The sexual experiences she invokes, however, are strictly "autoerotic." Risolo attempts to bring Mrs. Ramsay out of the closet—but leaves this reader unconvinced. I believe McKenna is closer to the mark.

2. For lesbian readings of Woolf's novels see Cramer, "Underground," on *Mrs. Dalloway*; Tvordi on *The Voyage Out*; Oxindine on *The Waves*; and Olano, "'Women Alone.'"

3. See Irigaray's *Speculum* for discussion of the totalizing nature of what she calls "phallocentrism."

4. Just as patriarchal realism is persistently mistaken for reality itself, so have (esp. male) readers of this novel often mistaken the apparent reality in the foreground for the reality of the novel as a whole—something that I believe accounts for its having been so massively misread. The same thing can be said for *Between the Acts*.

5. Jane Marcus' reading of Mrs. McNab, as an "unacknowledged bearer of culture" or even a "female Orpheus" whose "semiotic burble" points to "the origins of art in women's work" ("A Rose" 12, 11), is relevant here. I confess to being utterly perplexed by Mary Lou Emery's version of McNab—as "a violently masculine figure" (221), "a militarized, masculine force" (226)—especially in light of James Haule's discovery that in an earlier version of "Time Passes" "men were violently and mindlessly destructive. Women, in the figure of the ancient charwoman and the ghost of Mrs. Ramsay, cooperated with nature" (173).

6. See especially J. H. Miller and Zwerdling, "Coming of War." Feminist critics, too, focusing on the loss of the mother in this section, have spoken of it largely in terms of death and emptiness. Marcus points to "the horror and chaos of the universe, devastation and meaninglessness" (*Patriarchy* 6), while Lidoff argues that "Time Passes" is a "linguistic recapitulation of mother-loss as self-loss" (49).

7. It also mirrors the trajectory of recent lesbian literature, as sketched by

Farwell, in which "the mother as an image of female creativity is subsumed by the larger image of the lesbian, the one whose creativity springs from her primary attention to women" (75).

8. Lilienfeld too reads the novel as a revisioning of archetypes, in particular that of the Great and Terrible Mother ("'Deceptiveness of Beauty'"). See also Dibattista. Irigaray explores similar territory in "And the One Doesn't Stir without the Other," her meditation on the symbiotic nature of the mother-daughter relationship.

9. Here my reading conflicts with that of DuPlessis, who states that it is simply the admitting of "vulnerability, need, exposure and grief" (97) that enables the completion of Lily's painting. Lidoff similarly argues that it is Lily's grief that heals her. What these readings fail to account for is that none of Lily's earlier cries of longing, intense as they were, produced any results.

10. Daugherty echoes this perception: "Lily's desire . . . and her questions . . . assume that Mrs. Ramsay is a person worthy of her (and our) attention. And these are just the questions a patriarchal society never asks of Eve, of Mary, of women—'how does it feel to be you'?" (300).

11. Lilienfeld makes a similar point: "At the end of her journey . . . Lily has replaced within herself the figure of the archetypal Great Mother. . . . [She] has redefined the archetype and has located within her own being and objectively on her own painting the resources she once saw only in Mrs. Ramsay's holy sepulchre" ("'Deceptiveness of Beauty'" 361–62). See also Newman's provocative analysis of To the Lighthouse in terms of what she calls "the mother/virgin opposition." "In Lily's figure," Newman writes, "Woolf faces and refutes the 'choice' between mother and virgin" (59). Much of my thinking about To the Lighthouse, and Newman's as well, evolved from months of discussion in a feminist study group in western Massachusetts in the early 1980s.

12. I owe this insight to an unpublished essay by Kathy Newman that reads the novel in terms of myths of creation and interprets Part III as a vision of parthenogenesis. "In order to journey to creative autonomy," Newman writes, "the Daughter must somehow recognize in the Mother the original impulse to create that has been perverted for male purposes" ("To the Lighthouse: Virginia Woolf's Myth of Creation," manuscript).

13. Weil (94). In "Femme versus Lesbienne" Causse writes, "Only the lesbian can render to the biological woman the honor due her" (21).

14. Eileen Barrett's essay on Between the Acts reinforces my point about the apparent grip of patriarchal realism in this novel; Isa, for example, is referred to as "locked in patriarchal time and performing on a patriarchal stage" (24). Barrett's essay likewise points to the ultimate disruption and subversion of the patriarchal surface by matriarchal myth. See also Cramer, "Matriarchal."

15. Laurence attributes the "anxious rhythms" of the novel to "the daily 'zoom' of war," which, she claims, now enters Woolf's writing for the first time, along with the voice of the media. She refers to the effect of these voices as "modern, dissonant music" ("Facts" 239).

16. See also Barrett (26–27).

17. Barrett suggests that the play La Trobe intends to stage at the end of the novel might itself be an Eleusinian mystery play (35).

Works Cited

Abel, Elizabeth. *Virginia Woolf and the Fictions of Psychoanalysis.* Chicago: U of Chicago P, 1989.

Alpers, Antony. *The Life of Katherine Mansfield.* NY: Viking, 1980.

The Alyson Almanac, 1994–95 Edition: The Fact Book of the Lesbian and Gay Community. Boston: Alyson, 1993.

Annan, Noel. "The Cult of Homosexuality in 1850–1950." *Biography* 13.3 (1990): 189–202.

Appelbaum, Stanley, ed. *Introduction to French Poetry.* NY: Dover, 1969.

Auerbach, Nina. *Communities of Women: An Idea in Fiction.* Cambridge: Harvard UP, 1978.

Backus, Margot Gayle. "Judy Grahn and the Lesbian Invocational Elegy: Testimonial and Prophetic Responses to Social Death in 'A Woman Is Talking to Death.'" *Signs: Journal of Women in Culture and Society* 18 (1993): 815–37.

Baker, Houston A., Jr. *Modernism and the Harlem Renaissance.* Chicago: U of Chicago P, 1987.

Baldanza, Frank. "Virginia Woolf's 'Moments of Being.'" *Modern Fiction Studies* 2 (1956): 78.

Baldwin, Dean R. *Virginia Woolf: A Study of the Short Fiction.* Boston: Twayne, 1989.

Banks, Joanne Trautmann. "Four Hidden Letters." *Virginia Woolf Miscellany. Special Summer Issue* 43 (1994): 1–3.

———. "Virginia Woolf and Katherine Mansfield." *The English Short Story: 1880–1945.* Ed. Joseph Flora. Boston: Twayne, 1985. 57–82.

Barnard, Mary, trans. *Sappho: A New Translation.* Berkeley: U of California P, 1958.

Barrett, Eileen. "Matriarchal Myth on a Patriarchal Stage: Virginia Woolf's *Between the Acts.*" *Twentieth Century Literature* 33 (1987): 18–37.

Barrett, Eileen, and Patricia Cramer, eds. *Re:Reading, Re:Writing, Re:Teaching Virginia Woolf: Selected Papers from the Fourth Annual Conference on Virginia Woolf.* NY: Pace UP, 1995.

Barry, Kathleen. *Female Sexual Slavery.* Englewood Cliffs, NJ: Prentice-Hall, 1979.

Bartlett, Neill. *Who Was That Man?: A Present for Mr. Oscar Wilde.* London: Serpent's Tail, 1988.

Bazin, Nancy Topping. Roundtable Discussion. Fifth Annual Conference on Virginia Woolf. Otterbein College. Westerville, Ohio. 17 June. 1995.

———. *Virginia Woolf and the Androgynous Vision.* New Brunswick, NJ: Rutgers UP, 1973.

Beckson, Karl, and Arthur Ganz. *Literary Terms: A Dictionary.* NY: Farrar, 1989.

Bell, Diane, and Renate Klein, eds. *Radically Speaking. Feminism Reclaimed.* Melbourne, Australia: Spinifex, 1996.

Bell, Quentin. *Virginia Woolf: A Biography.* 2 vols. NY: Harcourt, 1972.

Bell, Vanessa. *Selected Letters of Vanessa Bell.* Ed. Regina Marler. NY: Pantheon Books, 1993.

Bellamy, Suzanne. "Bessie Guthrie." *Australian Dictionary of Biography, 1940–1980.* Ed. John Ritchie. Concord, MA: Paul and Co., 1996.

———. "Bessie Guthrie." *200 Australian Women.* Ed. Heather Radi. Sydney, Australia: Women's Redress Press, 1988. 220–22.

———. "The Creative Landscape." *Australia for Women—Travel and Culture.* Ed. Renate Klein and Susan Hawthorne. Melbourne, Australia: Spinifex, 1994. 373–79.

———. "Form—'We Are the Thing Itself.'" *All Her Labours: Embroidering the Framework.* Sydney, Australia: Hale and Iremonger, 1984. 68–84.

———. "Freedom from Unreal Loyalties." *Different Lives.* Ed. Jocelynne Scutt. Sydney, Australia: Penguin, 1987. 188–99.

———. *Mapping the Coming Women.* Melbourne, Australia: Spinifex; Bridgeport, Ct: Sanguinary/Bloodroot, forthcoming.

———. "The Narrow Bridge of Art and Politics." *Radically Speaking: Feminism Reclaimed.* Ed. Diane Bell and Renate Klein. Melbourne, Australia: Spinifex, 1996. 130–42.

Bennett, Paula. "Critical Clitoridectomy: Female Sexual Imagery and Feminist Psychoanalytic Theory." *Signs: Journal of Women in Culture and Society* 18.2 (1993): 235–59.

Benstock, Shari. "Expatriate Sapphic Modernism: Entering Literary History." *Rereading Modernism: New Directions in Feminist Criticism.* Ed. Lisa Rado. NY: Garland, 1994. 185–96.

———. *Women of the Left Bank: Paris, 1900–1940.* Austin: U of Texas P, 1986.

Berkman, Sylvia. "Ida Constance Baker." *Adam: International Review* 370–75 (1972–73): 107–10.

Bicknell, John. Telephone Interview. 13 July 1995.

Blackstone, Bernard. *Virginia Woolf: A Commentary.* London: Hogarth, 1949.

Blanche, Jacques-Emile. "*Un nouveau roman de* Virginia Woolf." *Les Nouvelles-Littéraires* (February 16, 1929): 9.

Boddy, Gillian. *Katherine Mansfield: The Woman and the Writer.* Ringwood, Australia: Penguin, 1988.

Bodenheimer, Rosemarie. *The Politics of Story in Victorian Social Fiction.* Ithaca: Cornell UP, 1988.

Bradbury, Malcolm. *The Modern World: Ten Great Writers.* NY: Viking Penguin, 1988.

Bridgman, Richard. *Gertrude Stein in Pieces.* NY: Oxford UP, 1970.

Briggs, Julia, ed. *Virginia Woolf: Introductions to the Major Works*. London: Virago, 1994.

Brimstone, Lyndie. "Towards a New Cartography: Radclyffe Hall, Virginia Woolf and the Working of Common Land." Hobby and White 86–108.

Brossard, Nicole. "Kind Skin My Mind." *The Aerial Letter*. Trans. Marlene Wildeman. Toronto: The Women's Press, 1988. 121–22.

Broumas, Olga. *Beginning with O*. New Haven: Yale UP, 1977.

Brown, Sally. "'Hundreds of Selves': The British Library's Katherine Mansfield Letters." *British Library Journal* 14 (1988): 154–64.

Browne, Stella. "Studies in Feminine Inversion" (1923). *The Sexuality Debates*. Ed. Sheila Jeffreys. NY and London: Routledge and Kegan Paul, 1987. 606–12.

Burke, Kenneth. *A Rhetoric of Motives*. 1950. Berkeley: U of California P, 1969.

Butler, Judith. *Bodies That Matter: On the Discursive Limits of "Sex."* NY: Routledge, 1993.

———. *Gender Trouble: Feminism and the Subversion of Identity*. NY: Routledge, 1990.

———. "Imitation and Gender Insubordination." *Inside/Out: Lesbian Theories, Gay Theories*. Ed. Diana Fuss. NY: Routledge, 1991. 13–31.

Campbell, David A., trans. *Greek Lyric*, vol. 1. Cambridge: Harvard UP, 1982.

Carby, Hazel. *Reconstructing Womanhood: The Emergence of the Afro-American Woman Novelist*. NY: Oxford UP, 1987.

Card, Claudia. "What Is Lesbian Philosophy? A New Introduction." *Adventures in Lesbian Philosophy*. Ed. Claudia Card. Bloomington: Indiana UP, 1994. ix–xxii.

Carpenter, Edward. "Homogenic Love" 1894. *Sexual Heretics: Male Homosexuality in English Literature from 1850 to 1900*. Ed. Brian Reade. NY: Coward-McCann, 1971.

———. *Love's Comming-of-Age: A Series of Papers on the Relations of the Sexes*. 1897. NY and London: Mitchell Kennerley, 1911.

Case, Sue-Ellen. "Toward a Butch-Femme Aesthetic." *Making a Spectacle: Feminist Essays on Contemporary Women's Theatre*. Ed. Lynda Hart. Ann Arbor: U of Michigan P, 1989. 283–99.

Castle, Terry. *The Apparitional Lesbian: Female Homosexuality and Modern Culture*. NY: Columbia UP, 1994.

Caughie, Pamela L. *Virginia Woolf and Postmodernism: Literature in Quest and Question of Itself*. Urbana: U of Illinois P, 1991.

Causse, Michèle. "Femme versus Lesbienne." *La Parole Méteque* 16 (1990): 20–22.

Clements, Patricia, and Isobel Grundy. *Virginia Woolf: New Critical Essays*. London: Vision Press, 1983.

Clements, Susan. "The Point of 'Slater's Pins': Misrecognition and the Narrative Closet." *Tulsa Studies in Women's Literature* 13 (1994): 15–26.

Collecott, Diana. "What Is Not Said: A Study in Textual Inversion." *Sexual Sameness: Textual Differences in Lesbian and Gay Writing*. Ed. Joseph Bristow. NY: Routledge, 1992. 91–110.

Cook, Blanche Wiesen. "'Women Alone Stir My Imagination': Lesbianism and the Cultural Tradition." *Signs: Journal of Women in Culture and Society* 4 (1979): 718–39.

Cramer, Patricia. "Notes from Underground: Lesbian Ritual in the Writings of Virginia Woolf." Hussey and Neverow-Turk, *Miscellanies* 177–88.

———. "Virginia Woolf's Matriarchal Family of Origins in *Between the Acts*." *Twentieth Century Literature* 39 (1993): 166–84.

Crompton, Louis. *Byron and Greek Love*. Berkeley: U of California P, 1985.

Crone, Nora. *A Portrait of Katherine Mansfield*. Ilfracombe, England: Stockwell, 1985.

Daly, Mary. *Gyn/Ecology: The Metaethics of Radical Feminism*. Boston: Beacon Press, 1978.

———. *Pure Lust: Elemental Feminist Philosophy*. Boston: Beacon Press, 1984.

Daugherty, Beth Rigel. "'There She Sat': The Power of the Feminist Imagination in *To the Lighthouse*." *Twentieth Century Literature* 37 (1991): 289–308.

Daugherty, Beth Rigel, and Eileen Barrett, eds. *Virginia Woolf: Texts and Contexts: Selected Papers from the Fifth Annual Conference on Virginia Woolf*. NY: Pace UP, 1996.

Davis, Thadious M. *Nella Larsen, Novelist of the Harlem Renaissance: A Woman's Life Unveiled*. Baton Rouge: Louisiana State UP, 1994.

De Grazia, Edward. *Girls Lean Back Everywhere: The Law of Obscenity and the Assault on Genius*. NY: Vintage, 1993.

DeJean, Joan. *Fictions of Sappho: 1546–1937*. Chicago: U of Chicago P, 1989.

de Lauretis, Teresa. *The Practice of Love: Lesbian Sexuality and Perverse Desire*. Bloomington: Indiana UP, 1994.

DeSalvo, Louise A. *Conceived with Malice: Literature as Revenge*. NY: Penguin Plume Books, 1994.

———. Introduction. *The Voyage Out*. By Virginia Woolf. NY: Signet Classic, 1991. v–xvii.

———. "Lighting the Cave: The Relationship between Vita Sackville-West and Virginia Woolf." *Signs: Journal of Women in Culture and Society* 8 (1982): 195–214.

———. *Virginia Woolf: The Impact of Childhood Sexual Abuse on Her Life and Work*. Boston: Beacon, 1989.

DeShazer, Mary K. *Inspiring Women: Reimagining the Muse*. NY: Pergamon Press, 1986.

Dibattista, Maria. "*To the Lighthouse*: Virginia Woolf's Winter's Tale." Freedman 161–88.

Dick, Susan. Editorial Procedures. *The Complete Shorter Fiction of Virginia Woolf*. Ed. Susan Dick. San Diego and NY: Harcourt Brace Jovanovich, 1989. 7–13.

Dijkstra, Bram. *Idols of Perversity: Fantasies of Feminine Evil in Fin-de-Siècle Culture*. NY: Oxford UP, 1986.

Dowling, Linda. "Pater, Moore, and the Fatal Book." *Prose Studies* 7.2 (1984): 168–78.

Downing, Christine. *Myths and Mysteries of Same-Sex Love*. NY: Continuum, 1989.

Dreiser, Theodore. *Sister Carrie*. Columbus, Ohio: Merrill, 1969.

Duggan, Lisa. "The Trials of Alice Mitchell: Sensationalism, Sexology, and the Lesbian Subject in Turn-of-the-Century America." *Signs: Journal of Women in Culture and Society* 18 (1993): 791–814.

DuPlessis, Rachel Blau. *Writing beyond the Ending: Narrative Strategies of Twentieth-Century Women Writers.* Bloomington: Indiana UP, 1985.

Dworkin, Andrea. *Woman Hating.* NY: Harper and Row, 1976.

Easson, Angus. *Elizabeth Gaskell.* London: Routledge and Kegan Paul, 1979.

Eberly, David. "Incest, Erasure, and The Years." Hussey and Neverow, *Emerging Perspectives* 147–51.

———. "Talking It All Out: Homosexual Disclosures in Woolf." Neverow-Turk and Hussey, *Themes and Variations* 128–34.

Eisenberg, Nora. "Virginia Woolf's Last Words on Words: *Between the Acts* and 'Anon.'" Marcus, *New Feminist Essays* 253–66.

Eliot, T. S. *The Waste Land. A Facsimile and Transcript of the Original Drafts Including the Annotations of Ezra Pound.* Ed. Valerie Eliot. London: Faber and Faber, 1971.

Ellis, Havelock. *Sexual Inversion.* 1897. Vol. 2 of *Studies in the Psychology of Sex.* Third Edition, Revised and Enlarged. Philadelphia: F. A. Davis, 1928.

Ellison, David R. "Comedy and Significance in Proust's *Recherche*: Freud and the Baron de Charlus." *Modern Language Notes* 98 (1983): 657–74.

Emery, Mary Lou. "'Robbed of Meaning'": The Work at the Center of *To the Lighthouse.*" *Modern Fiction Studies* 38.1 (1992): 217–34.

Faderman, Lillian. *Surpassing the Love of Men: Romantic Friendship and Love between Women from the Renaissance to the Present.* NY: William Morrow, 1981.

Faderman, Lillian, and Brigitte Erikssons, eds. and trans. *Lesbian-Feminism in Turn-of-the-Century Germany.* Iowa City, IA: Naiad Press, 1980.

Farwell, Marilyn R. "Toward a Definition of the Lesbian Literary Imagination." Wolfe and Penelope, *Sexual Practice/Textual Theory,* 66–84.

Fassler, Barbara. "Theories of Homosexuality as Sources of Bloomsbury's Androgyny." *Signs: Journal of Women in Culture and Society* 5:2 (1979): 237–51.

Fleishman, Avrom. "Forms of the Woolfian Short Story." Freedman 44–70.

———. *Virginia Woolf: A Critical Reading.* Baltimore: Johns Hopkins UP, 1975.

Forster, E. M. "Arthur Snatchfold." *The Life to Come and Other Short Stories.* NY: W. W. Norton, 1972. 97–112.

———. *Howards End.* NY: Vintage Books, 1960.

———. *The Longest Journey.* NY: Knopf, 1961.

———. *Maurice: A Novel.* 1971. NY: W. W. Norton, 1993.

———. "Rede Lecture." *Recollections of Virginia Woolf by Her Contemporaries.* Ed. Joan Russell Noble. London: Peter Owen, 1972. 195–96.

———. "Terminal Note." *Maurice: A Novel.* 1971. NY: W. W. Norton, 1993. 249–55.

Foster, Jeannette. *Sex Variant Women in Literature.* 1956. Baltimore, MD: Diana Press, 1975.

Fowler, Rowena. Introduction. "Virginia Woolf and Katharine Furse: An Unpublished Correspondence." *Tulsa Studies in Women's Literature* 9:2 (1990): 201–27.

Freedman, Ralph, ed. *Virginia Woolf: Revaluation and Continuity.* Berkeley and Los Angeles: U of California P, 1980.

Frye, Marilyn. "To See and Be Seen: The Politics of Reality." *The Politics of Reality: Essays in Feminist Theory*. Trumansburg, NY: Crossing P, 1983. 152–74.

Furbank, P. N. *E. M. Forster: A Life*. London: Heinemann, 1977.

Fuss, Diana. *Essentially Speaking: Feminism, Nature, and Difference*. NY: Routledge and Kegan Paul, 1989.

Gaard, Greta. "Identity Politics as Comparative Poetics." *Borderwork: Feminist Engagements with Comparative Literature*. Ed. Margaret Higonnet. Ithaca and London: Cornell UP, 1994. 230–43.

Garrity, Jane. "Encoding Bi-Location: Sylvia Townsend Warner and the Erotics of Dissimulation." *Lesbian Erotics*. Ed. Karla Jay. NY: New York UP, 1995. 241–68.

Gaskell, Elizabeth. *The Letters of Elizabeth Gaskell*. Ed. J. A. V. Chapple and Arthur Pollard. Cambridge: Harvard UP, 1967.

———. *The Life of Charlotte Brontë*. Ed. Alan Shelston. NY: Penguin, 1975.

Gasset, Jose Ortega y. "The Nature of the Novel." *Hudson Review* 10:1 (1957): 23.

Gates, Henry Louis. *The Signifying Monkey: A Theory of African-American Literary Criticism*. NY: Oxford UP, 1988.

Gerin, Winifrid. *Charlotte Brontë: The Evolution of Genius*. London: Oxford UP, 1967.

———. *Elizabeth Gaskell: A Biography*. Oxford: Clarendon Press, 1976.

Gilbert, Sandra M., and Susan Gubar, eds. *The Norton Anthology of Literature by Women*. NY: W. W. Norton, 1985.

Gillespie, Diane F. *The Sisters' Arts: The Writing and Painting of Virginia Woolf and Vanessa Bell*. Syracuse: Syracuse UP, 1988.

Glendinning, Victoria. *A Biography of Vita Sackville-West*. NY: Alfred A. Knopf, 1983.

Gordon, Ian. Introduction. *The Urewera Notebook*. By Katherine Mansfield. Oxford: Oxford UP, 1978. 11–30.

Gordon, Lyndall. *Virginia Woolf: A Writer's Life*. NY: W. W. Norton, 1986.

Gottlieb, Laura Moss. "The Years: A Feminist Novel." *Virginia Woolf: Centennial Essays*. Ed. Elaine K. Ginsberg and Laura Moss Gottlieb. Troy, NY: Whitson, 1983. 215–29.

Grahn, Judy. *Another Mother Tongue*. Boston: Beacon Press, 1990.

———. *Really Reading Gertrude Stein*. Freedom, CA: Crossing Press, 1989.

Greenberg, David F. *The Construction of Homosexuality*. Chicago and London: U of Chicago P, 1988.

Grindea, Miron. "Only One K. M.?–Notes and Footnotes to a Biography." *Adam: International Review* 370–75 (1972–73): 2–18.

Grosskurth, Phyllis. *Havelock Ellis: A Biography*. NY: Alfred A. Knopf, 1980.

Gubar, Susan. "The Birth of the Artist as Heroine: (Re)production, the Kunstlerroman Tradition, and the Fiction of Katherine Mansfield." *The Representation of Women in Fiction*. Ed. Carolyn Heilbrun and Margaret Higonnet. Baltimore: Johns Hopkins UP, 1983. 19–59.

Hafley, James. "On One of Virginia Woolf's Short Stories." *Modern Fiction Studies* 2 (1956): 13–16.

Haller, Evelyn. "Isis Unveiled: Virginia Woolf's Use of Egyptian Myth." Marcus, *A Feminist Slant* 109–31.

Halliday, W. R. *Greek Divination*. London: Macmillan, 1913.

Hamilton, Edith. *Mythology*. NY: Mentor, 1940.

Hankin, C. A. *Katherine Mansfield and Her Confessional Stories*. London: Macmillan, 1983.

Hanscombe, Gillian. "Katherine Mansfield's Pear Tree." Hobby and White 111–33.

Harding, Sandra. *Whose Science? Whose Knowledge? Thinking from Women's Lives*. Ithaca: Cornell UP, 1991.

Harrison, Jane Ellen. *Prolegomena to the Study of Greek Religion*. Second Edition. Cambridge: UP, 1908.

———. *Themis: A Study of the Social Origins of Greek Religion*. Cambridge: UP, 1912.

Harvey, Sir Paul, Comp. *The Oxford Companion to Classical Literature*. Oxford: Oxford UP, 1937.

Haule, James M. "*To the Lighthouse* and the Great War: The Evidence of V. Woolf's Revisions of 'Time Passes.'" Hussey, *Virginia Woolf and War* 164–79.

Hawkes, Ellen. Introduction. "Virginia Woolf's 'Friendships Gallery.'" *Twentieth Century Literature*. 25. 3/4 (1979): 270–302.

———. "The Virgin in the Bell Biography." *Twentieth Century Literature* 20.2 (1974): 96–113.

———. "Woolf's 'Magical Garden of Women.'" Marcus, *New Feminist Essays* 31–60.

Heacox, Thomas. "Proust and Bloomsbury." *Virginia Woolf Miscellaney* 17 (Fall 1981): 2.

Heilbrun, Carolyn. "Virginia Woolf in Her Fifties." Marcus, *A Feminist Slant* 236–53.

Heilbut, Anthony. *Thomas Mann: Eros and Literature*. NY: Alfred A. Knopf, 1996.

Hichens, Robert. *The Green Carnation*. 1894. NY: Mitchell Kennerley, 1908.

Hoagland, Sarah. *Lesbian Ethics: Toward New Value*. Palo Alto, CA: Institute of Lesbian Studies, 1989.

Hobby, Elaine, and Chris White, eds. *What Lesbians Do in Books*. London: Women's Press, 1991.

Hoffman, Charles G. "Virginia Woolf's Manuscript Revisions to *The Years*." *PMLA* 84.1 (1969): 79–89.

Holledge, Julie. *Innocent Flowers*. London: Virago Press, 1981.

Holleyman, George, and Treacher. *Catalogue of Books from the Library of Leonard and Virginia Woolf*. Brighton, England: Holleyman and Treacher, 1975.

Hull, Gloria T. *Color, Sex, and Poetry: Three Women Writers of the Harlem Renaissance*. Bloomington: Indiana UP, 1987.

Hussey, Mark. "Refractions of Desire: The Early Fiction of Virginia and Leonard Woolf." *Modern Fiction Studies* 38.1 (1992): 127–46.

———, ed. *Virginia Woolf and War*. Syracuse: Syracuse UP, 1991.

———. *Virginia Woolf A to Z: A Comprehensive Reference for Students, Teachers, and Common Readers to Her Life, Work, and Critical Reception*. NY: Facts on File, 1995.

Hussey, Mark, and Vara Neverow, eds. *Virginia Woolf: Emerging Perspectives: Selected Papers from the Third Annual Conference on Virginia Woolf*. NY: Pace UP, 1994.

Hussey, Mark, and Vara Neverow-Turk, eds. *Virginia Woolf Miscellanies: Proceedings of the First Annual Conference on Virginia Woolf.* NY: Pace UP, 1992.

Hutchinson, George. *The Harlem Renaissance in Black and White.* Cambridge: Belknap-Harvard UP, 1995.

Huxley, Aldous. *Chrome Yellow.* NY: Buccaneer Books, 1991.

Irigaray, Luce. "And the One Doesn't Stir without the Other." Trans. Helene Wenzel. *Signs: Journal of Women in Culture and Society* 7.1 (1981): 60–67.

———. *Ethique de la différence sexuelle. The Irigaray Reader.* Ed. Margaret Whitford. Cambridge, MA: Basil Blackwell, 1991.

———. *Speculum of the Other Woman.* Trans. Gillian Gill. Ithaca: Cornell UP, 1983.

———. *This Sex Which Is Not One.* Trans. Catherine Porter. Ithaca: Cornell UP, 1985.

Jay, Karla. "Lesbian Modernism: (Trans)forming the (C)Anon." *Professions of Desire: Lesbian and Gay Studies in Literature.* Ed. George E. Haggerty and Bonnie Zimmerman. NY: Modern Language Association, 1995. 72–83.

——, ed. *Lesbian Erotics.* NY: New York UP, 1995.

Jay, Karla, and Joanne Glasgow. Introduction. *Lesbian Texts and Contexts.* NY: New York UP, 1990. 1–10.

Jeffreys, Sheila. "Does It Matter If They Did It?" Lesbian History Group 9–28.

———. *The Lesbian Heresy: A Feminist Perspective on the Lesbian Sexual Revolution.* North Melbourne, Australia: Spiniflex, 1993.

———. *The Spinster and Her Enemies: Feminism and Sexuality 1880–1930.* London, Boston, and Henley: Pandora, 1985.

Jensen, Emily. "Clarissa Dalloway's Respectable Suicide." Marcus, *Virginia Woolf: A Feminist Slant* 162–79.

The Jerusalem Bible: Reader's Edition. Ed. Alexander Jones. Garden City, NY: Doubleday, 1966.

Johnson, Jeri. Introduction. *The Years.* By Virginia Woolf. Briggs 305–48.

Jones, Danell. "The Chase of the Wild Goose: The Ladies of Llangollen and *Orlando.*" Neverow-Turk and Hussey 181–89.

Kaplan, Sydney Janet. *Katherine Mansfield and the Origins of Modernist Fiction.* Ithaca: Cornell UP, 1991.

———. Roundtable Discussion. Fifth Annual Conference on Virginia Woolf. Otterbein College. Westerville, OH. 17 June 1995.

Kaye, Elaine. *A History of Queen's College, London: 1848–1972.* London: Chatto, 1972.

King, James. *Virginia Woolf.* NY and London: W. W. Norton, 1995.

Klepfisz, Irena. *A Few Words in the Mother Tongue: Poems Selected and New (1971–1990).* Oregon: Eighth Mountain Press, 1990.

Knopp, Sherron E. "'If I Saw You Would You Kiss Me?': Sapphism and the Subversiveness of Virginia Woolf's *Orlando.*" *PMLA* 103.1 (1988): 24–34.

Koestenbaum, Wayne. *Double Talk: The Erotics of Male Literary Collaboration.* NY: Routledge, Chapman and Hall, 1989.

Kooistra, Lorraine Janzen. "Virginia Woolf's *Roger Fry* and Fact in Life-Writing." *Woolf Studies Annual* 2 (1996): 26–38.

Lansbury, Coral. *Elizabeth Gaskell: The Novel of Social Crisis.* London: Paul Elek, 1975.

Larsen, Nella. *Quicksand and Passing.* Ed. Deborah E. McDowell. New Brunswick, NJ: Rutgers UP, 1986.

Laurence, Patricia Ondek. "The Facts and Fugue of War." Hussey, *Virginia Woolf and War* 225–46.

———. *The Reading of Silence: Virginia Woolf in the English Tradition.* Stanford: Stanford UP, 1991.

Leaska, Mitchell A. Introduction. *The Letters of Vita Sackville-West to Virginia Woolf.* Ed. Louise DeSalvo and Mitchell A. Leaska. NY: William Morrow, 1985. 11–46.

———. *The Novels of Virginia Woolf from Beginning to End.* NY: John Jay P, 1977.

———. "Virginia Woolf, the Pargeter: A Reading of *The Years* and *Three Guineas.*" *Bulletin of the New York Public Library.* 80.2 (Winter 1977): 211–20.

Lee, Hermione. Introduction. *To the Lighthouse.* By Virginia Woolf. Briggs 157–86.

Lehmann-Haupt, Christopher. "Of Homoerotic Elements in Mann's Work and Life." *The New York Times.* 21 Mar. 1996. C18.

Lesbian History Group, eds. *Not a Passing Phase: Reclaiming Lesbians in History.* London: Women's Press, 1989.

Levine, Lawrence W. *Black Culture and Black Consciousness: Afro-American Folk Thought from Slavery to Freedom.* New York: Oxford UP, 1977.

Levy, Heather. "'Julia Kissed Her, Julia Possessed Her': Considering Class and Lesbian Desire in Virginia Woolf's Shorter Fiction." Hussey and Neverow, *Emerging Perspectives* 83–90.

Lidoff, Joan. "Virginia Woolf's Feminine Sentence: The Mother-Daughter World of *To the Lighthouse.*" *Literature and Psychology* 32.3 (1986): 43–59.

Lilienfeld, Jane. "[The Critic] Can't Say That, Can She? Naming Co-dependence and Family in *To the Lighthouse.*" Hussey and Neverow, *Emerging Perspectives* 151–56.

———. "'The Deceptiveness of Beauty': Mother Love and Mother Hate in *To the Lighthouse.*" *Twentieth Century Literature* 23.3 (1977): 345–76.

———. "'Like a Lion Seeking Whom He Could Devour': Domestic Violence in *To the Lighthouse.*" Hussey and Neverow-Turk, *Miscellanies* 154–63.

———. "Love, Subversion, and Sisterhood: Relations between Charlotte Brontë and Elizabeth Gaskell." Presentation to National Association of Women's Studies. Bloomington, IN, May 1980.

———. *The Necessary Journey: Virginia Woolf's Voyage to the Lighthouse.* Diss. Brandeis University. 1975.

———. "Verbal Violence: Reciprocity in *Shirley* and *North and South.*" Presentation to Northeast Victorian Studies Association. Philadelphia, April 1980.

Lorde, Audre. "Uses of the Erotic." *Sister Outsider: Essays and Speeches.* Freedom, CA: Crossing Press, 1984. 53–59.

MacIntyre, C. F. Notes. *French Symbolist Poetry.* Trans. and ed. MacIntyre. Berkeley: U of California P, 1958. 115–47.

Mansfield, Katherine. "Bliss." *The Short Stories of Katherine Mansfield* 337-42.

———. "Carnation." *The Short Stories of Katherine Mansfield* 321-24.

———. *The Collected Letters of Katherine Mansfield.* Ed. Vincent O'Sullivan and Margaret Scott. 3 vols. Oxford: Clarendon P, 1984.

———. *The Letters and Journals of Katherine Mansfield: A Selection.* Ed. C. K. Stead. London: Penguin, 1977.

———. *Letters between Katherine Mansfield and John Middleton Murry.* Ed. C. A. Hankin. London: Virago, 1988.

———. *Poems of Katherine Mansfield.* Ed. Vincent O'Sullivan. Auckland: Oxford UP, 1988.

———. *The Short Stories of Katherine Mansfield.* NY: Alfred A. Knopf, 1937.

———. "The Unpublished Manuscripts of Katherine Mansfield." Ed. Margaret Scott. *Turnbull Library Record* 3.1, 3.3 (1970): 4–28, 128–36.

Mantz, Ruth, and John Middleton Murry. *The Life of Katherine Mansfield.* London: Constable, 1933.

Marcus, Jane. "Britannia Rules the Waves." *Decolonizing Tradition: New Views of Twentieth Century "British" Literary Canon.* Ed. Karen R. Lawrence. Urbana: U of Illinois P, 1992. 136–62.

———. "Liberty, Sorority, Misogyny." *The Representation of Women in Fiction.* Ed. Carolyn G. Heilbrun and Margaret R. Higonnet. Baltimore: Johns Hopkins UP, 1983. 60–97.

———, ed. *New Feminist Essays on Virginia Woolf.* Lincoln: U of Nebraska P, 1981.

———. "The Niece of a Nun: Virginia Woolf, Caroline Stephen, and the Cloistered Imagination." *Virginia Woolf and the Languages of Patriarchy.*

———. "A Rose for Him to Rifle." Introduction. *Virginia Woolf and the Languages of Patriarchy* 1–17.

———. "Sapphistry: Narration as Lesbian Seduction in *A Room of One's Own.*" *Virginia Woolf and the Languages of Patriarchy* 163–87.

———. "Taking the Bull by the Udders: Sexual Difference in Virginia Woolf–A Conspiracy Theory." *Virginia Woolf and the Languages of Patriarchy* 136–62.

———. "Thinking Back through Our Mothers." *New Feminist Essays* 1–30.

———, ed. *Virginia Woolf: A Feminist Slant.* Lincoln: U of Nebraska Press, 1983.

———. "Virginia Woolf and Her Violin: Mothering, Madness and Music." *Mothering the Mind. Virginia Woolf and the Languages of Patriarchy* 96–114.

———. *Virginia Woolf and the Languages of Patriarchy.* Bloomington: Indiana UP, 1987.

———. "*The Years* as Götterdämmerung, Greek Play, and Domestic Novel." *Virginia Woolf and the Languages of Patriarchy* 36–56.

Mares, Cheryl. "Reading Proust: Woolf and the Painter's Perspective." *The Multiple Muses of Virginia Woolf.* Ed. Diane F. Gillespie. Columbia: Missouri UP, 1993. 58–89.

Marks, Elaine. "Lesbian Intertexuality." *Homosexualities and French Literature.* Ed. George Stambolian and Elaine Marks. Ithaca: Cornell UP, 1979. 353–77.

Marxist-Feminist Literature Collective. "Women's Writing: *Jane Eyre, Shirley, Villette, Aurora Leigh.*" *The Sociology of Literature,* 1848. Ed. Francis Barker et al. Essex: U of Essex P, 1978. 185–206.

McDaniel, Judith. "Why Not Sally?" *Sinister Wisdom* 1.2 (1976): 20–33.

McDowell, Deborah E. Introduction. *Quicksand and Passing.* By Nella Larsen ix–xxxv.

McEldowney, Dennis. "The Multiplex Effect: Recent Biographical Writing on Katherine Mansfield." *ARIEL* 16.4 (1985): 111–24.

McKay, Claude. *Home to Harlem.* 1928. NY: Pocket Cardinal, 1965.

McKay, Nellie Y. "The Souls of Black Women Folk in the Writings of W. E. B. Du Bois." *Reading Black, Reading Feminist: A Critical Anthology.* Ed. Henry Louis Gates, Jr. NY: Meridian-Penguin Books, 1990. 227–43.

McKenna, Kathleen. "The Language of Orgasm." Barrett and Cramer 29–38.

McLaughlin, Ann. "The Same Job: The Shared Writing Aims of Katherine Mansfield and Virginia Woolf." *Modern Fiction Studies* 24 (1978): 369–82.

———. "An Uneasy Sisterhood: Virginia Woolf and Katherine Mansfield." Marcus, *Virginia Woolf: A Feminist Slant* 152–61.

McNaron, Toni. "'The Albanians, or Was It the Armenians?': Virginia Woolf's Lesbianism as Gloss on Her Modernism." Neverow-Turk and Hussey 134–41.

———. "Billy Goat to Dolphin: Letters of Virginia Woolf to Her Sister, Vanessa Bell." *The Sister Bond.* Ed. Toni McNaron. NY: Pergamon, 1985. 91–103.

———. "A Journey into Otherness: Teaching *The Well of Loneliness.*" *Lesbian Studies Present and Future.* Ed. Margaret Cruikshank. NY: Feminist Press, 1982. 88–92.

———. "Mirrors and Likeness: A Lesbian Aesthetic in the Making." Wolfe and Penelope, *Sexual Practice/Textual Theory* 291–306.

Meese, Elizabeth. *(Sem)erotics: Theorizing Lesbian : Writing.* NY: New York UP, 1992.

———. "When Virginia Looked at Vita, What Did She See; or, Lesbian: Feminist: Woman—What's the Differ(e/a)nce?" *Feminist Studies* 18.1 (Spring 1992): 99–117.

Meisel, Perry. *The Absent Father: Virginia Woolf and Walter Pater.* New Haven: Yale UP, 1980.

Mepham, John. "Mourning and Modernism." Clements and Grundy 137–56.

Meyerowitz, Selma. "What Is to Console Us?: The Politics of Deception in Woolf's Short Stories." Marcus, *New Feminist Essays* 238–52.

Meyers, Jeffrey. *Katherine Mansfield: A Biography.* London: Hamish, 1978.

———. *Homosexuality and Literature, 1890–1930.* Montreal: McGill-Queen's UP, 1977.

Miller, Elaine. "'Through All Changes and through All Chances': The Relationship of Ellen Nussey and Charlotte Brontë." Lesbian History Group 29–54.

Miller, J. Hillis. "Mr. Carmichael and Lily Briscoe: The Rhythm of Creativity in *To the Lighthouse.*" *Modernism Reconsidered.* Ed. Robert Kiely and John Hildebidle. Cambridge: Harvard UP, 1983. 167–89.

Minow-Pinkney, Makiko. *Virginia Woolf and the Problem of the Subject.* Brighton, England: Harvester, 1987.

Moi, Toril. *Sexual/Textual Politics: Feminist Literary Theory.* 1985. London: Routledge, 1988.

Moon, Kenneth. "Where Is Clarissa? Doris Kilman in *Mrs. Dalloway.*" *Clarissa Dalloway.* Ed. Harold Bloom. NY and Philadelphia: Chelsea House, 1990. 147–57.

Moore, Leslie. *Katherine Mansfield: The Memories of LM.* NY: Taplinger, 1972.

Moore, Madeline. *The Short Season between Two Silences: The Mystical and the Political in the Novels of Virginia Woolf.* Boston: George Allen, 1984.

Moore, Thomas. *The Life, Letters, and Journals of Lord Byron.* 2 vols. London: J. Murray, 1830.

Mossberg, Barbara. "Double Exposures: Emily Dickinson's and Gertrude Stein's Anti-Autobiographies." *Women's Studies* 16 (1989): 239–50.

Murray, John, ed. *Lord Byron's Correspondence, Chiefly with Lady Melbourne, Mr Hobhouse, The Hon. Duglas Kinnaird and P. B. Shelley.* London: John Murray, 1922.

Naremore, James. *The World without a Self: Virginia Woolf and the Novel.* New Haven: Yale UP, 1973.

Neaman, Judith. "Allusion, Image, and Associative Pattern: The Answers in Mansfield's 'Bliss.'" *Twentieth Century Literature* 32 (1986): 242–54.

Neuman, Shirley. "Heart of Darkness, Virginia Woolf, and the Spectre of Domination." Clements and Grundy 57–76.

Neverow-Turk, Vara, and Mark Hussey, eds. *Virginia Woolf: Themes and Variations: Selected Papers from the Second Annual Conference on Virginia Woolf.* NY: Pace UP, 1993.

Newman, Kathy. "Re-membering an Interrupted Conversation: The Mother/ Virgin Split." *Trivia, A Journal of Ideas* 2 (1983): 45–63.

Newton, Esther. "The Mythic Mannish Lesbian: Radclyffe Hall and the New Woman." *The Lesbian Issue: Essays from SIGNS.* Ed. Estelle Freedman, Barbara Gelpi, Susan Johnson, and Kathleen Weston. Chicago: U of Chicago P, 1984. 7–25.

Nicolson, Nigel. *Portrait of a Marriage.* NY: Atheneum, 1973.

———, ed. *Vita and Harold: The Letters of Vita Sackville-West and Harold Nicolson.* NY: G. P. Putnam's Sons, 1992.

North, Michael. *The Dialect of Modernism: Race, Language, and Twentieth-Century Literature.* NY: Oxford UP, 1994.

Olano, Pamela J. "'Throw Over Your Man, I Say, and Come': Reading Virginia Woolf as a Lesbian." Unpublished paper. 1991.

———. "'Women Alone Stir My Imagination': Reading Virginia Woolf as a Lesbian." Neverow-Turk and Hussey 158–71.

O'Sullivan, Vincent. "The Magnetic Chain: Notes and Approaches to K. M." *Landfall* 29 (1975): 95–131.

Ovid. *Metamorphoses.* Trans. A. D. Melville. Oxford: Oxford UP, 1978.

Oxford English Dictionary. Compact ed. Oxford: Oxford UP, 1971.

Oxindine, Annette. "Sapphist Semiotics in Woolf's *The Waves*: Untelling and Retelling What Cannot Be Told." Neverow-Turk and Hussey 171–81.

Parks, Adam. "Lesbianism, History, and Censorship, *The Well of Loneliness*, and the Suppressed Randiness of Virginia Woolf's *Orlando.*" *Twentieth Century Literature* 40:4 (Winter 1994): 434–60.

Penelope, Julia. *Call Me Lesbian: Lesbian Lives, Lesbian Theory.* Freedom, CA: Crossing Press, 1992.

Petry, Ann. *The Street.* Boston: Houghton Mifflin, 1946.

Phillips, Kathy J. *Virginia Woolf against Empire.* Knoxville: U of Tennessee P, 1994.

Poole, Roger. *The Unknown Virginia Woolf.* Cambridge: Cambridge UP, 1978.

Poovey, Mary. *Uneven Developments: The Ideological Work of Gender in Mid-Victorian England*. Chicago: U of Chicago P, 1988.

Porter, Roy, and Lesley Hall. *The Facts of Life: The Creation of Sexual Knowledge in Britain, 1650–1950*. New Haven and London: Yale UP, 1995.

Potts, Abbie Findlay. *The Elegiac Mode: Poetic Form in Wordsworth and Other Elegists*. Ithaca: Cornell UP, 1967.

Proust, Marcel. *Remembrance of Things Past*, vol. 1. NY: Vintage Books, 1982.

Radicalesbians. "The Woman Identified Woman." *Radical Feminism*. Ed. Anne Koedt, Ellen Levine, and Anita Rapone. NY: Quadrangle Books, 1973. 240–45.

Radin, Grace. "'I am Not a Hero': Virginia Woolf and the First Version of The Years." *Massachusetts Review* 16.1 (1975): 195–208.

———. "'Two Enormous Chunks': Episodes Excluded during the Final Revisions of *The Years*." *Bulletin of the NY Public Library* 80 (1977): 221–51.

———. *Virginia Woolf's The Years: The Evolution of a Novel*. Knoxville: U of Tennessee P, 1981.

Radner, Joan Newton, ed. *Feminist Messages: Coding in Women's Folk Culture*. Urbana: Illinois UP, 1993.

Raine, Kathleen. "Virginia Woolf at Girton." *Virginia Woolf: Interviews and Recollections*. Ed. J. H. Stape. Iowa City: U of Iowa P, 1995. 15–17.

Raitt, Suzanne. *Vita and Virginia: The Work and Friendship of V. Sackville-West and Virginia Woolf*. Oxford: Clarendon P, 1993.

Raymond, Janice G. *A Passion for Friends: Towards a Philosophy of Female Affection*. Boston: Beacon Press, 1986.

Restuccia, Frances. "'Untying the Female Tongue': Female Difference in Virginia Woolf's *A Room of One's Own*." *Tulsa Studies in Women's Literature* 4.2 (1985): 25–64.

Rich, Adrienne. *Of Woman Born: Motherhood as Experience and Institution*. NY: W. W. Norton, 1976.

Risolo, Donna. "Outing Mrs. Ramsay: Reading the Lesbian Subtext in Virginia Woolf's *To the Lighthouse*. Neverow-Turk and Hussey 238–48.

Rivers, J. E. *Proust and the Art of Love: The Aesthetics of Sexuality in the Life, Times, and Art of Marcel Proust*. NY: Columbia UP, 1980.

Rohrberger, Mary. *The Art of Katherine Mansfield*. Ann Arbor: U of Michigan P, 1977.

Roof, Judith. "'The Match in the Crocus': Representations of Lesbian Sexuality." *Discontented Discourses: Feminism/Textual Intervention/Psychoanalysis*. Ed. Marleen Barr and Richard Feldstein. Urbana: U of Illinois P, 1989. 100–116.

Rose, Phyllis. *Woman of Letters: A Life of Virginia Woolf*. London: Routledge, 1978.

Rosenman, Ellen Bayuk. *The Invisible Presence: Virginia Woolf and the Mother-Daughter Relationship*. Baton Rouge: Louisiana State UP, 1986.

———. "Sexual Identities and *A Room of One's Own*: 'Secret Economies' in Virginia Woolf's Feminist Discourse." *Signs: Journal of Women in Culture and Society* 14 (1989): 634–50.

Rubin, Gayle. "The Traffic in Women: Notes toward a Political Economy of Sex." *Toward an Anthropology of Women*. Ed. Rayna Reiter. NY: Monthly Review P, 1975. 157–210.

Sackville-West, Vita. *Challenge.* NY: George H. Doran, 1924.

———. *Country Notes in Wartime.* London: Hogarth Press, 1940.

———. *The Letters of Vita Sackville-West to Virginia Woolf.* Ed. Louise DeSalvo and Mitchell A. Leaska. NY: William Morrow, 1985.

———. *Passenger to Teheran.* London: Hogarth Press, 1926.

———. "Virginia Woolf and 'Orlando.'" *The Listener.* Jan. 27, 1955. 157–58.

Savage, George H. "Case of Sexual Perversion in a Man." *The Journal of Mental Science* 30 (1884): 390–91.

Schlack, Beverly Ann. *Continuing Presences: Virginia Woolf's Use of Literary Allusion.* University Park: Pennsylvania State UP, 1979.

Schoppmann, Claudia. *Days of Masquerade: Life Stories of Lesbians during the Third Reich.* Trans. Allison Brown. NY: Columbia UP, 1996

Scott, Bonnie Kime, ed. *The Gender of Modernism: A Critical Anthology.* Bloomington: Indiana UP, 1990.

Sears, Sally. "Notes on Sexuality: *The Years* and *Three Guineas.*" Bulletin of the New York Public Library 80.2 (Winter 1977): 211–20.

Sedgwick, Eve Kosofsky. *The Epistemology of the Closet.* Berkeley and Los Angeles: U of California P, 1990.

———. "The Privilege of Unknowing." *Genders* 1 (1988): 102–24.

Shengold, Leonard. *Soul Murder: The Effects of Childhood Abuse and Deprivation.* New Haven: Yale UP, 1989.

Showalter, Elaine. *Sexual Anarchy: Gender and Culture at the Fin de Siècle.* NY: Penguin, 1990.

Silver, Brenda. "What's Woolf Got to Do with It? Or, The Perils of Popularity." *Modern Fiction Studies* 38.1 (1992): 21-60.

———, ed. *Virginia Woolf's Reading Notebooks.* Princeton: Princeton UP, 1983.

Sinfield, Alan. "Closet Dramas: Homosexual Representation and Class in Postwar British Theater." *Genders* 9 (Fall 1990): 112–31.

Singh, Amritjit. "Black-White Symbiosis: Another Look at the Literary History of the 1920s." *The Harlem Renaissance Re-examined.* Ed. Victor A. Kramer. NY: AMS Press, 1987. 31–42.

Smith, Angela. "Katherine Mansfield and Virginia Woolf: *Prelude* and *To the Lighthouse.*" *Journal of Commonwealth Literature* 18.1 (1983): 105-19.

———. "Katherine Mansfield and Virginia Woolf." *Short Fiction in the New Literatures in English: Proceedings of the Nice Conference of the European Association For Commonwealth Literature and Language Studies.* Ed. J. Bardolph. Nice: Charlet, 1989. 17–21.

Smith, Patricia Juliana. "'And I Wondered If She Might Kiss Me': Lesbian Panic as Narrative Strategy in British Women's Fictions." *Modern Fiction Studies* 41 (1995): 567–607

———. *Lesbian Panic: The Homoerotics of Narrative in Modern British Women's Fiction.* NY: Columbia UP, 1997.

———. "Marie Corelli." *Gay and Lesbian Literary Heritage.* Ed. Claude J. Summers. Boston: Henry Holt, 1995. 176.

Smith-Rosenberg, Carroll. "The Female World of Love and Ritual: Relations between Women in Nineteenth Century America." *Signs: Journal of Women in Culture and Society* 1 (1975): 1–29.

Snyder, Jane McIntosh. *Sappho: Lives of Notable Gay Men and Lesbians*. NY: Chelsea, 1995.

Spender, Dale. *Women of Ideas and What Men Have Done to Them from Aphra Behn to Adrienne Rich*. London, Boston, Melbourne, and Henley: Ark Paperbacks, 1983.

Spraggs, Gillian. "Divine Visitations: Sappho's Poetry of Love." Hobby and White 50–67.

Squire, Susan. "'A Track of Our Own': Typescript Draft of *The Years*. *Modernist Studies* 4 (1982): 218–31.

Stein, Gertrude. "Ada." *Geography and Plays*. NY: Haskell, 1967. 14–16.

———. "As a Wife Has a Cow: A Love Story." *Selected Writings of Gertrude Stein* 543-45.

———. *The Geographical History of America; or, the Relation of Human Nature to the Human Mind*. Intr. Thornton Wilder. NY: Random House, 1936.

———. "Melanctha." *Three Lives*. NY: Random House, 1936. 85–236.

———. "Miss Furr and Miss Skeen." *Geography and Plays* 17-22.

———. *Selected Writings of Gertrude Stein*. Ed. Carl Van Vechten. NY: Random House, 1990.

Stephen, Leslie. "Charlotte Brontë." *Hours in a Library*. Vol. III. NY: G. P Putnam's Sons, 1894. 1–30.

Stephen, Leslie, and Sidney Lee, eds. *The Dictionary of National Biography*, vol. 1. Oxford: Oxford UP, rep. 1959-60.

Stevenson, Robert Louis. *The Strange Case of Dr. Jekyll and Mr. Hyde*. NY: Bantam Books, 1981.

Stewart, Garrett. "Catching the Stylistic D/rift: Sound Defects in Woolf's *The Waves*." *ELH* 54 (1987): 421–61.

Stimpson, Catharine. "The Female Sociograph: The Theater of Virginia Woolf's Letters." 1984. *Where the Meanings Are*. NY: Methuen, 1988. 130–39.

———. "Zero Degree Deviancy: The Lesbian Novel in English." *Feminisms: An Anthology of Literary Theory and Criticism*. Ed. Robyn Warhol and Diane Price Herndyl. New Brunswick: Rutgers UP, 1991. 301–15.

Stoneman, Patsy. *Elizabeth Gaskell*. Bloomington: Indiana UP, 1987.

Strachey, Ray. *The Cause: A Short History of the Women's Movement in Great Britain*. 1928. London: Virago, 1978.

Sturgeon, Mary. *Michael Field*. NY: Macmillan, 1922.

Symonds, John Addington. *A Problem in Greek Ethics Being an Inquiry into the Phenomenon of Sexual Inversion Addressed Especially to Medical Psychologists and Jurists*. 1883. London: Private Publisher Unidentified, 1901.

———. *A Problem in Modern Ethics Being an Inquiry into the Phenomenon of Sexual Inversion Addressed Especially to Medical Psychologists and Jurists*. London: Private Publisher Unidentified, 1896.

Tec, Nechama. *Dry Tears: The Story of a Lost Childhood*. NY: Oxford UP, 1984.

———. *When Light Pierced the Darkness: Christian Rescue of Jews in Nazi-Occupied Poland*. NY: Oxford UP, 1986.

Thompson, D'Arcy Wentworth. *A Glossary of Greek Birds*. Oxford: Clarendon Press, 1895.

Tomalin, Claire. *Katherine Mansfield: A Secret Life*. London: Viking P, 1987.

Transue, Pamela J. *Virginia Woolf and the Politics of Style*. Albany: State U of New York P, 1986.

Tvordi, Jessica. "*The Voyage Out*: Virginia Woolf's First Lesbian Novel." Neverow-Turk and Hussey 226–37.

Tyler, Lisa. "'I Am Not What You Supposed': Walt Whitman's Influence on Virginia Woolf." Daugherty and Barrett 110–16.

Uglow, Jenny. *Elizabeth Gaskell: A Habit of Stories*. London: Faber and Faber, 1993.

Vanita, Ruth. "Love Unspeakable: The Uses of Allusion in *Flush*." Hussey and Neverow, *Emerging Perspectives* 248–57.

———. *Sappho and the Virgin Mary: Same-Sex Love and the English Literary Imagination*. NY: Columbia UP, 1996.

Waldron, Philip. "Katherine Mansfield's *Journal*." *Twentieth Century Literature* 20 (1974): 11–18.

Walkowitz, Judith R. *City of Dreadful Delight: Narratives of Sexual Danger in Late-Victorian London*. Chicago: U of Chicago P, 1992.

Washington, Mary Helen. "'The Darkened Eye Restored:' Notes Toward a Literary History of Black Women." Introduction. *Invented Lives: Narratives of Black Women 1860–1960*. Ed. Mary Helen Washington. Garden City, NY: Anchor Press-Doubleday, 1987. xv–xxxi.

Weeks, Jeffrey. *Coming Out: Homosexual Politics in Britain from the Nineteenth Century to the Present*. Revised edition. London and NY: Quartet Books, 1990.

———. *Sex, Politics and Society: The Regulation of Sexuality since 1800*. Second edition. London: Longmans, 1989.

Weil, Lise. "Conversation with Michèle Causse." *Trivia, A Journal of Ideas* 20 (1992): 90–104.

Weston, Jessie. *From Ritual to Romance*. NY: Doubleday Anchor Books, 1957.

White, Chris. "'She Was Not Really Man at All': The Lesbian Practice and Politics of Edith Ellis." Hobby and White 68–85.

Whitman, Walt. *The Complete Poems*. Ed. Francis Murphy. Harmondsworth: Penguin, 1975.

Wilde, Oscar. *The Picture of Dorian Gray*. NY: Harper and Row, 1965.

Willis, J. H., Jr. *Leonard and Virginia Woolf as Publishers, Hogarth Press, 1917–1941*. Virginia: UP of Virginia, 1992.

Wilson, Deborah. "Fishing for Woolf's Submerged Lesbian Text." Barrett and Cramer, *Re:Reading* 121–28.

Wittig, Monique. "The Point of View: Universal or Particular." *The Straight Mind and Other Essays*. Boston: Beacon P, 1992. 61–67.

Wolfe, Susan J., and Julia Penelope. "Sexual Identity/Textual Politics." In Wolfe and Penelope, *Sexual Practice/Textual Theory* 1–24.

———, eds. *Sexual Practice/Textual Theory: Lesbian Cultural Criticism*. Cambridge, MA: Basil Blackwell, 1993.

Woolf, Leonard. *Downhill All the Way, 1919–1939*. London: Hogarth P, 1967.

Woolf, Leonard, and James Strachey, eds. *Virginia Woolf and Lytton Strachey: Letters*. London: Hogarth P, 1956.

Woolf, Virginia. "'Anon.' and 'The Reader.'" Ed. Brenda R. Silver. *Twentieth Century Literature* 25. 3/4 (1979): 356–441.

———. *Between the Acts*. San Diego and NY: Harcourt Brace Jovanovich, 1941.

———. *The Common Reader. First Series*. 1925. Ed. Andrew McNeillie. NY: Harcourt Brace Jovanovich, 1984.

———. *The Common Reader. Second Series*. 1932. Ed. Andrew McNeillie. NY: Harcourt Brace Jovanovich, 1986.

———. *The Complete Shorter Fiction of Virginia Woolf*. Second edition. Ed. Susan Dick. NY: Harcourt Brace Jovanovich, 1989.

———. *The Diary of Virginia Woolf*. 5 vols. Ed. Anne Oliver Bell. NY: Harcourt Brace Jovanovich, 1984.

———. *The Essays of Virginia Woolf*. 6 vols. Ed. Andrew McNeillie. NY: Harcourt Brace Jovanovich, 1987.

———. *Flush*. NY: Harcourt Brace Jovanovich, 1933.

———. "Friendships Gallery." Ed. Ellen Hawkes. *Twentieth Century Literature* 25. 3/4 (1972): 270–302.

———. *Jacob's Room*. NY: Harcourt Brace Jovanovich, 1923.

———. "Kew Gardens." *The Complete Shorter Fiction of Virginia Woolf* 90–95.

———. "The Lady in the Looking-Glass: A Reflection." *The Complete Shorter Fiction of Virginia Woolf* 221–25.

———. *The Letters of Virginia Woolf*. Ed. Nigel Nicolson and Joanne Trautmann. 6 vols. NY: Harcourt Brace Jovanovich, 1975–80.

———. *Melymbrosia*. Ed. Louise DeSalvo. NY: New York Public Library, 1982.

———. "Memoirs of a Novelist." *The Complete Shorter Fiction of Virginia Woolf* 69–79.

———. "Modern Fiction." *Common Reader: First Series* 146–54.

———. *Moments of Being*. NY: Harcourt Brace Jovanovich, 1976.

———. "Moments of Being: 'Slater's Pins Have No Points.'" *The Complete Shorter Fiction of Virginia Woolf* 215–20.

———. "Mr. Bennett and Mrs. Brown." *Essays* 3: 384–89.

———. *Mrs. Dalloway*. 1925. San Diego, NY, and London: Harcourt Brace Jovanovich, 1981.

———. "Mrs. Dalloway in Bond Street." *The Complete Shorter Fiction of Virginia Woolf* 152–59.

———. "The Mysterious Case of Miss V." *The Complete Shorter Fiction of Virginia Woolf* 30–32.

———. *Night and Day*. NY: Harcourt Brace Jovanovich, 1920.

———. *Orlando*. NY: Harcourt Brace Jovanovich, 1928.

———. *The Pargiters: The Novel-Essay Portion of 'The Years'*. Ed. Mitchell Leaska. NY: Harcourt Brace Jovanovich, 1977.

———. *A Passionate Apprentice: The Early Journals 1897-1909*. Ed. Mitchell Leaska. San Diego: Harcourt Brace Jovanovich, 1990.

———. "Professions for Women." 1942. *The Death of the Moth and Other Essays*. NY: Harcourt Brace Jovanovich, 1970. 235–42.

———. *Roger Fry: A Biography*. NY and London: Harcourt Brace Jovanovich, 1940.

———. *A Room of One's Own*. NY: Harcourt, 1981.

———. *The Second Common Reader*. 1932. Ed. Andrew McNeillie. NY: Harcourt Brace Jovanovich, 1986.

———. "A Society." *The Complete Shorter Fiction of Virginia Woolf* 124–36.

———. "The Sun and the Fish." *The Captain's Death Bed and Other Essays*. NY: Harcourt Brace Jovanovich, 1950. 211–18.

———. *Three Guineas*. NY: Harcourt, 1938.

———. *To the Lighthouse*, 1927.

———. *The Virginia Woolf Manuscripts* from the Henry W. and Albert A. Berg Collection at the NY Public Library. M41 [The Years] Holograph draft (incomplete); M42 [The Years] The Pargiters; a novel-essay based upon a paper read to the National Society for Women's Service, London. Holograph, unsigned, dated 11 Oct. 1932–15 Nov. 1934. 8 vols.

———. *Virginia Woolf's "Orlando": The Original Holograph Draft*. Ed. Stuart Nelson Clarke. London: S. N. Clarke, 1993.

———. *The Voyage Out*. NY, Harcourt Brace Jovanovich, 1920.

———. *The Waves*. NY: Harcourt Brace Jovanovich, 1931.

———. *The Waves: The Two Holograph Drafts Transcribed and Edited by J. W. Graham*. Toronto: U of Toronto P, 1976.

———. "A Woman's College from Outside." *The Complete Shorter Fiction of Virginia Woolf* 145–48.

———. *The Years*. NY: Harcourt Brace Jovanovich, 1937.

Wright, Richard. *Native Son*. NY: Harper and Row, 1940.

Yarrell, William. *A History of British Birds*. 3 vols. London: John Van Voorst, 1856.

Young, Ian. "The Flower beneath the Foot: A Short History of the Gay Novel." *The Male Homosexual in Literature: A Bibliography*. Ed. Ian Young. Metuchen, NJ: Scarecrow P, 1975. 149–61.

Zimmerman, Bonnie. "Is 'Chloe Liked Olivia' a Lesbian Plot?" *Women's Studies International Forum* 6.2 (1983): 169–75.

———. "Lesbians Like This and That: Some Notes on Lesbian Criticism for the Nineties." *New Lesbian Criticism: Literary and Cultural Readings*. Ed. Sally Munt. NY: Columbia UP, 1992. 1–15.

———. "Perverse Reading: The Lesbian Appropriation of Literature." Wolfe and Penelope, *Sexual Practice/Textual Theory* 135–49.

———. "What Has Never Been: An Overview of Lesbian Feminist Criticism." *Feminist Studies* 7.3 (1981): 451–75.

Zwerdling, Alex. *Between the Acts* and the Coming of War." *Novel* 10 (1977): 220–36.

———. *Virginia Woolf and the Real World*. Berkeley and Los Angeles: U of California P, 1986.

Index

Silence (*Cont.*) Woolf's desire to oppose, 55. *See also* Censorship; Ellipses; Evasion
Sissinghurst (Sackville-West's home), 19, 229
Sister Carrie (Dreiser), 97, 100
Sisters' Arts, The (Gillespie), 44
"Slater's Pins Have No Point" (Woolf), 9, 13, 61, 68–75, 122
Smith, George, 47, 48
Smith, Patricia Juliana, 124–25, 128–45
Smith-Rosenberg, Carroll, 40–41
Smyth, Ethel, 6; friends of, 163n. 6; influence of, on Woolf, 53–55, 184, 223; as lesbian, 119; Woolf's relationship with, 38, 46, 164n. 17, 224–25, 230, 232, 233
Snyder, Jane McIntosh, 69
"Society, A" (Woolf), 76n. 20, 78, 86–89, 93
Sonnets (Shakespeare), 171–72, 177, 179n. 13
Soul: death of, 100, 106–12; imagery for, 156, 161–62; theory of trapped, 148, 149, 158
Spaniel imagery, 169
Spraggs, Gillian, 69, 71, 86–87
Stein, Gertrude, 3, 4, 100, 210; lesbian codes in works by, 119–20; as lesbian modernist, 9, 78–80, 89–93
Stephen, Adrian, 5, 51
Stephen, Julia, 102–3
Stephen, Laura, 52
Stephen, Sir Leslie: and Brontë and Gaskell, 50, 54; and his children's education, 51; death of, 52; friends of, 169–74; grief of, 104; library of, 46, 55, 101; publishing connections of, 39; Woolf's feelings for, 41
Stephen, Thoby, 43, 51
Stevenson, Robert Louis, 81
Stewart, Garrett, 204, 215–17
Stimpson, Catharine, 61, 72
Strachey, Lytton, 17, 23, 222; homosexuality of, 117, 120, 149, 165, 166, 174; misogyny of, 27, 165, 168; as part of Woolf's literary tradition, 168, 176, 182; and Woolf, 5, 163n. 7, 167, 176, 180
Strachey, Ray, 146
Strange Case of Dr. Jekyll and Mr. Hyde, The (Stevenson), 81
Street, The (Petry), 97

"Studies in Feminine Inversion" (Browne), 150
Studies in the Psychology of Sex (Ellis), 148
Suicide: in Bellamy's family, 22, 31; Larsen's attempts at, 96, 103; in *Mrs. Dalloway,* 153–54, 162; of Shakespeare's "sister," 203; in *The Waves,* 125, 203–4, 215–17; Woolf's, 11, 103, 215; Woolf's attempts at, 164n. 17, 215. *See also* Death
"Sun and the Fish, The" (Woolf), 227, 236
Surpassing the Love of Men (Faderman), 40
Swann's Way (Proust), 233, 235–37
Swinburne, Algernon Charles, 168, 250–51
Sydney (Australia) Mardi Gras, 28
Sylvia's Lovers (Gaskell), 53
Symbolists, 66, 67
Symonds, John Addington, 151; homosexuality of, 120, 149, 163n. 10, 164n. 13, 170; theories of, 149, 153, 158, 169
Symonds, Madge. *See* Vaughan, Madge Symonds
Symposium (Plato), 131, 167

Taylor, Henry, 240n. 11
Taylor, Mary, 46
Teachers and students: Case and Woolf as, 231; Dickinson and Woolf as, 38; in Mansfield's life, 66–67; in Mansfield's works, 61–62, 64–65; in Woolf's works, 61, 68–75, 141–42. *See also* Mentorship
Tears. *See* Water imagery
Tec, Nechama, 126n. 4
Tender Buttons (Stein), 79
Thackeray, William Makepeace, 47, 52, 225
Three Guineas (Woolf), 23; anger in, 53, 54; Brontë references in, 39, 51–52; female grief in, 254; as influence on Bellamy, 26, 27–28; lesbianism in, 147; manuscript of, 25; on marriage, 146–47; question of writing directly in, 55, 117; sources for, 163n. 3
Three Lives (Stein), 100. *See also* "Melanctha"
"Throw Over Your Man . . . " (Olano), 41
Tiger imagery. *See* Animal imagery
Time and Tide (periodical), 148, 227
Tiresias, 256